TO FATHOM MORE

African American Scientists and Inventors

Edward Sidney Jenkins

with contributions by

Patricia Stohr-Hunt
Exyie C. Ryder
S. Maxwell Hines

University Press of America, Inc.
Lanham • New York • London

Copyright © 1996 by
University Press of America,® Inc.
4720 Boston Way
Lanham, Maryland 20706

3 Henrietta Street
London, WC2E 8LU England

Library of Congress Cataloging-in-Publication Data

Jenkins, Edward S.
To fathom more : African American scientists and inventors / Edward
S. Jenkins ; with contributions by Patricia Hunt, Exyie C. Ryder, S.
Maxwell Hines.
p.   cm.
Includes index
1. Scientists--United States--Biography. 2. Afro-American scientists-
-Biography. 3. Afro-American inventors--Biography, I. Title.
Q141.J46   1996   509.2'273--dc20   95-45159 CIP

ISBN 0-7618-0214-2 (cloth: alk: ppr.)
ISBN 0-7618-0215-0 (pbk: alk: ppr.)

⊖™The paper used in this publication meets the minimum
requirements of American National Standard for information
Sciences—Permanence of Paper for Printed Library Materials,
ANSI Z39.48—1984

For My Wife
Emily

and

My Late Parents
Sadie and Priestly Jenkins

ACKNOWLEDGEMENTS

I cannot possibly thank all the people who contributed to this book. Inevitably in the attempt, someone important will be left out. Nonetheless, at the very least I acknowledge my indebtedness to several scholars whose painstaking and revealing research and writings provided much of the information used in this text. My admiration and respect for them stand equally with my appreciation. I am also grateful to several persons who granted me extensive interviews, always at the expense of their valuable time, and provided valuable insights and information available no where else. Archival treasures from libraries, newspapers, museums, and other sources greatly enriched the content of this book and helped answer many of the author's questions. I acknowledged these indispensable sources in related reference sections at the end of various chapters.

Thanks also to my wife Emily for her sacrifices, our sons Edward Jr. and Rodney for their encouragement, and to Joyce Buchnowski and Julie Henry who took on the daunting task of trying to correct a few of the chapters.

Buffalo   ESJ
February, 1996

CONTENTS

CONTENTS

PREFACE

Science is a human endeavor, its branches interdependent, its essence tied to other disciplines, its edifices to the past conjoined. Upon contributions from Africa and Asia, the Greeks, Romans, Islamic Science, and Europeans, from Ancient Civilizations, the Medieval Period, the Rennaissance, the Enlightenment and Modern Times, its culture and architecture were crafted. The present structure of science and technology might be likened to an intricate but beautiful web system that stands as a grand monument to human strivings and achievement. That monument owes its success to no one man or woman, no one people or country, no one time, space or civilization but to many of each.

This work, *To Fathom More . . .*is a historical account of one entity − 17 American men and women of African descent who made important contributions to science and society. It is an incomplete story because others of the same ethnic heritage could just as well have been included. The intent and ambitious hope of *To Fathom More . . .* is to add a word of a sentence to the remarkable history of science and technology.

Science and inventors born during the 19th century take up considerable space in this text. They were gifted and unusual persons who, given the daunting conditions of their lives, never should have made their marks as scientists and inventors. The same can be said of African American scientists and inventors before this period and since. That they prevailed, and doggedly pursued their interests in science and technology, could alone make them admirable for their uncommon aspirations and strength of character. The pleasant truth however, is that they were included on merit. For all of them, their lives and works, their thoughts and feelings, make an interesting, but in their case insufficiently examined, commentary about the nature of science, and of the inventive, imaginative, mind.

These men and women, who like all of us were and are less than perfect, nonetheless rose up, followed their visions to a higher plane, and made the seemingly improbable come through, through their discoveries and inventions.

Chapter I _____

Benjamin Banneker - Eighteenth Century Astronomer
(1731-1806)

Sometime during the second half of the 17th century, a young English milkmaid named Molly Welsh collected a pail of milk. The cow kicked the bucket over spilling it all. The owner of the cow, not believing his worker's story that the spillage was accidental, filed a charge of theft. The milkmaid was arrested, tried, and convicted of a felony crime. Under the uncharitable law of that time in England she faced severe punishment - perhaps the dungeon or even worse, the gallows. Fortunately Molly could read so the courts took her literacy in consideration and acted with what it regarded as leniency. For her alleged crime she was sentenced to the American colonies where she served time as an indentured servant. After her required years in bondage, or more, Molly regained her freedom but she was forbidden by her sentence to return to England and whatever family or friends she may have had there.

Then virtually alone in the New World the true mettle of Molly asserted itself. She acquired some land in the wilderness west of Baltimore, Maryland near the Patasco River and made plans to build a farm for her livelihood. Trees had to be felled, stumps, and underbrush cleared away, a most formidable task, before engaging the hard labor of preparing the soil for cultivation. Among other things, Molly needed shelter for herself and for storage of the harvest she hoped to reap. Despite her grit and determination however, she had to acknowledge that she needed help. She saw only two choices: failure or the purchase of slaves. This placed her in a difficult failure or the purchase of slaves. This placed her into a difficult situation because, out of her moral convictions and her own trying experience, she abhorred the institution. After agonizing, Molly Welsh decided to purchase two slaves but vowed to set them free as soon as the farm was up and running.

Molly purchased two African men recently brought to America aboard a slave ship. Of the two, one man applied himself diligently to his work assignments but the other was recalcitrant and difficult, exasperating Molly to no end. Nevertheless he was said to be "bright with dignified manners and contemplative habits". He had a gift for fixing things and engineered a system for irrigating the farm the only such system in the region. It served them well. Molly learned that he was the son of an African Chief and that his name was Bannka and Banneky.

After several years the farm became productive, whereupon Molly, true to her vow, gave the men their freedom. She then married Banneky, once again demonstrating rare courage because in being wedded to a black man she risked punishment, loss of possessions, and even her freedom. The new bride took her husband's name that through misspelling and more common use became Banneker.

By virtue of their origin, culture and background, and their different stations in the colonies, Molly and Banneker were an unlikely couple. Contrary to widespread obsession with skin color in America, they took his dark hue and her blond hair and fair skin as only superficial and therefore unimportant differences. Together the couple forged a living out of the wilderness and only his prior death years later broke the bonds of their marriage. Molly named the first of four daughters born to this union, Mary, who it is said, grew into a striking figure, slim and graceful, with skin complexion likened unto "pale copper". Mary lived into her seventies and her hair, long and black, never turned gray.

Mary and Robert

When she became of age, Mary, like her mother, married a

newly freed slave. Before the union, Molly Banneker had already given counsel to her daughter and took care to ensure that she married the "right man". The result of their quest was a then slave on a nearby plantation named Robert. Stories varied but according to several accounts, Mary and her mother purchased Robert's freedom. By other version however, he purchased his own freedom. Whatever the truth, when Robert married the beautiful Mary, he took the name of his father in-law as he had no surname of his own in America.

By all reports the couple had a good marriage. Robert was a hard-working resourceful farmer who managed well. He was a caring family man, of the Christian faith and said to have been religious in his ways. Similar to her mother, Mary gave birth to four children, her first born, a son, Benjamin, three girls, Molly, named for her grandmother, Minta, and a third whose name does not appear in known records. Quite possibly her name began with the letter "M". In accordance with the laws of the time, because the mother was free, the children were born free and so remained.

Robert and Mary Banneker provided a good home for their children though the work was hard. Mary, an intelligent and resourceful person, proved to be an authority on beneficial herbs found in the region. Benjamin and his sisters pitched in on the farm where they produced tobacco, corn, and other staples and there were fruits as well. The Bannekers sold tobacco to the local general store in exchange for clothing, certain food products and other needed items. They also grew livestock and poultry for milk, meat and eggs. Sometimes Benjamin and his father hunted and fished to supplement their diet.

Discovering Books

Benjamin Banneker was born November 9, 1731. His grandmother taught him to read from the only book she owned, the Bible. The lad learned quickly, delighting in the opportunity to read recorded words. As he advanced in skill and understanding, Benjamin and his proud grandmother spent many pleasant hours reading the Bible to each other. They also enjoyed telling one another biblical stories and each found great beauty in the text. From these memorable sessions, Ben developed a love for literature that he treasured all his life.

When Grandma Molly learned that a new school had opened in the region, she lost no time in enrolling Ben as a pupil. Two other blacks were among the students who attended the integrated school under the tutelage of a Quaker Master. Again the lad proved to be an apt student, eager to learn and so enamored with his teacher's books that he usually stayed inside to read them during recess rather than play like the others.

The schoolmaster introduced Benjamin to a new subject – mathematics. Immediately captivated by the precision, exquisite beauty, and practical application of the subject Ben studied with zeal and concentration. Soon he began to use mathematics whenever possible at the school and at home around the farm. Sometimes he created imaginary problems as a hobby to break the monotony of farm work. From the day of his introduction to the discipline, mathematics became a lifelong passion and defining essence of Benjamin Banneker.

The youngster attended school until he earned the equivalent of an eight-grade education. At that point the schoolmaster "graduated" Ben saying there was no more he could teach him. He urged his star pupil to continue his education elsewhere.

The notion appealed to Ben but his father needed his help with the farm work. Also it is not likely he had the resources, nor accepting institutions to further his education in colonial America. At that point Ben's formal education ended but his devotion to learning never waned.

"A Venerable and Noble Figure"

One story has it that as a young man Benjamin fell in love with a beautiful slave woman and she with him. They tried to run away so she could also be free and they would marry, but, having suffered betrayal, were caught in the attempt. The captors threatened Benjamin's life and returned the slave to her plantation. There, distraught over her fate and separation from her intended, the young slave committed suicide. As he mourned loss, a grieving Benjamin Banneker vowed his undying love to her memory. He never married.

Banneker was 28 years of age when his father died. That left him and his mother alone on the farm. His sisters had married and were living on their own land. In adulthood, Benjamin Banneker was described as being dark brown in complexion and of medium height. A contemporary pictured him as a "venerable and noble figure," his posture always erect, and his rainments always clean. A quiet man, his demeanor was "soft and gentle", and though well spoken, he did not intrude on others.

A man named Charles Dorsey worked at the Ellicott store frequented by Banneker. He looked forward to Banneker's visits, finding him a fascinating man. Dorsey once said of his customer:

> He often came to the store to purchase articles for his own use, and after hearing him converse, I was always anxious to wait on him. After making his purchases, he usually went to the part of the store where George Ellicott was in the habit of sitting, to converse with him about the affairs of our government, and many other matters. He was very concise in conversation and exhibited deep reflection. His deportment, whenever I saw him, was perfectly upright and correct, and he seemed to be acquainted with everything of importance that was passing in this country.

As much as he loved mathematics, Banneker read other works with equal interest. His list included works by Addison, Pope, Shakespeare, Milton and Dryden. Later, he read extensively in astronomy. There is some indication he was acquainted with Newton's *Principia*.

It is difficult in modern times to fully appreciate the long hours, the gritty and exhausting labor required to keep a farm going in 18th Century America. The work was especially difficult when it had to be done alone, as was the case for Banneker. Nevertheless, undeterred by hard work, he ran a diversified and successful farm. His crops included tobacco, corn, a fruit orchard, and garden produce. Banneker raised poultry, kept a few cattle, and bee hives. With his rare and uncommon time for leisure, he played the flute and the violin, self-taught and learned for his personal pleasure but to entertain others as well. To Banneker, music and mathematics were sources of beauty.

Looking into the World of Insects

Banneker was as much a keen student of nature as he was of recorded knowledge, learning much through observation and reflection. He often recorded his experiences including inferences and predictions based on observations. Consider these two examples.

One such study helped him to independently predict the return of the insect cicada, more commonly known as locusts. The animals appeared periodically in the region and in hordes. Though not destructive of crops, nor disease bearing, they were noisy day and night, without letup. Such cacophony made them annoying and distracting to many, but sources of wonder and cause for speculation by a few. Based largely on his observations and recollections of past event, Banneker concluded that the animals were cyclical, appearing every 17 years. Then he accurately predicted their return in the year 1800 at which time the locals would have to endure another noisy episode.

Banneker had a penchant for making analogies. He likened the short but spirited life of the big bugs to a comet that blazed brilliantly but only briefly before fading away. In his description of the life cycle of the cicadas, he recorded that the body of the female was adapted to laying eggs in the tree branches. These eggs, he said, "by some occult cause penetrates to great depths in the earth, and there continues for the Space of Seventeen years". Banneker wrote that he believed the cicadas were "merry creatures", because they "sang" during their short lives from birth to death. Near the end of their life cycle the tail of the insect just broke or rotted off. Apparently they felt no pain because they "continued Singing until they die".

Banneker also gave his explanation of a certain puzzling behavior among bees. Bee owners noticed that sometimes a whole colony would fly away without apparent reason. Banneker studied the phenomenon and eventually came to believe that the "home bees" were invaded by stronger bee forces. The "home bees" would resist, fighting valiantly but would lose to superior warriors. The victors would take much of the honey and force the vanquished bees to fly away with them.

Mathematical Puzzles and the Striking Clock

Banneker's mastery of mathematics often led others to seek his help. How much seed should one purchase to plant a given acreage, how much lumber for a certain construction? Such mathematical knowledge was not widespread in colonial America so his help was very valuable. He always responded willingly and without request for favor. His other preoccupation was more abstract. Despite the hard work of the farm, he frequently corresponded with literate men of leisure about mathematical puzzles. Banneker usually found the solution, returning the answer in rhyme. Thus was he able to combine his love of literature with his devotion to mathematics.

One correspondent sent a puzzle asking Banneker to determine the number of leaps required for a hound, trailing at a certain distance, to overtake a shorter leaping hare. Banneker returned the answer:

Eight hundred leaps the dog did make
And sixty four the hare to take.

Not only did Banneker solve puzzles but he created some and expressed them in rhyme. He sent one such puzzle to his longtime friend George Ellicott:

Make me a vessel if we can agree,
The top and bottom diameter define,
To beat that portion as fifteen to nine,
Thirty-five inches are just what I crave,
No more and no less in depth will I have
Just thirty nine inches this vessel must hold.

Benjamin Banneker saw his first watch, courtesy of a friend. He marveled at the precise workings of the timepiece and asked to borrow it for study. The loan of the watch was an act of faith and show of high regard, for such a valuable instrument was anything but commonplace in the land.

Banneker studied the watch carefully. He mapped out the relations between the gears, wheels, and all moving parts that enabled the watch to keep track of time. Then, in a decision that was amazing, even for him, Banneker decided to build a clock for his own use. He felt he could construct a clock, using as a model the watch and a picture he had seen of a clock.

It should be kept in mind that clocks and watches during that period were made by skilled artisans, forerunners of scientific instrument makers, and originators of the principles of technology. Years of apprenticeship, under the watchful eye of a master craftsman, were required before being declared qualified to produce these magnificent timekeepers. The watchmakers had special tools and the best available metals at their disposal. Banneker had none of these. Undaunted by the lack of training, guidance by a master, or tools and materials, Banneker still believed he could produce a working model of this wonderful instrument.

With care and patience, plans took shape. All parts had to be accurately designed and proportionately larger than the inner workings of the watch he had seen. His knowledge of mathematics served him well. Having no metals, he used wood, and absent special instruments he used knives, files and whatever was available. His work, by and large, had to be done at night by the light of candles or oil lamps, and after farm chores were done. Sometimes he had to redo parts that were not accurate enough or, to his dismay, broke in the making. Nonetheless, he continued work on his tedious task.

Finally though, after two long years, Benjamin Banneker succeeded in making a striking clock out of wood. With minor adjustments, it is said to have kept perfect time for over 20 years, some reports state up to 40 years.   People came from miles around to see his remarkable creation.

"A Mind of Unusual Force"

George Ellicott introduced Banneker to astronomy after the latter's 58th birthday. It was a defining moment of his life. The preface of an almanac that Banneker published August 20, 1791, described the event:

> . . . George Ellicott lent him his Mayer's Tables. Ferfufon's Aftronomy, Leadbetter's Lunar Table, and fome aftronomic instruments but without accompanying them with either hint or inftructions that might further his ftudies, or lead him to apply to any ufeful refults. Thefe books and inftruments, the firft of the kind he had ever feen, opened a new world to Benjamin, and from thenceforth he employed his leifure aftronomical refearches.

Ellicott planned to return shortly and explain the technical concepts to his friend. An intrigued and impatient Banneker could not wait. He soon lost himself in deep and concentrated study, and in the challenge of a new and exciting science. In a surprisingly short time, he learned to plot positions of the sun, moon, planets, and to predict solar and lunar eclipses. Banneker predicted the solar eclipse of April 14, 1789. Because of his unfailing devotion to accuracy, he discovered an important error in one of the books Ellicott left him for use as a reference. Banneker went on to prepare numerous tables of measurements and calculations. Much of his data exist today. His research in astronomy, without the benefit of formal instruction caught the attention of some scholars in England. Moses Sheppard of England wrote:

> When we remember that Banneker was destitute of all means thought to be essential to the acquisition of astronomical knowledge, his aspiration to understand the organization of the Solar system must have been sustained by a mind of unusual force, which place him in the case of great men of every age.

The New Federal City

Along the way Banneker also became a surveyor. When America's first Head of State, President George Washington, appointed a commission to layout a new capitol for the nation, he included Andrew Ellicott, who in turn requested that Benjamin Banneker be added to the roster. Ellicott regarded Banneker as the most able astronomer among them, a skill essential for accurate location of sites and precise recordingss. He also knew his astronomical and surveying skills, linked together, would prove to be valuable. When informed that Banneker was a black man learned in science, mathematics, and surveying, Washington, under whose command blacks fought during the Revolutionary War, approved Ellicott's request without delay or qualms. By all accounts members of the commission accepted Banneker without prejudice or condescension.

Banneker's assignments were particularly burdensome, as he was no longer a young man. He spent nights plotting and recording essential astronomical data for the layout of Federal City, later Washington, D.C. and during the day presented the data to the men in the field. He also helped the surveyors plot various sites such as the United States Capitol Building, the White House, Treasury. and other buildings. There was insufficient time for him to sleep and rest.

Before the work could be completed a crisis developed around the head of the Team of Engineers, Pierre L'Enfant of France, who had fought with the Americans during the Revolutionary War. A rift between the Frenchman and some American officials, the relation with United States Secretary of State Thomas Jefferson being particularly strained, put the project in jeopardy. One night the angry L'Enfant left abruptly, taking all the plans with him. Upon discovery of his departure, and all the plans with him that represented great labor, an atmosphere of despair descended on the commission. Washington called the group together, explained the situation, and estimated there would be a delay of up to two years. Banneker offered a solution. Having seen all the plans, he felt confident that with a little help could reproduce them in a matter of days. Washington was skeptical believing the plans were too intricate, and too extensive for anyone to recall so much. Ellicott spoke up, telling the president that his friend had an unusual memory. He suggested that Washington authorize Banneker to proceed and asked that he be allowed to assist him where needed. Washington agreed, gave the authorization, and Banneker completed the drawings in a few days. That is why some historians call him "The Man Who Saved Washington, D.C."

Banneker's Almanac and Ephemeris

Banneker launched a new and ambitious project at the age of 60. With encouragement from the Ellicotts, he decided to write and publish an almanac and ephemeris. First introduced to the American colonies in 1639, almanacs provided useful information for a society where nearly everyone lived on a farm.

Tedious and time-consuming labor went into developing the almanac and ephemeris. Always meticulous, Banneker worked to be as accurate as possible. He published his first combined *Almanac and Ephemeris* in 1792. Nights he spent making and recording observations. During the day he worked on his calculations and developed tables. The almanac included a calendar of days, months weeks of the year. It contained information about medicine, the weather, seasonal suggestions, tides, ecclesiastical festivals, literature, poetry, quotations and essays. Banneker published "Tables of Federal Money" as established by Congress (e.g. 10 mills = 1 cents, 10 dimes = 1 Federal Dollar, 10 Dollars = 1 Eagle, etc). Monetary exchange tables explained the translation of money from England, Germany, China and other countries into American currency. For the traveller, he included information on road and highway connections. Other sections provided information on the federal government, such as the judiciary, its structure and some of its activities.

The ephemeris and almanac carried precise and detailed tables showing calculated positions of heavenly bodies from day to day at regular intervals. Navigators needed such information to find their way when at sea. He predicted several eclipses: the dates and times of lunar eclipses for February 25th and August 21st. Banneker predicted solar eclipses for March 12th and September 5th pointing out that the September eclipse could best be observed in London, England. Ferguson's formula, which rested on principles discovered by Sir Isaac Newton served as the basis for his calculations. Banneker found and corrected an error in Ferguson's formula, which led to greater accuracy in his calculations. That did nothing to diminish his respect and admiration for Ferguson, nonetheless in consistency with his belief that knowledge in science is dynamic not static, he wrote in his journal, "It seems to me that the wisest of men may at certain times be in error . . ."

The 1795 Banneker almanac carried a detailed account of a yellow fever epidemic. Published in chronological order of the spread, it contained useful epidemiological information and was among the first such published efforts in America.

Banneker published his almanac for some ten years until advancing age robbed him of the stamina needed to continue. Apparently no serious objection to his works surfaced due to his race though there was no attempt to hide its authorship by a black man. In fact, at one time it was said that the almanac rivaled Benjamin Franklin's *Poor Richard Almanac* published between 1732 and 1757. Armstead Williams of England called Banneker's astronomical calculations so "through as the excite the approbation of Pitt, Fox, and Wilburforce".

The most sensible of scientific Researchers

Much of Banneker's philosophical positions about science are revealed in his writings and quotations in his almanac. Some of them were contemporary and others remarkably modern. He clearly believed in empirical research but held that scientists should not be guided by dogma but should always keep an open mind for new information. Though scholars had amassed great stores of information, he believed that by far the greater volume of knowledge remained undiscovered. A quotation in his almanac expressed that view:

> The most sensible of those who make scientific researches is he who believes himself to be farthest from the goal and whatever advances he had made in his road, studies as if he yet knew nothing and marches as if he were only yet beginning to make his first advance.

Many people of his time believed Venus to be a star. It was a common misconception. So Banneker explained the nature of planets and how they were different from stars. It was clear that his distinction between the stars and known planets were correct but he could not resist going beyond observed knowledge to speculate that they could support life. In his 1792 almanac he wrote:

> That which we alternately call the morning and evening star, . . . is a planetary world, which with the four others [planets . . . vary their mystic dance, are themselves dark bodies and shine only by reflections . . . with all accommodating of animal subsistence.

Having so long studied the heavens, Banneker concluded that space was vast, much more than he had originally realized. The earth, which appears so large to its inhabitants, was, by comparison, exceedingly small. Beyond the distant planets were comets and constellations that gave off their own light. How could one explain such awesome bodies in the great expanse of space? Here Banneker the scientist would turn to his religion for answers. He believed that a supreme being was the architect and director of the universe. God placed those glittering worlds in place so that humankind could better understand his great might and unmatched powers. In all, he felt that there was a lesson on perspectives that rulers on earth and their countries should learn:

When I take the universe for my standard, how scanty is their size [earth kingdoms] and how scanty their figures [rulers].

Production of My Arduous Study

It has been noted that neither Banneker, nor his mother, sisters, or maternal aunts, were ever slaves, a legacy of Molly Welsh, and a condition unusual for blacks in America during times of slavery. The family could own property, and did. With his relative freedom, Banneker could receive some formal education, later exploit his exceptional mental powers with profound results, and did. His grandmother, an Englishwoman, once an indentured servant in the colonies, gave him the gift of being able to read and love of literature. The Quaker religion expanded his former schooling and introduced him to the wonders of mathematics. Then largely through self-education Banneker, an American farmer, became a man of letters, science, and mathematics. He studied the structure of American government and made a lasting contribution to the laying out of the nation's capitol. Not to be overlooked, he engaged other learned men in dialogue through writings, read widely, and held conversations with the likes of the Ellicotts and other Quakers. Though quiet spoken, the institution of slavery troubled him and he wished he could do something about it.

When Banneker completed the manuscript for his first almanac, he sent a copy of it and a cover letter to the erudite Secretary of State, Thomas Jefferson. In the letter he appealed to Jefferson to use his considerable influence to end slavery in the land on moral and constitutional grounds, even though Jefferson also owned slaves. Knowing that many scholars and theologians had portrayed blacks as sub-humans, this in order to justify slavery, Banneker sought to persuade Jefferson otherwise through a display of his almanac.

In his letter of August 19, 1791, Banneker first acknowledged Jefferson's high government position as a "distinguished and honorable station" which he approached from a humble position.

He acknowledged that none knew better than Jefferson how the "free" society held blacks in low regard, that they considered them "rather brutish than human, and scarcely capable of mental endowment." Banneker hoped to point out how false were those views . The Bible, he said, teaches that one "Universal Father" created all. That being the case, he said, then "however diversified in situation and color, we are all of the same family and stand in the same relation to Him." Therefore no less an authority than the Bible obligated Christians to "extend their power and influence to the relief of every part of the human race."

In a further effort to make the case that people of all colors deserved to be free, Banneker wrote of himself that he was a member of "the African race . . . of the deepest dye". He was a free man and blessed not to be " under that state of tyrannical thraldom and human captivity to which many of my brothers are doomed". He went on an asked Jefferson to remember when he and others chaffed under the tyranny of the " British Crown", longing to be free.

The freedom granted the American colonies, Banneker argued, came from Divine intervention; it was a special blessing from heaven meant not for one people but a universal gift to be shared. Withholding that blessing from others he suggested countered God's intent.

Continuing his plea, Banneker referred to Jefferson's words in the Declaration of Independence. He regarded it as inspired message, eloquent, and timeless. Banneker continued:

> Sir . . . you publicly held forth this true and invaluable doctrine which is worthy to be recorded and remembered in all succeeding ages, 'We hold these truths to be self-evident, that all men are created equal, and that they are endowed by their creator with certain inalienable rights, that amongst these are life, liberty, and the pursuit of happiness.'

It is of some interest that Banneker's assessment of the longevity of Jefferson's message proved to be prophetic. He considered the document to be profound, worthy to be honored and remembered throughout the ages. (Some of Jefferson's colleagues, though recognizing its grace and profundity, nevertheless thought that after a decade or two, it would fade into oblivion). From that point Banneker argued that it was hypocritical to sanction the institution slavery while simultaneously embracing the letter and spirit of the constitution. He went on to write;

> . . . how pitiable it is to reflect that altho you were so fully convinced of the benevolence of the father of mankind, and of his equal and impartial distribution of these rights and privileges . . . that you should counteract his mercies, by detaining in fraud and violence so numerous a part of my brethren.

Moving toward closure in his letter, Banneker addressed Jefferson as one scientist to another, and described the conditions under which he wrote his almanac and ephemeris:

> This calculation Sir, is the production of my arduous study, in this my advanced stage of life; for having long had unbounded desires to become acquainted with the secrets of nature, I have had to gratify my curiosity herein, through my own assiduous applications to astronomical study in which I need not recount to you the many advantages and disadvantages I have had to encounter.

Banneker's letter and almanac and ephemeris represented an early effort to influence national policy and practice based on scientific theory and law.

Jefferson responded to Banneker's letter with dispatch. He thanked the astronomer and said he earnestly wished for [more] proof "that nature has given to our [black] brethren talents equal to that of other colors of men . . ." That was as much a commitment as he would make. On the other hand, he did not regard the almanac and ephemeris lightly. Jefferson informed Banneker that he had sent a copy of the manuscript to Monsieur de Condorcet of the Academy of Sciences in Paris. This was one of the two leading, most influential science societies in the world during the late 18th century, the Royal Academy of Science in England being the other.

The Great Temple of Nature and Science

As mentioned, Banneker's physical decline due to advancing age caused him to stop publishing the almanac after about ten years. Still his mind remained alert, and he continued to study, observe the heavens, and make entries into his journal. He sold his farm to the Ellicotts with the provision he continue to live there under an endowment from them until his death. He based the terms of the sale on the value of the farm and his life expectancy. The Ellicotts agreed to the terms and became owners of the Bannekers' property. No longer having to support himself by farming, the old scientist spent more time in astronomical observation though at further price to his health.

Growing feeble, he faced other problems as well. Devious teenagers pilfered fruits from his orchard, which was among the best in the region. They stole other of his possessions as well. Now weakened and as usual, unassertive, Banneker could do little to stop them. His house was broken into by vandals and there was an attempt to burn his cabin. Even worse there is some indication of an attempt on his life.

Though a religious man, Banneker never formally affiliated with an established religion. He did attend some of the Quaker Meetings, usually entering quietly and departing in like manner. Silvio Bedini, who wrote an excellent biography, on Banneker, found a comment by Martha Ellicott Tyson who summed up the religious life of the man she knew. She wrote, "His life was one of constant worship in the great temples of nature and science".

Some biographers claimed that Banneker was occasionally given to excessive drinking. The author Shirley Graham (*Your Most Humble Servant*) appeared to dispute that view as did another Banneker biographer Will Allen. According to Allen, Banneker told about being introduced to alcoholic beverage during his assignment on the Federal City project. Of that experience

Banneker said, "I feared to trust myself even with wine, lest it steal away the little sense I have".

On October 9, 1806, Banneker left his cabin for a customary stroll. He met an acquaintance and while they spoke, suddenly felt ill. The acquaintance helped Banneker back to his cabin where he laid down and without speaking again, quietly expired. He passed away exactly one month short of his birthday.

Having been instructed in the event of his death, a nephew of Banneker took his books, astronomical instruments, calculations and valuable journal to George Ellicott. His Bible and certain other items went to his sisters. All other possessions were to be disposed of at the discretion of the family.

Burial took place in an unmarked grave two days after his death. A good estimate has been made of the site of his remains but the exact location is unknown. On the day of his internment, fire consumed his cabin, the cause suspect but undetermined. The building and all its content burned to ashes, Could it have been arson? There appears to be no hard evidence, only speculation and spontaneous combustion appears an unlikely cause.

The *Federal Gazette* announced Banneker's death in the obituary section October 28, 1806. The article described him as "a black man, an immediate descendent of an African father . . . well known in his community for his quiet demeanor, and among scientific men as an astronomer and mathematician".

Records identify the location of the Banneker farm. Having flourished from its founding by Molly Welsh, and continued until the decease of her only grandson, it gradually returned to its original state of trees and brush. Who and what Banneker was may have been lost but for the Ellicott's serving as temporary depository of his papers, some dedicated scholars who retrieved and studied them, and the Maryland Historical Society. Today he is remembered and honored through many books, articles, papers, visuals and audios, monuments and some schools bearing his name. It is also possible to visit his farm site.

Banneker never lost his sense of wonder about the universe. His religiosity, humility, and gratitude to his Maker is seen in a a passage from one of his several essays entitled "A Remarkable Dream", dated October 10, 1762.

Though I could not live many hours, nor did I believe I should if the Almighty in the extending of his Boundless-Goodness - had not Had Regard to me a poor unworthy creature and caus'd that Suffocating smell to pass from me, and gave me to trust in that melted my spirit into contrition before him & enabled me to vent my Sorrow in many Tears, after which my Toss'd mind was favored with a Calm.

References and Publications for Further Reading

Adams, Russell L., 1964. *Great Negroes Past and Present,* Chicago: Afro-Am Publishing Co., Inc,

Allen, Will, W. 1971. *The Afro-American Astronomer,* Freeport, New York: Books for Libraries Press.

"Banneker's Almanac and Ephemeris, 1793 and 1795", in *Afro-American History Series,* Wilmington, Delaware, Scholarly Resources, Inc.

Bedini, Silvio, 1971. *The Life of Benjamin Banneker, Astronomer and Scientist,* New York: Charles Scribner's Sons.

Clash, M. G. 1971. *Benjamin Banneker, Astronomer and Scientist*, Champaign, Illinois: Gerard Publishing Company.

Cromwell, John W., 1969. *The Negro in American History*, (Reprint of the 1914 Edition), New York: Johnson Reprint Company.

Graham, Shirley, 1949, *Your Most Humble Servant,* New York, Julian Messner, Inc.,

Green, Richard L. 1985. *A Salute to Black Scientists and Inventors,* Chicago: Empak Enterprise, Inc.

Haber, Louis, 1972. *Black Pioneers of Science and Invention,* New York: Harcourt, Brace and World.

Jenkins, Edward S., "Benjamin Banneker and Science Education", in Herget, Don Emil, 1990. *More History and Philosophy of Science in Science Teaching,* Proceeding of the First International Conference, Tallahassee, FL: Science Education and the Department of

Philosophy,

LePhillips, Phillip, "The Negro Benjamin Banneker, Astronomer and Mathematician, Pleas for universal Peace", *Record of the Columbia Historical Society,* (1917), 20:114-120.

Black Achievers of Science, Chicago: Museum of Science and Industry, 1988.

William, W., *History of the Negro Race in America from 1619 to 1880,* New York : Putnam's

Note: On October 9, 1995, the 189th anniversary of Benjamin Banneker's death, biologist-artist Pauline Smith-Carusi, her husband Chris and sons Mark, Galen and Glen, visited his farmland in Baltimore County, Maryland. They trekked over the the the area, writing notes, taking pictures along with sketches made by Smith-Carusi. Among other things they hiked along "Rock Creek", named by Molly Banneky. They also located the probable site of Benjamin Banneker's cabin near what is now the intersection of Odella and Westchester Street. A crumbling two-story unpainted frame building, overgrown by trees, saplings. and fallen branches, stands nearby.

A sign points the way to the Mount Gilboa A. M. E. Church, and underneath is a smaller incription showing the direction to the "Historical Home of Benjamin Banneker's Obelisk". They found no posted signs or any items informing the visitor of the nearby former Banneker farmland, nothing on the land itself. They explored a neglected, undeveloped historical site. Also on the Banneker side of the Odella-Westchester intersection is a meat packing/processing factory, along with cattles,cattle pens and related facilities.

A five foot tall granite obelisk, in honor of Benjamin Banneker, stands behind the Mount Gilboa A. M. E. Church on Westchester Avenue near the Odella intersection. It bears the inscription: "Benjamin Banneker, 1706-1831, Scientist". A bronze plaque explains that the monument was place near the unmarked gravesite of Banneker. The obelisk, erected in 1977, was the work of the Maryland Centennial Commission and the State Commission on Afro American History.

The Escape

George and Mildred Gaines McCoy felt the same compelling urge to be free. They did not want to live out their days as chattel slaves so in secrecy and with some apprehension, the couple weighed their chances for success if they attempted to run away. Could they avoid betrayal and escape undetected? Could they survive the rugged journey, walking and running hundred of miles north into a "free state?" If they failed, could they face the shame and endure the punishment that would be meted out to them for trying to escape? If they succeeded, could they survive the harsh and bitter cold of a northern winter? If they survived, could they start from scratch, poor and penniless, and support themselves in an alien land? Perhaps more important, could they overcome the shackles of mind and body, conditions imposed on them unending from birth that taught them to accept slavery as their natural destiny and their lot as inferior beings? To all questions they answered yes and decided to run away.

During the fall of 1837, The McCoys escaped but continued into Canada. They went there because the Federal Fugitive Slave Law allowed slaveowners to enter any state in the Union and claim their "property." The McCoys did not want that to happen to them.

The Fugitive Slave Law was controversial in some areas of the North. Angry free blacks were known to use threats, other times force, to protect friends and relatives from former owners who tried to return them to the plantation and sympathetic whites sometimes joined forces with black resistors. Such contentious behavior angered slaveowners who felt humiliated when forced to return home empty-handed. They pressed their representatives in Congress to strengthened the Fugitive Slave Law and make it more effective. Subsequently southern congressmen, themselves slaves holders, introduced new and more powerful legislation that people like the McCoys and their sympathizers feared. They threatened to leave the Union if the law did not pass, and many northern congressmen, cowered, uncaring, or in agreement with their views, joined them in voting for the measure.

The new legislation ordered law enforcement officers to capture and hold for return any fugitive slave within their jurisdiction. It empowered them to create any force necessary to subdue persons resisting the apprehension of escaped slaves. Anyone aiding, harboring, or concealing a fugitive slave risked heavy fines, arrest, or both. Encouraged by the new law, armed gangs roamed the countryside, supposedly looking for fugitive slaves. In practice they often took any person of African lineage, free-born or manumitted, into custody and turned them over for a bounty.

Then, even the Canadian sanctuary came under attack. One case concerned a man named Parker who escaped from a plantation and found refuge in Kingston, Ontario, Canada. Upon learning of Parker's whereabouts, Governor Johnston of Pennsylvania declared him to be an escaped criminal. He tried to use terms of the Webster-Asburton Treaty to demand that Canada extradite Parker to the United States as a criminal. The British Governor refused. He pointed out that the Webster-Asburton Treaty pertained to criminals. Slaves, he ruled, were not criminals but were "fugitives from justice." That being the case, the Webster-Asburton Treaty did not apply to Parker. With that ruling Canada remained a safe haven for Parker, the McCoys, and all fugitive slaves in that country who escaped from the United States.

George McCoy enlisted in the Canadian army and saw active duty. He served a specified period of time, thereafter receiving an honorable discharge and a 160-acre tract of land. George and Mildred McCoy started a family and reared their 12 children in Colchester, Ontario. From there they could go to the banks of Lake Erie and look across its narrow end at the United States.

Life was not easy for the McCoys. They lived in poverty at first, barely able to sustain themselves. Being ill-clothed and inadequately housed they suffered through the frigid winter months. Nonetheless, they would sacrifice the warm climate for their freedom. They vowed never to be slaves again.

Lawrence Carter of Detroit once interviewed some acquaintances of the McCoy's third oldest son. They learned from them that in Canada the McCoy family experienced a social life and some sense of community with a colony of hardy ex-slaves living in nearby Buxton, Ontario. In fact, that may have been the McCoy's original settlement. Gravestones in the Buxton area, west of Chatham, testify to the existence of that Canadian community.

To Scotland

Elijah, the third son of Mildred and George McCoy, was born May 12, 1843. He was a child of incessant curiosity who learned quickly and well. Especially did he show a fondness for mechanical things and a knack for repairing them. When Mildred and George were slaves, not only did they want freedom, they also dreamed of seeing their children get an education.

In Elijah they saw the best promise for fulfillment of their dream. As the boy continued to make progress, and his talents with mechanical things became more evident, they decided to send him to Scotland where he could study engineering. It was a visionary judgment that ranked high, and in some respects not unlike their decision to run away to freedom. Somehow, they could contemplate education at a level far beyond their own limited experience, where even simple reading and writing skills were considered notable accomplishments among people of many persuasions.

At the age of 15, Elijah boarded a ship for a long journey across the Atlantic to Scotland, and the University of Edinburg. He felt lonely at first in this strange land among strange people. Soon though, Elijah adjusted to the people and the environment and, determined not to betray the trust of his parents, applied himself industriously to his studies. Meanwhile, George McCoy worked several jobs, putting in long and tiring hours to support his son abroad and his family at home. Elijah resided in Scotland for five long years until he met all the requirements for certification as an engineer. The McCoy family celebrated his achievement in their hearts, quite proud of this fulfilling historical moment made by an offspring of ex-slaves.

Elijah returned home to Canada but remained for only one year. He crossed the border into the United States, the country of his parent's birth. A brutal Civil War was over, Union forces won, preserved the Union and ended slavery. McCoy knew Michigan was a busy, leading industrial state so he settled southwest of Detroit in Ypsilanti. What more logical place for an engineer, eager and prepared, to begin his career?

A proliferation of signs announcing openings for trained engineers confirmed his beliefs. McCoy applied for an opening at the Michigan Central Railroad. Though qualified by the credentials he presented, the company rejected his application because of his race. Disappointed yet determined, McCoy applied for another vacancy, then another, and another, but always with identical results and for the same reason. It was difficult to accept but he had to face the reality that no firm was going to employ him as an engineer. The young engineer agonized over his fate, the years of study, the sacrifices, hopes, and dreams of his parents now seemed for naught.

Still McCoy knew he had to earn a living but not in the profession for which he had trained. Reluctantly he accepted the only type of employment opened to a black man , which was shoveling coal into a steam engine firebox and lubricating machines by hand. Sometimes the work was hazardous, especially to fingers and hands. It was not uncommon for workers to suffer serious injuries to arms, legs and other parts of the body.

The Automatic Lubricator

Moving surfaces, when in contact, create friction. To reduce undesirable friction, surfaces must be as smooth as possible, and in the case of most machines, lubricated. Without lubrication, the higher friction causes results in temperature increase, sometimes to extremely high levels. Under such conditions, engine efficiency suffers, and severe damage leads to early wearing out. As an engineer, McCoy understood the principles of friction and the benefits of lubrication but with his advanced knowledge and training he was clearly underemployed. The routine tasks of his job did not offer the challenges his education prepared him to address.

It was in this banal environment that an inspiration emerged. McCoy reflected on the critical engineering problem common to machines with moving parts and this was friction. Regardless of the smoothness of the surface, friction was a problem. A number of other conditions obtained. Among them, the necessity for "down-time, that is stopping, lubricating and restarting industrial machines. Such an operation, though unavoidable, was costly, wasting valuable production time and limiting profits. On the railroad, "down time" to lubricate trains caused delays and inconveniences for passengers and slow delivery of commerce. McCoy pondered the problem: "Could it not be possible to make machines lubricate themselves without stopping?" He began to visualize a revolutionary type of machine - one that would lubricate itself!

He reviewed numerous machines, their intricate construction, and how they worked. From that point he considered ways and means of creating and arranging coordinating parts that would self-lubricate, in the right amount, and at the right intervals. McCoy set up a makeshift shop behind his house so he could build and test models. He used his own meager funds for research and then scrounged around for scrap metals to build his new device. He cut scraps and shaped them to fit his designs. Week after week, month after month, he built, tested, re-tested, modified, changed, and occasionally discarded parts. Sometimes things went smoothly, other times discouragingly slow or not at all. But his faith and vision persisted. They kept him going.

Finally in 1872, after two years of labor, Elijah McCoy built an automatic lubricator for machines. He was granted patent, No. 129,843 on July 23, 1872. With that invention came a new era in machine lubrication and a forward step in the industrial world.

After the first product went into operation, McCoy's astute mind saw how it could be improved. He worked quickly and in just two weeks patented a second device called an "Improvement in Lubricators for Steam-Engines" (No. 130,305, August 6, 1872). Less than nine months later, he filed for another patent under the title "Lubricators" (No. 139,407, May 27, 1873). A part of the description for that lubricator read:

> This lubricator oils chiefly when steam is exhausted, which is the time when oil is most needed; but if it is desired to provide for oil when the engine is working, it can readily be accomplished by simply making a channel or groove in the valve.

McCoy then solved another nagging industrial problem with his invention patented June 2, 1876 (No. 179,585). He introduced an improvement to an existing double-seated valve stating:

> I have found, by practice, that I cannot inject cold oil in a cylinder using steam packing, which is very much needed when such packing gets gummed up. To obviate this difficulty is the object of my invention. . .

Another of McCoy's inventions corrected a persistent problem in the railway industry. Lubricators on train locomotives were losing oil when the operator cut the steam off. Train locomotives also lost oil when they stopped at stations or slowed down on steep grades. McCoy found the conditions within the system that created the problem. He called it an "absolute and useless waste of lubricant". He solved that problem with another invention patented October 21, 1881. (No. 255, 443). His invention of September 13, 1898 allowed lubrication to be distributed through pipes under different pressures (No. 610, 634). Still another invention improved on this principle (No. 611,754).

McCoy's devices used lubricants of various weights and viscosities. They were adaptable to machines of different sizes, speeds and conditions of variable pressures. The machines varied from steam engines to airbrakes. Sometimes a single machine required several dissimilar lubricants and his inventions met those needs. Despite creation of such intricate devices, of all his inventions, observers rank as most ingenious the solid or graphite lubricator, patented in 1915.

The "Real McCoy"

The *Detroit News* reported that "From then [1872] until 1915, all railroad locomotives and steamships in the United States, and most foreign countries, were equipped with McCoy's `sight feed' and `gravity feed' lubricators. He helped to modernize the industrial world as his inventions encouraged universal adoption of automatic lubricating machines. Production costs dropped, profits increased, and conditions for safety improved.

According to Gordon Tschiarhart, between 1872 and 1920 McCoy was responsible for at least 87 inventions. He patented 57 of them. Most were lubricating devices. Some of his minor and lesser known inventions included an ironing board, wagon tongue, rubber heel for shoes, a metal table and a lawn sprinkler.

Not surprising, others moved into the automatic lubricator business. None however, matched McCoy's high standard of design, rigorous construction, durability, and dependability of performance. His was the choice of those who wanted the best. To avoid getting inferior substitutes, buyers often asked, "Is this the *Real McCoy?*" Thus was born an enduring American expression symbolic of pride in quality and authenticity.

Striking Appearance

Professional engineering journals cited many of McCoy's inventions. As word of his creations spread, several groups invited the inventor to address their group or serve as their consultant. Others who never met the McCoy, knew of him through reading engineering journals. Unfortunately, some persons and groups withdrew their invitation when McCoy's race became known to them. For the same reason, some refused to use his products despite their superior quality.

By demeanor, McCoy was a proud man though not very talkative. A figure of dignified bearing, he was physically strong and active most of his life. Lawrence Carter described his meeting the elderly McCoy:

> I often encountered McCoy on the Oakland Streetcar . . . He was spruce, erect, with a gray-streaked Patriarchal beard. He always stood at the rear of the streetcar, leaning on his cane. His appearance was striking even in advanced age. His eyes, bright and extremely piercing, would challenge you if you stared at him.

Carter remembered another image of McCoy. It had to do with a photograph that hung on the wall of a dentist, Dr. James B.

Goggins, that showed McCoy in the cab of the first locomotive equipped with "his lubricating system," which was adopted by the Canadian National Railways.

> When McCoy came in to visit Dr. Goggins he would often stand and gaze at the photograph of himself in that first locomotive outfitted with his lubricating system. He never talked much. Unlike most old men, he was not addicted to long boring tales about the past.

Despite his low-key mannerism, McCoy sometimes showed impatience with others. Monroe Walker, when researching material on McCoy's life, interviewed Karl Hamilton, president of the Detroit Historic Sites Committee. Said Hamilton, "He [McCoy] was a genius and geniuses are not [always] congenial people. He was impatient with ordinary people for not being able to fathom what he was talking about."

Carter reported that on another occasion McCoy had it out with the president of Stroh Brewing Company. It seems that Stroh said he wanted an aluminum can McCoy devised, as a souvenir. What started as a lively conversation between the two men ended up in a shouting match. McCoy stormed out. Shaken by the experience, Stroh retreated and asked for a drink. Then he had some unkind words to say about McCoy. Said Hamilton of McCoy, ". . . he was an educated engineer. . . a genius who was greatly misunderstood." It is of some interest that today most beer is sold in aluminum containers.

Another account involved McCoy and a well known citizen. Robert Willis, Detroit's oldest black lawyer, was given to long discourses, not all of them factual. Quite often his stories were boring, but no one told him so. On one such occasion McCoy was present:

> [Willis] launched into a windy tale about the panic of 1893 and [stories about] Coxey's army. McCoy cut him off sharply and called him a liar and [an] old windbag. Soon attorney Bob was fast asleep

of McCoy.

Set High Goals

In 1873, Elijah McCoy married Mary Elizabeth Delaney. Their union, which lasted for 50 years, ended only by her prior death. Mary McCoy was devoted to the cause of community advancement and gave support and leadership to several local organizations. She was an early worker in the women's suffrage movement.

Nine years after their marriage, the McCoys moved from Ypsilanti to Detroit, residing at various locations before settling at 5370 Lincoln Drive. Like his wife, McCoy was active in the community and supported various causes aimed at improving the lot of local citizens. His primary interests were the youth of Detroit, for in them he saw hope for the future. Each week McCoy volunteered time to work in a local youth center where he urged young people to set high goals and to work hard toward realization of their dreams. He stressed the importance of a good, solid, and fundamentally sound education. The price of such an education was serious, dedicated and purposeful study. McCoy disliked idleness, encouraging instead productive use of spare time. From such applications, he promised, good things can happen. He sounded like Erick From who wrote:

> There is no meaning to life except the meaning that man gives his life by the unfolding of his powers, by living productively.

Final Years

Sadly, the final years of McCoy's life were not kind to him. His wife died in 1923 and her passing affected him deeply. He grieved her loss and felt quite alone without her. Then his health, always marked by its vigor, went into sharp decline. With proceeds from all his remarkable inventions, McCoy should have been well off financially, but he was not. Ernest Browne, a Detroit citizen who spent an entire year researching the life of McCoy, concluded that the inventor was the victim of unscrupulous dealings. Monroe Walker came to a similar conclusion:

> Because of the widespread discrimination at the time, it was virtually impossible for him to gain access to corporate chiefs without white help. He frequently had to completely or partially assign his lucrative patents to white companies and individuals to raise research funding for his inventions.

Browne also said that McCoy was 'fleeced' by business partners even as they helped set up a company called the McCoy Graphite Lubricator Company. Later they renamed the company the McCoy Lubricator Company.

When his wife passed the bright spark of life began to fade from the old inventor. Then troubles mounted. Age, infirmities, and the pain of betrayal from business associates took their toll. McCoy became cranky and easily irritated. His once brilliant and productive mind faltered. A forlorn attempt at another invention failed costing him what little money he had left. He lost his business, his home, and the weight of betrayals and losses troubles made him bitter. As his robust health sank, McCoy became a poor, pathetic figure. He wandered about virtually homeless, yet too proud to ask for help. In 1928, a doctor hearing an old black man claiming to have been a great inventor, thought him crazy. The physician diagnosed McCoy as a man "suffering from delusions of grandeur" and committed him to the Eloise Infirmary (later named the Wayne County Hospital). There, languishing in virtual obscurity, he spent his last days. On October 10, 1929, alone and almost forgotten, Elijah McCoy died. He was 86 years old.

The county planned to bury McCoy in a pauper's grave. Fortunately, some old friends learned of his passing, collected money and gave him a decent burial. They laid him to rest in the Detroit Memorial Cemetery in Warren.

Remembering

Some 46 years after his death, the Detroit Historical Society placed a marker for McCoy at 5730 Lincoln Drive, the site of his former home. It had become an empty lot. Officials of the Henry Ford Museum in Dearborn also placed one of his lubricators on display. In further tribute, they named a street at the Ford Research Park Development the Elijah McCoy Drive.

On the strength of his inventive genius, Elijah McCoy vindicated the hopes and dreams of his parents when they took a risky flight to escape their enslavement. They wanted to be free, and wanted their children to be born free and later educated. By dent of his mind and determination, their free son Elijah rose above the restrictions of his environment, and his creativity flourished to the benefit of industrial progress. Though we know a great deal about Elijah McCoy, as one writer said, much about him remains shrouded in mystery. But we do know his life was real, his numerous creations were real, and that he, Elijah McCoy, was *The Real McCoy.*

References and Sources for Further Reading

Adams, Russell, L., 1964. *Great Negroes, Past and Present,* Chicago: Afro-Am-Publishing Company.

Baker, Henry E., 1969. *The Colored Inventor,* New York: Ronald Press and New York Times. .

Burt, McKinley, 1969. *Black Inventors of America,* Portland, Oregon, National Book Store.

Carter, Lawrence, "The Real McCoy, *Detroit News,* February 1, 1981, pp. 7, 11.

Foner, Phillip S., 1983. *History of Black Americans from the Compromise of 1850 to the End of the Civil War,* Westport CT: Greenwood Press.

Green, Richard (ed), *1985., A Salute to Black Scientist and Inventors,* Chicago: Empak Enterprises.

Haskins, Him, *1991. Outward Dreams: Black Inventors and Their Inventions,* New York: Walker and Company.

Hayden, Robert C., *1992. Nine African American Inventors*, Frederick, MD: Twenty-First Century Books.

James, Portia, 1989. *The Real McCoy: African-American Invention and Inventors, 1619-1930*, Washington, D. C.: Smithsonian Institution Press.

Klein, Aaron, 1970. *Hidden Contributor: Black Scientists and Inventors in America*, Garden City, New York: Doubleday and Company.

Sterling, Philip, and Rayford Logan, 1961. *Four Took Freedom*, Garden City, New York: Zenith Books.

Taylor, Julius (ed), 1955. *The Negro in Science*, Baltimore, MD: Morgan State Press, .

Tschiarhart, Gordon, "City Asked to Name Research Park Road for Black Inventor, *The Detroit News*, April 2, 1975, Sec. C

Walker, Monroe, "Forgotten Genius: His Inventions Made Millions; He Died Broke, *The Detroit News*, February 3, 1983, p.1A

Winslow, Eugene, 1974. *Black Americans in Science and Engineering, Contributors of Past and Present*, Chicago: Afro-American Publishing Co. inc.

Chapter III_____

Lewis Howard Latimer-
Inventor and Humanist
(1848-1928)

They called him a handsome man with winning ways. His fair skin and wavy hair made him stand out among his people. Nonetheless he chaffed under the lowly conditions that allowed others to treat him badly, and worse he saw no end in sight. His name was George Latimer. His father was white, his mother black, so in keeping with the laws and customs of the times, George Latimer, like his mother, was a slave.

George lived and labored on a plantation owned by James B. Gray in the Commonwealth of Virginia. The thought of living in bondage for the rest of his life on this plantation filled him with dread and misgivings so he decided he would run away to freedom-again. His flight though could not be alone for George simply could not leave his beautiful brown-skinned wife, another slave named Rebecca Smith-Latimer, behind. She was pregnant and the couple wanted their child to be free at birth, and for life.

By The Overground Railroad

Rebecca agreed to risk the flight to freedom with her husband though she knew as well as he that capture meant severe punishment, humiliation, and possibly worse. They therefore planned carefully for a long and arduous journey. Their strategy, though clever, was risky. They would run away-not by the underground railroad but the overground railroad. The fair skinned George would pass himself off as a slave master and if anyone inquired, he was taking his "property" to the next county. On October 4, 1842, the couple stole away and headed north At first they hid on a boat, then continued their escape by land. The exhausting trek and constant fear of being caught, severely tested the mettle of George Latimer and his courageous, pregnant wife but they persisted. Finally, after traveling some 600 grueling miles, George and Rebecca Latimer reached the Commonwealth of Massachusetts where at last, they were free!

Or so they thought. Gray learned of the Latimers' whereabouts and set out to bring them back. Under terms of the Fugitive Slave Law he went to Massachusetts and demanded the return of his slaves. Glennette Tilley Turner, author of the book *Lewis Howard Latimer*, said that " James B. Gray arrived in Boston and had Latimer arrested." She reported that news of his arrival spread quickly and "nearly 300 African American men assembled around the courthouse to prevent Gray from taking Latimer out of the city illegally." Protests erupted at the historic Faneuil Mall, and in nearby towns and cities. Abolitionists Frederick Douglass and William Lloyd Garrison joined the campaign to free George Latimer while sympathizers hid his wife.

Several black men guarded the jail hoping to thwart Latimer's re-enslavement. Turner also said another campaign was in the making:

Other abolitionist were busy trying to purchase Latimer
from Coolege [deputy keeper of the Suffolk County jail].
One was an African-American whose name is unrecorded
The other was Dr. Henry Bowditch. . . A black minister,
The Reverend Samuel Caldwell, acting on behalf of some
members of his church . . . purchased Latimer for $400.00.

When he heard the story, John Greenleaf Whittier wrote a long 24 stanza poem about slavery and the Latimers. In it he attacked both slavery and the Fugitive Slave Law, calling each cruel and immoral acts. Whitttier also defended Massachusetts citizens against Virginians who threatened them when they provided safe havens for the likes of Latimer. Here are three of the stanzas:

> From rich and rural Worcester, where through the clam repose
> Of cultured vales and fringing woods the gentle Nashua flows,
> To where Wachuset's wintry blast the mountain larches stir,
> Swelled up to Heaven the thrilling cry of "God Save Latimer!"
>
> We wage no war,-- we lift no arms, -- we fling no torch within
> The fire - damps of the quaking mine beneath your soil of sin;
> We leave ye with your bondmen, to wrestle while ye can,
> With the strong upward tendencies and godlike soul of man!
>
> But for us and for our children the vow which we have given
> For freedom and humanity is registered in heaven;
> 'No slave-hunt in our borders, -- no pirate on our strand!
> No fetters in the Bay State, -- No slave upon our land!

Then black citizens, joined by whites raised funds to buy the Latimers' freedom and break the chains of their bondage. The grateful and relieved couple finally realized their ambition never to be slaves again. Their family increased by four children and William, George, Margaret, the only daughter, and Lewis the youngest child, were born and remained free as their parents had dreamed.

Nevertheless the family faced great hardships. George Latimer could not find work on a regular basis although he had various construction and other skills. Without a regular income, he was unable to provide the bare necessities for his wife and children. Distraught, and despairing, and feeling his family would be better off without him, one day George Latimer left without notice, abandoning Rebecca and the children. Somehow, the family survived and seemingly without lasting rancor toward him. All the children grew to adulthood and Lewis, the youngest, though he never saw his father again, learned about him years later through correspondence with Frederick Douglass.

The remainder of this story is about Lewis, who was born September 4, 1848 in Chelsea, Massachusetts, near Boston. Years later this son of former slaves was recognized by the likes of Thomas A. Edison for his contributions to the emerging electrical industry and in various ways, to the nation.

Obliged to Serve

On April 12, 1861, Civil War broke out between the northern and southern states. Confederate forces of the south attacked Fort Sumpter in South Carolina, and southern states proclaimed themselves seceded from United States. President Abraham Lincoln vowed that the nation would not be divided and led the Union forces in war against the rebellious states. Slavery of course, was a central issue and much the cause of the conflict. The Latimer brothers, pondered the situation. They were poor and life was a struggle. Still they were free, and each of them shared their parents abhorrence of slavery. Frederick Douglass, who along with others helped their parents win permanent freedom, urged blacks to fight and forever break the chains of slavery. The Latimer brothers felt obliged to join a cause they believed to be in the interest of freedom. All three brothers signed up for duty and served with the Union forces during the Civil War.

Despite the gravity of the war however, black men desiring to fight for their country were not readily accepted into the armed forces of the Union. Though black fighting men had proven their valor during the Revolutionary War and the War of 1812, many whites still doubted their courage and discipline on the field of battle. Black leaders protested the exclusion and demanded the right to enlist in ground and naval forces. Thousands of young black men pressed the issue. Finally, with the war increasing in intensity and casualties mounting, the Union changed its policy. Black men answered the call and went to war.

Young George Latimer fought with the 29th Connecticut Volunteer Infantry. Accounts vary about his brother William. He either served with a land unit like George, or with the navy. Lewis enlisted in the United States Navy at the age of sixteen. He was assigned to the gunboat, the *U.S.S. Massasoit*.

The *Massasoit* got its name from the late chief of the Wampanoag Indian. Chief Massasoit gave food and provided other necessities to the early settlers at Plymouth, Massachusetts. His compassion helped ensure their survival during their first bitter winter on the continent. The gun boat bearing his name sailed south to take part in a military campaign on the James River in Virginia.

Sailing under the command of Lt. G. Watson Sumner, the *Massasoit* reached the James River on January 24, 1865. As General Tecumseh Sherman of the U. S. Army prepared for his famous march to the sea, Confederate Commander General Robert E. Lee tried desperately to control the James River. Its strategic position made the river critical to Confederate defense plans. So when the *Massasoit* and other gunboats sailed into the James, they ran into stiff resistance, coming under heavy fire from Confederate batteries dug in the swamps along the banks of the river. Other batteries at a place called the Howlett house commanded a vantage point for firing on the approaching Union boats. In the ensuing battle, the *Massasoit* was rocked by several hits as the Confederate forces repeatedly hurled "shot and shell" at them. One shell ripped into the starboard wheel and cut it entirely in two. Other hits broke the "supporting shaft," cut the escape steampipe and damaged the boatswain department, bulwark, and paddle wheel. Under the attack men on the gunboat were thrown to deck and some suffered wounds from Confederate fire. The *Massasoit* fought back, and fired on the attackers in the swamps. Despite the opposition, Union forces made their way up the river and rained shells on the swamps and Howlett house. After a fierce battle with casualties on both sides, the Union forces secured the river.

After the vicious battle, Lt. Sumner praised his men for their conduct under fire. He wrote in his report:

> Too much credit cannot be given to the officers and crew for the manner in which they conducted themselves during the action. It being the first action they participated in, they deserve special commendations, acting as they did, like veterans.

Fighting in Virginia to help free the slaves, near where his parents had escaped slavery so he and his siblings could be born free, must have caused Lewis Latimer to ponder the fate that brought him to that land. No doubt victory that day had a special meaning to the quiet, reserved young man from Chelsea, Massachusetts.

Thereafter the James River remained under the control of Union forces until the end of the war. The *Massasoit* also carried out several other assignments after the James River campaign. For a while they guarded the mouth of the river, acting as a deterrent against any Southern ram that might try to reach the Atlantic. On other assignments, the ship carried dispatches to General Sherman in North Carolina and patrolled the North Carolina Sounds. Listed as a cabin boy, Latimer also pulled duty as a landsman, patrolling the shore to guard against enemy attacks on the gunboat from land.

Like everyone else in the campaign, North or South, black or white, Latimer faced the danger of being killed or wounded in battle. But he faced an additional peril because Confederate forces generally did not classify captured black soldiers and sailors as prisoners of war. Under that policy they claimed special exemption from international law, and black prisoners suffered the highest rate of death among all prisoners from torture, neglect, and starvation.

Office Boy, Draftsman and Alexander Graham Bell

When General Robert E. Lee surrendered at Appomattox, the terrible war, a lamentable chapter in American history, ended in victory for the Union forces. Latimer received an honorable discharge from the United States Navy and went home. His brothers also returned safely following their honorable discharge from duty in the army. The Latimers were proud to have served their country in time of war, and to have helped preserve the Union. They also did their part to end nearly 250 years of slavery for blacks in America, helping in the process to free the country as well.

Many years after the Civil War had ended an interesting scenario took place in a New York City school. A young Winifred Latimer

Norman, granddaughter of Lewis Latimer, sat in a history class in Queens, New York. When the subject of the Civil War came up, Winifred told the teacher and her classmates that her grandfather had fought in that war as a U. S. Navy enlisted man. There being no mention of black servicemen in their textbook, none of them believed her. Days later her class attended a parade of Civil War Veterans in New York joining the festive crowd along the streets. Then came the band, followed by a group of Civil War Veterans in step, marching smartly under the colors. Then she saw her grandfather among them, erect, with military bearing, and decked sharply in his uniform. Excitedly she waved and called out to him. Latimer spotted his granddaughter, smiled broadly, and waved back. It delighted young Winifred that her classmates could see proof of her claim, but most of all, she was so proud of her grandfather.

Upon his return to Boston after the war, Latimer immediately sought employment. Unfortunately, like his father before him, he found the task daunting in the face of rejection after rejection. Nevertheless the young war veteran persisted.

Eventually, his tenacity, and critical help that Turner revealed came from a colored maid who recommended him, paid off. Crosby and Gould, a prominent law firm located at 34 School Street that specialized in patent applications, hired him as an office boy. Latimer did his job well, and to the satisfaction of his employers but stimulated by this environment aspired to be more than an office boy. His formal education, barely at the fourth grade level, was limited but he was a voracious reader who could absorb, retain and fathom vast quantities of written material.

In particular the work of the draftsmen captured Latimer's imagination. So much did he admire the care, detail, and precision of their work that, during his spare time, he devoted much energy to the study of mechanical drawing. The decision by Latimer to educate himself in this technical field, where African Americans were rare if not totally absent, when previously he could barely find work as an office boy, was an act of considerable optimism. Still he went ahead, using some of his meager income of three dollars a week, to buy books on mechanical drawing and to purchase second-hand tools and materials. Latimer studied hard. He spent hours in practice.

Occasionally when stumped by some technical matter, the aspiring young draftsman received help from a sympathetic worker at the firm.

Finally, confident that he could do the work of a draftsman, Latimer astonished his boss by requesting a promotion from office boy to that loftier position. He showed him some of his drawings and one of the draftsmen spoke up in his favor. Though reluctant initially, his boss relented and gave his office boy, the Civil War Veteran, a chance.

Latimer made good on his opportunity as his work fully met the high standards required by Crosby and Gould. He labored with such skill and dependable work ethics, that eventually the firm made him its Chief Draftsman.

Meanwhile, Latimer met and became friends with a teacher of deaf children named Alexander Graham Bell. The men found common ground in their love of music, the classics, and elocution. One day Bell told Latimer he wanted to obtain a patent for his invention, the "talking wire". He asked if Latimer would help him by doing the technical drawings. He also needed assistance in describing his invention in the language of patent applications, and according to the specification required by the United States Patent office. Latimer agreed. In 1876, Alexander Graham Bell procured a patent for his historic invention, the telephone, first called the talking wire. Perhaps no invention in the history of communication, and few of any kind, has had a more profound effect on the people of the world. Years later Latimer confessed that neither he nor Bell fully understood the importance of the telephone at that time, or the profundity of its impact.

Latimer, apparently moonlighting, could assist Bell with the patent application because of his draftsman's skill and the experience of his own first invention. On February 10, 1874, he and Charles W. Brown of Salem, Massachusetts obtained a patent for their invention of a new, improved, and useful Railway Car Water Closet (toilet). The two men had observed that railway water closets on trains were so designed that the bottom opened when in use and closed when the lid dropped. Any passenger venturing to use the closet when the train was in motion faced a perilous suction effect that brought in fast flying "dust, cinders, and other matter thrown up from the track. "

The number and speed of such particles was ". . . so great as to forbid or discourage use of the apparatus except under extreme conditions."

The men considered a water closet that would eliminate the hazard and would be easy to use. They worked together on the problem with Latimer making the sketches. Finally they came up with what they felt was the solution. The Latimer-Brown Water Closet used a pivoted bottom. Raising the seat automatically closed the bottom, making it safe to use. Closing the seat automatically opened the bottom, allowing the content to be discharged. Many railroads soon adopted their invention permitting passengers to obtain relief in safety and comfort. Their Water Closet was particularly appreciated by long distance railway passengers.

"My Love and I"

In matters of his social life, Latimer met and began dating Mary Wilson of Falls River, Massachusetts. Comely and graceful, Miss Wilson had large brown eyes and black hair that she wore swept back to just above her shoulders. On November 10, 1873, at the age of twenty five, Latimer won her hand in marriage. Later the couple moved to Connecticut, before relocating to New York City. The love and affection they had for each other held fast for more than fifty years broken only by her prior death. Latimer also wrote poetry and among the more than 100 poems he composed, many if not most were dedicated to or inspired by his Mary. One of his poems, "My Love and I" told how they could speak to each other without uttering a single word:

My love and I we side by side are sitting,
While fast the evening hours sweetly flitting;
Speechless tho' answering sigh to sigh
 Can, without word their wealth of love impart;
The touch of loving hand, or glance of eye
Needs but the language of an answering sigh.

Mary as ever and always his Venus. Though her light brown skin, black hair, brown eyes, and other features differed from the goddess of Greek fame, to him she was no less a goddess. He wrote another poem entitled the "The Ebon Venus" just for her.

I love her form of matchless grace,
The dark brown beauty of her face,
Her lips that speak of love delight,
Her eyes that gleam as stars at night.

O'er Marble Venus let them rage
Who set the fashion of the age;
Each to his taste; but as for me,
My venus shall be ebony.

Hiram Maxim

Hiram Maxim may better be remembered for his invention, the Gatlin Gun. It preceded the machine gun and various automatic weapons of today. He is less well known for his association with the United States Electric Company of Bridgeport, Connecticut where Latimer called him "chief engineer and inventor." There Maxim played a prominent role as a pioneer in the commercial use of electricity. His company produced various electrical products including dynamos used to generate current electricity. At that time, the commercial use of electricity was a new and yet to be realized dream. Like any new advancement in science and technology, much needed to be learned about the nature of electricity, and how this strange, fascinating, phenomenon could be used for the benefit of society. Ability, skill, knowledge, and bold imagination were very much in need.

One day Maxim happened to see Latimer at work. Surprised at what he saw, Maxim suddenly realized he was staring at the draftsman. Composing himself, he somewhat awkwardly apologized, explaining he did not mean to be rude. He simply had never seen such talent in a black man and in fact the very possibility never occurred to him. The two men began to talk and as they learned more about each other, a bond of mutual respect began to form. Although Latimer had not been schooled in electricity, Maxim recognized his skills and realized he was a man of imagination, a quick study and well-informed. He explained to Latimer what his company did, and about the promising commercial use of electricity. He also talked about how the industry needed people of vision, skill, and dedication and who were not fearful of this potentially powerful source of energy. Maxim then offered Latimer a position with his company.

Latimer pondered the offer. How could he know if the position with Maxim would work out? Should he take the risk? Still the work going on at the United States Electric Company intrigued him. He saw possibilities of a technological breakthrough that could change the way humankind lived. So Latimer accepted the offer and the challenge. In 1880, at the age of 32, he joined the United States Electric Company of Bridgeport, Connecticut.

There is no way to predict with certainty when or whether persons of special gifts will realize their potential and manifest their creativity. Still, it may be suggested that certain conditions in society favor the nourishment and development of a creative mind. In Massachusetts, and later Connecticut, though somewhat circumscribed by race and economics Latimer had opportunities to develop his talents. These opportunities would not had been vouchsafed for him in slavery and his creativity could never have emerged as it did. In the case of Latimer, he fully availed himself of what opportunities he had, and society benefited.

At the United States Electric Company Latimer carefully studied the known scientific principles of electricity. He closely observed the various manufacturing processes and became fully acquainted with all the procedures. As he put it :

> Within a week from the time we first met I was installed in Mr. Maxim's Office busily following my vocation of mechanical draughtsman, and acquainting myself with every branch of electrical incandescent light construction and operation."

Maxim helped Latimer whenever needed. In a relatively short

time, he became a qualified engineer.

Some believe that Latimer enjoyed his most creative years in the electrical field while with Maxim's Company. On September 13, 1881, he and Joseph Nichols of Brooklyn, received a patent for their invention, an improved electrical lamp. Their lamp allowed " a more perfect contact between the lamp filaments and the electrical conducting wires" and in the process removed what previously been a source of discontent among producers and users of electrical lamps. Most important, with their invention it became possible to make electrical "connections without the use of screws, pins, [or] similar accessories". Their more simple design reduced electrical resistance, which allowed a better flow of current to the filament, improved the efficiency and, most dramatically, the luminosity of electric lamps. In addition, they worked out a manufacturing process that made the production of their lamp simpler, faster, and cheaper.

On January 17, 1882, Latimer received a patent for an invention often cited as his most important creation. Others dispute this however, believing his water closet holds that distinction. For this creation he improved the filament of incandescent lamps. What he referred to as a "Process of Manufacturing Carbons," produced the best electrical lamp filament made prior to the use of metallic filaments. Latimer engaged a law in thermodynamics, which held that things tend to expand when heated. He believed that if the materials and the mold for making the filaments expanded at or near the same rate, then one would obtain an improved product. So he designed procedures and constructed materials for producing an electric lamp filament in a new way. When he subjected his filaments to test, Latimer found that they were less fragile than other products on the market, burned brighter and lasted significantly longer. The "Latimer Filaments" were more consistent in quality, could be manufactured in greater numbers, in less time and at lower cost. The "Latimer Filaments" were used in all of the Maxim lamps.

Latimer worked out complete details for the manufacture of every invention he crafted though for some he never received credit. The efficiency of his mass production procedures continued to help lower the production cost of the Maxim lamps. This allowed them to be sold more cheaply.

Later Latimer teamed with John Tregoning of Philadelphia to invent another improvement in electric lighting, a new and standard switch for use with the Maxim lamp. This also helped to advance the industry. Years later, the original model became a part of a collection at the Edison Institute in Dearborn, Michigan. He and Tregoning also patented an improved "Globe Supporter for Electric Lamps." This device, which could also support lamp shades, secured the globe and made it less likely to be broken by jarring. As the inventors pointed out, it did not tend to swing with the wind, and most important, allowed for quicker, easier change of lamps.

Let The Electric Light Shine

About this time, the country was on the verge of a new and exciting phase of the industrial revolution. A number of visionaries saw great possibilities of using electricity to light large buildings, streets, and ultimately homes throughout the country. Because the industry was so new, the technology for achieving these goals was in its infancy, not surprisingly there were skeptics. In fact most of the population doubted if electricity would ever replace oil and gas for lighting. In this environment, when Maxim's company obtained a contract to wire a building in New York, he saw this as a pivotal test case. Success was critical to the credibility of his company and the electrical industry in general. Maxim therefore turned to Lewis Latimer, who knew the industry "inside and out", and assigned the job to him. Latimer then supervised installation of the Maxim electric lighting system in the Equitable Building. It was the first building to be wired for electrical lighting in New York. In a subsequent assignment, Latimer directed installation of the first electrical street lamps in New York City. Then he went to Philadelphia and constructed an electrical plant for the *Philadelphia Ledger*.

Later, the U. S. Electric Company signed a contract for its first foreign installation - in Montreal, Canada. Again Maxim appointed Latimer to carry out the assignment. In preparation for the project, Latimer taught himself French, the language of primary use in Montreal and during the installations, he often wrote his instructions to workers in their language. His knowledge of French proved quite helpful and he completed the project on schedule. Seeing the value of knowing other languages, Latimer taught himself German so he could read some of their technical literature as well.

Even though these installations were successful, Latimer and other electrical industry pioneers realized they still had much to learn. He told what it was like for them in those early days:

> Electrical measurements had not then been invented and all our work was by guess. Official bell wire was the only kind then on the market, and our method of figuring was a good guess what size wire would carry a certain number of lamps without dangerous heating.

He went on to speculate that initially, lack of knowledge and experience may have been responsible for some fires considered mysterious at the time. From these initiatives, electrical pioneers like Latimer continued to improve, refine, and upgrade the industry.

His next commission took him to London, England for his most challenging assignment to date. Again, as the person who best understood all phases of the manufacturing process, Maxim assigned Latimer to build and put into operation a complete Hiram-Weston Lamp Factory, the first ever in Great Britain. Arriving in London he went to work without delay. First he supervised the construction of the plant and upon its completion taught workers how to produce the carbon filaments using the Latimer system. He also taught them glass-blowing technique for producing lamp globes. The complex tasks however, were compounded by personality difficulties he had not anticipated. Apparently due to certain class distinctions in the English society, it appeared that he was expected to assume a subordinate position when in the company of plant officials. In his "Electrical Recollections", Latimer wrote:

> My assistant and myself were in hot water from the first moment to the end of my engagement, and as we were incapable of

assuming a humility that we could not feel there was a continual effort to discount us and to that end the leading men would ask us about some process and failing to perform it would write to the U. S. saying that we did not understand our business. The people in the U. S. having tested us in many cases, simply wrote to us repeating the charge and we would see the leading men and explain and demonstrate the process to them so obscure. In nine months we had the factory in running order with every man familiar with the particular branch of the manufacture which fell to him, and as our easy independence was setting a bad example to the other workmen, we were released from our contract and permitted to return to the U. S.

Mary Latimer accompanied her husband to London so after completing the project, they remained in the famous city for a while. Latimer took a well-earned rest and the couple enjoyed a long-delayed honeymoon.

A Brief Commentary

Perhaps a brief commentary on artificial lighting may help illustrate the revolutionary changes that people like Latimer brought about. Before the advent of electric lights, many if not most business, entertainment, and recreational activities ceased at the end of the day. From the middle ages to the early 1800s, resin or pitch provided the best street lights available. Then gas lights came into use but according to Kate Bolton, even those were outshone by the light of the [full] moon. With its more powerful illumination, electric lights chased away the darkness of night and ushered a technological change that altered the social, economic, and recreational fabric of people around the world.

Departure from the Maxim Firm

For reasons not altogether clear, Latimer returned home from Europe and resigned his position at the U. S. Electric Company.

Turner offered several possible reasons for his leaving. She speculated that it may have been because Maxim had become increasingly occupied with his invention the Gatlin Gun at the expense of the electrical operations. She also noted that when Maxim wrote his autobiography, he never mentioned Latimer, and this may have led to some disillusionment. Large profits from Latimer's inventions went to the company, with little benefit to him, so this too could have been a factor. Even worse, Turner suggested that Maxim may have claimed some of Latimer's inventions as his own.

Latimer himself offered little explanation except a single but interesting comment that seemed to suggest during his absence certain forces worked to squeeze him out of any significant role with the company's future. In a passage from his essay on "Electrical Recollections" he wrote that upon his return home, "we [perhaps including his assistants] found the ranks closed up and every place filled." Perhaps Latimer's ground-breaking roles and inventions invoked jealousies and others sought to ensure he would not lead future projects.

So rather than being greeted with a substantial reward and promotion to higher rank when he came back, it appears Latimer was treated more like a pariah. Whatever the reason or reasons, the relationship between Latimer and Maxim cooled. There is no indication of any future reconciliation but Latimer later spoke kindly of Maxim for helping him to understand all phases of the electrical industry.

On the other hand, two events brought joy to the Latimer household after their return from England. Their family grew to three in 1883 with the birth of Emma Jeanette, the first of the Latimers' two daughters. After that a second daughter was born and named Louise, after her father. The two children brought great pride and happiness to the couple. In one sense both daughters followed after their father who in addition to his devotion to the sciences and technology, had a great love for the arts and humanities. More will be said about this subject later.

With Thomas Alva Edison

When Latimer left the U. S. Electric Company he worked for the Olmstead Company in New York. In 1884, while in their employ, Thomas Alva Edison, the most renown inventor in history, approached Latimer and asked him to join his firm at 65 Fifth Avenue. Edison hired Latimer on the strength of his credentials as an inventor, draftsman, thorough knowledge of electricity and the electrical industry. Moreover it was a time of frequent litigations over patent rights and Latimer had a good grasp of patent law. In addition, having instructed himself in French and German, Latimer could translate many of the scientific and technical journal articles into English. His versatility, and reputation for integrity made him a valuable asset to the Edison company.

With Thomas Edison, Latimer initially worked as a draftsman in the engineering department and later was made Chief Draftsman. Soon however, he began to devote a great deal of his time to the legal department as expert witness for the Patent Control Board. At first he was *the* legal department for Edison's firms. Latimer was a powerful force for Edison in courts where patent rights were in dispute. Often, his drawings were critical elements during court testimony. Robert Koolakian, Associate Curator, Edisoniana added:

> Because of his vast experience with Edison patents, he was called to testify as a patent authority in a number of infringement cases involving the two companies. In an era characterized by widespread patent abuse, he was particularly adept in defending original Edison patent claims.

When Latimer appeared as a witness, he consistently gave clear and precise testimony. Aided by his habit of careful observations, rich background knowledge and remarkable memory, he always included particulars that helped confirm the accuracy of his remarks. In one case, for instance, he gave a 13 page written testimony in support of Edison under the title, "Mr. Latimer's Theory on the Goebel Lamp Case." He offered detailed technical information as to whether one Charles Perkins invented a lamp, the origin of which was under dispute. In 1889, ("Deposition of Lewis H. Latimer"), he testified in a dispute about Maxim's claimed to have used, by a certain date, what he referred to as a "brush shifting system of regulation in which the commutator bushes of an auxiliary machine were shifted to vary the current exciting the field of the main machine." Latimer had previously run a plant arranged on that system so he was aware of the time sequence. His exact and detailed testimony lent credence to Edison's position, not Maxim. During that same year, he gave valuable testimony for Edison in the United States Circuit Court, Eastern District of Missouri, against the Columbia Incandescent Lamp Co. This was yet another challenge to Edison over the invention of the incandescent lamp.

A Book on the Principles of Incandescent Lighting

In 1890, Latimer published the definitive book on applied electricity called the *Incandescent Electric Lighting, A Practical Description of the Edison System.* It was one of the first books of its kind and found widespread use as a handbook by electrical engineers. The text, which was distinguished by its clarity and efficiency of words, explained fundamental principles of electricity, conversion of mechanical energy to electrical energy, series and parallel electric circuitry, the conversion of electrical energy to light energy, and a wealth of related information. He identified as his intended audience, technicians, "students who proposed to follow [electricity] as a profession . . . [and] the wont among the laity".

Analogies and his own drawings supplemented his narratives for greater clarification of scientific and technical concepts. Explanation of each scientific principle in the production and use of electricity provided background and logic for subsequent discussion. In his writing, Latimer patiently moved from the simple to the complex. He provided clear examples to show how a dynamo produced electricity. He explained and compared the better known direct current electricity with the newer alternating current electricity and discussed advantages and disadvantages of each. His book also showed how to construct series and parallel electrical circuits and this helped to sharpen the distinction between the two.

It is important to remember that such matters were little understood, or not at all, during this time in history. All too often, myths supplanted real understanding about current electricity and lighting. Latimer wanted to dispel as many such myths as possible. Always Latimer got directly to the point. His book was relatively small, but thorough and comprehensive. Robert G. Koolakian, the Edisoniana Curator wrote of Latimer's book: "This treatise is considered a milestone among the contributions made by the Edison Pioneers . . ."

Most references to Latimer's book overlook its contribution to the history of science and technology. The text revealed the reluctance of people during the late 19th century to adopt electricity for their use. They had many doubts about its utility and future. Latimer realized that few shared his vision of the role electricity was destined to play in the civilized world. So in his book, he repeatedly emphasized the importance of central electrical power plants to meet the need of large population centers. An interesting commentary in his book revealed that " . . . many doubted the possibility of lighting large districts from a central station as successful as with gas". Somewhat surprising was the revelation that among the doubters were ". . .men who stood high in electrical circles."

Of the electrical generators then in use, most were small, with limited capacity, and scattered unevenly across the countryside. Latimer saw that producing electricity in this manner was costly and inefficient. He, along with a small group of electrical pioneers, understood that large central stations produced electricity more efficiently, reliably and cheaply. By using central stations, he explained, the cost of electrical energy could be brought " . . . within the reach of those who otherwise could not afford it".

Not many copies of Latimer's book exist today. One is in the

Library of Congress, another in the archives of the State Library of New York in Albany, one in a library in New York City and a few other locations.

Inventions During the Edison Era

Oddly enough, it appears that Latimer had few if any inventions in the field of electricity after he went to work for Edison. A possible explanation is that he was so consumed by his other responsibilities, that it left little or no time for creativity in the fast-moving industry. Other possibilities include the loss of the creative spark or that whatever he may have invented was assigned and credited to the Edison's firm.

This is not to say he was no longer productive. There is a Copy of Claims Allowed, dated October 10, 1891, by Latimer entitled "Means for Producing Luminous Effects". In this invention he described the circuitry for "one or more [moving] endless belts bearing electric lamps connected together and arranged in one or more circuits to a source of electricity . . . ".

In a document not dated, Latimer presented his plan for a city-wide "Electrical Fire Extinguishing System." In an example of urban planning, he proposed that the city be divided into fire districts. His system included a motor and pump that would be located at strategic central points." Each resident would be within the reach of two pumps and each business structure four pumps. Later, many municipalities adopted plans similar to that espoused by Latimer.

Latimer also patented inventions outside the electrical fields after he joined Edison. On April 12, 1896, he received a patent for an "Apparatus for Cooling and Disinfecting." That apparatus was based on the principle of cooling by evaporation the same basis for cooling by more complex modern refrigerators and air conditioners. Latimer's conditioners might be called a passive cooling device since it required no moving parts. Many modifications of his apparatus can be found in cooling devices developed since his time. Latimer explained that his invention could be used for "Cooling, Deodorizing, or Disinfecting Apartments and other buildings", including homes and hospitals. Later that year, he and Joseph Nichols invented and obtained a patent for a "Locking Rack for Hats, Coats, and Umbrellas.

In 1898, Latimer invented an electric elevator and sought to interest the Westinghouse Company in its manufacture. Some discussions ensued but the outcome is not known. In 1901, he invented an elastic tread vehicles but failed to convince anyone, General Electric included, of its merit.

Mergers and Changes

Through merger, the Edison Electric Company expanded and became the General Electric Company. This major change left two industrial giants, General Electric and Westinghouse, in near total control of the electrical industry. To protect themselves against patent theft and to mount strong defense in patent lawsuits, they established a joint Board of Patent Control. Latimer was the key figure on the board and served in that capacity for 15 years. How he managed to work in that demanding position so well and for so long is a matter of wonder since he had vision problems that should made reading materials very difficult.

Latimer left the General Electric Company in 1911. He then worked as consultant to Edwin W. Hammer, Patent Solicitor and engineer of New York City, and the firm of Hammer and Swartz. In 1924 at the age of 76, Lewis Latimer finally retired.

The Edison Pioneer and Renaissance Man

On January 24, 1918, in a significant show of high regard for him, a small group invited Latimer join them as one of the 28 charter members of the Edison Pioneers. Only by invitation could one become a member of the organization. The two major requirements for membership were, (a) the individual had to have worked with Thomas Edison and (b)the person had to have made contributions of such magnitude as to be acknowledged as a one of the "creator of the electric industry". Latimer cherished the honor perhaps above all others as it meant his peers placed him and his contributions as a peer with such giants as Edison and George Westinghouse. An interesting sidelight is that though Latimer lived comfortably, he alone of the pioneers did not become wealthy. Generally acknowledged to have been the most versatile and among the most able of the pioneers, some felt he should enjoyed similar rewards. There is no indication however, that Latimer ever dwelled on the matter at all.

More than an inventor, Latimer also studied the arts and humanities because he believe that civilized society recorded its great ideas in books, he sought to know and understand them through reading. As mentioned earlier, he was a voracious reader. Judge Gerald Latimer Norman of Brooklyn, whose mother was Emma Latimer-Norman, remembered several conversations with his grandfather. He recalled with admiration, the elder Latimer's great love of knowledge and wisdom, and astounding capacity for recall. His personal library contained more than 1,000 books.

Latimer expanded his skills acquired as a draftsman and trained himself in painting. At various times he used ink, charcoal, and oils with many of the oils showing pastel shadings. Most of his paintings were of portraits or landscapes but perhaps his better known were "The Italian Boy", "The Beggar" and an unnamed painting of a small child. His granddaughter, Dr. Winifred Norman Latimer, believed that the painting was of his daughter and her aunt, Louise. Some of his painting were accepted for display in art galleries.

Latimer held a life long passion for music. His favorites were church hymns, Negro spirituals, the classics and popular music of the day. He taught himself to play the flute, violin, piano and organ. Sometimes he played to entertain his friends. Occasionally he filled in at church when the organist was absent. At home, Latimer played violin-piano duets with his daughter Emma, a Julliard graduate and accomplished pianist. Music brought him joy, pleasure, and relaxation. His daughter Louise studied art.

The Negro Associates, who conducted extensive research on the life and works of Lewis Latimer, praised his achievements in science/technology, admired his extensive knowledge of the humanities, law, and civic affairs. It was this group of scholars who bestowed upon him the title, "The Renaissance Man". That is how his grandchildren, Gerald Latimer Norman and Winifred Latimer Norman remembered him.

So did Latimer's friends. On his 75th birthday they collected as many of his poems as they could find, which numbered more than 100. Under the title, *Poems of Life and Love*, they published a book of his verses, and affectionately had them bound in special Italian leather. The limited edition consisted of just 50 copies that they distributed among family and admirers.

Latimer's poetry dealt with a range of topics. Among the poems his friends located, one showed his feelings about the permanency, or stability of friendship. A stanza from his poem, *Friends* read:

> Years waxed and years waned,
> Youth it has left us
> But friendship remained
> And now as with white locks
> I bend o'er life's page
> The friend of my childhood
> Is the friend of my age.

Seemingly, Latimer never ran out of ideas. Sometimes he expressed his creativity in inventions, most in electricity, sometimes in poetry, essays, or music, and at other times through his paintings on canvass. Nonetheless even he had moments when his best efforts at producing new ideas proved fruitless. This is suggested in his poem called *Thinking*, part of which read:

> Like pendulum, the brain
> Swings one way with a single thought
> And back with it again;
> And if one asks the victim

Of his mental to and fro,
Now tell me what you are thinking?
They answer, "I don't know."

Latimer believed that the inventor, in following an idea, should have a thorough understanding of the scientific laws and theories related to the project under consideration. Then through rational thought, and at times intuitive revelations, these laws and principles should be applied to creating something new. Those who relied on magic and superstition to control or influence nature were misguided and doomed to failure. In a short essay called *Life*, he wrote:

> The folly of outraging all of nature's laws, in the hope of producing a predetermined unnatural result is something the world goes on repeating through the ages, utterly oblivious to inevitable failure.

It appears that even as a young child, Latimer expressed an interest in poetry. This was revealed in an ardent letter sent to him on May 15, 1893 by a boyhood acquaintance Annie E. Johnson of Nahauh. She wrote about some of her recent travails, including deeply felt losses in the passing of her mother and husband. In her closing lines she appeared to brighten up, apparently feeling some relief in being able to express her sorrows to a friend. She wrote:

> I write in confidence, and freely, remembering the old days and "little Lewis' who had a blank book with 'scraps' on the cover and poems and drawings, inside even then.

Latimer sought to publish some of his poetry and met with some success. Charles A. Dixon, editor and publisher of *Leisure Time, The Society Journal*, of Philadelphia was so impressed that in a letter to Latimer dated May 12, 1888 he wrote:

> Let me tell you that poetry is your 'forte'. Every one of your poetic effusions pleased me so much, that I couldn't leave one of them out.

Not only did they please me individually, but they have "taken by
storm" every one who has read them that I have seen. You strike
the popular chord in all of these verses.

In the Interest of the Country at Large

Despite the hectic pace of his life, Latimer took time out for
civic duties as well. He felt it a responsibility of every citizen
to make constructive contributions to society. Latimer helped
organize and held office in Huntsman Post of the Grand Army
of the Republic, consisting of Civil War Veterans. He always
took part in their annual parades, insisting on walking, not riding
until age and infirmity made walking impossible. At various
times he served as adjutant and secretary of the organization. He
taught a course in mechanical drawing to immigrants. When first
asked to do so, he begged off because of his already heavy load.
Then recalling that people of good will had helped his parents to
freedom, he agreed to teach the course.

Latimer also helped organize a Unitarian Church in his
hometown of Flushing. He served as an elder among other things.
It was in connection with the church that Gerald Latimer Norman
remembered an incident that showed his grandfather's strength.
It seems that the organ needed to be moved to another placed in
the sanctuary. Several men tried to do so, failed and threw up
their hands in resignation. The wiry, slightly built 5 feet, 9 inches
Latimer, impatient to have the organ moved, relocated it to the
desired place - alone.

He also spoke out when and where he saw evidence of
injustice. When Queens Mayor Seth Low removed a black man,
S. R. Scottron from the school board, he left the African-
American community without representation. Latimer joined a
citizens' political action movement in an effort to correct what
they saw as a blatant wrong. The group held a rally and issued
a public statement expressing their grievance.

In followup of the rally, Latimer wrote a letter directly to the
mayor. He argued that Scottron was qualified to serve, that he
was a " . . . good citizen, a worthy gentleman, and one whose

influence . . . warrants the assertion that he would be a fit representative of any of her people, regardless of race." To reappoint Mr Scottron, he said, was morally right. The population not now represented in the school board, he said, was significant and not without political clout. He argued that "There [were] upward of 25,000 colored voters representing upward of 125,000 individuals, unquestionably Americans by reason of ancestry, birth, and education." For the record, he failed in his efforts. The mayor ignored the protests, did not acknowledge Latimer's letter, and did not reappoint Scottron or any black to the school board.

Latimer believed that racial discrimination was detrimental, not just to its victims but to the whole of society. The Negro American, he felt, had an obligation to oppose injustice, for none knew better the pains of its abuse. When the National Conference of Colored Men invited him to address their convention in Detroit Michigan. But he sent them a letter, December 12, 1895, apologized for his absence and pledged his support. In part his letter read:

> It is necessary that we show by our martyrdom under the lash . . . that we are looking to the interest of the country at large when we protest any injustices meted out to any class or condition of our citizens.
>
> . . . the community which permits a crime against its humblest member to go unpunished is nursing into life and strength a power that will ultimately destroy its own existence.

His Genial Presence

As mentioned, the Latimer daughters, like their father, were drawn to the humanities. Louise studied art, and graduated from the Pratt Institute of Brooklyn. Emma Jeannette ("Jean"), graduated from the Julliard School of Music. For a while she contemplated a career as a concert pianist but put all such ambitions aside when she married a local school teacher. Their two children, Gerald Latimer Norman and Winifred Latimer

Norman, have already been mentioned on previous occasions.

Family and friends described the old inventor as a caring and devoted father and husband. Articulate in speech and writing, he had an excellent command of the language. Considered to be "quiet, with urbane manners, he nonetheless held strong convictions. Latimer presented a distinguished figure with erect posture.

The Negro Associates also said that Latimer was careful not to intrude on others. The personal view people had of him varied. Some, in deference to his reputation as a great inventor, held him in awe. His quiet demeanor caused others to perceive him as somewhat distant and aloof. Nonetheless, those who knew Latimer found him consistently "warm . . . friendly, and with a good sense of humor." He was a seeker of good company, and many sought his companionship in turn. For all his achievements, and the people he knew in high places, Lewis Latimer was "modest, self-effacing . . . not given to vanity".

The Latimer home in Queens, New York was something of a cultural and social center. His friends often congregated there, and visited with each other. Of course it did not hurt to dine at the Latimer table as Mary Latimer's reputation as an excellent cooking was well deserved. Young people of ambition sought the old inventor for counsel, especially those who wanted tips on how to survive in technical and professional fields where few or no African-Americans ever worked. They were encouraged to excellence by Latimer, and inspired by his calm, reassuring comportment and record of achievement.

"A Great Work for All People"

In January of 1924, Lewis Latimer suffered a stroke that forced him into retirement. His beloved wife of nearly 50 years had passed away a year earlier and he felt her loss deeply. Family and friends worried as they witnessed his decline. Latimer's grief, compounded by his illness, slowly but visibly sapped his strength and once indomitable spirit. On December 11, 1928, almost five years after his stroke, Lewis Latimer died. He was 80 years old.

The Edison Pioneers paid a moving tribute to their departed comrade as they chronicled his life story and his contributions to the electrical industry. They praised Latimer for "His keen perception of the possibilities of electric light and kindred industries. . . ." and they cherished their association with him. The Pioneers acknowledged Latimer's passing with sadness, grateful that they had known him and confessed that they would miss him too.

We barely mourn his inevitable passing so much as we rejoice in pleasant memory at having been associated with him in a great work for all people. Broadminded, versatile in the accomplishment of things intellectual and cultural, a linguist, a devoted husband and father, all were characteristic of him, and his genial presence will be missed from our gathering.

The Pioneers also recorded that Latimer's "remains [were] sent to Fall River, Mass. Where, at his previous request they were cremated and placed in the same grave with the remains of his beloved wife. They declared further that "Mr. Latimer was a full member, and an esteemed one of the EDISON PIONEERS."

He was preceded in death by his parents and brothers, and survived by his sister, Margaret Hawley of Connecticut, two daughters and two grandchildren.

In His Honor

The Lewis H. Latimer Gardens in Flushing, New York, were named in his honor. A community center and an elementary school also bear his name. The Schomberg Public Library in New York City named a wing after him and there is a Lewis H. Latimer Street in New York.

In a collective effort, the Queens Historical Society, General Electric Foundation a local black Baptist church, and his grandchildren saved his former home from destruction. It is now an historical landmark and serves as a museum in Queens, New York.

Other tributes include a biographical videotape by the Unitarian Universalist Associates. At various times several of his inventions and documents have been on display at the Smithsonian and the Anacostia Neighborhood Museum in Washington, D.C., the Edison Institute in Dearborn, Michigan, and other locations. The General Electric Foundation funds and the National Society of Black Engineers administers an annual Lewis Latimer Achievement Awards for college scholarships.

The life of Lewis Latimer exemplified what ability and determined effort can achieve when men and women are free and doors open to their merit.

What tho' I suffered through the years
Unnumbered wrongs, unnumbered fears,
My soul doth still forbid me tears,
Unconquered and unconquerable.
What tho' my bed of thorns be made,
My soul soars upward, undismayed
Unconquered and unconquerable.
What tho' by chains confined I die,
My soul will upward fly
Unconquered and unconquerable.
I scorn the hand that does me wrong
Though suffering days and years be long,
My soul still chants that deathless song,
Unconquered and unconquerable.

-by Lewis Latimer. The manuscript, preserved by his granddaughter, Dr. Winifred Latimer Norman, and published in a brochure "Remembering Lewis Latimer" by the Lewis H. Latimer Fund, Inc. The fund is dedicated to preservation of his home as a museum.

References and Publications for Further Reading

Bolton, Kate, 1979: "The Great Awakening of the Night: Lighting America's Streets, *Landscape*, 23: 41-47.

Dedication Journal: *Lewis H. Latimer Gardens*, New York, June, 1971.

Dictionary of American Naval Fighting Ships, Volume IV, Washington, D.C.: Navy Department, Office of the Chief of Naval Operations, Naval History Division, 1967. (Courtesy Arnold and Karen Markoe).

Finkelstein, Mel, "Inventor's House is Moved: As Shulman Hail His Works," *New York Post, January 14, 1988.*

Fried, Joseph, "A Campaign to Remember an invention," *New York Times,* August 6, 1988, New Jersey, Connecticut Issue, pp. 27, 28.

_____, "G.E. Offers $25,000 to Help Save House of Queens Inventor," *New York Times,* August 9, 1988, B3.

Green, Richard, 1985. *A Salute to Black Scientists and Inventors,* Chicago: Empak Enterprises,

Haber, Louis, 1970. *Black Pioneers in Science and Invention,* New York: Harcourt, Brace, and World, Inc.

James, Portia P., 1989. *The Real McCoy: African-American Inventions and Innovations, 1919-1930,* Washington, D.C.: Smithsonian Press..

Iverem, Ester, "Latimer House Finds A New Home", *New York Newsday,* December 14, 1988, City Edition.

Latimer, Lewis Howard, 1890. *Incandescent Lighting: A Practical Description of the Edison System,* New York: D. Van Nostrand.

Logan, Rayford and Michael Winston (ed.), 1980. *Dictionary of American Negro Biography,* New York, D. Van Nostrand.

Rawson, Edward K., and Charles Stewart (ed.), 1900. *Official Record of the Union and Confederate Navies in the War of Rebellion,* Series I, Volume II, Washington, D.C.: Government Printing Office.

Sertima, Ivan Van (ed.), 1983. *Blacks in Science, Ancient and Modern,* New Brunswick, New Jersey: Transaction Books.

The Negro Associates, 1964. *Story of Lewis Latimer,* New York, The Negro Associates, Thomas Alva Edison Associates, 1973. *Lewis Howard Latimer, A Black Inventor: A Biography and Related Experiments You Can Do,* Detroit, Michigan: Thomas Alva Edison Foundation.

Turner, Glennette, T., 1991. *Lewis Howard Latimer,* Englewood Cliffs, New Jersey: Silver Burdette.

Winslow, Eugene (ed.), *Black Americans in Science and Engineering: Contributors of Past and Present,* New York: Afro-American Publishing Company Inc. for General Electric Company, 1974.

The following documents were provided by the Henry Ford Museum & Greenfield Village Research Center.

Bowser, Aubrey, "Lewis H. Latimer, Edison's Assistant, Dies at Age of 81," *Amsterdam News*, December 19, 1928.

Koolakian, Robert G., "Lewis *Howard Latimer* in *Thomas Alva Edison's Associate, Lewis Howard Latimer: A Black Inventor*, Dearborn Michigan, A Special Bicentennial Exhibition, Greenfield Village and Henry Ford Museum, February 17, 1975.

Latimer, Lewis, "Means for Producing Luminous Effects, *Copy of Claims Allowed*, Filed October 10, 1891.

Latimer, L. H., "Electrical Fire Extinguishing System (Undated).

Latimer, L. H., *Electrical Recollections*, (Undated)

Letter to L. H. Latimer from Charles A. Dixon, Editor and Publisher, *Leisure Hours: The Society Journal*, Philadelphia, April 23, 1884.

Letter to Latimer from Annie E. Johnson, Nahauh, July 12, 1893.

Letter to L. H. Latimer from Frederick P. Fish, New York, May 19, 1898.

Letter to L. H. Latimer from Frederick P. Fish, New York, March 5, 1901.

"Lewis H. Latimer," *Amsterdam News, Wednesday,* December 19, 1928. (Editorial).

DISPOSITIONS and other testimony pertaining to legal cases:

"Disposition of Lewis H. Latimer," Trial of Charles G. Perkins, United States Electric Company, 1889.

"Memo, - -Mr. Latimer's Theory on the Goebel Lamp Case"

Testimony of Latimer: "Edison Electric Light Co. *et al*, vs. Columbia Incandescent Lamp Co. *et al."*

Poem, "Massachusetts to Virginia", by John Greenleaf. Whittier, written after George Latimer and his wife Rebecca, parents of Lewis Latimer, escaped from Virginia to Massachusetts..

LATIMER'S PATENTS REVIEWED

U. S. Patent No. 147,363, *Closets for Railroad Cars*, February 10, 1874.

U. S. Patent No. 247,097, *Electric Lamp,* September 13, 1881.

U. S. Patent No. 252,386, *Process of Manufacturing Carbons,* January 17, 1882.

U. S. Patent 255,212, *Globe Supporter for Electric Lamp,* March 21, 1882.

U. S. Patent No. 334,078, *Apparatus for Cooling and Disinfecting,* January 12, 1886.

U. S. Patent No. 557,076, *Locking Racks for Hats, Coats, and Umbrellas,* March 24, 1896..

Special appreciation to the late Judge Gerald Latimer Norman and Dr. Winifred Latimer Norman, grandson and granddaughter of Lewis Howard Latimer, for valuable information and insights.

Chapter IV_____

Daniel Hale Williams, Trail Blazing Heart Surgeon and Builder of Hospitals

With quick steps the boy walked out of his father's barber shop and down Main Street in Hollisdaysberg, Pennsylvania. Familiar with the sights and sounds of this part of town, he did not hesitate on his way home. The lad felt good as he thought about the work he had done helping his father. He liked doing odd jobs at the barbershop because one had to learn these things to become a barber. Someday he would be in the business like his dad.

The youngster, Daniel Hale Williams was born January 18, 1856, the fifth child Daniel and Sarah Price Williams' seven children. Dan's siblings, Anne Effine, Henry Price, Sarah, (Sally), and Ida were older than he, and Alice Price, and Florence May were younger. Their father, Daniel Williams Jr. was of black, German, and Scotch-Irish, ancestry. His reddish hair and light skin made him look more white than black. Their mother Sarah was black and Indian with long, black hair and skin of a darker hue than her husband.

The Williams were free blacks and none of them ever experienced slavery. Their father owned a barber shop downtown. With income from his business, and some wise investments, Daniel Williams Jr. provided a comfortable home for his family. Nevertheless, they never forget that many blacks lived in slavery and that their own lives were not without constraints.

During family gatherings, Dan and Sarah Williams would tell the children about their family ethnic background. They told them about a cousin on their mother's side, the famous abolitionist and orator, Frederick Douglass. The children also learned about their uncles, aunts, and cousins and where many of them lived. They also taught the children about the importance of a good education because they thought it was critical to the welfare and survival of black people in this country.

Family

One day Daniel's father made a surprised announcement. They were leaving Hollisdayburg and moving to Annapolis, Maryland. The Civil War was over and with it the end of slavery. Blacks could now move about without showing papers proving they were free. The elder Daniel Williams decided to devote more time working for full and equal rights for African Americans. The decision meant giving up a lucrative business and economic security. Nonetheless, his new mission required that he travel about the country, and he looked forward to preaching to a larger audience about the importance of education. Beside, he reasoned, perhaps in a milder climate he could get rid of that nagging cough that wouldn't go away.

So the family packed up and moved to Annapolis where some relatives lived. The children were anxious to see Grandma Ann Wilks Price who told them exciting stories about Frederick Douglass and his great work. The author Lillie Patterson wrote that Grandma Price who had been held in bondage but was freed before the war - told her grandchildren stories about what it was like to be a slave. The children, Dan in particular, were amazed when she told them how she was freed:

 `Your grandfather bought me,' she said softly. Grandfather Henry Price had worked hard, she told Dan. He saved his money and invested in stocks and real estate. The money from his investments went toward buying slaves so he could set them free.

Grandma Price took the children to the cemetery to visit their grandfather's grave. She proudly pointed to the inscription on his headstone that read:

Sacred to the memory of REVEREND HENRY PRICE who died in Annapolis February 20, 1863 in the 71st year of his age. By Faith he lived on earth, in Hope he died, by Love he lives in Heaven.

The transition to Annapolis went well for the children but not for their father. He looked tired and drawn. His cold kept growing worse but he wouldn't rest. His work was just beginning, he said, there was so much to do. He simply had no time to rest. But his condition deteriorated. Hard, painful coughs racked his chest. Despite his determination to continue his mission, the elder Williams grew weaker at an accelerated pace. Finally he saw a doctor who told him he had the fearsome disease tuberculosis also known as consumption.

The doctor urged immediate medical treatment and complete rest. but Williams refused. Then one day, he collapsed and not long afterward, Sarah Price Williams was a widow.

"We Colored People Must Cultivate The Mind"

Almost immediately, Sarah Williams realized she could not support herself and the children. Her husband had always taken care of everything. Without him, she could not manage. With sadness she broke up her family and all the children went to live with different relatives except young Dan. His father's death affected him deeply, and the already shy lad became more reclusive. His mother arranged for Dan to live with a friend, Mr. Mason, in Baltimore. She hoped that he could help her son by teaching him how to make shoes.

Mr. Mason was a kindly man and Dan liked him. Unfortunately, he hated making shoes. The work, the smell, and the idea of making shoes for the rest of his life filled him with despair. Dan became restless and increasingly unhappy. He was also disappointed at not being able to attend school. His father had often said to his children, "We colored people must cultivate the mind." Dan remembered those words and vowed that somehow he would find a way to get more schooling and cultivate his mind.

One day Dan decided to run away and join his mother. She and two of his sisters lived with one of his father's cousins 90 miles west of Chicago in Rockford, Illinois. Dan desperately wanted to see his mother and sisters but at 12 years of age did not have fare for the long journey. How could he ever make it from Baltimore to this place way out west!

Nonetheless, a desperate Dan felt he had to do something. One day, without telling anyone where he was going, the boy ran to the railroad station. There he found an agent who had been a friend of his father. He begged the agent to give him a pass so he could join his mother and sisters in Illinois. The agent looked into the eyes of a sad and lonely child. Moved by compassion, he gave Dan a pass along with instructions about getting to Rockford.

A few days later Sarah Williams answered a knock on the door and was stunned to see her slender, red-haired son standing before her. After the spontaneous mother-son embrace, and answers to many questions, the still tired, hungry lad pleaded that he be allowed to stay. He did not want her to go back to Baltimore.

Let's Move, There is a School in Janesville

After the initial shock, but still incredulous, Sarah listened to her son. Dan begged his mother to let him stay. He would not be any trouble, he said, and he would work hard to earn his keep. His mother agreed that if her 12 year old son could somehow manage to travel all the way from Baltimore to Rockford alone, he shouldn't be sent back. Yes, he could stay. At least part of the family was together again.

But not for long. This time it was his mother who became restless. She wanted to return east to Maryland. Sarah Williams missed her two youngest children who were still there. She just had to go back. As for Daniel, well he could return with her or remain in the Midwest with his sister Sally. No doubt fearful he would have to go back to the shoe business, Dan elected to stay.

After a while, Dan and his sister Sally moved to Edgerton, Wisconsin and they found the town to their liking. Sally made hairpieces and Dan cut hair. Dan still wanted to get an education but there was no school for him in Edgerton. Later, he learned that in a nearby community called Janesville, Wisconsin, he could get an education.

Dan went to Janesville to look things over. While there he met a black man named Harry Anderson. A warm-hearted and friendly man, Anderson, who owned a barber shop, needed another barber. Dan applied for the job and to his delight Anderson agreed to take him on. In the excitement, the young man had overlooked one important item - he had no place to stay. Anderson invited Dan to live with his family. But what about his sister Sally? No problem, Andersons told him. They would make room for her too. Harry Anderson and his pleasant, Irish-born wife Ellen gave Dan and Sally a warm welcome to their home. Along with their own three children, the Williamses became very much a part of their family. In addition to being a barber, Anderson doubled as a musician. Music held an important place in the Anderson family tradition. When they learned that Dan had a good singing voice, and some skill playing the guitar, he became even more an integral part of their lives. Dan and Sally had a family again.

A Pivotal Decision: To be a doctor

Dan enrolled in the Janesville Classical Academy. The headmaster of the academy accepted him after a strong recommendation by Orrin Guersey, a local businessman. Guernsey, a customer at the Anderson barber shop had been impressed by Dan's love of books and his eagerness to learn. In accepting Dan, the headmaster risked objection from parents. Despite Dan's Caucasian appearance, he expected they would not be pleased upon learning that his student "had Negro blood in his veins." But he felt that Dan deserved an opportunity to get an education and enrolled him into the academy.

Anxious to get on with his education, Dan paid his fees with money earned at the barber shop and playing music with the Anderson band. He studied hard and earned very good grades. Dan enjoyed a good relation with his schoolmates being among the most popular of the students in school. In 1877, at the age of 21, Daniel Hale Williams graduated from the academy. He knew his father would have been pleased.

After graduation, Dan wondered about his next step. His brother Price, who practiced law in Philadelphia, suggested that Dan might want to join him in the legal profession. Dan considered the offer but only briefly. He realized that he had no more interest in law than in the shoemaking business.

One day the young man read a newspaper article about a local physician, Dr. Henry Palmer. The story gave a dramatic account of Dr. Palmer's valiant effort to save a victim of multiple bullet wounds. From that time on, Daniel Hale Williams knew he wanted to be a medical doctor.

Apprenticeship

By some accounts Dan had met Dr. Palmer who regularly got his hair trimmed at the Anderson barber shop. Others claimed that he met the physician only when his band played for a party at the Palmer's home. Perhaps both claims are true.

Dr. Palmer had a busy practice and throughout the state, others in medical circles thought highly of him. Active in the American Medical Association, Palmer had once been vice president of the prestigious medical society.

To become a physician, Dan needed a period of apprenticeship under a practicing physician. What better person than Dr. Palmer.

So he took a bold step and made an appointment with the physician. He told Dr. Palmer how much he wanted to be a doctor, and asked to be taken on as an apprentice. Palmer noted his sincerity but he knew that sincerity was only part of the requirement. Speaking to Dan, the physician weighed his words carefully. Medicine was an honored profession, he said, but not easy. First the apprentice had to go through a long period of hard, intense, work and study. Doctors sometimes had to keep all night vigils with their patients, even after a hard day's work. Then they had to treat patients the next day because people would still be sick or injured. At other times, without being forewarned, doctors might have to travel through inclement weather to treat patients. Sometimes, despite the doctor's best efforts, the patient died. Such conditions could be heart-wrenching, but the physician had to go on. Dr. Palmer admonished Dan to think about these challenges, and come back later with his decision.

Dan did not take Dr. Palmer's warnings lightly but nothing he heard discouraged him. He was willing to pay the price in work and study, and to make whatever sacrifices necessary. Impressed, Palmer agreed to train Dan for the medical profession.

Initially Dan carried out routine chores. Gradually, under the watchful eye of his mentor, he started to treat patients. First the doctor allowed him to treated minor cuts, aches and pains and later, fractures. Meanwhile, Dan studied medicine by reading all the books and medical journals in Dr. Palmer's office. On trips to and from the homes of patients, the two men talked about their latest or upcoming case and about medicine in general. Dan was growing as a doctor and Harry Anderson encouraged him all the way.

Times Are Changing, Go To Medical School

Dan worked as an apprentice for almost two years. As he neared the end of his training, Dr. Palmer told him that times were changing. Medicine was moving to the point where apprenticeship would no longer suffice. Soon, he said, doctors would have to go to medical school and be licensed to practice medicine. He urged Dan to enroll in a good medical school to prepare himself for the changing times.

Dr. Palmer recommended the Chicago Medical School that was affiliated with Northwestern University. He had sent his own son there earlier. He offered to support Dan's application with a strong letter of recommendation.

Dan liked the idea of going to medical school. He wanted to be a good doctor; a well-prepared doctor. He knew his father would have approved. He didn't have the money, and he could not work while in school, but he felt he couldn't stop now. Dan looked for a way.

The Chicago School of Medicine accepted Dan's application. Palmer's letter of recommendation presented him as person of ability, skill, devotion, and stamina. Nonetheless the lack of money remained a problem so Dan worked at various jobs. He labored long hours helping to string wires for the new inventions, the telephone, and the incandescent electric lights. Unfortunately he did not earn enough money for medical school.

Dan wrote to his mother for assistance. She replied that she was sorry but her own financial situation prohibited her from helping. Perhaps later. Finally he turned to Harry Anderson who in an act of faith and confidence in his young friend, co-signed for a loan from a local bank. To get a place to stay, he wrote to a Mrs. Jones, another friend of his late father, asking her to accept him as a boarder. Mrs. Jones had a comfortable home located not far from the medical school. Yes, she would accept him.

When Mrs. Jones' saw Dan she was struck by the strong resemblance of the handsome young man to his late father. She welcomed Dan into her home and allowed him to stay without the usual advanced pay.

In the fall of 1880, Dan enrolled in medical school. The first year was demanding and he had little time for social life. He did not mind. Medical school was exciting and challenging. Beside, he had no money and he really was indebted to Mrs. Jones. Sometimes Dan wondered just how long she would "carry him."

The second year seemed better because he was more familiar with the pace and requirements of the professors. Money problems still plagued him, but thanks to timely help from Harry Anderson, he remained in school.

Finally the big day for Daniel Hale Williams arrived; graduation. During the last week of March, 1883. a large gathering attended the impressive commencement ceremonies of the Chicago School of Medicine. Dan was among the 36 graduates who had completed all the requirements for the M. D. degree. Finally, he heard his names called. "Dr Daniel Hale Williams." Dignified and erect in his bearing, the slender young man strode briskly to the stage and received his diploma.

Dr. Dan

Following graduation, Dr. Daniel Hale Williams opened an office in Chicago at 31st and Michigan Avenue. He set up practice in an area known as the South Side, in a racially mixed neighborhood. The new doctor soon built up a good practice, with patients from both races. Dr. Dan, as he became affectionately known, kept regular office hours and made house calls. He also served as the attending physician at the Protestant Orphan Asylum. Later, the City Railroad Company contracted for his services to treat an assortment of accidents that occurred with considerable frequency. With his earnings he began to repay Harry Anderson. He acknowledged his indebtedness to Anderson, not only for the loans, but also in caring for him like a son.

In a short time, Dr. Dan built a good reputation as an excellent doctor and skilled surgeon. Due to circumstances of the time, many of his operations took place on kitchen and dining room tables in the homes of patients. Young doctors found it difficult to acquire hospital affiliations and private hospitals usually did not accept black patients. The few hospitals that accepted blacks were usually dreary places, poorly kept, and more associated with poorhouses, insane asylums, and places to die than to get well. Such conditions left the young physician almost no alternative but to operate in the home of patients.

To help prevent infection, Dr. Dan always scrubbed his "operating rooms" and cleaned them with antiseptics. He sprayed the air with carbolic acid and all sheets had to be "antiseptic clean". He made sure that all surgical instruments were sterile. Patients saw in his manners an air of assurance and his words underscored that he knew his business. Dr. Dan also projected a sense of warmth and caring that helped put his patients at ease. More important, his patients enjoyed a high rate of recovery.

From 1884 to 1891, Dr. Dan also served on the surgical staff of the South Side Dispensary. This gave him access to medical facilities for some of his operations. At the Dispensary, he gave demonstrations and lectures to medical students, winning their admiration for his knowledge, clarity of presentation, and surgical dexterity. One of his students was Charlie Mayo, later of the internationally acclaimed Mayo Clinic.

A Hospital For Everyone

Despite his successes, it bothered Dr. Dan that many blacks had to undergo surgery in homes when they needed to be in a good hospital. That led him to think about building a hospital. He envisioned a place where serious cases among blacks could be treated with dispatch, and under the best conditions possible. He wanted a medical facility that respected the patients and gave them a sense of dignity. His hospital would accept people of all races, treat them with courtesy, and handle their cases with the best medical skill and efficiency.

He knew he would have to mount several obstacles to make his dream a reality. His problems had many prongs. Chicago Hospitals would not accept blacks into their nursing training programs nor black doctors as interns. His quick mind accurately assessed the growing health needs of people in the area in contrast to the serious shortage of well-trained nurses and doctors. This intolerable situation had to change. Clearly something had to be done. Dr. Dan conceived the idea of building in Chicago, an interracial hospital where black and white doctors would practice medicine together. Young blacks and whites would train together and become doctors and nurses. He dreamed of a hospital that would not only help solve medical problems and heal the sick, but also would foster better racial cooperation, understanding, and mutual respect in the interest of common good. The idea was perceived by many as revolutionary.

Dr. Dan unveiled his plan to local medical and civic leaders. He explained his philosophy of a new hospital for *all* the people of the Southside and their medical needs. Though some were skeptical, none dismissed his message nor doubted his sincerity. After the initial introduction, Dr. Dan began the next phase of his campaign. With fervor he preached the sermon of possibility; that this was something they *could do*. Not only could the people of the region build a hospital, but they could build a *good* hospital, one of first rank, and located right there in the Southside. He repeatedly reminded them that their hospital would not be exclusive or restrictive to any one race like the other private hospitals in the city. It would be an interracial hospital.

He had little trouble selling the need for a hospital that would accept blacks. The need was obvious. But some people expressed reservations about the practicality and workability of an interracial hospital. A few critics believed it would be best to focus on a hospital for blacks rather than to risk almost certain rejection by white doctors, white nurses, and surely white patients. Although Dr. Dan might look white, he had cast his lot with the black race. Would not whites reject him too?

Still Dr. Dan felt strongly that a hospital should serve all people and he held his ground. Sick people were sick people he observed, and should that not be reason enough, the Hippocratic Oath obligated the medical profession to heal all sick people. He repeatedly urged that the southside hospital not follow the lead of those who would make exceptions to this solemn obligation. Yes, he continued to argue, the hospital should be opened to everyone. It would be the right thing to do.

Seeing his sincerity, and admiring his dedication to the noble principles of his profession, hospital supporters agreed to pursue his course. Black ministers, so important in the campaign, embraced the cause and enlisted the support of their congregations. Soon there were fund raising activities. Traviata Anderson, Harry Anderson's daughter who was like a sister to Dr. Dan, used her musical talents and sponsored concerts. A special committee solicited support from the business community. Some of Chicago's leading and most influential business leaders lent their backing. As people united behind the crusade, scores donated bed linens, pillows, mattresses, beds, cots, kitchen utensils, mops, buckets, and other items. The organizers used cash contributions for the building fund, medical instruments, medical supplies, and medical drugs. The community united behind the cause.

As the campaign moved ahead, the building committee considered a name for the hospital. Some suggested the Williams Hospital after Dr. Dan, but he opposed the idea. He urged instead that the hospital be given a neutral name. The final choice was Provident Hospital. The committee then acquired a three story structure that would accommodate a 12 bed hospital. They thought that would be a good start.

On May 4, 1891, Provident Hospital opened it doors to the public. Many people contributed to the success of the campaign, but it was a particular source of pride to the African Americans people of Chicago that they could plan and build a hospital. Perhaps their example would inspire blacks in other parts of the country to build good hospitals. This was especially important as usually they were denied access to hospitals already in place.

Set Standards of Excellence

Even after the hospital opened, many citizens continued to make much needed contributions to help with operating expenses. Dr. Dan worked tirelessly to make the facility a success, sometimes going as long as 24 hours without sleep. It was not unusual to see him scrubbing and disinfecting rooms during the late hours of the night. Aseptic cleanliness was high on his list.

Hundreds of young women applied for the new nursing program. The first class consisted of only seven of the top applicants. Dr. Dan felt they would be the nucleus of a program that would meet the high standards of excellence he sought.

He also assembled an outstanding interracial staff of doctors for Provident Hospital. It was a testimony to his reputation that he could attract some of the best doctors in the city. Many provided their services free of charge.

Then Dr. Dan ran into a difficult problem. A black physician, Dr. George Hall, applied for hospital affiliation. The author Helen Buckler, described the unpleasant aftermath.

> Hall had been practicing medicine for about two years, mainly in the red light district. His medical degree came from an Eclectic School. He was not well trained. From Dr. Dan's point of view he was not qualified. Others on the board, more sentimental, eager to have another Negro on the roster, perhaps liked Hall's affable ways, urged his appointment. Dr. Dan finally compromised by allowing Hall to be appointed to the children's department.

Despite his eventual acceptance, Dr. Hall took offense at his initial rejection. Though Dr. Dan accepted the majority view, Dr. Hall never forgave him for what he regarded as an unpardonable slight. He vowed to exact vengeance on Dr. Dan, and in time, he did.

A Medical Breakthrough

On the hot, humid, night of July 9, 1893, a fight broke out in a bar near Provident Hospital. During the altercation, a man named James Cornish, suffered a stab wound to his chest. Friends carried Cornish to Provident Hospital where Dr. Dan examined him. The wound itself did not appear to be too serious and there was very little bleeding. But the patient's condition soon began to deteriorate. He complained of pain around his heart, his breathing became labored, his pulse weakened, and he perspired profusely. Dr Dan surmised that the patient was bleeding internally and without medical intervention Cornish would soon die.

Dr. Dan considered his options. The only way to stop the bleeding would be to operate but he faced a long-standing tradition in the medical profession that considered it patently imprudent to operate on the heart. Dr. Stephen Johnson, in his book, *The History of Surgery, 1896-1955,* expressed the accepted view of the time.

Many of the leading surgeons of the day felt it unwise to suture a human heart. Billroth, who dominated European surgery, is said to have remarked, `A surgeon who tries to suture a human heart deserves to lose the esteem of his colleagues.

Wrenching words but a human life was at stake.

Dr. Dan decided to operate though he knew that failure would severely damage his well-earned reputation as a physician and surgeon. He also faced another and very critical problem. The conditions for the delicate operation were far from ideal but he had performed surgery under difficult conditions before. Herbert M. Morais, in his book, *The History of the Negro in Medicine,* described the major challenges faced by Dr. Dan.

Dr. Dan, . . . set to work with no x-ray pictures to direct him, no trained anesthetist to assist him, no blood transfusions to keep the patient alive, no chemotherapeutic drugs to correct infection, no artificial airway to keep the windpipe open . . .

Preparations were made and hospital staff swiftly wheeled Cornish into the operating room. Dr. Dan moved decisively, with skilled, deft, movements. He operated quickly, but not hurriedly or recklessly, and opened the chest or thoracic cavity of the patient. Upon exposing the pericardium sac, the double membranous sac that completely encloses the heart, he reached perhaps the most critical point in the operation. In the pericardium are roots of major heart blood vessels and the space between the two layers of the pericardial membranes contains a fluid used to lubricate the vital, pulsating organ. Dr. Dan located the knife puncture in the pericardial sac, he found bleeding from a major blood vessel. Continuing, he saw a cut in the throbbing heart.

The heart wound was small and he decided to leave it alone. It could heal without his intervention. The wound in the pericardial sac was serious and had to be repaired. The surgeon immediately began to suture the pericardium and the large blood vessels that had been damaged. That was no easy task. He had to select the right suture material and technique on the spot. No previous operations of this kind existed to serve as a guide. The pericardium moves and jumps almost as much as the heart itself so the task of stitching was most delicate. Nonetheless, he successfully completed he task and moved out, suturing the openings he had made. Finally, Dr. Dan completed the ground-breaking surgery and bandaged the patient's chest. James Cornish was still alive. A great sigh of relief went out in the operating room along with congratulations for a masterful job.

Then the waiting began. Could a patient undergoing such a surgery continue to live? Would he fully recuperate and live an active life again? For the next few days, Dr. Dan kept vigil. On one occasion the patient had to be returned to the operating room to remove fluid from the pleural cavity but after that, Cornish rallied.

The doctors who watched the operation knew they had witnessed medical history in the making. On July 22, 1893, the feat was reported in a newspaper, *Chicago Daily Inter-Ocean* where the headlines read, "Sewed Up His Heart."

Of course what Dr. Dan actually had done was to operate on the pericardium. Had the heart been more severely damaged, there is no reason not to believe he would have sutured it also. After Dr. Dan's surgery on Cornish, several reports belatedly claimed that H. C. Dalton, of St. Louis, not Daniel Hale Williams, was the first to perform a successful operation on the pericardium. According to those accounts, Dr. Dalton's operation was performed on September 6, 1891, on a 22 year old man who had suffered a stab wound to the chest. That was two years before Daniel Hale Williams operated on James Cornish.

All agreed though that Dr. Dan never heard of the Dalton surgery. The author Lewis Fenderson researched claims about the Dalton surgery and found nothing to substantiate it. What he found was a report in the March 2, 1897 of the *The New York Medical Record*. According to the *Record*, ' . . .this case [James Cornish], is the first successful or unsuccessful case of a suture of the pericardium that has ever been recorded'."

Dr. Dan did not participate in the controversy. The important thing was after 51 days, James Cornish left the hospital a well man.

In 1897 Dr. Dan published a full account of the procedure in the *Medical Records*. The title of the article was, "Stab Wound of the Heart and Pericardium - Suture of the Pericardium - Patient Alive Three Years After. " The patient, James Cornish returned to a physically active life and lived an additional twenty years.

Move To Washington

When elected to his second term as President of the United States, Grover Cleveland named Judge Walter Q. Gresham Secretary of State. The Cleveland Administration's agenda included a project to improve and upgrade Freedman's Hospital in Washington, D.C. Judge Gresham urged Dr. Dan to apply for the job of chief surgeon, offering to back him for the position. The proposition caught the southside physician by surprise. He had thought of no position other than serving at Provident Hospital. He initially thought it would be disloyal of him to go any other place. Not so, Gresham countered. Provident was now functioning quite well. On the other hand, conditions at Freedman's were deplorable and because of its larger size Dr. Dan could actually help many more of his people than at Provident.

Freedman Hospital, affiliated with the medical school of Howard University, was originally established to treat the sick and injured among former slaves. The thousands of emancipated blacks who came to Washington, D. C., lived under pathetic and unsanitary conditions which, not surprisingly, adversely affected their health. According to Herbert M. Morais, ". . . of the 31,500 Negroes living in Washington and Georgetown, in 1866, almost 23,000 suffered some illness." These people needed medical care and Freedmen Hospital was their hope.

Eventually, Dr. Dan yielded to persuasion and submitted his application. Many doctors from across the country, black and white, sought the position. Dr. Dan's impeccable record, and glowing letters of recommendation, enabled him to outdistance all others. He accepted the proffered appointment and moved to Washington.

It did not take long for Dr. Dan to realize that he faced a monumental task at Freedman's. Hospital buildings and facilities were hopelessly inadequate. The author Helen Buckler gave an account of the physical plant.

". . . four two-story frame pavilions built a quarter century before still in use . . . deteriorated through age, constant use, and insufficient repair . . . temperature regulation was impossible . . . water closet arrangements were primitive and unsanitary. Furnishing was poor.

Buckler continued her description:

The operating room was in the `Brick,' . . . building which housed classrooms of the medical department . . . the administrative offices . . . and the apartment office of the surgeon -in-chief. Surgical patients had to be carried on stretchers from the wards into the open, regardless of the weather or their condition, and carried back to the wards after their operation. Convalescent patients had likewise to expose themselves to the weather in going to their meals. Bed patients received food which had been carried in trays across the yard from the kitchen, and the food was cold.

Dr. Dan also found inefficiency in staff, facilities and the organizational structure. Antiquated medical practices,   due to ignorance, carelessness, or both abounded. Not surprisingly, the death rate was frighteningly high. Disturbed by what he found, Dr. Dan vowed that such conditions must prevail no longer. His people deserved the same kind of first-class medical attention as anyone else. He went to work.

Anyone who assumes a new position and makes major changes, is likely to encounter resentment. Dr. Dan, though aware of the possibility, reorganized the entire hospital. He modernized and upgraded hospital operations, and created new departments including medicine, dermatology, respiratory and bronchial, gynecology and added pathology and bacteriology services. He established nurses training and medical internship programs.

The new Chief Surgeon then took on the delicate task of evaluating the staff. Unfortunately, a number of them would have to be replaced. He recruited new doctors, including specialists he needed, appointed them to the appropriate departments. That meant replacing many general practitioners who previously occupied those positions. The incoming doctors were reputable physicians, black and white, all highly competent, well-trained, and current on the most recent developments in medicine. Outside the hospital he found that black doctors were isolated and local medical association closed to them. During his experience in Chicago, Dr. Dan had found that meeting with other doctors and exchanging ideas proved mutually beneficial. So he joined interested physicians who formed an interracial group that promoted a flow of ideas and exchange of information with obvious good results.

During Dr. Dan Williams' first year at Freedman the mortality rate dropped sharply. Of more than 500 surgical cases, only eight died. He performed most of the operations himself. Surgery almost always took place in lecture-demonstration settings to allow physicians, medical students, and others to observe his techniques and procedures. In addition, Dr. Dan taught classes at the Howard University Medical School. He conducted clinics at other medical schools as well. Medical care at Freedman improved dramatically.

Medical Successes and Personal Loses

One day in 1895 an ambulance brought a diminutive woman in critical condition to Freedmen's. She had gone to another hospital but, despite her grave condition, was turned away. No room they said. The staff at Freedman looked at each other knowingly for they had seen this before. They knew that one so sick would never have been turned away from that hospital, except that she was black. Worse, the patient had been misdiagnosed as having the dropsy, the error probably due to a hasty examination of an unwanted patient.

Dr. Dan and his staff immediately recognized that the patient was pregnant and about to deliver. Shortly after arriving at Freedman's she went into convulsion, which suggested serious complications. The examination also revealed that her birth canal was too small to deliver the baby, so to save her life, surgery would have to be performed. Dr. Dan faced a critical dilemma. Should he try to save the life of the mother, the child, or both? To attempt to save the mother through surgery was risky. To try to save both would imperil mother and child. After viewing the alternatives and the risks, Dr Dan decided to perform a Caesarian section. He would try to save mother and child. The decision to do so was based on his moral conviction of duty to save life, on confidence in his understanding of the medical problem, and his skill and experience as a surgeon.

The term Caesarian comes from the Latin word *caedere,* meaning "to cut". A Caesarian then is birth by incision through the abdominal walls. Legend has it that Julius Caesar was delivered in this manner, thus the name of the operation. Ancient Roman law mandated the procedure in the event of the death of the mother prior to normal delivery.

As late as the 19th century, the mortality rate for patients undergoing the Caesarian procedure was as high as 50 per cent, so few western doctors performed the operation. Many of them, declaring that the life of the mother came first, performed a less risky procedure called fetal craniotomy, which unfortunately meant sacrificing the life of the child. Although it was a medically acceptable procedure, Dr. Dan rejected that option.

Proceeding with the surgery, Dr. Dan gave full details to those around him, what he was doing and why. Operating in his usually skilled and efficient manner, he removed the baby from its womb. The patient, who had been on the verge of death, survived, and made a complete recovery. Dr. Dan saved both mother and child.

During this period he endured sadness when death took some of this personal loved ones away. His famous cousin Frederick Douglass passed away and later he mourned the loss of his beloved "sister" Traviata. She died of tuberculosis. Death claimed Dr. Henry Palmer under whom he did his medical apprenticeship, and Judge Walter Gresham, who supported him for the position at Freedman's. Perhaps the heaviest loss of all, was the death of his brother Price.

But there was also happiness in his life. He met Alice Johnson, a local school teacher and daughter of one of his patients. Alice Johnson's mother, Alice Walker, was the daughter of an unwed mulatto, a slave, and a white father. Her father was the famous sculptor, Moses Ezekial. Alice Walker carried the racial traits of her father, almost to the complete exclusion of any other. Alice Johnson inherited much of her mother's light skin color. Lillie Patterson said of the young school teacher, "Whenever she walked down the streets heads usually turned and stared, so striking was her beauty."

As time passed, Dr. Dan and Alice saw more and more of each other. He enjoyed her company immensely and she his. On April 2, 1898, Daniel Hale Williams took Alice Darling Johnson as his wife.

Politics and Medicine

Under the Williams administration Freedman Hospital made significant improvements in health care and teaching. The image of the hospital changed from that of low regard to respectability. Nevertheless, with its dependency on the federal government for support, Freedman could not escape the whims of politics. Increasingly Dr. Williams found himself spending as much time fighting political battles as he did on his medical and hospital administration duties. A panel even sought to discredit him on flimsy charges of malfeasance. It pained him that some he had tried most to help, betrayed him for political gains.

The political maneuvering and especially the duplicity, caught him off guard. Unprepared for such behavior, he had neither the disposition or desire to engage such acrimony. As a consequence the doctor became somewhat overly sensitive and to a certain extent too distrustful of others.

As each new battle for turf surfaced, Dr. Dan armed himself with the record of achievement and positive change that took place under his administration. On these he made his defense. With the weight of evidence clearly on his side, he won each battle. But he came to realize, much to his dismay, that such political distractions were not likely to go away. He saw that to his adversaries, the quality of health was priority only if it provided a political advantage. With each new administration would come a new agenda and political infighting would continue, often to the detriment of good medical practice.

To the surprise of many, Dr. Dan submitted his resignation. He announced that he had achieved his major objectives, and his work at Freedman done. Then in February, 1898, with his new wife, Dr. Dan returned to Chicago.

A Tireless Crusader

Back in his "home city," Dr. Dan rejoined the staff of Provident Hospital. He continued an active role in the National Medical Association, which he helped to organize in 1884. The NMA was formed because the American Medical Association refused to accept black doctors to its membership. Dr. Charles V. Roman the described mission of the National Medical Association with these words.

Conceived in no spirit of racial exclusiveness, fostering no ethnic antagonisms, but born of the exigencies of the American environment, the National Medical Association has for its object the banding together for mutual cooperation and helpfulness, the men and women of African descent who are legally and honorably engaged in the practice of the cognate professions of Medicine, Surgery, Pharmacy and Dentistry.

Dr. Dan often conducted clinics to demonstrate recent developments, and to advance the cause of good medicine. He had a special interest in conducting clinic at Meharry Medical College where he was an adjunct associate professor of medicine. Meharry, located in Nashville, Tennessee, was organized in 1875 to prepare blacks to treat the critical health needs of their people. Dr. Dan sought to enhance that mission. His clinics were always well attended by doctors and medical students who expressed unabashed admiration for his masterful demonstrations, clean techniques, swift and skill performance.

Dr. Dan was a also a tireless crusader for the building of new hospitals. In those cities where blacks were denied treatment in local hospitals, which was most cities, he brought the message that they should build their own, "like we did in Chicago." But he would not leave it there. He laid down guidelines, based on his own experience, and on what he knew to be marks of excellence in a hospital.

Trouble at Provident

Many friends and former patients were delighted to have Dr. Dan back at Provident. But others, particularly Dr. George Hall, did not welcome his return. While Dr. Dan was in Washington, the political-minded Hall had succeeded in attaining a position of influence and power at Provident. At every opportunity, he made life uncomfortable for Dr. Dan and waged a relentless campaign of deception and false innuendoes designed to demean him. Dr. Dan had no commitment to his own people, he would say. Dr. Dan and his wife were snobbish, they did not wish to mingle with dark-skinned blacks and common people. Dr. Hall pledged to punish Dr. Dan, to destroy him, to make his name forgotten in his time, and after his passing.

Despite the heavy-handed charges, Dr. Dan did not defend himself, though he could and likely should have tried to set the record straight. He could fight his way across much of the country from Baltimore to Rockford as a boy. He could fight his way into medical school and later to build a hospital for the underserved. But when it came to quibbling, gossiping and bickering, even when he was being hurt, he could not engage. It was not his way. In a rare effort, he once wrote that all attempts on his part to develop a better relation with Dr. Hall had met with failure. On the other hand, as Dr. Dan simply could not conceal his disdain for the professional incompetence of his adversary, his demeanor further aggravated the situation. The gulf remained, even widened, and their collective strengths never served Provident.

In 1912, the prestigious St. Luke Hospital asked Dr. Dan to join its staff as associate attending surgeon. Some of his colleagues urged him to decline because St. Luke did not accept other black physicians on its staff. They argued that his interest in St. Luke would paint him as having become responsive to wealthy whites to the neglect of his own people. But Dr. Dan felt that by going to St. Luke, he would be opening the door to other blacks. He believed his new association could help bring about the day of interrracial medical healing when black doctors, like all others, could treat their patients at any hospital in the city. Dan Williams also felt he could learn things at St. Luke that would be beneficial to doctors and patients at Provident.

Once again Dr. Dan never went public with his motives, even though stung by the criticism against him. Consequently some thought the worse of him because they heard only one side which, unexamined seemed plausible to them.

Meanwhile, Dr. Hall pressed the attacks. He exploited others and with his charm and affability, swayed many to his way of thinking. Even so, a small core would not forget how much Dr. Dan had done. They pointed to his peerless skills as a physician of the highest order, to how he had built Provident from a dream, to how he had helped countless patients, had aided many professional men and women, and how his pioneering contributions had helped advance the cause of medicine. They remained loyal, and supported Dr. Dan as a good and honorable man and respected physician. The controversy therefore joined and the two camps took aim at each other. The fight even went beyond Provident and Chicago to other parts of the country.

Despite the attacks, Dr. Dan accepted the position at St. Luke. In response the Provident Board, no doubt influenced by Hall, ordered him to bring all his patients there. Dr. Dan was incredulous and refuse to comply. Sadly, the man who founded Provident, and who had turned vision into reality, felt compelled to resign. He then went to St. Luke to work full time.

More than any others, the whole affair deeply wounded Dr. Dan. He lost faith and began to withdraw as a leader, and an active participant in medical circles. He stepped aside when his influence and creative powers were probably at their peak. Sadly he also ceased publishing, abandoned his crusading for hospitals, and many other activities as well.

Idlewild

After moving to Chicago, the Williams' were delighted when Alice became pregnant. With great anticipation, they looked forward to adding to their family. But their joy turned into concern when the pregnancy became difficult. Then, in the summer of 1899, their child was stillborn. Not only that, but Alice barely survived a difficult surgery. After that, she could not conceive again. Alice Williams then drew within herself and for a while, a strain descended upon the marriage.

Nonetheless, there were some good times in their lives. Dr. Dan and several black men purchased some land in Idlewild, Michigan for a summer resort community. Impressed by the rich growth of trees and tranquil setting, Dr. Dan envisioned the community, not only as a place for rest and relaxation, but a good setting to promote cultural activities, and advance knowledge about health care.

The Williamses built a summer home in Idlewild that stood amongst tall stately trees overlooking an inviting lake. There Dr. Dan could relax, engage in the joy of some outdoor activities such as cutting wood for the fireplace, but always taking great pain to save as many trees as possible. He was among the early conservationists. Most especially, Dr. Dan took great pride in his flowers and they, along with children who came to know him well, were his great love. He also kept in touch with young medical students, including the hosting of an annual social event for them at Idlewild. Always there for future doctors, he informed, advised, counseled, and sometimes provided money for those in the pinch. He remembered his difficult days as a young medical student.

Then misfortunate struck. What the Williamses had hoped would be years of joy and pleasure at Idlewild received a severe jolt when Alice was diagnosed as having Parkinson's disease. Parkinson's disease is a neurological disorder. It occurs when there is an inadequate level of dopamine, a chemical that transmits messages from what is known as the substantia nigra of the brain to parts of the organ that controls muscular movements. Victims of Parkinson suffer from tremors, weakness, and gradual loss of muscle control. Though in recent years medicine has made great strides in treating Parkinson's disease, its cause is yet unknown and medical cures remain elusive. So when Alice Williams was afflicted, medical science knew far less about the cause or treatment of the affliction.

Although in full anticipation her gradual decline, Alice Williams faced her condition bravely. Her husband, the compassionate physician, devotedly attended to her needs. Even when she was confined to a wheelchair such courage as she displayed earned the respect even of her detractors. And when Dr. Dan would take her to Idlewild, the setting proved to be a helpful refuge. In 1924 however, after an extended illness, she died. Then only a year after the death of his wife, Dr. Dan's grief was compounded by the passing of his dear friend and father surrogate, Harry Anderson. Further stress ensued when a misunderstanding with some members of his extended family caused them to turn their backs on him. The next year, in 1926, he suffered a severe stroke that left him partially paralyzed.

The old warrior valiantly tried to fight back. His love for medicine yet sustained and for his profession transcendent. He even talked about another interracial hospital, maintained his interest in young doctors and medical students as he continued to give them his counsel. Still the sadness and loneliness that intruded in his life wrought a bitterness of spirit compounded by episodes of forgetfulness. Then came more strokes that made of his life a painful existence. His physical condition deteriorated and the brilliance of his mind dimmed. On August 4, 1931, five years after his first stroke, Dr. Dan expired at his beloved Idlewild.

His remains were returned to Chicago where he was interred in the Graveland Cemetery. Inexplicably, the man who made such brilliant, ground-breaking contributions to medicine was laid to rest in an unmarked grave, a condition later corrected.

"To Have Known Him Was A Pleasure"

During his lifetime Daniel Hale Williams ranked among the foremost physicians of his day. He shined brightly as a healer and surgeon of unusual skill. Williams also contributed to medical progress through his publications, clinics, lectures and speeches. His articles appeared in such journals as the *New York Medical Record, The Chicago Medical Record, The Annals of Surgery, The Philadelphia Medical Journal,* and others. Dr. Dan worked to establish hospitals that would provide good medical care for the neglected. He established programs that provided medical training and internships opportunities for talented and aspiring people shut out. In every instance, excellence was his goal.

Dr. Dan was active in the National Medical Association, in civil rights movements, in civic programs such as the YMCA, and other ventures. Few tried harder than he to climb the high and rugged mountains to interracial cooperation, mutual respect and understanding in the field of medicine.

From 1887 to 1891, he was a member of the Chicago Board of Health. Dr. Dan was Rank Colonel on a board of surgeons that examined potential medical officers for service in the war against Spain. In 1899, he was appointed to the Chicago Board of Public Health. He served on the surgical staff of Cook County Hospital from

1900 to 1906 and from 1907 until his death. During World War I, he was the medical examiner on the State Board of Appeals. Dr. Dan was also Clinical Instructor at the Chicago Medical College. Somewhere along the line, he perfected the technique for suturing the delicate spleen to halt hemorrhaging.

Perhaps a further commentary on the Provident controversy is in order. The initial victory went to Dr. Hall where some of vengeful mind, removed all traces of Dr. Dan's connection, including his role as founder. Fortunately, that oversight was corrected at the insistence of James Gordan, a member of the original hospital committee.

Among his many honors, Wilburforce University of Ohio awarded him an honorary doctorate as did Howard University in Washington, D.C. When he helped organize the NMA, he was elected vice president only because he would not accept the presidency. Perhaps his most honored recognition came when he was made a charter member of the prestigious American College of Surgeons. Today, books, chapters in books, and many articles are written about him. Some of his publications are read even today by serious students of medicine.

When Dr. Dan passed, the news wires around the country announced his death. In article after article, accounts of his deeds were recounted. So impressive were his medical feats that many were move to anoint him, a "miracle man." But perhaps none of the tributes spoke more eloquently about Dr. Dan than a neighbor. He wrote,

> . . .To have known him was a pleasure - to know him intimately was a priceless privilege. He was at once an inspiration and an aid. To emulate his simplicity, his kindly spirit and his great modesty is to pay tribute to the truly great. . .

All this would seem to make his burial in an unmarked grave seem implausible. That situation was later corrected.

References for Further Reading

Buckler, Helen, *1968. Daniel Hale Williams, Negro Surgeon,* New York: Pittman Publishing Co., . (A definitive text on Dr. Dan)

Fenderson, Lewis H., *1971. Daniel Hale Williams: Open Heart Doctor,* New York: McGraw-Hill Book Company.

_____, "Daniel Hale Williams (Dr. Dan)," in Logan, Rayford and Michael R. Winston (ed), pp. 654-655, *1982. Dictionary of American Negro Biography* W. W. Norton and Company.

Haber, Louis, 1970. *Black Pioneers* of Science and Invention, New York: Harcourt, Brace and World, Inc..

Hayden, Robert C., *1971. Seven Black American Scientists,* Reading, Massachusetts: Addison-Wesley Publishing Company.

Johnson, Stephen L. 1970. *The History of Cardiac Surgery, 1895-1955,* Baltimore, Maryland: The Johns Hopkins Press.

Klein, Aaron, E., 1970. *Hidden Contributors: Black Scientists and Inventors in America,* Garden City, New York: Doubleday and Co.

Meriwether, Louise, 1972. *The Heart Man: Dr. Daniel Hale Williams,* Englewoods Cliffs, New Jersey: Prentice Hall, Inc.

Morais, Herbert, 1969. *The History of the Negro in Medicine* New York Publishers, Inc., Patterson, Lillie, 1981. *Sure Hands Strong Heart: The Life of Daniel Hale* , Nashville, Tennessee: Abingdon, (Another definitive book on Dr. Dan).

Poor, John N., 1964. "Daniel Hale Williams", pages 252-253, in Malone, Dumas (ed.), *Dictionary of American Biography,* New York: Charles Scribner's Sons.

Stratton, Madeline Robinson, 1965. *Negroes Who Help Build America,* Boston: Ginn and Company.

Thomas, Clayton (ed), 1985. *Taber's Cyclopedic Medical Dictionary,* Philadelphia: F. A. Davis Company..

Chapter V_____

Granville T. Woods-Railway Inventor
(1856-1910)

The British invented the railroad, and after many trials and errors proved that it could work. The first rails were made of a variety of materials, including stones and wood. It took a while before technology produced the tough, smooth steel rails.

The railroad industry in the United States really began around 1830. During the 19th century the railroad industry laid tracks westward from the center of government, industry, trade and commerce in the east, to points south and west. Eventually rails stretched across the great rivers, vast plains, and deep canyons of America. They went through miles of wilderness and swamps, and over, around, or through granite rocks of the towering Rockies. Like no other form of transportation, the railroads connected one American city to another, and those cities to towns, villages, and hamlets all joined. Unlike Europe where railways only connected large population centers, American railways also reached sparsely settled places or lands not settled at all. Small, obscure, and lonely settlements became names and faces to other parts of the country.

Where the railroads went, new places came into being and sometimes small settlements flourished and grew into large cities. The railroad linked the Atlantic to the Pacific, the East to the distant West, and the North to the South.George Douglas wrote that "Americans saw the railroad inextricably bound up with their national destiny". He said it was through the railroad that the

United States truly became united.

Passengers who boarded trains during the early days of railway travel, rode under spartan conditions. They sat on hard wooden benches in cars heated in winter by pot-bellied stoves that were hazardous in the event of an accident or sudden stops. Out West, trains might be delayed or stopped collison with animals or by snow piled up at the pass. During the summer heat, particles from the locomotive stacks often swept into open windows of the cars while at other times trains encountered swarms of locusts Sometimes there were attacked by Indians trying to protect their land or by bandits seeking to rob trains and passengers of their wealth.

Nonetheless, none of these travails halted growth of the railways during the nineteenth century. The quality of rails and trains in the United States lagged those of Europe but the nation soon became a world leader in total rail mileage. The sheer size of the country and willingness of rail barons to take risks accounted for much of the expansion. Railway empire builders dreamed grandiously of linking the whole country, East to West, and North to South. Also the federal government viewed railway expansion as being in the nation's interest and supported the industry with measures that included land grants and low interest loans. Even so, all these efforts would have been less successful had not a few Americans of inventive genius raised the level of speed, safety, comfort and reliability. One such creator was Granville Woods, an American of African descent.

An Unlikely Inventor

There is come controvery about Woods' birth..One account claimed that Woods was born in Australia and at the age of sixteen immigrated to the United States with his parents. Most sources however, are in agreement that Woods' parents were free blacks and that he was born April 23, 1856 in Ohio. The latter versions appears more plausible and as it provides the most consistent and comprehensive explanation of this unusual man.

Granville's parents were Tailor and Martha Woods. He had a brother named Lyates but beyond that little is known of his family and his early life. Still, when informed of Woods' achievements later in life, and the impact his contributions had on industrial progress, its seems reasonable to speculate that he came from a family of discipline, character, and progressive orientation.

Though the Woods lived in a free state, certain laws constrained them and made fragile their limited freedom. In 1804 and 1807, Ohio, the first Northern State to do so, codified what became known as "Black Laws", that regulated and restricted the rights of "black and mulatto" people. By statue the state denied them equal educational opportunity, equal economic opportunity, denied them justice before the courts, and exacted a telling price in human dignity. The law, also specific to blacks, required them to post a $500 bond before they could move to Ohio. Blacks could not serve in the militia, could not testify against whites in the courts, and could not build schools to educate their young. Custom, combined with codification, deprived blacks of true freedom.

Above the Froth

When forced to live under demeaning circumstances, some despair, withdraw, or become bitter and hostile. Creativity is stunted and self-esteem suffers. Others somehow rise above the froth, grow, believe in themselves and define their lives by loftier standards. The latter group included Granville Woods.

By all accounts, Granville's formal education, such as it was, ended at the age of 10 and he went to work. The lad found employment with a railroad company in the machine shop where his innate talents emerged. By thoughtful application of hands and mind, he quickly became a skilled machinist and blacksmith. Granville found wonder in the world of machinery; mechanical things fascinated him and stimulated his imagination.

Not satisfied with his limited formal education, Granville took private lessons and, whenever possible, enrolled in night school.

Granville spent the days of his apprenticeship working, observing, learning all phases of machine shop operation. The knowledge and skills he acquired provided a foundation that, later in life, allowed him to exploit his inventive nature.

Westward Ho, and Back

In 1872, after six years on the job, and sixteen years old, Granville moved to Missouri where he found employment with the Iron Mountain Railroad. His first job was as a locomotive fireman but he advanced rapidly to become a train engineer. At the age of seventeen Granville sat in the driver's seat of a powerful engine, perhaps amongthe youngest locomotive engineer in the country.

Granville devoted his leisure time to study, avoiding the fast life that attracted so many of his acquaintances. Mostly he read books about the then new field of electricity, becoming increasingly fascinated by its magic and the possibilities it held for humankind. For some reason or reasons, he soon moved eastward to Springfield, Illinois where he found employment in a different area, a steel mill.

All the while the young man from Ohio kept thinking about electricity and possible uses for it in the future. His optimism however went counter to most, including men of letters and those of high industrial standing. Woods may also have wondered if his race might prevent any possibility of his being a player in the creative application of electricity for society. If so, did not deter his continued efforts toward understanding known laws and theories about this phenomenon.

In 1875 the nineteen year-old Woods moved again, this time to New York. He reasoned that since resources in electricity were greater there, so would be his opportunities. After finding employment in a machine shop, where he worked by day, at night he enrolled in college and studied electrical and mechanical engineering. The courses were challenging but he was up to the task. Woods completed the course of studies in two years and was graduated, an achievement not shared by many Americans of any description during the nineteenth century.

Then came the downside. Despite numerous openings in the area, and being qualified by experience and formal education, his race blocked all job appointments as either a mechanical or an electrical engineer. Though numerous rejections tested his resolve, Woods refused to lose hope. His tenacity paid off when, on February 6, 1878, Woods boarded the British steamship *Ironside,* as an engineer!

The oceans were new to him, its unbroken vastness, and restless ways, fascinating. On clear nights, the heavens could be seen as never before, sparkling stars, planets shining, moon changing, all captivating to the mind. At other times though, the elements challenged his courage when howling winds and crashing waves tossed the ship about.

Possibly more interesting were the different countries as Woods' ship visited new lands with new people and cultures foreign to him. He saw sights he only read about, heard sounds, breathe air, and smelled odors previously only dreamed about. Perhaps, at least for awhile he felt as the poet Brooke Atkinson who wrote, "Land was created to provide a place for steamers to visit".

Despite his adventures on the steamer, or perhaps because of them, after two years as an ocean voyager, Woods returned to land and the United States. He found employment with the railway again, this time as an engineer with the Danville and Southern Railroad. He continued to explore an idea that came to him while at sea when he pondered the question, could existing steam boilers be made to work with greater efficiency. If so, how? Woods imagined new possibilities, made sketches and tested elements of his ideas whenever possible. For the time being electricity, though not forgotten, took second place. He returned to Cincinnati and in a bold decision, resigned his job to devote full time to his idea of building a better steam engine.

'A New and Improved Boiler'

The Reverend William J. Simmons, a contemporary of Granville Woods, and who corresponded with him, provided some insight into the character trait that drove the young engineer to persist and that sustained him during difficult times.

> Mr. Woods says that he has been frequently refused work because of the previous condition of his race, but he has great determination and will never despair because of disappointments.

Woods had a burning desire to put his training as a mechanical and electrical engineer into use. At this time, he put his "great determination" to test when he decided to work on a new and improved steam engine. He well realized that the inventor must first engage in serious study and reflection to achieve the goal of a new innovation. At times the very effort may invite ridicule from others. Always there is the possibility of failure but he had faith that his idea would work. Of course on rare occasion the inventor may stumble, so to speak, on a new idea or revelation by chance but that never comes in the absence of trying even if in another direction. The great Louis Pasteur of France, chief architect of the germ theory put it into perspective when he said that, "Chance favors the prepared mind".

Woods' familiarity with the steam engine grew out of his educational background and his experiences with trains and ships. It may be recalled that he also apprenticed as a mechanic and blacksmith. When Woods studied engineering he learned more about the scientific principles involved in the working of the steam engine, a man-made marvel and critical force in the industrial revolution. So after extensive investigation and thought, Woods came to the conclusion that he could build a better steam engine and he "rolled up his sleeve", physically and mentally, and set out to do just that. After considerable expenditure of both, and money as well, he completed his work on a new steam engine and applied to the U. S. Government for a patent.

The patent was sought to give Woods the right of ownership in the form of temporary monopoly over the invention. (Currently in the United States, that period is seventeen years). His patent application had to meet strict government specification, defining the invention and all its parts in clear, concise language. The inventor had to explain what the invention did, how it operated or functioned, and what made it novel or unique. Paper used in the application, language, writing and margins, formulas, symbols, all had to meet government standards. Drawings had to accompany all narratives and the margins, lines, shadings, legends, etc. had to obey guidelines. Also before patents are issued, lawyer and application fees, which can be expensive, must be paid.

On June 3, 1884, Granville T. Woods obtained a patent for his new Steam Boiler Furnace (Patent No. 299,894). He increased the efficiency of the steam boiler furnace by "promoting [more complete] combustion" which, of course, economized fuels. This he accomplished by having a partial vacuum created during boiler operation, which forced more air through the combustible material, thus producing more complete burning. Woods' boiler also forced combustible gases to recycle which achieved even greater economy. He stated in his patent application that the "temperatures were highly increased and kept above the point of thorough combustion". His steam boiler furnace made an important contribution to industrial progress which, at that time, depended heavily on steam-driven machines.

Invention for the Telephone and Railway Telegraphy

After the steam boiler patent, Woods turned his attention to electricity and magnetism and their application to human communication. In just five months after his steam boiler furnace project, and perhaps encouraged by its success, he obtained another patent, this one an invention that improved the telephone transmitter (December 2, 1884, Patent application No. 308,876). Alexander Graham Bell invented the telephone October 10, 1876, and with the aid of Lewis Latimer, himself an inventor, successfully obtained a patent for his device. From that start, Bell continued to make improvements on what may be the most significant human innovation in the field of communication. His success attracted others to the field as well. Woods' invention of 1884 improved transmission of the human voice signal.

Only four months later, April 7, 1885, Granville Woods patented another telephone invention, this one of greater applicability. He referred to it as an "Apparatus for Transmission of Messages by

Telephone and Electricity". The versatile device could be used by both telephone and telegraph operators. Woods sold this patent to the American Bell Telephone Company.

With many more ideas to pursue, he decided to organize his own company to handle his inventions. He called it the Woods Electric Company of Cincinnati. His next invention was a "Telephone System and Apparatus", for which he received a patent (No. 371,241) on October 11, 1887. He wrote that his invention differed from "ordinary methods of electrical transmission of speech. . . .First, he said, "I employ in the primary or local circuit under control of the sending diagram a non-continuous or intermittent current". With this innovation, Woods obtained a current of "far greater inducing strength". The result was that his apparatus made possible clearer transmission of "speech and other sounds" than any currently in use. Woods also improved the diaphragm of the telephone receiver for truer reproduction of the voice. In addition, unlike existing receivers, his invention overcame certain interferences from neighboring transmission lines. The Woods apparatus could transmit messages over a greater distance than any other telephone apparatuses.

So Moving Trains Can Talk to Other Moving Trains: The Induction-Telegraph System Invention

In 1887, William Simmons, wrote about a major problem in the railway industry - increasing train accidents. He quoted a passage from the *Scientific American* that reported the seriousness of the problem.

Only last week [there was] a collision between two freight trains at New Brunswick, New Jersey, on the line of the Pennsylvania railroad, in which two lives were lost and property to the value of half a million dollars destroyed. It was of course by mere chance that these trains were not carrying passengers.

From his experience as a locomotive engineer, Granville Woods knew the dangers first hand. Trains were becoming faster heavier, and more powerful. As a result when trains collided, they caused great destruction, loss of life and property. The problem was, what to do about it; how could train transportation be made safer? Should they be made lighter, less powerful, and slower, or was there a better and more acceptable way? The report in *Scientific American* acknowledged that the telegraph had helped, but not enough. Simmons went on to say that the only way to prevent train collisions, would be to have men guard every "point" on the railroad. The men could never be distracted from their duty, they could never rest or sleep, and they would have to have supernatural eyesight that could pierce the thickest fog.

One scheme known as the "block system" had been tried, but this was not satisfactory. Woods asked, what if moving trains could speak with each other? What if experienced station managers, men who knew the railway system thoroughly, could coordinate movements and contact moving trains at any point? Would that not help? Woods thought so.

Similar to other successful inventors, one of Woods' strength was his capacity to draw on scientific principles and make creative applications. In this case he reviewed the principles of current electricity, magnetism, electromagnets, and the phenomenon of induction. Then he engaged the complex, logical connections, and found a way to make these things work for the benefit of humankind.

Out of this came his invention that Woods called the "Induction Telegraph System." He obtained a patent for this invention November 15, 1887 (No. 373,915). In his patent application he explained:

> My invention relates to a system of electric communication between two moving railway trains or vehicles, or between the same and a fixed station or stations, and transmits the signals to and from the vehicles . . . "

Simmons corresponded with Woods about the system. He said the inventor told him that his telegraph served both a technological and social/civic function. In his letter to Simmons, Woods explained that his invention was:

> . . . for the purpose of averting accidents by keeping each train informed of the whereabouts of the one immediately ahead or following it; in intercepting criminals; in communicating with stations from moving trains; and in promoting general, social and commercial intercourse.

Simmons reported on one of the best descriptions of Woods' invention that appeared in the January 14, 1886 issue of the *Catholic Tribune* :

> By means of this system, the railway dispatcher can note the position of any train on the route at a glance. The system also provides means for telegraphing to and from the train while in motion. The same lines may also be used for local message without interference with the regular train signals.
> . . .In fact, two hundred operators may use a single wire at the same time.

With this invention, railway communication improved significantly and train travel became much safer. It was one of Woods' major contributions to the industry.

The Edison Challenge

Others were working on the same train - to - train communication idea so Woods' invention was a race against the competition. According to several sources, when Woods sought to patent his invention, a formidable opponent challenged him. Thomas Edison, acknowledged as the greatest inventor in history, and another man named Lucius Phelp (or Phelps), claimed that Edison was the original inventor of the Induction Telegraphy. Woods defended himself against these claims, twice against

Edison and once against Phelps. Testifying for Edison was one of his employees, and an inventor and acknowledged patent expert, Lewis Latimer A brief comment about Mr. Latimer.

Lewis Latimer was a Massachusetts-born son of runaway slaves. A veteran of the Civil War, former employee in a patent law office, a self-taught draftsman, electrical engineer, inventor, linguist, and author, Latimer came with impressive credentials. Latimer did the drawings for Alexander Graham Bell and helped him prepare his patent applications for his invention, the telephone. He invented an improved Water Closet for trains, and had several inventions that improved the electrical incandescent lamp. Some observers called his procedures for manufacturing a superior carbon filament a major advancement in incandescent lamps efficiency. Latimer wrote the first book on incandescent lighting using the Edison system. He was known for his memory of details and his integrity. So versatile was Latimer in various fields: the electrical industry, patent laws, draftsmanship, poetry, art, and languages, that many called him the Renaissance Man.

In nearly every case where Latimer appeared as an expert witness, Edison won. Two of the few cases where Latimer was on the losing side were during Edison's two challenges to Woods. Probably, it was the first time two black Americans inventors took opposing sides in a patent dispute.

An article in the *Catholic Tribune* supportive of Woods stated that "Mr. Woods has all the patent office drawings for these devices, as your correspondence witnessed." The writer went on the record that,

> The patent office has twice declared Mr. Woods prior inventor of the induction railway telegraph against Mr. Edison, who claims to be the prior inventor. The Edison and Phelps company are now negotiating a consolidation with the Wood's Railway Telegraph company.

Reportedly, after his second loss, Edison attempted to buy Wood's Company and offered him a position with the Edison company. In some respects, it was a tempting offer. Woods would have an opportunity to work with a man acknowledged to be without a peer as an inventor. He would be associated with a powerful company and given job security without all the risks associated with his own small company. Nevertheless, he declined, preferring to be free to follow his own interest, and chart his own creative course.

Among several other Woods communication inventions was the Relay-Instrument (Patent No. 213,823). This invention improved his Inductive Telegraphy System and the Railway Telegraphy (Patent No. 217,858). The new Woods system made use of telegraph lines running next to train tracks and devices, which could then interact with his system installed in car roofs for "static-conduction telegraphy." Woods' invention allowed train personnel to operate their devices without interfering with the ordinary use of the adjacent wires.

Most of Woods inventions involving electrical devices, used alternating currents and the phenomenon known as electromagnetic induction. Electric motors, telephones and telegraphs depend on the proper arrangements and use of electromagnets. The basis for this is that magnetic energy can be converted into electrical energy, and electrical energy into magnetic energy. By using electrical energy to make electromagnets, we have our most powerful magnets. Moreover, when using electromagnets, the magnetism can be turned on and off as desired, polarity can be altered, and the magnetic strength varied. Electromagnets are essential to modern technology.

Woods' use of electromagnetic induction was based on principles discovered by two great scientists during the 1830s. One was the American Physicist Joseph Henry, and the other the English physicist/chemist, Michael Faraday. Woods made extensive use of the phenomenon by which an alternating current in one electromagnetic arrangement *induces* current in another, separate electromagnetic arrangement. This is electromagnetic induction.

The Galvanic Battery

The oldest method of producing current electricity is by use of the galvanic battery. The galvanic battery, is named after the 18th century Italian scientist Luigi Galvani. It is commonly known as a "battery" or sometimes an "electrical battery". A battery consists of two or more cells properly combined. Galvani, by chance, discovered the phenomenon of current electricity in frog legs. A classic debate in science historyntook place between Galvani and his compatriot Alessandra Giuseppe Antonio Volta, about the nature of current electricity. Actually Volta is the father and inventor of the electrical battery as we know it today.

In the modern Galvanic battery, as it was called by Woods, the basic concept is the same as that described by Volta. Chemical energy is converted to electrical energy. The electrical cells that make up an electrical battery, consists of unlike electrodes, such as copper and zinc for instance, or zinc and carbon, and an electrolytic chemical solution, usually an acid or base. Positive electrodes or anodes, and negative electrodes, or cathodes, are immersed in an aqueous or moist chemical electrolytic solution. An example of an electrolyte is a solution of sulfuric acid or ammonium chloride (sal ammoniac). Direct current electricity is produced from chemical actions taking place in the unit. The chemical battery was once the only source of current electricity.

Woods noted that despite commercially produced electricity (from large generators), people still needed the chemical battery. For relatively small voltage requirement and where a portable source of electricity is needed they turned to the battery. So he asked of himself, can the battery, as presently in use, be improved?

As in other cases during his productive career, he thought it possible and went to work. On July 9, 1887, Woods obtained a patent, (Patent No. 387,839), for a new Galvanic Battery. Woods explained in his patent application how his invention was "new", "useful", "simple", "cheap", "convenient", and "durable" for ordinary purposes . . ." What was innovative about his battery was the design, but also the structure and results he obtained. The electrodes could easily be removed, cleaned, and replaced if desired, and the chemical solution of *sal ammoniac* could conveniently be replenished. These arrangements made for a longer life, therefore a cheaper battery. Woods placed the zinc electrode in the center, and arranged strips or pencils of carbon in a concentric pattern around the zinc with electrodes separated by insulation. The sturdy Woods Galvanic Battery could withstand jolts and could easily be transported from one place to another.

Brakes for the Train

Woods shifted his attention to some of the problems plaguing the braking system of trains. His formal education as a mechanical and electrical engineer, and experience working in a machine shop, and later as a locomotive engineer, provided valuable background for this new and bold venture. He observed that as locomotives became increasingly massive, faster, and powerful, and as trains added more boxcars, the strain on existing braking systems increased as did risk to safety. His answer was an Electro-Magnetic Brake Apparatus for which he obtained Patent No. 371,655 on October 2, 1886. Woods explained that his braking system used "a current of electricity passing from a generator carried upon a locomotive engine or car for setting, controlling or releasing brakes". Even as his system was a significant advancement in train brake control, he had other ideas.

The automatic airbrake, invented by George Westinghouse was a major advancement in train braking systems. After Westinghouse obtained his airbrake patent (No. 88929, April 13, 18869), the Steubenville Accommodation (Panhandle Railroad) running out of Pittsburgh, Pennsylvania was the first to use it. Other train lines followed.

Still there were problems. Under certain conditions the airbrakes did not respond throughout the length of the train. At other times the brakes failed to release immediately on command when applied. After studying the problems, Granville Woods decided to work on an invention that would correct these shortcomings and significantly improve the airbrake in operation. Following the submission of a very detailed design, Woods received a patent on June 10, 1902, (Patent No. 701, 981), for an Automatic Airbrake.

Woods observed that many railway accidents occurred because the air brakes failed to meet expectations. He studied all the chambers and moving part, all the pistons and valves finding his background in mechanics and his experience as a railroad man useful in the analysis process.. Woods wanted airbrakes that responded more quickly and reliably, released immediately upon command, and stopped in a shorter distance. To achieve his objectives, he designed new valves and other working parts. Putting all together Woods succeeded in inventing a new air brake that worked more efficiently and reliably for normal braking and emergency stops. Dependable braking systems, he pointed out, were at times the difference "between life and death".

Woods' brake also held steady and reliably when the train traveled down a long grade. The brakes controlled speed over an extended period. This was accomplished by building in an efficient recharging process.

Deeply interested in the Woods' invention, George Westinghouse sought him out. Following negotiations between the two inventors, Westinghouse purchased Woods' invention and assigned it to the Westinghouse Air Brake Company of Pittsburgh, Pennsylvania.

An Electric Railway System

Woods later became interested in the electric train. The first public electric railway operated in Germany in 1883. In the United States, the Baltimore and Ohio constructed the first electrical train system, a limited version in 1895, and operated an electric rail line through a tunnel. With the growing demand for moving large numbers of people in big cities, the electric train had at least one major advantage. Unlike the steam engine, it would not discharge smoke and steam in densely populated areas. By the 1920s, electrified rail lines appeared in Europe, the United States and Canada. Woods' inventions, beginning in the 1880s, helped advance this mean of transportation.

Even though versions of the electric trains were struggling in Europe, Woods saw the potential benefits and the future needs. On August 23, 1886, he applied for a patent on his newest invention, the "Elecro-Motive Railway." (Patent 385,034). He assigned the patent to his own company, the Woods Electric Company of Cincinnati, Ohio. This invention helped to improved construction and operations of electrical railways.

On May 2, 1887, Woods patented another pioneering invention, the "Overhead Conducting System for Electrical Railways (Patent 383,844). This improved the performance of electrical trains as well as safety of operations. The Woods concept is used even today.

In 1890, Woods moved back to New York. On August 31, 1891, he completed a major development, the "Electric-Railway System" (Patent 463,020). His design provided for the construction of "a cheap, simple and efficient electric railway. . . [that] could use existing lines or new lines. A new advancement was made by excluding the overhead lines. Instead, the main feeder for current to the motors of the train was a "hermetically-sealed channel in the road bed . . .". This provision reduced the chance of accidental electric shocks. An important element in the system's design was its ability to simplify location of damaged electrical terminals. With early detections of damages, needed repairs could be made with a minimum of delay.

Another, and even more intricate system, the "Electrical-Railway Conduit", involved underground systems for electric trains. Woods patented this system in the United States in 1892, and renewed it in 1893 (No. 509065). He also obtained a patent in Canada in 1893 (No. 41,806). This invention helped solved the vexing problem of current leakage in underground systems. In keeping with his usual pattern, Woods designed his invention for installation at the lowest possible cost. At every point and connection, insulation was secure. His arrangements also protected critical electrical boxes against moisture that might lead to deterioration.

On October 30, 1896, Woods filed a patent application for another complex system, the "Electric-Railway System" (718,183). This system also involved supplying current to a train from a central system through "conductors along the roadbed". By using electromagnetically controlled switches, he reported "perfect safety from shock." In keeping with his usual concerns about costs, Woods made his train system economical to construct, operate, and easy to control. He engineered a flexible system knowing that the future would bring many changes in the industry as the number of passenger and their needs changed. For the new invention he specially designed some 64 switches, shunts, coils and other parts. Woods continued to patent inventions that resulted in major improvements in the electrical railway system well into the 20th century.

The Scale Can Be Large or Small

As can be seen, most of Woods inventions in transportation and communication had large-scale industrial applications. Often, the Ohio-born inventor was ahead of his times. A somewhat different, but still related creation of the versatile inventor was his Amusement Apparatus (Patent No. 639,692). He obtained a patent of a race track for motor driven cars. Any motorcar could be used but, not surprising, Woods recommended electric-driven vehicles. The scale of the track could be large or small and adapted for use indoors or outdoors. The cars could be human driven or could run without people in direct control. Track construction design included an eight-figure pattern. Many model tracks have since used a conception similar to what was originally conceived by Woods.

Times are Changing

Studies of Woods suggests he had unusual powers of imagination and curiosity coupled with strong and steady work habits. He read widely, could absorb and retain details, and had an insatiable desire to learn what is known, to analyze and overcome shortcomings, and create apparatuses and systems beneficial to the industrial world. Various accounts credit him with from 60 to over 150 inventions but the exact number is not known. Part of the confusion stems from the fact that he did not secure patents for all of his inventions and some were sold to interested parties. Woods said a number of his inventions were lost due to "outright theft". That his creations paid a pioneering and significant role in communication, transportation, and the electrical industries is a solid claim.   Clearly he helped modernize the electrical rail system.

As Woods grew older he pondered the changing technology among his many fields of interest. The world was moving on. His own inventions and those of men like the incomparable Thomas A. Edison, Lewis Latimer, and George Westinghouse were being changed by a new generation of scientists, engineers and technologists. This new breed was better educated and more thoroughly grounded in the laws and theories of science and abstract mathematics. He and his contemporaries were pioneers who provided the creative bases but now there were new tools in the hands of a new generation. According to William Katz:

> Woods observed that the young man who wanted to get ahead would have to get himself educated. He believed that men such as himself would no longer function in the new and advanced technological age.

Education and the Future

This was progress but it also gave him pause. What about black people just emerging from more than two centuries of slavery and its aftermath? Would they be left further behind? The prejudices they faced were real and not to be taken lightly, but that was not his only concern. There was a critical need among African Americans for an education they did not now have in sufficient numbers.. He said that the colored youths without education would find themselves pitifully underemployed in the twentieth century. He spoke out for education and presented his ideas about the kind of schooling needed.

It should come as no surprise that the centerpiece of the Woods' education plan would be about technical training. He believed that for his plan to be implemented new schools had to be founded. The existing institutions would could not accommodate his curriculum. These new schools, he felt, should teach the latest knowledge about mechanics to "put into the hands of our boys and girls the actual means of livelihood." Nevertheless, he felt that technical training alone would not prepare the youths for the future. Woods felt that character should also be taught. Young people needed to understand the virtue of determination. That meant having a strong inner feeling of worth and a tough hide. Out of his own experiences, Woods knew that even with an education, black students would face some difficult times. So he proposed that schools also prepare students how to handle rejections without despairing or losing their confidence. He urged that they obtain a superior education and never quit. He once told a group of young black people:

> Refuse to become discouraged. Continue to apply for work after more than one refusal. The reason will include prejudice, but not always.

Some Footnotes

Some historian contend that the attention Woods received never matched his considerable achievements. Nothing this writer found suggests that Woods worried about that but there is no denying his bitterness about people stealing his creations. Still in his lifetime, some recognized his accomplishments. A newspaper account appearing in *The Cincinnati Sun,* referred to him as the successor to Thomas Edison. Others, called him the "Black

Edison." An article in the *Cincinnati Colored Citizen* said Woods was the "best known electrician of the day". *The Catholic Tribune* cited Woods as the "equal, if not superior to any inventor in the country . . ." Another writer called him a genius, ranked among the best.

By most accounts Woods never married. A short paragraph in a Westchester County newspaper referred to a "comely" African American woman who gave her name as Susie Elizabeth Woods. She said she was the inventors' wife. Another account claimed, but seems not to have confirmed Woods going to Westchester County seeking her whereabouts. Beyond that, there is little reference to his marital status.

Woods died in a New York Hospital on January 30, 1910. Death came shortly after he suffered a stroke. He was 53 years old and almost until the end his mind still active and creative in thought. He was also practically broke. Part of the reason may have been that he spent large sums on legal cases involving patent disputes. It is not known who kept books for him and how well. Mae Claytor offered other observations: She wrote:

> Further research is necessary to explain why such a versatile inventor died in virtual poverty. He probably had to pay huge legal fees for defense in a suit for criminal libel in 1892. Woods had charged that his patents for an electric railway had been stolen by the manager of the American Engineering Company. Arrested and briefly held in jail for lack of money to pay his bail, he confronted powerful businessmen and politicians.

Woods is buried in a New York cemetery. An elementary school was named after him in Brooklyn, New York and dedicated in 1969. In 1974, Governor John Gilligan of Ohio issued a proclamation in his honor.

References and Books for Further Reading

Adams, Russell L., 1964. *Great Negroes Past and Present*, Chicago: Afro-Am Publishing Company, Inc.

Arduis, Susan B., 1991. *An Introduction to U. S. Patent Searching: The Process*, Englewood, CO: Libraries Unlimited.

Baker, Henry, 1913. *The Colored Inventor: A Record of Fifty Years*, New York. .

Claytor, Mae P, in Logan, Rayford W. and Michael R. Winston, ed., 1982. *Dictionary of American Negro Biography*, New York: W. W. Norton and Company.

Douglas, George H., 1992. *All Aboard: The Railroad in American Life*, New York: Paragon House,

Green, Richard L., ed., 1985. *A Salute to Black Scientists and Inventors*, Chicago: Empak Enterprises Inc.

Hayden, Robert C., 1972. *Eight Black American Inventors*, Reading, MA: Addison-Wesley Publishing Company.

James, Portia P., 1989. *The Real McCoy: African-American Invention and Innovations, 1613-1930*, Washington, D.C.: Anacostia Museum of the Smithsonian Institution, Smithsonian Institution Press.

Katz, William Loren, 1972. *Eyewitness: The Negro in American History*, Revised Edition. New York: Pitman Publishing Company, Inc.

Klein, Aaron E., 1971. *Hidden Contributors: Black Scientists and Inventors in America*, Garden City, New York: Doubleday and Company, Inc..

Low, W. Augustus, 1968. *Encyclopedia of Black America New York:* Arno Press.

Peters, Margaret, 1968. *The Ebony Handbook of Black Achievement*, Chicago: Johnson Publishing Company.

Prout, A. 1921. *A Life of George Westinghouse*, New York: American Society of Mechanical Engineers. .

Robinson, Wilhelmenia, S., 1968. *Historical Negro Biographies*, International Library of Negro Life and History.

Simmons, William J., 1888. *Men of Mark: Eminent, Progressive and Rising*, New York: Arno Press.

Turner, Glennette T., 1991. *Lewis Howard Latimer*, Englewood Cliffs, NJ: Silver

115

Burdette Press.

Stevenson, O. J., 1966. *The Talking Wire: The Story of Alexander Graham Bell*, New York: Julian Messner.

Winslow, Eugene, ed. 1974. *Black Americans in Science and Engineering: Contributors of Past and Present*, Chicago: Afro-Am Publishing Company, Inc.

Granville Woods Patents Reviewed

Steam Boiler Furnace, No. 299, 894 (June 19, 1883)
Induction-Telegraph System, No. 373,915 (May 21, 1885)
Telephone System and Apparatus, No. 371,241 (June 1, 1885)
Electro-Motive Railway, No. 385,034 (August 23, 1886)
Relay Instrument, No. 364,619, (September 17, 1886)
Electro-Magnetic Brake Apparatus, No. 371,655 (October 2, 1886
Railway Telegraphy, No. 373,383, (November 3, 1886)
Overhead Conducting System for Electric Railway, No. 383,844 (May 2, 1887)
Galvanic Battery, No. 387,839, (July 9, 1887)
Electric Railway System, No. 463,020 (August 31, 1891)
Electric Railway Conduit, No. 509,065 (October 14, 1892)
Electric Railway System, No. 678,086 (July 24, 1895)
Electric Railway System, No. 718,183 (October 30, 1896)
Electric Railway, No. 667,110 (September 29, 1897)
Amusement Apparatus, No. 639,692 (September 27, 1898)
Electric Railway, No. 687,098 (June 29, 1900)
Electric Railway, No. 729,481 (November 24, 1900)
Automatic Airbrake, No. 701,981 (February 5, 1901)

Chapter VI_____

Charles Turner, Pioneer Entomologist (circa 1867-1923

by Patricia Stohr-Hunt

It was three o'clock on the afternoon of September the seventeenth, 1913. For two days we have had frequent showers; even then, although the sun was shining brightly, there were numerous clouds in the sky, and any one of which, without a moment's notice, might float before the sun. The temperature was only 78 degrees Fahrenheit; but compared with the 73 degrees of the afternoon of the sixteenth and with the 63 degrees of the fifteenth, it seemed quite warm. The numerous nests of the ant Lasius Niger L., which had long existed unnoticed beneath the pavements and in the vacant lots of St. Louis, had suddenly been rendered conspicuous by the restless myriads of gigantic virgin females, miniature males, and small workers that were swarming from them and forming agitated masses of ants about each entrance.
Dr. Charles Henry Turner
Notes on the Mating of Lasius Niger L.

After reading the published works of Charles Turner, it is readily apparent that he made significant contributions to the field of science. Between the years of 1907 and 1923, he was one of the most productive entomologists in the country. He systematically observed the behaviors of smaller insects, especially bees and ants, and other animals as well. His ground breaking work helped lay the foundation for what eventually gave rise to behavioristic psychology. But Charles Turner was more than just a scientist.

He was also deeply concerned about the welfare and education of the black community. This humanitarian concern lead him to spend the last 17 years of his life teaching biology and psychology in a black high school in St. Louis, years when he could have held a prestigious professorship at the University of Chicago (Hayden, 1970).

His Education and Educational Career

Charles Henry Turner was born in Cincinnati, Ohio on February 3, 1867. The son of a church custodian and a registered nurse, Charles was a curious boy, who frequently asked questions about nature. His chief interest was with small animals that crawled or flew about (Hayden, 1979). It was in Cincinnati that Charles attended elementary school, high school, and college.

In 1891 Charles earned the Bachelor of Science degree from the University of Cincinnati. A year later, he earned a Master of Science degree. Charles could have devoted himself entirely to scientific research, but his devotion to family and community channeled his energies in a different direction. He taught at the University of Cincinnati (Hayden, 1970) and briefly in the public schools of Evansville, Indiana, but his commitment to the education of black people carried him south (Woodson, 1939).

In April of 1893, Charles Turner wrote a letter to Booker T. Washington, explaining that he was anxious to work among his own people. As a result of this communication, Charles Turner found himself employed at Clark University in Atlanta, Georgia, as a professor of biology. From then until 1908, he held several positions in education, including high school teacher, high school principal, and college professor (Hayden, 1970).

Though committed to education, Charles was also dedicated to the study of animal behavior. He managed to observe, experiment, and research during the hours he was not teaching. This work so interested him that he enrolled at the University of Chicago and resumed his study of biology. While there he not only began to distinguish himself in the field of entomology, but in 1907 he also earned the degree of Doctor of Philosophy, summa cum laude (Woodson, 1939).

An Exemplary Teacher

It is at this point that the story of Dr. Turner takes perhaps a surprising turn, for he did not elect to remain at the University of Chicago to continue his experiments. He turned down the possibility of continuing his scientific work at a research institution, well endowed with equipment and facilities, and chose instead to teach. Hired in 1908 to teach at Sumner High School in St. Louis, Dr. Turner taught there until his death.

As teacher, Dr. Turner was inspiring. He brought first hand information about animal behavior into the classroom by sharing his discoveries with his students, collected live plants and animals for study, required the use of microscopes for many lessons, and took the students out into the fields and vacant lots of St. Louis so that they too could discover the joy of observing and experimenting with science and nature (Hayden, 1970). These years as a teacher were productive ones professionally for Dr. Turner.

The Exciting World of Insects

Dr. Turner was a prolific writer and published more than fifty articles in such journals as the *Biological Bulletin*, the *Journal of Animal Behavior*, the *Journal of Comparative Neurology and Psychology*, the *Psychological Bulletin*, and the *Zoological Bulletin* (Hayden, 1970). For more than seven consecutive years he reviewed the current literature on the behavior of spiders and insects other than ants for the *Journal of Animal Behavior*, while reviewing the literature on the behavior of higher invertebrates for the *Psychological Bulletin*. He also wrote notes and book reviews for many journals publishing work on the behavior of animals. His work was highly regarded in the United States and in Europe, and his articles were referenced in many important

books of the time, such as *The Social Insects, The Ant Book* by
Turner's former professor William Wheeler, *The Animal Mind* by
Smith, and *The Psychic Life of Insects*, by Bouvier (Hayden,
1970).

Dr. Turner's strengths as a scientist included his keen powers
of observation, as he would often sit for hours and observe the
behavior of insects (Hayden, 1970). These skills were enhanced
by Dr. Turner's fastidious and precise record keeping. The data
he collected were detailed and explicit. His observations were
accompanied by exact times, weather and nesting conditions, and
often hand drawn diagrams or photographs. An excerpt from a
paper on the homing of ants presents some of his original
findings:

> I am uncertain of the species of ant used in this experiment, but
> it was one of the small southern camponotids. The ant had its
> home in the baseboard of our front porch. At the time this
> experiment was begun, many of them were busy moving to and
> from some aphids that were feeding on the leaves of a vine that
> shaded the portico. By searching, I soon found a leaf upon which
> there was only one ant. This leaf was removed and inserted, by
> the petiole, in a notch in one of the brick supports of the veranda.
> The hole in which I had placed the leaf was only two feet from
> the next opening. The ant acted as though dead for a while and
> then it thoroughly explored the leaf. From the leaf it mounted the
> pillar and went downwards (away from the nest) almost to the
> ground. It then went first to the right and then to the left and
> zigzagged upwards again to the leaf. After again exploring the
> leaf it returned to the pillar and, after passing up and down
> several times, returned to the leaf. After another exploration of the
> leaf it returned to the wall and after a little meandering returned
> to the leaf. After another exploration it returned and zigzagged
> slowly upwards until it reached the baseboard. Then it at once
> increased its speed and hastened to the nest.
> (Dr. Charles Turner, "The Homing of Ants: An Experimental Study of Ant
> Behavior".

Another of Dr. Turner's strengths was his ability to devise rather ingenious methods of experimentation. Take, for example, this unpublished experiment:

> The colony, which was housed in a Janet nest, usually kept a guard in the entrance. One day some strange ants forced their way past the guard to some food which I had placed inside the next. The guard, after fighting with them for a while, retreated into the inner chamber, rushed about among the ants and then returned to the fray, followed by several others. This looked like communication. To test the matter the following experiment was devised. I heated dissecting needles and glass stirring rods red-hot, to destroy any odor, and soon as they were cool, fought the guard with them. Soon it retreated into the inner chambers, rushed among the ants, and then returned, alone, to the outer chamber. Then I dipped the needle or the stirring rod into oil of cloves and again fought the guard. It again retreated to the inner chamber, rushed among them, and returned to the outer chamber. In this case, however, it was followed by several of its companions.
>
> (Dr. Charles Henry Turner, in Literary Notices, a review of *The Life History of the Carpenter Ant*).

Dr. Turner asked many questions about insects and other invertebrates. Can honey bees distinguish colors? Do mason wasps respond to light? How do ants find their way back to the nest? How do spiders feed? Such questions among many were answered by Dr. Turner through his skillful use of the scientific method. The titles of some of his many published works on these subjects include: The homing of ants: "An experimental study of ant behavior," "Do ants form practical judgements?", "The homing of the burrowing bee," "The homing of the mud dauber," "Experiments on color vision of the honey bee," "Behavior of the common roach in an open maze," and "The reactions of the mason wasp to light." Dr. Turner's written work represents not only a profound understanding of the animals he studied, but also a rare gift for communicating the results of scientific experimentation in an almost lyrical fashion. Not only are his works easy to read, but they are also enjoyable. In this excerpt from a paper on the behavior of parasitic bees, the reader is given a rare glimpse into the enjoyment and humor that Dr. Turner must have found in his work:

> The bees were fed on honey deposited either on glazed paper or in a Minot watch glass and placed on the floor of the cage. .... To feed from the small drop of honey on the paper never caused the bees any trouble; but the larger the amount of honey in the watch glass was, at first, a source of much inconvenience. It was amusing to watch a bee feeding from it. While feeding the bee was certain to get one of its feet into the honey. In striving to extricate the leg, the bee would invariable get another foot smeared. This would serve to complicate matters. Sometimes the bee would succeed in backing out, but more often it would wade through the honey to the opposite side of the glass. Then it would drag itself along to some good resting place and attempt to clean its besmeared body.
> (Dr. Charles Turner, Notes on the Behavior of a Parasitic Bee of the Family Sletidae).

Tribute to a Man

Dr. Turner's distinguished career as a teacher and scientist ended on February 14, 1923 with his death. In May 25, 1923, a memorial service was held for Dr. Turner in the auditorium of the high school he so dedicated his final years to teacher in (Hayden, 1970). In an appreciation speech given by Mr. A. G. Pohlman, Dr. Charles Henry Turner was remembered in a grand fashion.

> It has been said that the size of a man may be measured in terms of his influence for good and for the betterment of his fellow man. But just as striving to attain is more important to us than the desired thing itself, so we tend to look abroad for a truly great man, forsooth, he walks in our very midst. ... We have been misinformed in our ideas of great men. We have been misled into looking for magnificence and for vain-glorious trappings in which our fancy would clothe and important person. Indeed the humble

simplicity of the truly great man disarms us quite completely and we crane the neck to overlook exactly that which we seek. It is for you who know Dr. Turner to satisfy yourself that here indeed was a great man. ... Permit me, in the name of the Academy of Science, to pay our respect not only to Turner the Scientist, but also to Turner the Man. (A. G. Pohlman).

References and Further Readings

Academy of Science of St. Louis. *Transactions of the Academy of Science of St. Louis.* St. Louis, Missouri: Von Hoffman Press, 1932.

Drew, Charles R. (1950). Negro scholars in scientific research. *Journal of Negro History, 35*, 135-149.

Hayden, Robert C. *Seven Black American Scientists.* Reading, Massachusetts: Addison-Wesley, 1970.

Turner, Charles H. (1907). "The Homing of the Ants: An Experimental Study of Ant Behavior", *Journal of Comparative Neurology and Psychology*, 18, 521-523.

_____. (1911). Notes on the behavior of a parasitic bee of the family Sletidae. *Journal of Animal Behavior, 1,* 374-392.

_____. (1915). Notes on the mating of Laces Niger L.. *Journal of Animal Behavior, 5,* 337-340.

Woodson, Carter G. (1939). "Negroes distinguished in science". *Negro History Bulletin, 2,* 65-70.

Chapter VII_____

George Washington Carver- Pioneer Chemurgist
(circa 1864-1963)
by Exyie Ryder

George Washington Carver, the son of slaves, was born near the end of the Civil War in Diamond Grove, Missouri. His mother, Mary "Carver," belonged to a German immigrant couple whose names were Moses and Susan Carver. His father, it is believed, was a slave on a nearby plantation. George and his older brother Jim, grew up on the Carver plantation and accepted the Carvers as their parents. The boys had a happy childhood, spending most of their time fishing, helping with farm and household chores, and occasionally taking long walks in the woods.

George was a small and sickly child, so he usually worked inside the house cooking, doing laundry, and taking care of plants. Jim on the other hand, was healthier and physically stronger and consequently assisted with the farm work outside. At an early age, George showed a fondness for plants, especially wild flowers. Every year, he planted and maintained a beautiful flower garden.

One thing that puzzled George as a boy was how the Carvers, a white couple, got to be the parents of him and his brother. When he asked, he learned that his real mother, Mary, had been a slave on the Carver plantation. As the rest of the story goes, Mary and her sons were raided one cold rainy night by a band of nightriders who frequently roamed the countryside terrorizing residents and stealing slaves. On the night the thieves appeared at the Carver's house. Moses Carver fought back. In so doing, he was able to protect Jim; however, Mary and little George, an infant at the time, were captured. Several days passed and the Carvers heard nothing about Mary and her son. Fortunately, a few days later George was found.

The neighbor who found and returned George to the Carvers offered to exchange him for one of Moses Carver's racehorses. The Carvers were so happy to see little George alive that they gave up a three hundred dollar horse for him. And although they were saddened about Mary's abduction, they were nevertheless happy to be able to reunite George and his brother. The year was 1860.

Love of Learning

After spending the first 10 years of his life in Diamond Grove, George decided that he wanted to go to school. He informed the family of his decision, and told them that he wanted to learn how to read, write, and to study about plants. He added that since there was no school in Diamond Grove that he could attend, he was moving to a nearby town, Neosha, Missouri, where there was a school for colored children. In shock and disbelief, the family expressed their regret at his decision and tried to dissuade him by reminding him of his shyness and frailty. But with determination and assertion, George was certain he could take care of himself physically, and could earn enough money to provide for himself.

George left early one morning and arrived in Neosha, a town about seven miles from Diamond Grove, that afternoon. He met a couple named Andrew and Mariah Watkins who lived across the street from the school for colored children. Having no children of their own, Uncle Andy and Aunt Mariah as George affectionately came to call them, invited him to live with them and attend school in return for helping with the household chores. George was very grateful for having met them and remained in

Neosha until he felt that he had learned as much as the teachers in the little one-room schoolhouse could offer him.

George moved from Neosha, first to Fort Scott, Kansas then to Minneapolis, Kansas where he completed his high school education. The outstanding record he posted led to a scholarship offer from Highland University but he never enrolled THERE. When Carver appeared there for registration the president told him a mistake had been made because Highland did not enroll colored students.

The rejection stung but George was determined not to despair in his pursuit of higher education. He found a job and place to live and continued his quest. Within a few months Simpson College in Iowa accepted him. Because all students at the college were required to join the Army Reserve Officers Training Corp (Army ROTC), George became the first African American ROTC student in the United States. At Simpson College, he excelled. In art he did so well that his professor tried hard to persuade him to become a career artist. The idea appealed but Carver's acute interest in the sciences kept him from accepting. Science was destined to be dominant in his future but his interest in art sustained throughout his life. Thus he, in actively combining the two fields, demonstrated that science and the humanities could be accommodated within the same person.

A Faculty Position

In 1891, after completing his studies at Simpson College, George entered Iowa Agricultural College where he found the doors of science open to him. There he compiled an impressive record and in 1894 earned the B. S. degree. Iowa then appointed him assistant professor of botany, a first for a black American. Continuing his studies at Iowa, in 1896 he earned the M. S. degree in botany.

Carver's taught courses in botany and agriculture. He also managed the greenhouse, a responsibility he cherished because it allowed him to continue his plant experiments. The well-equipped laboratories, large libraries, and other facilities provided the intellectual stimulation he had yearned for most of his life. Carver published several papers based on his research.

At Iowa State College, Professor Carver conducted research in botany and plant diseases, and presented lectures and seminars on plant growth and crop rotation. He also shared his findings with the scientific community through publications that appeared in journals around the country. In a remarkably short time, Carver became well-known for his extensive knowledge of plants, soil, and plant diseases. Across the country he was regarded as an authority on these topics and was sought as a consultant by the federal government and other groups that needed his expertise.

Tuskegee Beckons

In the Spring of 1896, just as Carver's research and other professional activities were in high gear, he received a letter from Dr. Booker T. Washington, the director of Tuskegee Normal School in Tuskegee, Alabama. Washington invited Carver to join the faculty at Tuskegee, after having heard about his exciting work in agriculture at Iowa. Washington's mission at Tuskegee was to assist students in the rural Alabama region obtain an education toward elevating their standard of living. He felt that Carver's expertise and success in agriculture would have a positive impact on the school's program as well as in the community, where there was significant poverty and hunger.

When Carver finished reading the letter, he decided that he would accept the position and answer the call to serve his people. At that moment, he felt that it was what God wanted him to do. Although Dr. Washington told him that he could not promise him wealth, fame or working conditions like those at Iowa State, Carver still felt the urge to go where he was needed.

In the fall of 1896, George Washington Carver arrived at Tuskegee, Alabama, by train, eager to see the school and begin work. He found to his amazement, a situation far worse than he had imagined from reading Dr. Washington's letter of invitation. The people were malnourished, hungry, illiterate, jobless and poor; the soil was barren, over-worked, and infertile; the houses in the area were run-down shacks; and the agriculture department at the school consisted of one empty classroom and a cow.

Carver faced one of the biggest challenges of his life. He began to think about how he could develop an agriculture program, and at the same time, improve the lot of the people. There were two main obstacles to initiating his program. First, there was no money for a laboratory, equipment or books. Secondly, most of the students at Tuskegee shunned farming and told Dr. Carver that they were not interested in agriculture, but instead wanted to learn a skill or trade that would enable them to leave the farm and earn a decent living. The lack of interest in farming disturbed Carver, but he understood that they did not associate a formal education with farming. The parents, relatives, and neighbors of Carver's students were all farmers with no college education. He also understood that the students associated farming with being poor and with sharecropping. So he decided to change the image of farming from a demeaning occupation to a scientific endeavor. To elevate the notion and significance of agriculture, Carver decided to change the name of the department to "scientific agriculture." His main goal was to bring scientific agriculture - the study of the interaction of botany, chemistry, and soil science - to the college students, then to take its basic principles to the community in practical, understandable layman's terms.

Carver devoted his efforts to developing an agricultural department with a stimulating curriculum, competent professors, research laboratory, and enthusiastic, quality students. As more and more students became convinced that agriculture was an important and respectable field of study, enrollment in scientific agriculture surged. With the help of his students, Carver began collecting items to furnish and equip a laboratory. They collected pots, pans, tools, tubes, wire, and other items that could be useful in making laboratory equipment. The community responded with donations of everything imaginable, and Professor Carver accepted all, without reservation. Fortunately, Carver was resourceful and creative enough to construct much of the needed laboratory apparatus from the things people had either donated or discarded. Within a short time, Carver had a functioning, but crude, laboratory in which the students were able to conduct hands-on, minds-on experiments.

In addition to working with students in the classroom and in the field, Professor Carver also reached out to the community through his extension programs. This included the Movable Demonstration Wagon and the monthly "Farmer's Institute." These initiatives included lectures, agricultural short courses for community farmers, and bulletins on topics of practical use for farm families. Several thousand families were annually involved in these extension programs. Adhering to the Tuskegee philosophy of work and study, Professor Carver advocated the practical application of knowledge and skills to everyday living.

Professor Carver spent a considerable amount of time and effort teaching farmers about such things as crop rotation, topsoil maintenance and planting. He prepared and circulated a bulletin in which he provided information in everyday language that people in the area could easily understand.

One of his most arduous tasks was to help farmers repair the worn-out soil so that it could produce a healthy crop to feed the starving, impoverished people in the region. Beginning with a soil analysis, he discovered that the soil was depleted of nitrogen - an important nutrient of fertile soil. From his knowledge of soil science, he knew that the nitrogen deficit was a result of planting cotton in the same soil continuously for many years. Recalling that leguminous plants such as peas were capable of extracting nitrogen from the air and putting it back into the soil, Professor Carver addressed the problem by urging the farmers to plant peas on their land instead of cotton. He encouraged the farmers to alternate, on a yearly basis, the planting of cotton and peanuts in order to maintain healthy productive soil.

Within two years, Professor Carver demonstrated how effective the soil treatment had been. He displayed the large plump vegetables and fruits that replaced the scrawny ones that were grown on previously worn out soil. Farmers were amazed at the results. They could hardly believe that Professor Carver had produced high quality vegetables and fruits from the previously poor, rocky soil. Suddenly, all farmers were eager to learn the secret of scientific farming. In response, Professor Carver intensified his outreach courses extending them to farther outlying counties in the state. The extension classes were held once a month when Carver travelled to teach the farmers about crop rotation. Within a few years, cotton and peanut crops were bigger and better than ever before.

Community Outreach

Peanuts, or goobers as they were called, grew very well in Alabama, but farmers and housewives were unaware of their high nutritional value or the many ways that they could be cooked. When Professor Carver organized extension classes for women, one of his first topics concerned the food value of the peanut. In other classes, he demonstrated food preservation techniques so that during the winter, good nutritious food would be available. Carver also popularized accessible plants for dishes that were tasty, nutritionally desirable, easy to prepare, and economical. Among the foods he popularized was the garden tomato, which was plentiful, but had never been used as source of food by families in the area.

As he had done for the farmers, Carver prepared monthly bulletins that contained menus, recipes, and other household tips for housewives. Before long, there was a noticeable difference in the health of the people in the region, and malnutrition decreased.

Carver's work at Tuskegee became known throughout the world, and won him the respect and admiration of people of all races and socioeconomic levels. His research with the peanut resulted in more than 300 different products, some of which were cheese, paint, stain and flour. With the sweet potato, he was equally as creative, making products such as flour, stains and syrup. In 1921, his genius prompted the United Peanut Growers

Association, an all-white organization, to invite him to Washington, D.C. to appear before the Congressional Ways and Means Committee on its behalf. His demonstration with the peanuts and its value resulted in Congress passing a bill that imposed a protective tariff on peanuts imported from other countries.

Carver attracted the attention of Henry Ford and also Thomas Edison, the latter a prominent inventor, the former a leading industrialist, who tried unsuccessfully to lure him away from Tuskegee by offering him unlimited resources, state-of-the-art laboratories and lucrative salaries to work in their research facilities. But Carver was happy with his life and work at Tuskegee, and consequently was not tempted by the offers.

A Celebrated Scientist

Professor Carver's life evolved to one of celebrity status, although he remained humble and unaffected by the honors, awards, and recognition he received for his accomplishments. In 1916, he was made a fellow of the Royal Society of Arts in London. Other awards that followed included the National Association for the Advancement of Colored People's prestigious Spingarn Medal and numerous honorary doctorate degrees from various colleges and universities.

On Carver's fortieth year at Tuskegee, the Institute held a celebration honoring him for extraordinary achievements and services. By this time Professor Carver was 73 years old. His tenure at Tuskegee had been unusual, to say the least, for he never concerned himself about salary and always was committed to helping others. He had no interest in acquiring the comforts of luxury living.

The Carver Museum was founded and located on the campus of Tuskegee Institute. The institute housed hundreds of items that Carver produced during his lifetime. Among them are paints, dyes, preserved foods, artificial marble, crocheted tablecloths, and his paintings. The museum highlights Carver's life as a scientist, an artist, and a humanitarian. Carver helped create a new industry that brought billions of dollars to the South and the nation. As one writer put it, he was the first and greatest Chemurgist.

Today, scholarships, theaters, schools, awards, streets and cemeteries are named in honor of George Washington Carver. During his lifetime, he received three patents and identified two species of fungi that now bear his name.

On January 5, 1943, Carver died in his room on the Tuskegee Institute campus following a brief illness. He was 79 years old.

References and Literature for Further Reading

Adair, Gene. *George Washington Carver.* New York: Chelsea House Publishers, 1989.

Bontemps, Anna. *Story of George Washington Carver.* New York: Grosset and Dunlap, 1954.

Coil, Suzanne M. *George Washington Carver.* New York: Franklin Watts, 1990.

Fowler, Mary Jane and Fisher, Margaret. *Great Americans.* Grand Rapids, Michigan: Gateway Press, Inc., 1988.

Haber, Louis. *Black Pioneers of Science and Invention.* New York: Harcourt, Brace and World, Inc., 1970.

Moore, Eva. *The Story of George Washington Carver.* New York: Scholastica, Inc., 1971.

White, Ann Terry. *George Washington Carver: The Story of a Great American.* Eau Claire, WI: E. M. Hale and Company, 1953.

Chapter VIII_____

Garrett Augusta Morgan
Firefighters Breathing Helmet
(1875-1963)

Garrett Augustus Morgan was the seventh of eleven children in his family. He was born in the "black section" of Paris, Kentucky called Clayville, either in 1875, 1877 or 1879, on the fourth day of March. Garrett's parents, Sydney and Elizabeth Reed Morgan, most likely were born into slavery. Little else is known about them except that Sydney Morgan worked on the railroad and Elizabeth Morgan was the daughter of a preacher. In the small town of Paris, about 11 miles from Lexington, poverty was commonplace. As with most of the families in and around Paris, especially the black families, the Morgans were "dirt poor."

With only limited schooling available, Garrett completed the fifth grade Early on however, he showed a strong fascination for anything mechanical. But there was little opportunity to work with machines in his hometown and jobs of any kind were scarce. It is not surprising then that Garrett, being enterprising of mind, had ambition beyond the drab existence then in his home town. He left Paris. In 1895, and moved about 75 miles north to Cincinnati, Ohio. Garrett arrived rough-hewn, barely literate, and penniless.

In the city the young Kentuckyian found a job repairing sewing machines. He learned the principles of the appliances quickly, how they worked and how to fix them when they broke down.

Garrett remained in the Cincinnati about six years before moving to Cleveland in 1901. Jim Strang of the *Cleveland Plain Dealer* reported that Morgan ". . . spent his first three nights here [in Cleveland] sleeping in a railroad freight car with newspapers his only cover." He found work as a janitor in a sewing machine shop but quickly moved up to repairman. Before long Garrett began making innovative changes in the machines as well. One of his first inventions was a belt fastener for the drive belt that simplified the operation of the sewing machines. With no money to patent his device he sold the rights to a buyer whose name is unknown. According to various accounts, Morgan received $150.00 for the rights to his invention, which amount proved to be a small fraction of its worth.

Apparently Morgan handled his earnings well, as in only a few years in Cleveland he opened his own business. He sold and repaired sewing machines, and seeing a market for dry goods, began to manufacture clothing. Morgan specialized in making coats, suits and dresses that he sold to local citizens. A hard worker, he put in long hours, determined to build his business and make a success of his operations. His business grew to where he had to employ a 32-person workforce to meet demands. Morgan continued to invent, mostly item for making clothing and improvements on the sewing machine. He also created a woman's hat fastener, round belt fastener and friction drive clutch.

On September 22, 1908 Morgan married the lovely Maryanna Hasek, also of Cleveland. They bought a comfortable home at 5202 Harlem Avenue and never moved again. The couple had three sons, John Pierpoint, Garrett Jr. and Cosmos Henry.

Perhaps it was the tailoring business that promoted Morgan's interest in grooming. He developed and refined a substance for grooming hair. This proved to be an attractive product and of such demand that he founded the G. A. Morgan Hair Refining Company. Many years later, Morgan invented an electric curling comb especially designed for use with his products. By many accounts, the hair grooming business was especially successful and it provided lifelong support for him and his family.

A Weapon to Fight Fire

Fire is essential to the well being of humankind. Historians believe that long before recorded history, humans first saw fire under frightening conditions such as during a thunder storm when lightning struck a tree with a loud, ear splitting sound, setting it ablaze. Equally frightening, or more so, may have been the searing heat of magma flowing down a mountainside after a violent volcanic eruption. Also, the eerie burning of methane gas in a swamp lake could hardly have been reassuring. Gradually though, humans learned to start, control and confine fire and use it for their benefit. Fire could chase away the chill, overcome the gloom of darkness, ward off stinging insects, fight wild animals, and make raw food more palatable.

Many years later humankind learned, likely by accident, to extract metals from soils and rocks using fire. With metals they made better, stronger tools, ushered in the bronze age, then the iron age, and eventually the industrial revolution. Nevertheless, even today fire can rage out of control, cause great damage, and inflict severe suffering.

On one such occasion Garrett Morgan watched a fire sweep out of control in Cleveland, Ohio. As firefighters fought the flames he was struck by an idea of making a device that might aid in the fight against unwanted fire.

A Breathing device for Firefighters

Morgan studied the science of combustion - what makes things burn and what conditions extinguished flames. He observed the conditions under which firefighters worked during their dangerous missions and realized that in addition to the heat, a major problem was the dense smoke that made their eyes sting, restricted their vision and choked their breathing. Toxic fumes could deter them. Therefore he sought to construct a device that would allow firemen to enter a burning building, perform their duties and exit safely. Previous attempts to build a protective breathing apparatus for firemen failed outright or had such serious shortcomings as to be of little or no use. Some were too bulky, others had too short a working span, and all were unreliable. Morgan also observed that smoke and other fumes tended to rise during a fire. He researched the characteristics of noxious gases in such places as chemical laboratories and burning structures to see if he might also tackle those problems.

Morgan set standards for his breathing helmet. His device had to be reliable, portable, quickly donned, resistant to water and fire, and usable for an extended period. Like many, if not most new ideas, this project demanded long hours of work and reflection. Assisted by his brother Frank, Garrett worked on what he called a breathing helmet which turned out to be a forerunner of the modern gas mask. After each trial he made changes to better meet his standards. Sometimes progress went smoothly, at other times he had to go "back to the drawing board." Gradually his idea took shape. He designed a hood that fitted over the head made of material "impervious to water" and resistant to heat and flames. To this he attached tubes that brought in filtered, moistened and cooled air. He arranged the hood and tubes so they would not interfere with the work of the fireman. A transparent plate, made of mica and placed at eye level, enabled the firefighter to see all around. Morgan added an ear trumpet that permitted the wearer to hear with little or no obstruction. His breathing device also allowed the firefighter to control the quantity of air entering the hood, which was another important safety and comfort feature. He explained how this worked:

> This tube extends to the upper end of the hood and when the used air from the lungs is discharged into this tube it will act upon a light ball . . . This ball closes the [designated] opening and when raised the draft from the mouth will produce a current through this opening which will draw all the foul air from the upper end of the hood, and will increase the draft through the air inlet tube . . . by suction. In this manner the entrance of the fresh air can be placed under the control of the operator . . .

After describing how the device operated, Morgan then explained how it could be used. He wrote:

> The objects of the invention are to provide a portable attachment

which will enable a fireman to enter a house filled with thick, suffocating gases and smoke and to breathe freely for some time therein, and thereby enable him to perform his duties of saving life and valuables without danger to himself from suffocation.

Morgan also said that chemists and engineers could use his breathing apparatus to protect themselves when "obliged" to work in environments containing "noxious fumes or dust." His device had no buckling straps or fasteners that might delay its use. Robert Hayden wrote that the apparatus could be put on in just seven seconds and taken off in three. Prior to making it available to others, Morgan tested the breathing helmet under actual fire fighting conditions to ensure it would work. The first account of its use appeared in *The Plain Dealer* on September 16, 1912 when a chemical fire broke out in the city:

Spontaneous combustion in chemicals in the . . . National Electric Lamp Association at Hough Avenue N. E. and E. 45th-St caused the fire which was discovered by Frank Owen, the watchman. Sulphurous and phosphorous fumes were so thick he could not enter, and he turned in a fire alarm.

Engine Company 17 went to the fire. Capt. Joseph Andrews saw how thick and poisonous the smoke was and he donned his special breathing helmet and rushed through the smoke to the flames. A few squirts from the chemical extinguisher and the flame was out.

The article also reported that the Cleveland Fire Department had tried Morgan's apparatus in an "atmosphere permeated with formaldehyde." Officials praised the helmet and declared themselves well pleased with the results.

Morgan obtained U. S. Patent No. 1,118,675 for *The Breathing Device* following his application of October 18, 1915. Then, for three months he tried to raise capital so he could manufacture his invention. His initial offering of company stocks at ten dollars per share to people in his neighborhood, met with little success. With no other choice he went outside his community where he found willing investors, soon raised the capital he needed and formed a business partnership. Just two years later, the stocks in Morgan's company were worth $250 per share.

Crib Blast Heroes

The city of Cleveland looks out on Lake Erie, one of the five neighboring lakes called the Great Lakes of North America. These magnificent natural wonders hold 20% of all the fresh water in the world and they play a major role in the well being of the United States and Canada. In 1856, Cleveland officials approved a public works project to get more fresh water from Lake Erie for the city's growing population. In 1916, construction began to upgrade the existing system by adding a large 10-foot tunnel some 22,500 feet from shore. Before working on the tunnel, a shaft was constructed to the floor of the lake from a site called Crib No. 5. The men extended the shaft further down by digging through the sandy bottom of Lake Erie 119 feet below the surface. From there workers called sandhogs began digging the tunnel below the lake bed toward shore. Out some 16,000 feet, just over three miles from shore, that tunnel would connect with two seven-foot tunnels built earlier, to carry the water to filtration plants at the city's water works.

The project went as planned. Then on July 25, 1916, near the end of a workday, a mighty explosion rocked the area below the bed of the lake where many of the men worked. People on the surface hearing an ominous, rumbling sound immediately feared the worse. Apparently, the sandhogs had dug into a gas seepage and a spark or sparks from a worker's pick that struck a hard rock, ignited the gas causing an explosion. Smoke, debris, and gas filled the tunnel amid the cries and moans of injured and dying men. George Barmann of *The Plain Dealer* reported that 11 courageous workers quickly descended the shaft on a rescue mission. Down at the bottom, smoke, dust, debris and deadly toxic fumes engulfed them. Tragically, all perished. Hope faded.

Then someone remembered the Morgan Breathing Device. They found the inventor, and asked if he could help. Morgan contacted his brother Frank, and the two men rushed to the scene. Quickly, they donned their gear, descended the steep shaft and entered the dangerous tunnel. Above, a large crowd of citizens anxiously waited along with policemen and firemen. Barmann published Morgan's description of the condition inside the tunnel:

> I put on the mask and went down into the crib. There was a door into the tunnel, but I couldn't get it open. I could hear people pounding on the door.
> The door had a glass in it so I smashed the glass and I could hear the Gas and compressed air whistle out. Then I could open the door because the pressure was off.

Inside the Morgan brothers went about their grim rescue mission. Sometimes walking, other times crawling, they found men in various states of consciousness. Once located, the Morgan brothers brought victims out. Onlookers cheered. They went back again and found other workers at different locations.

Garrett and Frank Morgan wanted to continue but Bureau of Mines officials ordered them not to return. Morgan said he did not understand the directive because he felt no ill effect and no one gave them a clear explanation.

Despite having brought some of the men out of the tunnel, Morgan grieved that he could not save everyone. . The carnage he saw below the lake haunted him so severely that for years he had trouble sleeping. He said, "When I shut my eyes, I can see the men curled up in that death chamber."

Honors and Recognitions

Morgan's invention won him several prestigious recognitions. In New York, he received the First Grand Prize Gold Metal at the Second International Exposition of Sanitation and Safety. Prominent citizens of Cleveland gave him an award that recognized his invention and bravery. The Cleveland Association of Colored Men praised his valor and honored him for his inventive prowess. The International Association of Firefighters Chiefs gave him a metal and made him an honorary member.

Controversy arose about whether Morgan received a medal from the City of Cleveland. Most sources said he did not. After the lake rescue, the mayor of Cleveland, exuberant and lavish in his praise told Morgan and his brother that the city would never forget them and their courageous deed. He went on to promise compensation for life. Years later however, Morgan complained that he never received any pay or recognition of any kind from the city, nor did his brother. Nevertheless, Morgan cherished all commendations others saw fit to give him, he treasured each award and throughout the remainder of his life took great pride in their display.

Fire departments in several cities of Ohio, Pennsylvania and New York began using his Breathing Device and other fire departments showed interest as well. Some cities invited Morgan to demonstrate his apparatus though in the South he had to hire a white man to do the demonstration. In other instances, Morgan disguised himself as "Big Chief Mason," an Indian from what may have been a fictitious Walpole Reservation in Canada. According to Jim Strang of *The Plain Dealer,* that happened in New Orleans. There, when Morgan hid his identity, "He took a white friend Charles Salem to act as `Garrett A. Morgan' while he posed as Mason the demonstrator." A story in the New Orleans *Times Picayune,* October 14, 1914, reported that "Mason entered a tent filled with smoke while wearing his gear. He remained in it for twenty minutes without ill effect." Nevertheless, when it became known that the inventor was a black man, some cities canceled their orders.

As mentioned earlier, Morgan's invention was sometimes called a forerunner of the modern gas mask. He had envisioned his device being upgraded to carry an independent air supply. The military recognized the value of the mask during World War I when the Germans attacked Allies fighting forces with toxic gases. At the outbreak of World War II, every major country in the world had stockpiles of gas masks. As Morgan predicted, in chemical industries, mines, various businesses, even in some homes, gas masks proved valuable.

An Automatic Traffic Signal

The automobile has been a great transforming force in modern times. Perhaps no other mode of transportation has touched more lives in more places on a daily basis. The momentum for cars started began during World War I when the military used thousands of motorized vehicles to quickly deploy armed forces. After the conflict civilian demand for cars and trucks escalated and all sorts of new businesses such as dealerships, service stations, repair shops, tire factories, fuel and lubrication industries evolved. Licensing and other government regulations expanded and the need for more and better roads and bridges escalated. Great social and political changes throughout the nation followed. Potential for accidents also increased dramatically.

One day Garrett Morgan saw an automobile and a horse drawn carriage collide at a busy intersection. The accident left occupants of both vehicles shakened, the automobile and carriage seriously damaged, and the horse fatally injured. The incident confirmed what Morgan had thought all along that with more, bigger and faster cars, measures to promote greater traffic safety was critical. A good traffic signal, he thought, would help.

Morgan studied the traffic patterns to better understand the problem. He then set his objectives, sketched a general design and began the long and tedious process of transforming ideas to reality. Some ideas worked, others did not. Sometimes there were successes as he proceeded, other times failure. He nevertheless persevered and finally produced what he felt was a workable and useful automatic traffic signal. On November 20, 1923, Morgan received the United States Patent No. 1,475,024 for "a certain new and useful Improvement of a Traffic Signal."

Morgan explained that his invention should be placed at the "intersection of two or more streets . . . " There it could be conveniently "operated for directing the flow of traffic." He showed that his signal provided a clear, unambiguous and "visible indicator." The signal stopped all traffic before allowing some vehicles to move across the intersection while those in a traverse direction waited. That served to reduce accidents that "frequently occur by reason of the over-anxious waiting driver to start as soon as the signal to proceed is given". Morgan formulated a new system of traffic control. His basic ideas influence the movement of traffic on American streets today.

The signal was visible day and night. To improve affordability, he created a system that could be "readily and cheaply manufactured." The city of Cleveland installed an early working model, operated by hand, "at Vine Street and Mentor Avenue in Willoughby." They installed the second model at "E. Ninth and Euclid Avenue".

Morgan sold the rights of his invention to General Electric for $40,000. He wanted to remove himself as a problem of adoption. He felt it would be a tragedy if some cities failed to protect its citizens simply because of the inventor's race. It pleased him that, when marketed by General Electric, many cities bought and installed his invention. Morgan's signal, praised as the most functional and versatile of the time, continued in operation until replaced by the overhead electric traffic signal.

A Sense of Civic Duty

In addition to his inventions and business enterprises, the now urbane and courtly Morgan devoted much time and efforts to causes of civil liberties. He actively worked in organizations working for civil rights and a good, fair, more just society. In 1908 Morgan became a charter member and treasurer of the Cleveland Association of Colored People. He joined the National Association for the Advancement of Colored People when the two organizations merged.

During the 1920s, Morgan started a newspaper, the *Cleveland Call*, to dramatize the plight of blacks, and their general omission media. Later, the paper became the *Cleveland Call and Post*. Morgan also gave of his time and energy to such organizations as the Home of Aged Colored People, Phyllis Wheatley Association, Masonic Lodge, Elks Club, the Antioch Baptist Church and the Crispus Attucks Republican Home. Phyllis Wheatley, a slave owned and later set free by a Boston family gained recognition on two continents for the poetry she wrote. According to Carter G. Woodson, "She was a writer of such interesting verse that she was brought into contact with some of the best thinkers of that period." The Crispus Attucks Republican Home was named after a free black who lived during the American colonial period. Fatally wounded as a protester during the Boston Massacre, Attucks was the first to spill blood and die for American freedom.

In 1931, Morgan ran for the city council as an independent candidate. In his platform he pledged to fight for (1) an equitable representation in city government for people of his (the third) district, (2) relief for the unemployed, (3) improved housing conditions, and (4) more economic and efficient administration of public affairs. His progressive platform could not carry him however, and Morgan lost the election. Undaunted he continued to invest time and energy in the city and especially in his community. At Cleveland's Western Reserve University, he helped to organize a black fraternity as existing fraternities barred black students from membership.

I Dream a World

As mentioned earlier, when Morgan and his brother rescued workers down in the tunnel, the mayor of Cleveland praised their feat and promised the inventor that the city would take care of him for the rest of his life. Although Morgan and his brother felt no ill effects at the time, some researchers speculate that some gas may have seeped in. Others suggest being brought to the surface a bit too fast, not toxic gas seepage, contributed to his impaired health later in life. Whatever the reason or reasons, with advancing age Morgan's health declined sharply, just like his brother Frank who preceded him in death. Then his vision began to fail. In 1943, doctors diagnosed his eye condition as glaucoma and, despite annual visits to the Mayo Clinic, he gradually lost his sight to the point of near blindness. Burdened by heavy medical bills, the old inventor sought help from the city whose mayor promised, out of gratitude for his heroic service, the city would take care of him for the remainder of his life. Now however the city had forgotten the pledge and acknowledged no obligation to its famous citizen. As with his brother Frank, who only asked for a burial plot, Morgan was refused help of any kind.

Though constrained by his near blindness, frail health, and not much money, Morgan continued to be active. Even after being diagnosed legally blind, he invented a curling comb and a pellet to extinguished cigarettes "should the smoker fall asleep".

In 1963, with only 10 percent of his vision remaining, Morgan enjoyed a proud moment when he saw his inventions on exhibit in Chicago. A few weeks later, on July 26, 1963, the old inventor from Paris, Kentucky died. He was buried in Lake View Cemetery in Cleveland. His wife died five years later, on the same date.

Morgan's works, however, have not gone unnoticed. In 1967, the Shriners dedicated a plaque in recognition of his contributions to society. The plaque was displayed in the Cleveland Hall of Fame. On October 23, 1977, a historic marker in his memory was placed in a "four acre African-American Cultural Garden" of Cleveland. Three years later, Tyrone Williams, a local citizen, started a movement to preserve the Morgan home.

In 1987, 24 years after his death, Garrett Augustus Morgan was inducted posthumously into the Cleveland Hall of Fame. Commenting on the occasion, Tom Andrzejewski wrote that Morgan took his rightful place among "the heavyweights of history from the Western Reserve . . . presidents, industrialists, inventors and others who helped shape the world from Northern Ohio, and mainly from Cleveland." Among the illuminaries were President James A. Garfield, industrialist John D. Rockefeller, William H. Brett who created the world's first open shelf [library] system , the physicist Dayton C. Miller, first to photograph sound waves and take surgical x-rays, Rebecca Cromwell whose organization preceded the Red Cross and Rabbi-statesman Abba Hillel Silver.

Morgan used his inventive talents to rise above his humble beginnings. Through his inventions and civic work he sought a better society. His life suggests that he thought like Langston Hughes who wrote the memorable poem, *I Dream a World*.

A world I dream where black or white,
Will share the bounties of the earth

And every man is free,
Where wretchedness will hang its head,
And joy, like a pearl,
Attend the needs of all mankind,
Of such I dream-
Our world!

References and Publications for Further Reading

Adams, Russell L. 1964. *Great Negroes Past and Present*, Chicago: Afro-Am Publishing Company, Inc.

Andrzejewski, Tom, "Cleveland's Hall of Fame inductees left lasting marks", *The Plain Dealer*, (Cleveland, OH), August 12, 1988, B2.

Baker, Henry E., 1913. *The Colored Inventor: A Record of Fifty Years,* New York:, The Crisis Publishing Company.

Barmann, George J., "July 24, 1916: Death Lurked Beneath Lake", *The Plain Dealer,* (Cleveland, OH), July 24, 1966, 1AA, 5AA.

Bontemps, Arna, (ed.), 1963. *American Negro Poetry,* Clinton, MA: The Colonial Press, Inc.

Burt, McKinley, Jr., 1969. *Black Inventors of America,* Portland, OR: National Book Company.

"Crib Blast Hero Recalls '16 Deeds", *The Plain Dealer,* (Cleveland, OH), July 25, 1958.

Green, Richard, L. (ed), 1985. *A Salute to Black Scientists and Inventors,* Chicago: Empak Enterprises, Inc.

Haber, Louis, 1970. *Black Pioneers of Science and Inventions,* New York: Harcourt, Brace and World, Inc.

Hayden, Robert, 1972. *Eight Black American Inventors,* Reading, MA: Addison-Wesley, Hayden, Robert, "Garrett A. Morgan (1875-1963)" in Logan, Rayford and M. Winston (eds.), 1982. *Dictionary of American Negro Biography,* New York: W. W. Norton and Company.

Joyner, L'Tanya, "Saving of Morgan Home is urged", *The Plain Dealer,* (Cleveland, OH) August 18, 1980, B1.

Jackson, W. Sherman, "Big Chief Mason-Ingenious American", in Jenkins, Edward (ed), 1975. *American Black Scientists and Inventors*, Washington, D.C.: National Science

Teachers Association.

James, Portia P., 1989. *The Real McCoy: African-American Inventions and Innovations, 1619-1930,* Washington, D.C.: Smithsonian Institution Press.

Morgan, Garrett A. *Breathing Device,* Patent No. 1,113,675, October 13, 1914.

Morgan, Garrett, *Traffic Signal,* Patent No. 1,475,024, November 20, 1923.

Plaski, Henry A., and Ernest Kaiser, *Afro, USA,* New York: Bellwether Publishing Company, 1971.

Strang, Jim, "Garrett A. Morgan: Gas Mask Inventor dim memory here", *The Plain Dealer,* (Cleveland, OH), February 16, 1975, D43

"Tests New Device to Fight Flames", *The Plain Dealer,* (Cleveland, OH), September 16, 1912, 5.

Tripp, Rhoda Thomas (compiled by), *The International Thesaurus of Quotations,* New York: Harper & Row, 1970.

Williams, H. Lavette, "Garden dedication to memorialize gas mask inventor", *The Plain Dealer,* (Cleveland, OH), October 23, 1977, I35.

Winslow, Eugene, *Black Americans in Science and Engineering, Contributors of Past and Present,* Afro-Am Publishing Co., Inc., 1974.

Woodson, Carter G., *Negro Makers of History,* Washington, D.C.: Associated Publishers, Inc., 1928.

*Chapter IX*_____

Ernest Everett Just - Biology of the Cell (1883-1941)

Ernest Everett Just, the fourth child of Charles Fraser and Mary Matthews Just, was born August 14, 1883 in Charleston, South Carolina. Of three preceding siblings, the first was stillborn, the second died of cholera at age four, and the third succumbed to diphtheria at age two. Ernest, frail and sickly, caused his parents to worry that they might lose him too.

Historian Kenneth Manning in his definitive biography of Ernest Just, *Black Apollo of Science*, said that Ernest's grandfather, Charles Just, with part German ancestry, who grew up in Charleston, had been a slave but privileged with considerable freedom of movement. Charleston, originally named Charles Town after Charles II of England, and founded in 1680 on a bay between the Ashley and Cooper Rivers, is one of the oldest cities in the United States. It was a great trade center with an excellent harbor that looked out on a seven-mile inlet to the Atlantic Ocean.

After the Revolutionary War, Charles Town became Charleston. Because of its strategic location, many battles were fought in and around the city for control of its harbors, but none brought such mass destruction as the Civil War battles.

When Ernest was born, only 18 years after the war, Charleston had lost much of its glory. Notwithstanding, many of its residents insisted that despite defeat of Confederate forces and severe damages to its infrastructure, Charleston was a yet a splendid city; a jewel in the crown of American cities.

In August of 1886, when the still frail Ernest was only three years old, an unlikely phenomenon occurred. A series of small tremors struck the "Low Country" of South Carolina, including Charleston, followed by a quiet and tranquil period. On Tuesday, August 31, 1886 the calm continued and the weather, hot and humid, gave no hint of trouble. Dusk turned to a still, dark, sticky, night when abruptly and without warning the earth began to heave violently. The United States Geological Survey reported the event in graphic details:

> Suddenly at 9:05 P. M., the quiet was shattered by a roaring noise, a thundering and beat of the earth beneath the buildings, the screams of anguish and fear of the residents . . . the destructive shaking . . . built up to a violent oscillation and a roaring sound.

An earthquake, the worse ever recorded in the United States east of the Appalachians struck Charleston, creating great havoc. The upheavals, powerful and undulating, damaged every building in the city, most of them severely. The Just family, like other Charlestonians rushed outside to avoid being struck by falling objects as buildings twisted, sagged and in some cases came crashing to earth. Fortunately all escaped without injury and they, along with neighbors, spent the night under dark skies as aftershock after frightening aftershock followed the quake. Charlestown, having already suffered through a long war, was damaged even more by the quake.

In addition to having to cope with the aftermath of the powerful earthquake, the Justs were concerned about Mary. She was with child again so they worried about what effects the trauma might have on her health and that of her unborn child. Fortunately, owing to her fortitude, she suffered no ill effects and gave birth to a healthy baby boy They named him Hunter. About two years later Mary and Charles Fraser had their sixth and last child, a daughter they called Inez. All of their last three children lived to adulthood.

Then misfortune struck again. At 32, Charles Fraser died, leaving Mary with three small children to rear alone. Three weeks later, her father-in-law passed, following a short illness.

Best Suited for Strong Men

Having survived the earthquake and endured so many losses in her family, Mary must have wondered if her misfortunes would ever cease. She mourned her losses but with a young family to care for had little time for grief. To make matters worse, all the children were frail and often ill. She feared that in their weakened condition they might contract diphtheria or cholera as did her first three children. Or maybe the dreaded tuberculosis or consumption, no stranger to black Charlestonians, might strike her children down.

She faced other problems as well. He husband left heavy debts to pay. Then when Rutherford B. Hayes became president, his policies encouraged local power brokers, many vengeful following the war, to strip southern blacks of their newly acquired political rights. Small gains in civil rights, education and economics were eclipsed. In this atmosphere, and with incidents of violence on the rise, blacks also felt a pervasive fear for their personal safety. Hope dimmed. For them, these were not good times.

In such trying times, Mary Just turned to her religion faith to help counter the deepening mood of despair. She pondered the few options available. Her father in-law had been a skilled craftsman and entrepreneur and at one time, owned a construction company that built or repaired many of the wharves in the harbor. None of that was of any benefit or comfort now. Mary knew that there was usually work at the harbor, but even if she possessed the skills, the construction business did not provide jobs for anyone of her gender. Despite dim prospects, she remained determined to get a job.

Eventually Mary Just found employment in the phosphate mines on James Island off the coast of Charleston. The work was very hard and tiring, best suited for strong men. The rocks and dust left the laborers covered with grit and grime at the end of a long work-day. It hardly seemed a place for the widow of Charles Fraser Just, especially since she always placed a high premium on cleanliness. But nothing else paid as well for blacks, the debts had to be paid and the children cared for. Beside, she reasoned, with all the water available, she could wash the dirt and grime away. Yes, she and her children could keep clean. As for the hard work, she did not mind. With a job, she would pay off her late husband's debts and care for her family.

The determined young widow astutely managed the money she earned from her work in the mines. She regularly saved a small portion of her meager wages, planning to buy land of her own someday. Like cleanliness, ownership of property was important to her and the quest a part of her character. Eventually her frugal ways paid off and she saved enough money and purchased real estate on the island. It was a good beginning, a goal achieved.

Manning reported that somehow Mary Just found time for serious involvement in civic affairs. She campaigned in the interest of community progress and economic self-empowerment among her people. By dent of her vision and strivings, she became an accomplishing force in the community. According to Manning:

> She became a strong leader, canvassing the inhabitants, mostly the men, and persuading them to transform the settlement into a town. They called the town Maryville, after its prime mover. It was one of the first purely black town governments in the state, a model community for blacks, not only in South Carolina, but throughout the United States.

Along with cleanliness and ownership, Mary Just placed a high premium on education. Manning averred that she was "a woman of high character and fairly good education." He also said that when not working the mines, Mary Just taught religion, reading, spelling, and arithmetic, mostly to children but also to some adults who aspired to become literate. It appears she accommodated all of them. In other classes she taught the women to make hats and dresses.

Just went beyond her community, organized and taught classes in the City of Charleston. Education, she believed, could help lift her people, make them more self-sufficient, and lead to a better life. At every opportunity, the worker/schoolmarm preached good hygiene, exhorting her listeners to be clean. Out of genuine integrity, she lived and taught the creed: "Be clean, for cleanliness is next to godliness."

With License In Hand

Young Ernest attended his mother's school on the island and proved to be an apt student. The lad recognized the importance of his mother's mission and helped her as much as he could. Ernest was an obedient child and not at all a problem. Mary taught him that hard work, dedication to high standards, to neatness and cleanliness, were noble virtues. Such values influenced her son throughout his life.

Ernest's other lessons came from his own curiosity, and from his bent for observing things in nature. The abundant plant and animal life on the island captured his attention. The nearby Atlantic ocean, so vast, restless, and teeming with life, drew him into long periods of contemplation. Ernest often watched ships leave the Charleston Harbor and disappear over the horizon, and he wondered what mysterious lands lay at the end of so many trackless ocean trails. His thoughts may have been similar to those of the poet Lord Byron who wrote,

Roll on thy deep and dark blue ocean - roll!
Ten thousand fleets sweep over thee in vain;
Man marks the earth with ruin - his control!
Stops with the shore.

Ernest differed in style and behavior from his parents. His late father, handsome and gregarious, reveled in social circles, especially enjoying the company of women. His mother, strong, assertive, and persuasive, was a leader, a force in the community. Ernest though, tended to be shy and somewhat of an introvert. He did not always cope. When the outside world made him uncomfortable, he often withdrew, and found refuge in the bible and other books. The lad loved to read.

When Ernest reached the age of 13, his mother decideded she had taught him all she knew. She felt he should go away and further his education. Then Ernest could return to the island and teach things beyond her capability. That way education among the people of the island could be elevated.

With that in mind, Mary Just sent her eldest son to the state industrial school, now South Carolina State, to get his high school education. Ernest went to Orangesburg and studied in a program basically designed to prepare him to teach. He completed the program in three years, earning a certificate to teach in the "colored schools" of South Carolina. At the age of 16 Ernest returned to Maryville with license in hand, ready to begin his mission.

Best Not to Stay

He never did. During his three-year absence, Maryville changed. His mother, who tried valiantly to help improve the community, now faced opposition in almost everything she tried to do. Her goal had been to unite the people and improve their education and economy. But apparently forces of deceit and betrayal undermined her efforts. Those in opposition even tried to take from her personal things she had labored so hard to own. On top of that, her beloved school burned down and she could not afford to rebuild. Disappointed, the Justs felt it best that Ernest not stay. He should go on and further his education elsewhere. His potential must not be allowed to waste. Out of shattered dreams some good would come, through Ernest.

The industrial school had helped Ernest considerably but owing to its limited resources, did not provide the kind of quality education he needed. His mother wanted him to be so well prepared that he could qualify for any college.

The resourceful Mary Just learned of a school called Kimball Union Academy, in Meriden, New Hampshire. Although a great distance from Charleston, the New England institution offered a solid, rigorous, education.

They decided that Ernest would first sail to New York from Charleston. He could pay his fare by working aboard the vessel. Once in the New York, Ernest could find a job and earn money to help with the expenses at Kimball. On that bold blueprint, they made arrangements and Ernest left Charleston in the spring of

1900. Now a teenager, the slender youth with light complexion and brownish hair had inherited much of his father's good looks. As the vessel steamed out of the bay, he looked back at the bustling harbor his grandfather had helped build. His mother waved her farewell, sad, but bolstered by high hopes for his future. Her boy would get a good education.

New England, Kimball, And The Classics

Ernest arrived in New York City with five dollars in his pockets. He found a place to stay, and a job where he worked until it was time to enter school in New Hampshire. The youth marvelled at the large buildings wired for electricity and telephones, and the great mass of people from many different lands, so busy, always rushing about. Nevertheless, it appeared to him a contradiction that in the crowded streets, people still seemed so distant from each other.

In the autumn of 1900, Ernest left New York City for Meriden and Kimball Academy. The towering mountains of New Hampshire contrasted sharply with the flat lands in and around Charleston. The buildings seemed sturdy, but the architecture less grand than in his home town. And the sea, so much a part of his life in Charleston, was now a greater distance away. The weather, colder and much less humid than in South Carolina, gave early hints of the coming winter.

In some sense the people in this New England town were also different in their dialect, behavior, and customs. Ernest had come from a world largely black, to a land of whites. At Kimball, many came from family of means. He, of course, did not. Still he enjoyed a good and friendly reception, both at Kimball and Meriden, so the transition went well.

Ernest wasted no time in getting down to his studies. He took a few remedial courses in areas of his academic weaknesses, and majored in the classics. He earned top grades in nearly everything but had to struggle in mathematics. His teachers were excellent, approachable, and worked closely with him. Ernest credited them with being a major factor in his success, not only because of their good teaching, but also because they encouraged him all the way.

Understandably Ernest went through periods where he felt lonely and homesick. Mostly though, he felt comfortable at Kimball and in the village. He participated in several school activities and these helped fill the void. His oratorical skills blossomed. The youngster participated in the debate society, and became its elected him president. Ernest served as editor of the school's paper, and wrote many articles for the publication. Somehow he found time for other extracurricular activities as well. Nonetheless, studies came first and he completed the four-year course at Kimball in three years earning good grades.

Then came commencement, a time of excitement and colorful, impressive ceremonies. At graduation, Ernest received several honors in recognition of his high academic achievement. He knew his mother would have been proud had she been able to attend.

Sadly she could not. A year earlier, acting on a strange feeling that something was wrong, Ernest rushed home. Upon arrival he received the shocking news that his mother had died and had been buried only hours before his arrival. So, while many celebrated their graduation with family and friends, Ernest celebrated alone. Still he felt the warmth of his mother's spirit.

The Big Green

Now strictly on his own, Ernest vowed to continue his education. He knew his mother would have wanted that. In the fall of 1903, he enrolled as a freshman at Dartmouth College in nearby Hanover, New Hampshire.

Dartmouth, a private, liberal arts college, received its charter in 1769 from England's King George III. First located in Lebanon, (Columbia), Connecticut, its first mission was to educate the Indians. A few years later the school relocated to Hanover, aided by funds from the 2nd Earl of Dartmouth. The institution also changed its mission from educating Native Americans to educating sons of the privileged.

At first Ernest did not like Dartmouth. Unlike the warm and friendly atmosphere at Kimball, with caring and helpful teachers, here he experienced a colder, less caring demeanor. Also, Ernest tended to steer away from most things social and distanced himself from the passionate worship of the popular championship football team, called "The Big Green." He majored in the classics, which he liked and had done well in while enrolled at Kimball, intending to focus on Greek, his best subject at the academy. At first his academic performance was uncharacteristically spotty, not like the consistently excellent record he set at previous schools. Perhaps the long hours working to earn his keep, and adjusting to the new environment took their toll.

When during his sophomore year Ernest enrolled in biology, his outlook at Dartmouth changed dramatically and his academic performance improved sharply. For the first time since arriving at Dartmouth his considerable intellectual powers came alive. The course, "Principles of Biology" and a lecture on the cell theory, grabbed his attention more than any single experience at the Dartmouth. The professor, a Dr. William Patten, impressed him greatly with his expansive knowledge and teaching skills. Professor Patten, Dartmouth's noted biologist and chair of the biology department, was a dynamic teacher and compelling lecturer. In the years to follow, he played an important role in Just's scientific career.

In another biology course, a Professor John Gerould immediately recognized the young South Carolinian as a bright student with a quick intellect. He took pains to work with the now eager young student and gave him much needed encouragement. Though Just never lost his love for the classics, biology swiftly became his major interest.

In the tough, rigorous, biology program Ernest took every course offered by the department. He began to understand more fully the structure of biological sciences and its modes of inquiry. The plants and animals of his native South Carolina, especially on James Island took on new meaning to him. He always had a fascination for the sea, so it was not surprising that it intrigued him to learn that life began in the sea.

Ernest, reflecting on how scientists classify all living things, plants and animals, into large groups called phyla, and several subdivisions according to their characteristics, following the expanded Carl Linnaeus Taxanomic System, noted anew that all animal phyla are found in the sea. Also the Phylum Echinodermata was native only to the sea. How intriguing! The excitement spilled over into other phases of his life at Dartmouth. He began to like the place. During his senior year, Earnest devoted considerable time to undergraduate research in biology, learning how to unearth new information about life and the world. That was one of the defining experiences of his career at Dartmouth.

Because of his outstanding academic record, Just was named a Choate Scholar and elected to the Phi Beta Kappa academic honor society. He also earned the highest honors in the departments of history and biology, and graduated *magna cum laude,* (meaning "with high praise"). It was the top academic honor achieved by any Dartmouth graduate that year.

Nonetheless, Dartmouth basically ignored Just at graduation. Kenneth Manning described how the institution handled Just's achievement during commencement, and speculated on the cause:

> There were to be six speakers in all, the two top students and four of the other fifteen having commencement marks. For some reason, the faculty appointed six speakers privately but listed only five speakers publicly. Perhaps they had chosen Just privately but listed only five publicly. Perhaps they had chosen Just, then decided it would be a faux pas to allow the only black in the graduating class to address the crowd of parents, alumni, and benefactors. It would have made too glaring the fact that Just had won just about every prize imaginable.

Such matters did nothing to diminish the achievement of a goal, and the realization of a dream that Mary Just had held for her son. He had gone to a good school, and graduated with distinction. As Emerson had written:

The reward of a thing well done is to have done it.

To Howard University

In October 1907, Just accepted a teaching position at Howard University in Washington DC, at an annual salary of $400. Howard, founded in 1867 with private funds and federal government support, was named for its first president, General Oliver O. Howard. Initially planned as a national biracial institution, the university quickly became predominately black.

The academic administrators assigned Just to teach English and rhetoric, not science. In this field of his first love, he plunged into his work with zest and dedication, finding enjoyment in his work. In turn, his students responded favorably to his enthusiasm, pedagogy, and rich knowledge of the field.

Outside the classroom, Just became active in extracurricular activities, as he had at Kimball, serving as advisor to student groups. He organized a student dramatics club and under his tutelage the group became quite popular, much admired for their play selection and excellent stage productions. Just advised a group of young men who evolved into founders of a social fraternity, Omega Psi Phi, which group went on to become a national organization. He also helped students plan and carry out field trips, tennis matches, and swimming outings. The young professor was a busy man about campus, not unlike his mother on James Island.

Professor of Biology

Despite his success and pleasure working in the English Department, Just's stay was short. Howard wanted to improve its science department, which meant among other things strengthening the science faculty. In 1910, the administration moved him to the biology based on his impressive record in that science at Dartmouth.

Just missed teaching English, rhetoric and literature, but did not object as biology was clearly his calling. There are many differences in the two areas, one in the humanities, the other in the natural sciences though there is also common ground. Traditionally the two focus more attention on their differences than common goals with unfortunate consequences. Though each is needed for a well versed, and the proverbial well-rounded education to the benefit of society, and though a number of scholars recognize this truth, by and large their special interests, language, modes of inquiry and style clouds the view of one to the other. Just though was humanist and scientist, clearly aware of the interdependence between the fields, easily appreciated the wonderful values and strengths of each.

Regardless of where Just taught, he proved to be a well informed and inspiring teacher. He constantly challenged his students, exhorted them to study hard, and to "think."

Russell M. Ampey, Professor of Biology at Southern University and a former student of Just said that he and his schoolmates knew that Just represented the university in the world of science with distinction. They held him in high esteem, and followed his works closely. He explained why.

> "I, like others, viewed him with a considerable amount of awe, for we all knew he was a world authority. I read reams and reams of his papers. His writings were clear and concise and always well documented- strongly backed up by evidence. That's what made him so respected."

According to Ampey, Just would sometimes present his students with an intriguing problem and disappear. They were left to their own devices to work out laboratory procedures and visit the libraries at Howard and elsewhere in Washington, D. C., for needed information. When he reappeared, Just would test his students on what they had learned, asking penetrating questions. He held them to high standards and made it very clear he had no rewards for "small potato deeds." Ampey mused, "It was frustrating and ego-smashing, but in the end, we knew something."

Inspired by Just, Ampey went on to earn his doctorate in biology. He joined the faculty at Southern University in Baton Rouge and helped J. W. Lee, a respected science educator, build a strong biology department. Ampey also organized an E. E. Just Biology

Club, in honor of his former mentor.

It's Time To Move Ahead

After one year as assistant professor in biology, the university promoted Just to associate professor and the following year, full professor. Just also held a joint appointment as professor of physiology in the Howard University School of Medicine. Not long after that, he became chair of the department of biology. His salary rose to $2150, the maximum for a member of the faculty at Howard.

When Just received his bachelor's degree from Dartmouth, it was the realization of an improbable dream. His introduction to biology further stimulated his desire to pursue advanced studies in the life sciences. Toward that end, he soon began inquiring about opportunities for graduate studies.

Despite his record and manifest potential in science, Just received little encouragement for graduate work. This lack of support was consistent with the times when the scientific community did not treat women without prejudice to their gender, nor blacks without prejudice to their race. Despite this climate Just asked his former professor at Dartmouth William Patten for his support and letter of recommendation. Patten knew his former pupil would encounter racial obstacles in science so at first he sought to dissuade him from any such efforts. He finally gave in to Just's insistence and put him in contact with an old acquaintance, and renowned biologist at the University of Chicago, Dr. Frank R. Lillie. As he had promised, Patten supported Just by writing a strong letter of recommendation. On the strength of that recommendation, and Just's strong academic record at Dartmouth, Lillie invited him to the Marine Biological Laboratory in Woods Hole, Massachusetts, for summer study. Just was one of the few among many applicants selected by Lillie to study at the Woods Hole facilities.

Even so, Lillie wanted Just to know what he was getting into. He painted a bleak future for any African-American who successfully completed the rigorous requirement for the doctorate in science. Doors of large universities and research institutions with their well-equipped laboratories would be shut to him and shut tightly. He likely would experience frustrations when heavy teaching loads and lack of resources and support at black colleges would prevent him from conducting research on his own campus. Just listened but could not be dissuaded; he felt too strongly that he had to continue his education. He had faced obstacles before. It was time to move on.

The Marine Biological Laboratory

The Marine Biological Laboratory is located in Woods Hole, Massachusetts, a village at the southwest tip of Cape Cod. Initially called Woods Holl, the local United States Post Office changed its name to Woods Hole in 1896. That name for the village stands today. The islands of Nantucket and Martha's Vineyard are nearby.

The Marine Biological Laboratory was incorporated Tuesday, March 20, 1888. It owes its existence to the vision and hard work of many dedicated women and men who founded the laboratory and built it to prominence.

The founders of MBL had a vision of a vital American scientific laboratory dedicated to a better understanding of life through serious study and investigation of marine organisms. They also envisioned that the laboratory would be a center of excellence for instruction in biology, with a strong emphasis on marine biology. As Jane Maienschein of Arizona State put it, MBL was designed to be "a gathering spot for biologists . . . to work with their favorite marine organism . . . to converse with each other, and exchange ideas in a way that seldom happens in the more limited confines of university biology departments."

The founders hoped to make of Woods Hole a grand gathering of scientists. This institute would become no less than an "exemplar of community research in biology, a hotbed of intense, dedicated biology work."

But what attracted the founders to that Massachusetts village by the shores of the Atlantic? What were its redeeming qualities? According to Maienschein, the draw was both scientific and recreational. She wrote:

> [There were] a diversity of marine organisms whose relative simplicity made them particularly useful for understanding life processes. Biologists could get fresh supplies in sufficient quantities. [Also many] natural advantages . . . numerous harbors and lagoons, with muddy, sandy, or rocky bottoms, while the coast is so broken by bays, promontories, straits and islands as to afford the most varied habitats. In addition, the tidal currents churn up the food and oxygen supplies in the water and produce beautiful collections of organism from nearby Gulf Stream as well as the northern currents. The fresh water sands provide alternative supplies for materials.

Maienschein went on to describe other attributes. Woods Hole was accessible by all the prevailing modes of transportation including rail and water. It offered a pleasant summer climate suitable for recreating and bathing. Workers found its "lush greenery and flowers . . . thick woods . . . an ideal place for a laboratory but also an ideal place for summer residence."

Frank Battray Lillie

Frank Battray Lillie, Just's new mentor, was born and raised in Toronto, Canada. He did his undergraduate work at the University of Toronto, then went to Clark University in Massachusetts to study under Dr. Charles Whitman. Whitman in turn invited Lillie to Woods Hole to begin his graduate work. Lillie earned credits at Woods Hole, then went to the University of Chicago where he received his Ph.D. in biology. Six years later he was appointed a professor of embryology at Chicago, where his scientific work made him one of the most respected biologists of his day. Lillie developed the theory that specific substances found in the egg and sperm of living organism interact when egg fertilization takes place. His theory, *the fertilizin theory*, commanded the attention and respect of embryologists world wide.

In 1910, the University of Chicago appointed Lillie chairman of the department of zoology and later dean of biological sciences. He served as assistant director of Woods Hole from 1900 to 1908 before succeeding Whitman as director. Lillie remained in that capacity until 1925. From 1926 until his retirement in 1942, he served as president of the Woods Hole Corporation. Under Lillie's leadership, MBL gained national prominence, and later it ranked with the elite among such institutions internationally.

A virtual *Whos Who* among scientists worked and studied at Woods Hole. Among them were such notables as Louis Agassiz, Cornelia Chapman of Mt. Holyoke, the embryologist Edwin Conklin, the famous geneticist and first Woods Hole Nobel Laureate Thomas Hunt Morgan, the well known physiologists Jacques Loeb, Paul Reznikeff and many others whose works established them as leaders in their field. Among these men, and at this research institute, Ernest Just went to work and study.

Just at Woods Hole

When Lillie cautioned Just about problems he would encounter because of his race, he spoke from history and his knowledge of prevailing individual attitudes and institutional exclusions. No doubt, he also had in mind another African-American, Charles Turner, who earned a doctorate in entomology from the University of Chicago. Turner published a number of attractive scientific papers about insects. He developed a well-regarded theory called "turner circling" that explained certain behaviors among bees. Turner never worked at a major university on a tenure appointment and spent most of his professional life teaching high school biology. Jane Maiemschein, in her history of Woods Hole said that, ". . .the discomfort Blacks experienced at Woods Hole in the teens and twenties . . . was, of course, a

reflection of racism in the society as a whole . . ." Just was aware
of these conditions but he knew of no better way to follow his
urgings to scientific pursuit. The once dormant, though gifted
scientific talent in him had been aroused and he could not deny
his interests, nor his desire to better prepare himself in science.
His main goal was to study biology at Woods Hole. As for the
other problems, he would have to deal with them when the time
came.

When Just arrived at Woods Hole, he found a beehive of
scientific investigations and discoveries. Whitman had made new
discoveries and gained recognition for his investigations in
animal morphology, particularly   the leech, *Clepsine*. E. B.
Wilson conducted studies in cytology and embryology, including
his influential work on "The Cell-lineage of Nereis. " Jacques
Loeb's theory on multiple embryos explored new territory. Lillie's
investigation on the role of certain protoplasmic inclusions in the
development of the fertilized eggs continued to be fruitful.
Morgan experimented on regeneration in worms, medusae and a
number of other forms. Wilson, A. D. Mead, Morgan, and Loeb
probed the phenomenon known as parthenogenesis. Genetics,
evolution, physiology, animal tropism, and to a lesser extent
botany, were among the research areas scientists were finding
exciting. Many new and useful discoveries and evolving
biological theories came from these and other studies at Woods
Hole.

Just first went to the MBL in 1909 and returned every summer
until 1930. He took courses under several of the eminent
biologists and attended special lectures by scholars in various
fields. Lillie arranged for Just to receive credits through the
University of Chicago *in absentia.*

Just did well in all his courses at Woods Hole. More
challenging were his assignments as a laboratory assistant for
Lillie, a most demanding taskmaster. Just proved equal to all
assigned tasks, and the two men, so alike in temperament, got
along very well. For Just, Lillie was almost an ideal mentor, and
he knew he could learn much from him. Lillie in turn admired

Just's intellect, quick grasp, and devotion to tasks. A bond formed between them that led to a lifelong association and working partnership in science.

Or Like The Fragrant Breath Of Flowers

While attending one of the faculty receptions at Howard, Just met a young lady named Ethel Highwarden. A petite, stately, and delicate beauty, she carried herself in a proud and graceful manner. Ethel Highwarden taught German and French, languages familiar to Just. After they met, the two learned they had much in common, particularly their mutual interest in the languages and literature. After that first meeting, Just saw Miss Highwarden often. He courted her continuously, but in a manner deemed proper for the times - that is, under the watchful eye of her mother. Shortly after his promotion to full professor, Just asked Miss Highwarden to marry him and she said yes. On Friday, June 26, 1912, the lovely, Ethel Highwarden, her long black hair gleaming in the light, and the slender, handsome Ernest Everett Just became husband and wife.

> On that day, whatever the elements, a gentle breeze played a soft symphony among the trees. The myriad beauty of flowers and green carpets of grass painted a portrait of vivid beauty against nature's landscape.

Perhaps Just, himself an amateur poet, may have harbored thoughts much like the black inventor, linguist, artist, poet, and author Lewis Howard Latimer. Latimer wrote in tribute to his beloved wife Mary:

> Thy love is like the cooling shade of trees;
> Or like the fragrant breath of flowers;
> My thoughts fly to thee as the wayward bees,
> Return to seek again the honeyed bowers.

The Relation Of The First Cleavage Plane

The happy couple wanted to have a long honeymoon after the wedding, but Lillie urged Just to return to Woods Hole. That meant separation, and a difficult choice coming as it did so soon after their marriage. Nonetheless they canceled plans for travel to Europe so Just could continue his studies. He was investigating the breeding habits of the genus *Nereis*. The *Nereis* is a marine annelid, or segmented worm, also called *clamworm*. In addition, Just began investigating the sea urchin *Abacia*. Sea urchins of the Phylum Echinodermata, are spiny animals usually found on the bottom of the sea. Extinct species of the echinodermata fossilized better than most other prehistoric animals because of the nature of their skeletons. Paleontologists often study their fossils and from them have learned much about the distant and misty past.

In 1912, Just published his first scientific paper, entitled "The Relation of the First Cleavage Plane to the Entrance Point of the Sperm." In this paper, Just argued that when a sperm penetrates an egg, the location of the point of entrance determines the line of cleavage of the fertilized egg. The publication turned out to be of considerable interest to embryologists. Manning explained the impact of Just's first published paper:

> The article came up for discussions in domestic and foreign journals, including *Biological Bulletin* and *L'Annee Biologique*. Years later . . . Nobel Laureate T. H. Morgan [called it] the fundamental and authoritative study on the subject.

Just published four others articles during the next three years reporting his findings on the *Nereis*, and the flatworm, *Platyneris*.

Quadrangles And Gothic Style

In 1912, after his first publication, Just also advanced to the residency stage in his doctoral program. That, of course, meant a year full time, at the University of Chicago. But Just could not afford to spend a year without working and could not persuade Howard University to grant him a sabbatical. He was clearly disappointed but resigned himself to a delay in meeting the residency requirement for his degree. Three years later, with assistance from Lillie, Just finally convinced university officials that the status of the Howard and the medical school where he also taught, would be enhanced by his obtaining a doctorate. He then spent the 1915-16 academic year in Chicago, Illinois.

By all accounts, Just made a quick adjustment to the new environment of the Midwest. He found Chicago, second only to New York in population, a bustling center of education, commerce, transportation, and manufacturing. Just also discovered a world of culture, political involvement, and economic status among blacks such as he had not before seen. It was a good and enlightening social experience.

The University of Chicago opened its doors in 1892 on the south side of the city where it still remains. Originally a Baptist institution, it later became interdenominational. Just found the campus impressive with its limestone buildings, classic gothic architecture, storied quadrangles and energetic research among many disciplines. The University enjoyed an enviable reputation as a world renown institution of higher education and center of research.

The rigorous program, high academic standards, and general intellectual stimulation at the university gave Just a delightful challenge. In 1916, he completed all requirements for the Ph.D. in biology. At the time, few of his race had reached that pinacle, especially in the sciences. By his example, and his stellar achievement, Just inspired others to follow in his footsteps.

They Asked Him How He Did It

In the fall of 1916, Dr. Ernest E. Just returned to Howard with a consuming desire to spend more time in research. He continued to be interested in the workings of the cell, for this was information critical to understanding the mysteries of life. He was especially interested in the cytoplasm and cellular surface. Just felt that these two components of the cell held important secrets of life, even though most other biologists thought the nucleus commanded all cellular functions. But as Howard was not then a research university, it could not accommodate Just as he would like, perhaps not even to the extent the university would have liked. Patten and Lillie had warned Just earlier that neither white research universities, nor the nation's research laboratories would accept him, and black universities could not support his research interests. They predicted that he might be unhappy when work responsibilities and inadequate research facilities would make impossible his spending extended time in research. Indeed, though Just remained at Howard, he was not content. To at least partially compensate for this lack, Just repeatedly returned to Woods Hole during the summers, always arriving ahead of the crowd and getting down to work

After some strain during the early years, other residents at Woods Hole accepted Just fairly well. They respected him for his investigative breakthroughs, exceptional skill in the laboratory and excellent qualities of mind. His laboratory skills in particular were much admired. Just's innovations and improved procedures often led to better experimental results. Others frequently sought him out for assistance and information about investigation techniques. He always responded to any request for help. Such beneficence often meant setting aside some important work of his own, or breaking into his concentration as he formulated new theoretical considerations. Maienschein gave an example of Just's innovations and his response to the needs of others:

> It is clear that many scientists held the highest respect for Just's biological work on fertilization and the cell surface. As Paul Reznikoff recalled, Just was `one of the most remarkable men he had met, a meticulous researcher who was always ready to give up his own valuable time to help anyone with experimental work. While Reznikoff's group was getting about 60 to 70 per cent successful cleavage, Just would get 98 to 99 percent successful cleavage. They asked him how he did it. In his typical way he

showed them. He kept his starfish and sea urchins in a covered bucket, even during the very short time it took to move them into the lab. He thus avoided the accelerating and confounding effects of the sun.

At home however, Ethel Just was not pleased with her husband's absence each summer, and this caused tension within the family. They were now parents to three children, Margaret, born 1913; Highwarden, in 1917, and Maribel in 1922. She thought it his obligation as their father to spend more time with them.

Just noticed that many scientists brought their families to Woods Hole. They could enjoy the pleasant summers and outdoor recreations the area afforded while the scientists conducted their research. Just thought this would be a good place for his family also. That way he could continue his research and have more time for Ethel and the children. It would be good, he felt, for his family to escape the hot, humid, summer weather of Washington, D.C. Lillie advised against such a move, fearing the black family would not be well received by others at the Woods Hole.

Nevertheless, Just went ahead with his plans. He suffered disasterous results. Just's wife and children were shut out by the community. Though her husband had a small circle of intimate friends, Ethel appeared not to fit in with them. Maienschein's explanation that the same racism in society at large existed at Woods Hole seemed to have been borne out. Manning reported that when the Justs arrived in Woods Hole, "Families would not sit with them in the mess hall. The wives of MLB scientists made it quite clear to Ethel that she was not welcome."

Manning described Ethel Just, as a proud person who did not mix easily. When she saw herself being ostracized, she did not feel compelled to seek acceptance, or to extend herself for the approval of others. Moreover, the wife of Ernest Just did not at all take kindly to such slights as she and her family received, and therefore had no wish to spend the summer at Woods Hole among such people. She would not beg for their acceptance nor would she condescend to lower her status for their comfort. Manning also suggested that in part, Ethel Just was less well accepted than her husband because his complexion was fairer while she was of a somewhat darker hue.

So Just had to take his family back to Washington before the summer was over. Anger, frustration, and humiliation went with them. Arriving home, Ethel vowed that neither she nor the children would ever set foot in Woods Hole again. They never did.

Marine Organisms And Cellular Biology

In spite of social problems encountered at Woods Hole that summer, Just continued his research and publications on the cytoplasmic functions of the cell. He and Lillie collaborated on several scientific publications as equals. Just was also helped by his association with the embryologist Jacques Loeb and each held the other in high esteem. Nevertheless, Loeb later took strong exception when Just criticized his theory of parthenogenesis. Angered that Just publicly criticized some of his research and described his laboratory procedures as flawed, Loeb lashed out at him. A major rift developed between two gifted men of science.

In the meantime, not only did Just display exceptional laboratory skills, he also developed new procedures that helped advance the study of marine organisms. Because he spent so much time advising and helping others there is some wonder that he accomplished as much as he did.

What he accomplished was considerable. Just published nearly 70 papers in scientific journals, two books, contributed four book chapters, and several articles on subjects other than natural science. But things were changing and so was Just. Manning pointed to several areas of concern:

1. Beyond his small circle of close friends Just endured racial slights over the years. Sometimes he chaffed under

the memory of past experiences as having to mop floors and wait tables for janitors when he, a college professor, first went to Woods Hole to study. These incidents had a cumulative effect and over the years he became increasingly bitter and unhappy because of them.

2.   He displayed an exceptional knowledge of marine organisms in the region. One observer, impressed by his research said he was a genius in experimental design, and his laboratory techniques. Consequently students and other scientists visited his laboratory with considerable frequency. Though he accommodated all who made requests of him, Just began to weary of the interruptions and services that went largely unappreciated.

3.   The Woods Hole community began shifting to the physico-chemical study of living organism. Just felt that the merits of the new emphasis should not lead to abandoning qualitative biological studies that remained critically important in the study of life.

4.   His close friend and mentor Frank Lillie spoke of retirement and Just did not know what kind of support he could expect from his successor.

Woods Hole became increasingly less comfortable. He worked there during the summer of 1930 but unlike most previous years began to look elsewhere to continue his work. ·

Europe

Just wanted to devote himself more fully to his research with more time to think about his new theories about how the cytoplasm and cellular cortex behave. These were relatively unexplored domains. Some of his efforts to attract funding for a research center at Howard failed largely because grantors felt uneasy about the center's future after Just left. Howard still could not accommodate him as he would have like in terms of research support. To a certain extent he understood and tried to promote the university's mission.

An opportunity to pursue his research overseas gave him some out. In 1929, Just took a six months leave and went to Naples on a grant, acquired with difficulty, from the Rosenwald Fund. His daughter, Margaret, accompanied him. In Europe, he found welcome and, to an extent he had not known before, acceptance as an equal. Jane Maienschein explained why Just selected Naples as the site to conduct his investigations:

> [There was] a different set of organisms to work with and an international group of scientists using the absolute foremost of contemporary research techniques.

She also said that at the Stazione Zoologia, the research facility at Naples, Just found the "best equipment and materials needed". According to Manning, Just wanted to test his hypothesis that "the European sea worm *Nereis dumerilii,* and the American sea worm, *Platynereis megalops* were not one and the same thing." His hypothesis proved correct. Manning reported that Just conducted fertilization experiments with the *Echinarachnius,* an American sea urchin, and two European organisms, *Paracentrotus lividus* and *Echinus microtuberculatus.* He also conducted extensive and detailed morphological research on the *Amphioxus.* The American toiled arduously while in Naples and his work went well.

He also travelled extensively in Europe, initially with Margaret until she returned to America, and afterward with newly acquired friends. At other times he wrote poetry, one of which as reported by Manning, was an ode to the sea:

> Beyond the slowly moving purple sea
> Diamond dusted in the sun
> Hills now vaguely dimmed as mantled in the mist
> They rise and softly etched the sky.

Just remained in Europe for about eight months. He returned home only reluctantly. An invitation from the renown Kaiser-Wilhelm Institut brought him back to Germany, a country where he spent some time during his first visit. He arrived in January 1930 and remained until June 1930. Few foreigners and no American had ever been so honored. The Insitut provided state of the art facilities and Just discussed issues, trends and exchanged views with some of the foremost biologists of the day. Among them was Max Hartman, Germany's ranked embryologist.

Also in 1930, Just accepted an invitation from the Eleventh International Congress of Zoologists in Padua to present a paper. He discussed his theory that ectoplasm played a critical, though largely unrealized, role in the development of the cell.

Just wanted to remain in Europe and he explored every possible avenue to stay. He had access to the great laboratories on the continent, detected no mood or act to restrict him based on his race and felt acceptance on the merits of his scientific work. His research at the Kaiser-Wilhem-Institut went well and he had complete freedom to concentrate on his research. As he tried to extend his leave Just found that winning support from American agencies became a matter of constant struggle and increasingly difficult. Howard University also balked at yet another extension of his leave. The university wanted to build a strong graduate program with Just as the prime architect.

During his stay in Europe, Just became romantically involved with a German woman, also a gifted scientist. His marriage, already in distress prior to his leaving America, weakened, and the bonds that once held him to Ethel, stretched, strained, and broke for good. Meanwhile, in Germany the winds of political change blew fiercely. With the rise of the Nazis to power and the discomfort it brought, Just returned to Naples hoping to somehow avoid returning to America.

Nonetheless the pressures continued and his troubles mounted. Manning called Just's years between 1938 and 1940, "The Exile." His alienation from Howard increased and his bitterness toward America deepened. He desperately wanted to put America behind, remain in Europe, and devote himself fully to a life of research in science. He settled in Paris for awhile and worked at the Laboratoire d'Anatomie et d'Histologie Comparie of the University of Paris, and Sorbonnne's Station Biologique at Roscoff Finistere. Then war broke out, Germany conquered France, and detained many, including Just, in Concentration camps. Only by his wits, and the intercession of others who cared about him did Just manage to get out of the camp and return to America.

"To Set Forth Fundamental Methods"

In the long run, Just eventually helped lay the foundation for modern cellular and molecular biology. Basically, he began by adopting the long-standing assumption among biologists that the cell is the structural and functioning unit of living things. He firmly believed that only through creatively investigating the cell can scientist learn the fundamental principles of life itself. Accumulated evidence convinced cellular biologists, that marine animals were excellent organisms for such investigation. They noted, among other things, the comparable specific gravity of sea water and protoplasm. The internal fluids of marine animals and sea water closely match in important chemical content and concentration. Following such leads, scientists discovered close relations between cellular behavior and the environment.

At first Just's scientific investigations followed along the line of his mentor, Frank Lillie. He admired Lillie and respected him as a friend and great scientist. His fierce loyalty in defense of Lillie's theories sometimes brought him into conflict with others and subjected him to criticism from some quarters. In time however, Just expanded his investigations and became more independent of Lillie in thought and in research direction.

Nonetheless friends and foes alike acknowledged Just as a meticulous experimenter. Lillie attributed much of the soundness of Just's finding to "the very refined methods he had developed for works in this field." Friends urged Just to write a book about his methods and techniques. In the spirit of communication among scientists, they asked him to share his knowledge and procedures with a wider audience.

Just finally agreed, and wrote a book called *Basic Methods for Experiments on Eggs of Marine Animals*. In his text, he intended to ". . . set forth fundamental methods for the use of eggs and spermatozoa of marine invertebrates in experimental investigation." First Just described methods especially applicable "to those eggs and spermatozoa that are most commonly employed" and that were. . ." so general that they apply equally to games of the same species both in American and European waters . . .". He wrote, both for the beginner and the experienced embryologist," whose work demands individual extension of methods." He stressed the importance of studying the living egg in as "natural" an environment as possible. Nonetheless, Just cautioned that some studies could never be conducted without fixed eggs, preserved in non-living state. With that in mind, Just devoted considerable time and space in his book to explaining methods for preparing fixed eggs of superior quality. The book encompassed some of his major findings based on more than three decades of investigations in America and Europe.

Just's first and fundamental rule emphasized that all apparatus had to meet the test of "scrupulous cleanliness." Indeed, all traces, even of any cleaning agents had to be removed from glassware to be used. Next, the quality of the glassware should be the best available and free from contamination. He provided guidelines so the researcher would know how to avoid using contaminated apparatus. Just recommended that all precautions be taken to ensure that descriptions of normal development of organism be based on observations under conditions like those occurring in nature. Optimum conditions for investigation help guard against the investigator making interpretations that lead to erroneous conclusions. Lillie commented on Just's emphasis in this area:

His technical papers were characterized by intimate knowledge of material and use of it in optimum state; he was thus able to avoid the pitfalls of failing to distinguish between results due to unphysiological initial conditions in the real objects of his experiments, viz., the effect of altered physical and chemical conditions.

Just also advised that whenever possible, the investigator should collect his (or her) own organisms rather than using those collected by others. That way, one could best be sure of the highest quality in specimen to be used for study.. He provided meticulous details about culturing organisms to help ensure normal development. For instance, he stated that his "experience in rearing marine invertebrates from eggs - *Asteruas, Abacia, Echinarachinius, Platynereis, Pectenaria, Diopatra . . . "* and many others, convinced him that the most important understanding is simply knowing when to begin feeding them.

Just included detailed information on the best "Methods for Handling Eggs and Sperm in the Laboratory", again in the interest of valid results. He noted the importance of identifying which of four stages the particular egg was fertilizable, adding that sperms should be as fresh as possible to ensure greatest viability. He offered specific details on how best to handle eggs of such marine organisms as the *Arbacia, Echinarachins, Cumingia, Ciona,* and many others. His text, lucid, comprehensive and thorough, particularly useful to the investigator, covered such topics as, "General Working Conditions, Precautions and Prequisites", "Normal Development", "Methods for handling Eggs and Sperm in the Laboratory", "Some Methods for Preliminary Experimental Manipulations," "Methods of Fixation", "Methods of Clearing and Imbedding." In the appendix, Just also discussed, "Differences in eggs worthy of note", "Summary of means eliciting experimental parthenogenesis in various eggs", and "Protocol on fixation". He took pains to explain the benefits of using fixed materials pointing out their critical value in research.

Just frequently compared his procedures to those used by other embryologists, including such respected scholars as Jacques Loeb and T. H. Morgan. When he felt that procedures he devised were superior to theirs, and counter to accepted practice, he would say so. Sometimes his assertions, on occasion perceived by some as rather blunt, created considerable controversy. But he always took pains to support his position with research evidence.

The Cell Is More Than the Nucleus

Just published a second book in 1939, *The Biology of the Cell Surface.* He identified the fundamental biological problems of the day and brought together under one cover his experimental findings covering a 25-year period. His "new biology" and philosophical views were also carefully laid out in this publication. His stated object was to present his "interpretation of the drama of life unfolding before our eyes." Just went on to say:

> It thus became imperative for me to examine and to appraise hypothesis and factual evidence and to define first every problem .. . I had projected for my book. To all those who look with interest upon the manifestation of life in animals and in man, who desire to know more, and more exactly what answers to their questions concerning life biology can give, this book would speak.

Just further contended that it was the solemn duty of scientists, however esoteric the subject, to communicate to others with clarity:

> Even the most abstract truth needs to be expressed with simplicity and clearness and thus relate itself to everyday human experience . . . However cloistered biology may be as a scientific research, as the science of life and having appeal to all men it should make itself articulate beyond its cloistered walls.

On another subject, he readily acknowledged the growing importance of physico-chemical quantitative research because such studies revealed new information and fundamentally, helped make biology a more exact science. Nonetheless, he held that it would be a serious mistake to abandon qualitative research, as some advocated, because there would always be a "need for accurate description and accurate observations". He went on to say:

The demand for filling in gaps persist. Where minute details are wanting, they must be supplied. Wherever uncertainty or doubts intrudes concerning a descriptive datum, this should as far as possible be removed.

Just contended that purely descriptive studies must remain as an essential research tool because some biological phenomena are simply not quantifiable. What approach we use, whether theoretical or applied, should be influenced by purpose. In the final analysis, he wrote, "The main purpose of an experiment in biology should be the explanation of the naturally occurring phenomena." Therefore, according to Just, biology must employ both the tools of quantitative and qualitative research in its quest for truth.

As to his own theory of cellular behavior and development, Just considered his position "revolutionary." His observations convinced him that the widely held view of the primacy of the nucleus in cellular functions, and the relatively unimportance of the cytoplasm, were wrong. Instead, he asserted that the cytoplasm, and its outer cortex the cellular ectoplasm, were indispensable to cellular function. If we are to understand the cell, then we must understand the structure and function of the cell surface.

The cellular cortex he said, was considered by many scientists as being no more than a semi-permeable membrane; that the nucleus was the "kernal of life." Just did not agree. Any investigator, he said, who gives only scant attention to the cytoplasmic component, fails to account for "those protoplasmic systems which lack sharply defined . . . nucleus . . . such as the bacterium whose protoplasmic organizations fail to show a discrete nucleus as a living organism." In the development of life, the first step in the complex and miraculous processes of changing the egg into an identifiable organism, took place in the cellular cortex. This portion of the cell stood in contact with the external environment and keyed the cell response to it.

The fundamental roles of living protoplasm involving contraction, conduction, respiration, and water exchange, could never take place without an active and enabling role played by the ectoplasm. Regardless, whether development from an egg begins with fertilization, or with parthenogenesis (development of an organism from an egg without union with a sperm), it does not take place without cytoplasmic processes which, occur first. In the ectoplasm, Just said, one can see "activities that set apart the living thing from the nonliving . . . There one can find the cell accommodating itself to the external environment. More exactly, he stated ". . . in the region of the ectoplasm one observes . . . how life maintains itself ever in harmonious tempo with the ceaseless changes in its surroundings." In opposition to many of his contemporaries Just concluded that the nucleus was a dependent of the ectoplasm, not the other way around.

Lillie succinctly summed up Just's position on the cytoplasm of the cell and its implications:

> He conceived that the behavior of the ectoplasm is one prime factor in differentiation during development, and the building up of nuclear material another; there is a constant interplay of both with the general protoplasm.
> This led to an interpretation of the action of the gene in heredity and the conception was even extended to an interpretation of evolution.

What is Life?

Just rejected the doctrine of vitalism which postulated that a nonmaterial substance, or "vital process" in living things sets them apart from inanimate or nonliving objects. The vitalist say that this "vital process", is not, and cannot, be controlled by the laws that apply to nonliving materials. Just had a different explanation of life that will be discussed later. He also rejected the doctrine of mechanism that sought to explain things in terms of laws governing machines. Most mechanists, he felt, saw all things in terms of deterministic laws, nothing according to purpose. Just wondered why, when the physicist, even before the advent of quantum mechanics and relativity, agreed that not all of physics could be explained by mechanics, did some biologists find grounds for embracing that philosophy.

Just pointed out that living things consisted of the same "material compositions," molecules, atoms, electrons, etc. . . ." as could be found in the non-living things in its environment. It follows then that in many respects biology is the biology of chemistry and the biology of physics. Living things, he said, have no chemical element not found in the environment of which it is a part. Therefore, living things obey all known physico-chemical laws that govern the behavior of non-living things. That is why, as he suggested earlier, if we are to achieve a fuller understanding of the biological processes, the chemistry and physics involved had to be addressed. But he always warned that an understanding of a cell in any altered state did not necessarily reveal the chemistry and physics of the normal living cell. There is in life a phenomenon peculiar unto itself.

According to Just, what made living things different from nonliving things was not the chemical elements, which were common to all, but the organization of that chemistry. He wrote, "Clearly then, the state of being alive reposes in combinations, in the order of which the constituents are assembled both in space and time . . ." To Just, life was a marvelous, miraculous and special manifestation of nature and related to it. He wrote in his book, *The Biology of the Cell Surface:*

> We feel the beauty of Nature because we are a part of Nature and because we know that however much in our separate domains we abstract from the unity of Nature, this unity remains. Although we may deal with particulars, we return finally to the whole pattern woven out of these. So in our study of the animal egg: though we resolve it into constituents parts the better to understand it, we hold it as an integrated thing, as a unified system: in it life resides and in its moving surface life manifests itself.

Grants, Honors, And Recognitions

When Just returned to the United States from Europe in 1941, he was not a happy man, nor was he well. He had married while in Europe, his wife was pregnant, and his financial situation needed to care for his new family, strained. He wanted to continue work on basic research, but despite his proven record as a scientist there still were no such opportunities. To its credit, Howard retained him as a full professor and department chair despite his long and frequent absences.

At first Just did not realize the seriousness of his condition despite his weight loss and constant pain. Friends noted that he looked haggard and tired. When he finally consented to a see a doctor, his worse fears were realized. He had cancer. Just tried to carry on his duties at Howard, but he simply could not. On Friday, October 27, 1941, Ernest Just died at the home of his sister Inez in Washington, D. C. He was 58 years old.

Frank Lillie wrote a moving obituary for, and tribute to, his former student. It was published in the journal *Science* January 2, 1942. Lillie called it " . . . a sad task to write this short memorial of my former student, collaborator and friend . . .His death was premature and his work unfinished; but his accomplishments were many and worthy of remembrance." Lillie noted Just's accomplishments at Woods Hole and Europe, his philosophy (which was influenced in part by the writings of Kant, Hegel, Mach, Schrodinger, Heisenberg and a few others), and his constant struggles. He wrote:

> An element of tragedy ran through all Just's scientific career due to the limitations imposed by being a Negro in America, to which he could make no lasting psychological adjustments in spite of earnest efforts on his part . . . That a man of his ability, scientific devotion and of such strong personal loyalties as he gave and received, should have been warped in the land of his birth must remain a matter for regret.

During his life Just received a number of grants without which he could not have spent years abroad conducting research. In this he was supported in part by the Julius Rosenwald Fund, the

General Education Board, the Carnegie Corporation and the Rosenwald Foundation. Though there were differences with Howard, that institution showed considerable forbearance in granting him leaves when its own sense of mission would have been better served by Just's presence and work on campus.

Just received the first ever Spingarn Medal in recognition of his contributions to science and his campaign to help improve medical education at Howard and elsewhere. In accepting the award Just said that he felt unworthy, that the association might "do far better to honor some well known worker."Nonetheless, he said that the honor inspired him because it demonstrated that his "striving and learning were appreciated." With the award, he felt anxious to get on with his work and "any privations would be glory".

Just was also elected vice president of the American Society of Zoologists. He held membership in the American Association for the Advancement of Science, the Washington Academy of Sciences, the Ecological Society and the Societe des Sciences Naturelle et Mathematique de Cherburg. He also served on editorial boards of the *Physiological Zoology, Protoplasma: Zeitschrift fuer physikalische Cheme, The Biological Bulletin* and *Journal of Morphology.*

One of the greatest tributes to Just came over forty years after his death. In 1983, on the 100th anniversary of his birth, a commemoration was held in his native South Carolina in his honor. The Twenty-sixth Southeastern Conference on Developmental Biology, held a symposium on Cellular and Molecular Biology of Invertebrate Development at the Bell W. Baruch Institute for Marine Biology and Coastal Research in tribute to his work. J. D. Ebert said, "This symposium dedicated to Just is timely, an occasion not only to celebrate the one-hundredth anniversary of his birth, but also, in his name, to dedicate ourselves to a re-creation of a national spirit of science." Richard Sawyer credited Just with laying "a part of the foundation on which we [cellular biologists] stand today".

South Carolina State College, in conjunction with the South

Carolina Hall of Science and Technology, held a Commemorative Program in his honor. South Carolina Govenor Richard Riley issued a proclamation in his honor. A tribute, entered into the Congressional Record of the United States of America (August 4, 1983) called Just a "great scientist and a great man".

References and Literature for Further Reading

Academic American Encyclopedia,, 20:213, Dansbury, Connecticut: Grolier, Inc. 1989.

Adams, Russell, L., *Great Negroes Past and Present* Chicago: Afro-Am Publishing Company, Inc., 1964.

Black Achievers in Chicago: Chicago Museum of Science and Industry, 1988.

Cobb, W. Montague,"Ernest Everett Just, 1883-1941", *Journal of the National Medical Association,* 49: 349-350, September, 1957.

"Commemoration Program in Honor Ernest Everett Just, 1883-1941," South Carolina State College, October 21, 1983, courtesy of Minnie M. Johnson, Coordinator of Collection Development, Miller F. Whittaker Library.

Dawes, Ben, *A Hundred Years of Biology,* Edingburg: The Riverside Press, 1952.

Ebert, J. D., "Preserving The Anarchy of Science," in Sawyer, Roger H. and Richard M. Showman (eds.), *The Cell and Molecular Biology of Invertebrate Development,* Columbia, S. C.: University of South Carolina Press, 1985.

Haber, Louis, *Black Pioneers of Science and Invention,* New York: Harcourt, Brace and World, Inc., 1970.

Hayden, Robert C., *Seven Black American Scientists,* Reading, Massachusetts: Addison-Wesley Publishing Company, 1970.

Just, Ernest E, Basic Methods for Experiment of Eggs of Marine Animals, Philadelphia: P. Blakiston's Sons and Co., 1939.

_____ "Initiation of Development in the Egg of *Arbacia",* *The Biological Bulletin,* 43:384-391, 1922.

_____, *The Biology of the Cell Surface,* Philadelphia: P. Blakiston's Sons and Co., 1939.

Klein, Aaron E., *Hidden Contributors: Black Scientists and Inventors in America,* Garden City, New York: Doubleday and Company, Inc., 1971.

Lillie, Frank R., "Ernest E. Just," *Science,* 95:10-11, January 2, 1942.

_____., *The Woods Hole Marine Biological Laboratory*, Chicago: The University of Chicago Press, 1944.

Logan, Rayford and M. Winston (eds), *Dictionary of American Negro Biography,* New York: W. W. Norton and Company, 1982.

Maienschein, Jane, *100 Years Exploring Life, 1888-1988,* Boston: Jones and Bartlett Publishers, 1989.

Manning, Kenneth, *Black Apollo of Science: The Life of Ernest Everett Just,* New York: Oxford University Press, 1983. (This is the definitive work on the life of Ernest E. Just).

Mather , Frank L. (ed), *Who's Who Among Colored Americans,* Chicago, 1915.

1990 Encyclopedia Americana, 20:144, Dansbury, CT: Grollier, Inc.

Nuttli, Otto, Buddinger, G. A., and R. B. Hermann, *The 1886 Charleston, South Carolina Earthquake - A 1986 Perspective*, U. S. Geological Survey Circular 985, Washington, D. C.: U. S. Government Printing Office. 1986.

Robinson, Wilhemenia S., *Historical Negro Biographies,* Chicago; International Library of Negro Life and History, 1968.

Sawyer, Roger H., and Richard M. Showman, *The Cellular and Molecular Biology of Invertebrate Development,* Columbia, South Carolina: The University of South Carolina Press, 1985.

Wormley, Stanton L. and Lewis H. Fenderson, (eds.), *Many Shades of Black,* New York: William Morrow and Co., 1969

Chapter X_____

Louis Tompkins Wright, M.D.
(1891 - 1952)

Louis Tompkins Wright was born July 23, 1891 in the small town of LaGrange, Georgia, located southwest of Atlanta near the Alabama border. He was the oldest of two sons. His parents were Ceah Ketcham Wright, a physician and minister, and Lula Tompkins Wright. Ceah Wright, one of the first graduates of Meharry Medical College in Nashville, Tennessee, earned his M. D. degree in 1881. Founded in 1876, Meharry had as its mission to prepare former slaves and their descendants to be physicians who would provide critically needed health care for former slaves and their descendants. Following his graduation however, Dr. Wright practiced medicine for only a few years before turning to the ministry full time.

Lula Tompkins Wright, respected in the community for her personal character and devotion to family and church, was of fair skin, strong character, and strikingly beautiful. Unfortunately, in 1895, when young Louis was just four years old, the Reverend Dr. Ceah Wright died, leaving his young widow to rear their two sons alone. In the face of this loss, Lula Wright and her two boys drew closer and worked together for the benefit of the family.

Four years later Lula Wright married again. Her second husband was Dr. William Fletcher Penn, also a physician. Dr. Penn, the first African American graduate of the Yale School of Medicine earned his M. D. degree in 1898.

The family settled in Atlanta, Georgia. Soon they welcomed a new member when Lula Tompkins Penn gave birth to her third child, a girl who was given the name Jesse. Later, when Jesse Penn grew up, she married Dr. Harold West who served many years as president of Meharry Medical College.

Harvard Medical School

Dr. Penn was a caring father, both for his two sons and his daughter Jesse. His bonding with Louis grew particularly strong as the lad demonstrated he could shoulder responsibility. When a race riot broke out in the city, Penn gave Louis a rifle with the instruction that he was to protect his home, mother, and siblings. The atmosphere in the city was tense and the threat real. Though frightened Louis took his post, hoping he would never have to take rifle to shoulder, but determined to fight if necessary. Fortunately a white neighbor, concerned about their welfare, appeared suddenly and spirited the family to safety in his car. Young Louis never forgot that act of courage and altruism.

Louis attended college at Clark University, a small, all black church-supported school in Atlanta. Though mischievous at times, young Mr. Wright was a campus leader and, much to the joy and delight of his parents, an excellent student. In 1911 he earned a bachelor's degree in chemistry and was graduated valedictorian of his class. To Dr. Penn's delectation, Louis announced he wanted to become a physician. The two men talked, then agreed that Louis ought to attend the best medical school in the country which, clearly in their minds, was the Harvard University Medical School.

Because Louis was black, and his degree conferred by a relatively unknown, underfunded, Negro institution in the south, many of the locals considered the realization of such a goal improbable. Even friends wondered why he sought admission to Harvard, but though they regarded the notion as patently absurd, admired Louis for his ambition and resolve, and wished him success. It therefore came as a surprise, even to his ardent supporters, when Harvard Medical School mailed him a letter of acceptance.

Harvard was surprised too. When Wright presented himself to the admission office, school officials were nonplussed. There had been some mistake they said, a fortuitous, unfortunate error. They were expecting a graduate of the nearby and prestigious Clark University of Worcester, Massachusetts. No one there ever heard of that "funny little school in Atlanta." The officials tried to convince Wright that his obscure and small school could not possibly have prepared him to meet the high standards set by Harvard. Most likely he would not be able to keep pace with the best and brightest young minds prepared by the best and most prestigious colleges and universities in the land. Surely he could see that he would be better off somewhere else, couldn't he?

No he could not. He had no plans to return to Atlanta or go to any other school. So he stood there and argued with the Harvard officials. His gaze was intense and steady; he did not waver. Wright pointed out that his letter was official, it came from them and they said he was accepted. Surely they could understand that, couldn't they? Finally, a compromise was reached. Dr. Otto Folin of the chemistry department agreed to give him an oral test. Wright passed, and on Folin's recommendation the university accepted him as a student. Four years later Louis Tompkins Wright graduated from Harvard Medical school, *cum laude*, and fourth best in his class.

"Be Good And Good For Something"

Whatever folks back home thought of his chances, they supported Wright in his ambition. Professor Lawyer Tayler of the Department of Chemistry and Physics at Atlanta's Clark University wrote a letter describing Wright as a quick study. He said:

> He [Wright] seems to be able to take in and digest in one-third the time it does an ordinary student . . . as far as his character is concerned, I would rate it 100%.

A Reverend C. C. Neal said that Wright simply "led his class in everything."

His uncle, I. Garland Penn, who was a poet, wrote several letters on his behalf. He sent a letter of introduction to the

Reverend Ernest Lyman Milts, a friend living in the Boston area. Penn hoped the minister would be kind enough to look after his nephew who, after all was far from home in an alien environment. He said of his nephew:

> We are expecting great things of him and are counting upon him making good there, as he has done here in school. We are proud to say that he was valedictorian in his class and did good work.

> We are particularly anxious about his religious life while in Boston, and any advice and help given him will be greatly appreciated by his father and mother, and by me equally with them, in the future.

One letter from home to Wright was unusual and of particular interest. Dated January 12, 1912, the letter arrived unsigned. The writer informed Wright that she was in love with him. Nevertheless, he was not to worry, she said, because she was old enough to be his mother. The mystery person advised him to visit all the places in the region that were of historic interest. She admonished him to keep his feet warm to avoid "consumption." For good mental health she advised Wright to "laugh every chance you get."

The writer went on to tell Wright that she would like to send him $50.00 to help with his expenses, but could only send fifty cents, which she enclosed. Next came both financial and motherly advise. Wright was encouraged to value every nickel, count every blessing, be brave, and walk whenever he could. In the matters of morality, he should avoid temptation. Temptation, she warned, would appear when least expected. She wanted him to ". . .be good and good for something . . . [because] the world needs men pure hearted, wholehearted, faithful and loyal."

"Thoroughly And Enthusiastically A Doctor"

Each year Wright qualified for scholarship assistance, which was necessary to sustain him as a student at the Medical School.

In 1914, his application for pecuniary assistance asked for $1.50 per week for food and $4.00 per week for room.

A member of a local District Grand Lodge, B.J. Davis, had a chance to meet Wright. He was one of several persons contacted by Uncle Garland to kind of look out for the young man. Wright so impressed Davis that the Bostonian wrote a letter to his mother in Atlanta, praising her son.

> Your boy is thoroughly and enthusiastically a doctor. He has the proper ideal of his profession. . . I have never met a young man that impressed me so much with the integrity and loftiness of his purpose.

"On Account Of Your Being A Colored Man"

Historian Robert Hayden wrote that during Wright's third year at Harvard, officials told him he "could not go with his classmates to the Boston Lying-In Hospital to learn to deliver babies. . ." The medical school arranged to place him with a Boston-based black Harvard graduate explaining, `That is the way all colored men get their obstetrics.'

Wright protested. The catalog stipulated that students at the Harvard Medical School would study obstetrics at the Boston Lying-In. He was a student. He had paid his tuition. He expected what was promised in the catalog and the experiences provided all other medical students at the institution. Some of Wright's classmates, moved by the morality of his stand, supported him. Officials finally acceded, though not necessarily in good grace, and assigned Wright to the Boston Lying-In along with his classmates. His reception and the nature of his experiences there are not known to this writer.

Nevertheless his difficulties continued, and he could do nothing about the next distraction. His high academic standings, and overall qualifications easily met the requirements for induction into the Phi Delta Kappa of Medicine, the Alpha Omega Alpha Honor Society. Nevertheless he was blackballed and therefore denied admission. He watched as the society inducted others into its membership, some as far down as seventeenth in class ranking while he, fourth ranked, was snubbed. Wright suffered in silent anguish and years passed before he could overcome the bitterness for what he felt deeply was an unjust rejection.

When Louis T. Wright was graduated from the Harvard Medical School, family members expressed their joy and pride at what he had achieved. He was now a medical doctor. Not surprising, Uncle Garland was the first to write,

> One of the joys that come to all of us this week is the fact that you graduate from Harvard, one of the greatest schools in the world, with such high honors . . . We all send congratulations by the bushel.

And from his stepfather came a telegram.

> Congratulations my son. Your mother and all of us rejoice in the successful confirmation of ambition . . . proud to have such nice things said about you by all the people who have met you.

But then came the matter of his internship and disdain that neither his good academic record nor his determination could overcome. Every hospital in Boston rejected his application: Boston City Hospital, Peter Bent Brigham, Massachusetts General. All said no. So Dr. Wright applied to Vancouver General Hospital in Canada, hoping for a better reception there. A letter from Vancouver, dated April 17, 1915, summed up the hospital's position and it seems, all the other refusals:

> Though I have no doubt in the world that you would make an excellent intern in our hospital, but on account of your being a colored man, I would be unable to take you on the staff.
> I am very sorry indeed that I have to write you to this effect for I know your services would suit me.
>
> P. S. I am returning your photograph.

Dr. Penn then suggested that his son apply to Freedman Hospital, which was affiliated with the black Howard University Medical

School, in Washington, D.C. This time the news was good. His acceptance letter read: "You are hereby notified of your selection as intern in the Freedman's Hospital for a term of one year beginning July 1, 1915. (Signed) W. A. Warfield, Surgeon in Chief."

"Lichenification Occurs In All Positive Tests"

While at Freedman's, Dr. Wright became interested in the Schick Test for immunity to diphtheria. The disease diphtheria disease is caused by a rod-shaped bacterium, or bacillus, called *corynebacterium diptheriae*. This microscopic organism multiplies in the throat and gives off a powerful toxin. The toxin, not the organism, attacks the palate, larynx, and trachea. In the infected organ, a false membrane covers mucous surface making the tissue dysfunctional. Among the symptoms of diphtheria are husky voice, fever, sore throat, nasal discharge, pronounced weakness, and a strong, fetid odor of the breath.

In 1913, Dr. Bela Schick, a United States pediatrician, developed a test to determine the degree of immunity a person had to diphtheria. The test involved injecting 0.1 mL of dilute diphtheria toxin under the skin. If the test proved positive, meaning the person was susceptible, a red, inflamed area appeared in the skin at the point of injection.

According to the medical view of the time, Negroes were more susceptible to diphtheria than whites. Unfortunately, they believed that the Schick Test was not applicable to persons of African descent because of their dark skin. Doctors thought dark skin would not develop the telltale redness indicative of susceptibility to diphtheria. On that belief, they concluded the test was of no use for Negroes.

Dr. Wright questioned both of these assumptions. How did anyone know? Had any studies been conducted, had any data been systematically gathered? He checked the literature and could not find supporting scientific evidence. So, during his internship, Dr. Wright conducted controlled tests to see if the Schick technique could be used with people who had dark skin. In 1917, he published his results in the *Journal of Infectious Diseases*. His studies offered convincing evidence that the Schick Test could be used as effectively with Negroes as with persons of lighter skin. In the article he wrote:

It is interesting to note that in the Negro the reaction is as clear cut as in white . . . Lichenification occurs in all positive cases regardless of the color of the skin, and promises to be of value in differentiating positive from negative reactions in those rare instances where an increase of pigmentation does not take place for one reason or another.

The Doctor, The Military

Upon completing his internship at Freedman's Hospital, Louis Tompkins Wright, M. D., took the tough New York State Board Examination. He easily passed with a score of 93.4. Wright also took the board examinations in the states of Maryland and Georgia where in each case, he passed with the highest average for the year.

Not uncharacteristically, Uncle Garland sent warm congratulations when news arrived of his nephew's excellent showing. The young doctor then returned home to practice medicine with his stepfather. His stay in Atlanta was short as a grave crisis had gripped the nation. The United States, led by President Woodrow Wilson, entered World War I that had been raging in Europe for two years. America joined the Allies, led by Great Britain and France, in a global conflict of great destruction, against Germany and the Axis Powers. Immediately the armed forces faced a critical shortage of medical doctors. Responding to the nation's call for physicians, Dr. Wright left a promising practice and volunteered his services for the army. He was inducted into the medical corp as a second lieutenant at Fort McPherson, near Atlanta.

The exact reason Dr. Wright join the military is not known. Beginning with the Revolutionary War, blacks in uniform had fought, suffered and died in the nation's defense but full citizenship under the constitution remained a promise unfulfilled. Strangely, despite the critical need for more manpower, the federal government actually discouraged black enlistment by placing tight restrictions on them. The relatively few accepted into the military were typically consigned to service divisions. Moreover, in the history of black military service to the United States, only two Americans of African descent had ever received appointments as commissioned officers. One was Charles Young, the third black American West Point graduate (August 31, 1889), the other was Benjamin O. Davis Sr., a captain who later rose through the ranks. (During World War II, Davis was promoted to the rank of Brigadier General, the first ever for a black American). So the situation Wright entered did not look very promising given his race and temperament.

Nonetheless, black leaders urged their people to support the nation in a brutal war that, until that time in human history was unparalleled in global destruction. They also insisted that Negroes not be confined to service units and menial duties. Rather, they contended some must also be placed into combat units as well, and some must be trained as commissioned officers-as leaders. So perhaps then, in volunteering for service, Louis T. Wright acted in response to three principles: he was a patriot, love of country; a fighter for human rights, love for justice; and a well-prepared physician, loyal to his profession.

From Fort McPherson, Dr. Wright went to Officers Training School at Fort Des Moines, Iowa. The Des Moines OTS was specifically established to increase the number of Negro commissioned officers in the military. Upon completing his training, Dr. Wright was among 700 black inductees promoted to a higher rank. As a first lieutenant, he was assigned to Camp Upton, New York where, in addition to treating patients, he made another important contribution to medicine.

During World War I, the military worried about the possible outbreak of the acute contagious disease smallpox among enlisted personnel. The threat of an epidemic, or even a pandemic, due to this virus, heightened their concern pertaining to military readiness. Viruses are the smallest known infectious agents and can only be seen with an electron microscope. The smallpox virus is brick-shaped, enclosed in a complex double membrane that helps make it a very hardy organism. Some people have a natural immunity to the smallpox virus; others can acquire immunity through inoculation with a smallpox vaccine.

The immediate problem was that some people had to be inoculated more than once before there was "a take." This repetition slowed the process of immunizing military personnel, leaving many of them vulnerable to a disease that was could spread rapidly through the ranks. Dr. Wright thought he could speed the innoculation process by changing from the "scratch inoculation" technique to injecting the vaccine under the skin with a small hypodermic needle. This was called the intradermal or intracutaneous procedure.

Wright tested his hypothesis by inoculating 227 volunteers using the intradermal procedures. He achieved dramatic success with 160 takes from the first inoculation as opposed to 19 takes for the same number of persons using the "scratch" test. His intradermal method soon became standard army procedure because of its effectiveness and efficiency. Later he published a detailed account of his study and reported his findings in the *Journal of the American Medical Association*, August 18, 1918 under the title "Intradermal Vaccination Against Smallpox."

Among scientific researchers who took note of Wright's procedure were Hans Zinsser, an Immunologist and Bacteriologist at Harvard University, John Kolmer, Professor of Pathology and Bacteriologist in the Graduate School of Medicine, Philadelphia, and George Dock in Volume V of "Oxford Medicine." Several other persons in the foregoing and related fields cited Wright's works.

"That Fresh Funny Looking Girl"

On one weekend, Wright and some friends took a leave from Camp Upton and went to New York City. They visited a recreational center that local public-spirited citizens had organized for the entertainment of servicemen away from home. The organization was the forerunner of the United Service Organization, more commonly known as the USO, which became nationwide during World War II. The Center sponsored several activities such as music, dancing, games, refreshments, and the opportunity to meet new people.

Wright immediately took note of one volunteer at the center,

Corinne Cooke, a young lady of fair skin and vivid beauty
sensed being observed by a slim army lieutenant, but he
appeared to be somewhat shy. Many years later, in an interview
with Dr. E. M. Bluestone, she explained how she met Dr. Louis
Tompkins Wright, of Atlanta, Georgia.

> Dr. Wright asked some friends of his, pointing to me, who is that
> fresh, funny-looking girl . . . He had watched me work and was
> impressed with what I was doing. He loved efficiency . . . The
> next week a friend of mine called me and said, "Do you
> remember the little lieutenant who you met last week, well he
> wants to know if you are going to dance with him, and I said yes
> . . . After that, he never missed a week-end seeing me and writing
> to me, from then till the day he came back from the war twelve
> months later.

Before going off to war, the shy "little lieutenant" asked the
"fresh, funny looking girl" for her hand in marriage. To his
enduring delight, she said yes.

Wounded At Mt. Henri

The insistent demand by black leaders that black soldiers be
trained in the infantry, not just stevedore regiments, resulted in
the formation of the 92nd and 93rd divisions. These combat
units fought in many decisive World War I battles, including
those at Argonne, Maison-en-Champagne, and Metz. One
regiment, the 369th, was among the first of the American units
to engage the Germans in combat. For six months, the 369th
remained under fierce enemy fire without relief, longer than any
other fighting unit. Fighting battle after battle, the regiment
sustained more than 1500 casualties, yet never retreated, nor lost
a single prisoner to the enemy.

Wright took up position on the Argonne front with
companion unit, the 367th Regiment, working as Battalion
surgeon. Behind the roar of powerful cannons and the launching
of screaming shells, the Germans attacked Wright's unit

attempting to dislodge the Americans from their position. Heavy artillery fire was followed by infantry offensives including fierce hand to hand combat. Casualties mounted and Dr. Wright treated the wounded under fire. The 367th fought back, the lines held, each time forcing the enemy to retreat in the face of its losses.

The Germans then mounted a psychological offensive. They sought to exploit and aggravate discontent among black soldiers because of the way they were discriminated against in their own country. It might be argued that the Germans had reason to believe they could be successful in this attack. The historian Philip Drotning said that World War I found "black Americans existing in the most discriminatory environment since the end of the Civil War." He wrote that while the men fought the enemy, "Jim Crow laws spread like crabgrass." The President of the United States and Commander In Chief of all armed forces, Woodrow Wilson, ordered segregation in "restaurant and restroom facilities for federal employees, [and] offered a flood of discriminatory legislation."

Seeking to exploit these conditions the Germans showered the black American soldiers on the front line with propaganda leaflets. One of the leaflet Wright and the others received read:

> What is Democracy? Personal freedom, all citizens enjoying the same rights socially and before the law? Do you enjoy the same rights as the white people do in America . . . or are you rather not treated as second-class citizens. Can you go into [any] restaurant . . . theater . . . is lynching . . . a lawful proceeding in a democratic country?

Despite the propaganda onslaught, and their own long-standing grievances, the black American soldiers rejected the German propaganda and continued fighting for their country. Wright worked long hours under adverse conditions to help keep American forces in as good medical condition as possible. The French government, in recognition of their valor under fire, awarded the black Americans the Croix de Guerre. American Commanding General John "Black Jack" Pershing told them he was "proud of the part you have played."

Dr. Wright was later placed in charge of the Triage or 366th Field Hospital where his work was perhaps even more demanding and often tense. To improve treatment of the wounded against shock, he used gum acacia, being among the first to show its effectiveness. After the war, in a paper presented to the Medical Society of the District of Columbia, he gave a detailed account of the benefits of this procedure.

Phosgene is a toxic colorless gas, and when inhaled produces nausea and irritates the lungs. The chemical name for this gas is carbonyl chloride ($COCl_2$). On September 4, 1918, the Germans tried chemical warfare and attacked Wright's unit with the deadly gas. Not being armed with gas masks, Dr. Wright, like other American soldiers around him fell under the gas attack. He suffered severe damage to his lungs and the injury plagued him for the rest of his life. For three agonizing weeks the doctor lay among the disabled in a hospital. All the while he struggled to get on his feet so he could go back and help those who needed him. Wright rejected a medical discharge so he could return to the front. Though weakened, Wright went back to duty and assumed responsibility for the surgical wards. On November 14, 1918, he received the purple heart and an overdue promotion to captain. The end of the war found him treating the sick and wounded at the Metz front.

Captain Louis Wright was honorably discharged April 2, 1919. He went to New York and set up private practice but kept his ties to the army by signing up with the Medical Officers' reserves. He soon rose to the rank of Lieutenant Colonel. But his medical practice grew heavy, and he was still weak from the war damage to his lungs. Sadly, Wright's health forced him to resign from the reserves.

As Soon As There Is A Vacancy

After he set up practice in Harlem, Dr. Wright applied for a position with the staff at the Harlem Hospital. He did so despite being fully aware that throughout the city, and without exception, black physicians were shut out of such appointments. Wright's decision to fight against these barriers evoke comparison with his improbable application to the Harvard Medical College and challenge of conventional wisdom that the Schick Test could not determine if Negroes were immune to diphtheria.

Upon receiving his application, officials gave him the standard response to black applicants, they would call as soon as a vacancy occurred. Wright persisted even though each of his frequent inquiries received the identical reply: "Sorry, still no opening."

Finally, one white doctor, familiar with Wright's published works, joined the fight against racially based exclusion. This coalition gained other allies who helped bring mounting pressure for change. Faced with incessant demands, the establishment made a small concession by naming Dr. Wright and three other black doctors Adjunct Assistant Visiting Attending Physicians, the lowest rank possible.

Normally a physician of Dr. Wright's qualification would have placed far higher but, though demeaning, it was accepted as a baby step forward. Even so, four white doctors, irate that even so minor a concession was made, promptly resigned in protest. Other doctors, clearly angry, punished the hospital superintendent for approving those few, lowly appointments of blacks, publicly humiliating him with a demotion to the position of garbage inspector. Some hospital personnel greeted black doctors and nurses with open hostility.

Yet there was no turning back. The determined campaign led to movement in other quarters that offered additional small hope for equal treatment. Dr. Jane Wright, reflecting on the fight, recounted one hope for change.

> This incident led Mayor Hylan to order an investigation of the city's hospital system, especially [at] the Harlem Hospital. Through an agreement between the medical board . . . and the mayor, the hospital [could] admit Negro physicians as adjuncts in the various specialties and to accept Negro interns who passed entrance examinations.

Discrimination still obtained however as hospitals froze black doctors in their low rank, irrespective of qualifications. Meanwhile,

Dr. Wright sought membership in the American College of Surgeons. Again he met with determined and resourceful opposition. Fabrications and vague guidelines that changed without notice were used to discourage Wright and block his admission to the ACS. As was his wont, Wright persisted, asking only to be judged on merit. After an arduous and protracted campaign, and aided by influential white physicians who were his friends, the ACS approved his application for admission. He became only the second black physician ever to hold membership in the college. He followed Dr. Daniel Hale Williams, the first surgeon to operate on the heart.

Treatment Of Trauma

is many interests Wright's medical engagements were broad in scope. One of his early publications involved Alcohol on the Rate of Discharge From the Stomach." ed by articles relating to the Schick Test, intradermal oculation against smallpox, and use of gum acacia. ed as a surgeon in the Emergency Ward of the he operated on all kinds of traumas. Of particular were fractures, especially injuries to the neck and head. In 1936, he invented a special brace for fractures of the neck designed to reduce the risk of serious injuries, including paralysis, when the patient was moved. His publication in the *Journal of the American Medical Association* entitled,"A Brace for the Transportation and Handling of Patients with Injuries of the *Association* Cervical Vertebrae," described the structure and use of the brace.

Dr. Wright also wrote the chapter on head injuries in the 11th edition of Scudder's standard text on fractures. Frank Kingdon, in citing the publication wrote: "His authority is recognized beyond the bounds of his local habitation, for to Scudder's important book called 'Treatment of Fractures,' Dr. Wright contributed the definitive chapter on skull fractures and brain injuries."

In 1948, Wright created a special plate brace for fixation of fractured thigh and shinbones. He described his innovation in an article entitled, "Operative Reduction and Fixation by Means of a

Specially Designed Blade Plate for the Treatment of
Supracondylar and T-Fractures of the Lower End of the Femur
and the Upper End of the Tibia." The article appeared in the
Harlem Hospital Bulletin in June, 1948.

Dr. Max Thorek, Surgeon-In-Chief, of the American Hospital
in Chicago, followed Dr. Wright's contributions in another area
of medicine. Writing on the subject, "The Human Testis and its
Diseases," Thorek recognized Wright as a foremost authority in
the use of sodium iodide in treating gonorrheal epididymitis.

Anatomist, physician, and anthropologist Dr. A. Montague
Cobb cited Wright, not only for his large scale projects, but also
for the variety of his works as shown by publications on subjects
like " ainhum, Madelung deformity, dicumarol, etc." In various
medical journals, Wright published findings and innovative
surgical procedures for traumas of soft tissues as well as traumas
of bone and skull. These included the repair of ruptures and
injuries to pancreas, liver, kidney, spleen, intestines and
abdominal areas, as well as the treatment of gunshot and stab
wounds. His intensive work in the area of trauma helped elevate
Harlem Hospital to a position of national prominence.

"Dear Doctor: I Wish To Let You Know"

Frank Kingdon described the essence of Louis Wright the
physician. His office was spotless. Four bookcases were filled
with technical volumes and the latest periodicals. His hands were
sensitive and strong, "almost as expressive as his eyes." He
projected an impression of "efficiency and friendship, the doctor
who is the first friend of his patient." In the operation room,
Kingdon said of Wright's surgical hands, "They work with speed
and precision, skillful to the point of art. You understand as you
stand by why here is a surgeon truly honored among his fellow
practitioners. . . here is surgery at its most expert."

Herbert Footner, in the publication, *New York, City of Cities,*
reported that doctors told him that by any standards, Dr. Louis
Wright was a brilliant surgeon.

Then there was an unexpected testimony that came from an expert of another kind, this one from a grateful former patient. She wrote a compelling letter in longhand.

Dear Doctor:

I wish to let you know at this time, that at the close of this year, it is eleven years since the most wonderful job of Surgery you've ever done was performed, and that was on me. Its a funny way to put it but I am in the best of health, I have no re-occurrence of the old rectal disorder. I thought you might like to know.

Dr. Wright never discarded that letter.

Aureomycin

Antibiotics have been known to science since the days of Louis Pasteur. Nevertheless, only after Sir Alexander Fleming's serendipitous and landmark discovery of penicillin in 1929, and its purification by Sir Howard Florey, E. B. Chain and associates in 1939, did these amazing substances began to play an important role in treating infectious diseases.

Flemings discovered penicillin in a penicillium mold (e.g., *Penicillium notatum)*. Soon scientists, hailing penicillin as a miracle drug, were searching other molds and the soil for other antibiotics since. In 1948, the antibiotic aureomycin, was isolated and described by Benjamin Duggars. Duggars extracted aureomycin, or chlortetracycline hydrochloride from the mold, *Streptomyces aureofaciens.*

Wright was contacted and asked to conduct the first clinical test using aureomycin on patients. Sound clinical research data is a critical step, among others, in the long process of bringing a promising medical drug to the market. The request also spoke to confidence in Wright for his medical research skills.

Dr. Wright's mission was to describe and identify in precise details the possible medical benefits and side effects of aureomycin. First he took an extra precaution with his subjects. Before administering the drug to any patient, Dr. Wright tested aureomycin on himself. He then investigated the curative effects and toxicity on twenty-five human subjects at the Harlem Hospital, his patients suffering from such afflictions as acute peritonitis, colon ulcer, a stubborn infectious chlamydial venereal disease (lymphogranuloma venereum), and other soft tissue infections.

Wright announced his findings, in the *Journal of American Medical Association, New York Academy of Science* and the *American Journal of Surgery*. Altogether he published 30 papers on his investigations with aureomycin, including a paper on treating lymphogranuloma. His paper on the treatment of lymphogranuloma venereum, in particular was considered a classic in medical circles. Eight other papers dealt with Wright's investigations of another early antibiotics, terramycin. Studies of that nature help to show and confirm that this was what is known as a "broad-spectrum" antibiotic useful against both gram-positive and gram-negative bacteria..

"If We Are Not Citizens"

It pained Dr. Wright that the health of the Negro was significantly worse than that of the rest of the nation. Health facilities for the Negro were too few; and Negro doctors and nurses, so essential an element in better health delivery, were in short supply. Nonetheless, more than numbers had to be addressed as these alone could not tell the full story. High standards, ethical practices, and equality of opportunity, he insisted, should mark the establishment of facilities where black patients were treated and where black doctors and nurses were trained. Wright vigorously opposed any and all practices or facilities where black doctors, nurses, and patients were treated as second class citizens. He vigorously summed up the underlying philosophy he and his colleagues embraced. In a letter to Edwin Embree, President of the Rosenwald Fund, he wrote,

> If we are not citizens, we feel we should be honest with ourselves and say so. If we are not entitled to the rights of citizenship as guaranteed by the Constitution of the United States, we feel we should be honest with ourselves and with you. On the other hand, we feel that sound

progress, as far as the colored physician goes, is to work and struggle as members of all other racial groups have done, to improve ourselves, our contacts, and to establish our rights. No other position in our minds, can be compatible with self-respect or intellectual growth.

His wont was to be combative on such matters, a tendency that frequently led him into conflict with significant others, including some blacks. He took issue with executives of the Julius Rosenwald Fund who promoted segregated hospital. He simply saw no place for such medical facilities. In opposing the Rosenwald people, Wright took on a powerful adversary.

The Julius Rosenwald Foundation, named for the philanthropist Julius Rosenwald, and established in 1917, announced as its objective to make significant contributions to the "well-being of mankind." An early initiative offered help to the Negro in education by providing matching funds for building new and much needed school buildings. Widespread gratitude among blacks followed.

In 1931, the Rosenwald Fund started a new initiative, setting as goal to build several "Negro" hospitals around the country. One was planned for New York City. The Rosenwald people believed that such facilities would elevate the health of the Negro by providing greater access to health caregivers, and would open new opportunities for the training of Negro doctors and nurses.

When Wright and his associates learned of the Rosenwald plans, including the news that the segregated hospital was to be established in their area, they objected. No local leaders, they replied, people who knew their community best, were consulted before making the decision. Views of the indigenous were never sought, their expertise ignored when deciding to build a segregated facility in their community. They saw condescension in the Rosenwald people and viewed their initiative as arrogant, misguided, uninformed and therefore not wanted, however noble the intent.

Wright wrote another letter to the Fund again protesting their disregard for what locals wanted. He maintained that "The comptroller of the Rosenwald Fund should not have sole discretion in deciding what is good, and not good for the Negro." About the

the segregated facilities, he said that,

> All methods and movements practiced by the Rosenwald Fund
> fix for the Negro citizens a definite status less than that for the average
> American citizen. Setups are arranged for him that are different from
> those employed for other racial groups in America . . . The Negro
> citizen, for his own advancement and progress along racial lines, needs
> no separate institutions. What the Negro physician needs is equal
> opportunity in practice - no more, no less.

Dr. Wright explained that his own investigations consistently
showed that "segregated hospitals represented a duality of
citizenship in a democratic government that is wrong." Invariably,
he found such hospitals to be underfunded and limited in size.
Due to the shortage of money, they were "inadequately
equipped," shortchanged in personnel, and in every case
maintenance of facilities came up short. Negroes had to occupy
"worn-out hospital buildings," that whites had formerly occupied
and discarded as unfit for themselves." All this, he believed, led
to health facilities and environmental conditions that were "most
deplorable." Dr. Wright wanted to know how could the human
mind work at its best under such conditions?

Convinced about the fairness of his position, Dr. Wright
continued to ask, what could these discriminatory policies and
practices lead to except inferior health for the Negro patient, and
poorer training for Negro doctors and nurses. The results, he
argued, were intrusive and promoted an unfortunate but pervasive
mindset that sanctioned inequality. Wright said that in such
settings, many, if not most, white doctors developed a superiority
complex toward the Negro. At the same time, many, if not most,
colored doctors and colored citizens developed an inferiority
complex. "These two complexes obstruct clear thinking, mutual
understanding, and mutual respect."

To right some of these wrongs, Wright called for the
elimination of "Jim Crow" hospitals. He wanted instead,
institutions where doctors, nurses, administrators/staff, patients
and auxiliaries were truly integrated. "For social justice, in

health matters", he said, "is an essential ingredient in any sound health center." The idea of building a "Jim Crow" hospital for blacks, "contravenes the Constitution of the United States, bows its head before racial prejudice, and offers a minimum of health protection to the American people." He went on to submit that "We [The Manhattan Medical Society], believe the establishment of this principle of equal opportunity for all, regardless of race, in the North, is not too much to hope for."

Wright's opposition to the Rosenwald plan brought him in conflict with blacks as well as whites who thought it best to accept the Rosenwald grant on the Funds' terms. To them, it was not time, nor practical, to integrate all the hospitals of New York. They regarded Dr. Wright as too bold, too impatient, too militant.

So the fight was joined but Wright refused to give in. Eventually, a new coalition formed when several whites joined forces with Wright and the Manhattan Medical Society. Together they succeeded in blocking the proposed segregated hospital.

"Disease Draws No Color Line"

Dr. Wright called for placing the health of the Negro on the national agenda, based on need. He asked for "no favor or consideration" but also no "double standard." Any epidemic in the black community, he said, would eventually spread to the white community. Any epidemic in the white community would eventually spread to the black community. He declared that "There is no such thing as Negro Health, disease draws no color line . . ."

Wright also made no attempt to conceal his displeasure with the American Medical Association. The refusal of AMA to accept black doctors as members was, as he put it, a "travesty of justice." Rather than meeting its sacred obligation to protect the health of *all* Americans, the AMA stooped to prejudice medical schools and public health services, to the detriment of the health of the Negro.

Consistent with his belief that a disease is a disease without regard to color, Dr. Wright opposed the celebration of Negro Health Week. He called the observance an "idea dishonestly born." Health problems, he contended, could not be solved in a single week. Instead, he felt "We need the same year round attention given all races." In an address to the National Health Conference, Wright repeated his position,

> Tuberculosis is tuberculosis wherever found. Syphilis is syphilis wherever found. Health problems are health problems wherever found.

Some black leaders took exception to Wright's position. They found a need for Negro Health Week in order to urge and to raise consciousness about good health practices. Negro Health Week, they said, offered the best opportunity to organize and educate the population toward improving the health of the Negro. They believed that Negro Health Week was a good idea for a good cause.

A fellow physician, Dr. Daniel Taylor, sought the middle ground. He proposed that Negro Health Week should be observed for now, and that it not be dropped until a good substitute could be found.

Colored Patients And Colored Nurses

A new controversy surfaced when an article in the newspaper, *New York Age* charged the Presbyterian Hospital with discrimination against a Black patient. According to the *Age,* the hospital refused to admit Martha Hill Brown, wife of a prominent clergyman Reverend Dr. Jonas Brown, to a private room. Representing the Uptown Medical Association Wright sent a letter to the hospital asking about the allegation and about policy governing room assignment. A hospital representative, Dr. Dean Sage, responded to Wright's letter. Sage wrote that is was the hospital's desire not to have the incident tried in the public press. Instead, he preferred to discuss the matter with Dr. Wright through the privacy of a letter. The letter went on to say:

> We have endeavored to remain silent in the face of a concerted and bitter attack. I feel however that your identification with the Uptown Medical Association, and the high regard in which we all hold you, entitles you to a personal answer to the questions which you raise.

Sage claimed that someone called the hospital and canceled the private room for Mrs. Brown because the cost was too high. He was unable to give a name, he said, because the caller was not identified. He also he had no supporting record or information by which the call itself could be confirmed. Sage failed to explain whether or not hospital policy permitted decisions about private rooms to be made on an unsubstantiated basis.

Wright thanked Sage for his "kind letter." He agreed that current dialogue should take place in the absence of ". . . unwarranted statements in the press." However, he made known to Sage that he found his answers unsatisfactory. Still, he would withhold final judgment until more complete investigations could be made.

In the meantime additional charges of discrimination were levied against Presbyterian Hospital. Wright wrote Sage another letter wherein he presented the position of the Uptown Medical Association with respect to Presbyterian Hospital.

> 1. The Presbyterian Hospital was established to serve all people without discrimination. During the most recent fund-raising campaign, there was no evidence of discrimination.

> 2. After the fund-raising drive was over, the hospital began discriminating against colored patients who requested private rooms.

> 3. No Negro nurses are enrolled in the Nurse's Training School of Presbyterian Hospital.

In response, Sage stated that the Board of Managers had no

formal policy of racial exclusion and planned none. For some reason he did not want that remark to made public saying, "What I say is not for publication." He then defended hospital practice arguing that Presbyterian was fair and should not be held accountable for all the allegations being made against it. Sage's position was:

1. Except "in very rare instances," all other hospitals in New York excluded Negroes from their private pavilions.

2. No private hospital in New York accepted colored nurses in the Nurses Training School.

3. Negro applicants to the school could not meet hospital standards.

4. New York City itself segregated Negro nurses by confining them to Lincoln and Harlem Hospitals.

5. White nurses would not want to work with colored nurses. The presence of Negro nurses would upset hospital routine.

The exchange between the two men continued. Wright accused Presbyterian Hospital of acting in bad faith when it failed to honor its commitment of fairness and nondiscrimination. He charged that,

1. The attitude of the hospital was worse than that found in the old south. Even the white southerner of the 1920's would not refuse to ride an ocean liner because a colored passenger occupied a first class cabin.

2. As for the qualification of Negro applicants, one Harriet Edwards, with impeccable credentials, was refused admission to the nursing training because of her color.

3. The decision on "Negro candidates should not depend on the objection of white students." Board managers should be firm and just. Why wouldn't white nurses work with Negro nurses? White

students from the south do not fail to attend Radcliffe because Negro students are present.

4. The fact that Negro nurses are segregated elsewhere does not make it fair or just.

Despite the differences between them, the two men continued their dialogue. Wright felt that Sage was making an honest effort to improve policy and practice at Presbyterian and that he was making a sincere attempt to seek some common ground. He believed that among all races there were people of good will.

"On Account Of My Book"

When Wright attended the Harvard Medical School he met a senior Negro medical student name William Hinton. Hinton was graduated from Harvard *cum laude.* The two men became friends and the bond between them lasted for life. Dr. William Hinton, known as "Gus" to his friends, made his home in Canton, Massachusetts, near Boston. Dr. Hinton worked at the Wassermann Laboratory and was Director of the Laboratory Department of the Boston Dispensary. He developed a new and innovative program to train laboratory technicians to be highly competent in basic techniques and skilled in the latest procedures. Hinton lectured on a regular basis in Preventive Medicine and Hygiene at the Harvard Medical School. His effectiveness in his work and outstanding classroom presentation earned the enthusiastic admiration of his students who considered him a master teacher.

Hinton may be best known in medical circles for his development of a serum test for detecting syphilis. Syphilis was the most deadly sexually transmitted disease known to humankind prior to the AIDS pandemic. He announced the test in 1927 after twelve years of painstaking research. Among medical authorities, his procedures were hailed as an important and major advancement in the field. In 1931, Hinton made additional refinements in his test. Five years later, 1936, he published a well-regarded text in medicine, entitled *Syphilis and Its Treatment*.

He could not have anticipated, however, that becoming a foremost authority on syphilis would create an uncomfortable dilemma. When it happened, he contacted his former Harvard schoolmate Louis Wright, for advice, recalling the good counsel he had received from his old friend on other occasions.

The dilemma came about when the Manhattan Medical Society wanted to honor Hinton for his outstanding contribution to medicine. He would be the first recipient of a medal given in recognition of the most outstanding work by a Negro physician for the year. When informed of his selection, Hinton wrote Louis Wright and wondered:

> . . . how anxious I am to accept this award. I am hesitant about the racial question brought up on account of my book. MacMillan Company is using a review from the Southern Medical Journal, and I am afraid my race might have an unfavorable effect . . . I am wondering what your reaction to it might be.

Hinton feared that if it became known that he was a Negro, prejudice would prevent some doctors from using his test. He worried about the consequences, feeling that rejection of the Hinton Test, in the absence of something better, would be a tragedy. He also worried that if some doctors based their rejection on his race, many cases of syphilis might go undetected and scores of patients untreated. To make matters worse, those potentially undiagnosed and untreated patients might continue to transmit the disease to others. So, if he accepted the award offered by the Uptown Medical Society, his race would become known with a possible unfortunate consequence to medicine. If he did not accept the award, he feared members of the Society would be offended, and he did not want to do that.

Wright agreed with his friend that he was in somewhat of a dilemma. In his reply to Hinton, he assailed what he called "the Pharisees" who would place race above merit in medical practice. He assured Hinton that regardless of the public stance of these

"Pharisees" that "they know damn well you have the best test and your book is the best book written on the subject."

Wright knew of course that such talk, however sincere, would not solve the problem. He took the matter up with the Executive Board of the Medical Society and explained Hinton's predicament. The doctors were sympathetic though they lamented what they saw as the hypocrisy that created the quandry. They did not want Hinton to suffer further pain over the matter and worked out a solution. Wright wrote to Hinton on behalf of his colleagues:

> I have spoken to members of the executive committee. They agree with me that for you to be publicized at this time would certainly hinder widespread use of your test . . . Just write them a formal letter that you regret your inability to accept their invitation without writing the reason.

Dr. Hinton was not alone in bringing problems to Wright. Columnist and author George Schuyler wrote Wright about his visits to an insane asylum in Mississippi. He had an unusual request. Schuyler wrote that given the oppressive conditions under which they lived, he simply could not understand why every Negro in the State was not driven to insanity. He was incredulous to find that many blacks actually wanted to stay in Mississippi. Even more astounding to Schuyler was the fact that some of them who left, actually returned with relief. He thought that perhaps Dr. Wright, eminent brain surgeon that he was, might operate to find the reason for this most baffling case of human behavior.

Another example of the many requests to Dr. Wright came from the author, Shirley Graham. Graham, who had written a revealing book on the black astronomer and mathematician Benjamin Banneker, (*Your Humble Servant*) was concerned about the welfare of her son, who was in a nearby sanitarium. Through W.E.B. DuBois, she asked Wright to please look in on her son. She wanted to know how he was doing, and trusted Wright's expert judgment.

"His Story Is Good Enough To Be Told"

Friends and family worried about Dr. Wright and the backbreaking workload he carried. He put in long and exhausting hours as a physician and hospital administrator. His involvement in civic affairs, where he was usually the spokesperson, and his role as National Chairman of the Board of the National Association for the Advancement of Colored People were each in themselves the equivalent of a full-time job. Dr. Wright's schedule was enough to break the health of the strongest person, let alone one suffering from badly damaged lungs. One day he became ill, so ill in fact that he could not go further. Diagnosis brought devastating news. He had tuberculosis. He may have remembered that when he was a young medical student, his mystery writer told him to avoid the "consumption."

Tuberculosis is a dreaded and highly infectious disease. It is caused by the rod shaped bacteria or bacillus called *Mycobacterium tuberculosis.* Most frequently the disease affects the respiratory system, but may also attack bones, joints, the nervous system, skin and other parts of the body. Symptoms include severe coughing (often expectorating blood), chest pains, shortness of breath, fever, sweating, poor appetite, and weight loss. Wright's lungs, already damaged, were further debilitated by the disease. Under the relentless eroding effect of tuberculosis, Dr. Wright the active physician, became Dr. Wright the seriously ill, inactive patient. Both were heavy burdens to bear, particularly the latter.

When word of his illness became known messages of regret poured in and "Get Well" wishes flowed from many quarters. The Harlem Hospital immediately sent a letter covered with signatures: ". . .we are rooting for you and look forward to the day when you, well and strong, will join us again", they said. The NAACP felt his absence sorely; especially his leadership. Dr. M.O. Bousfield, often an antagonist over health policy, expressed his deep sorrow over Wright's illness. Dr. C.C. Stewart of Greensboro, North Carolina sent a message to "Cheer up and do your best to pull over the top." A friend from Jamaica wrote about his shock and sorrow saying, "I only hope you will soon be on the road to recovery."

Isolation and complete rest were described. For nine long and agonizing months Wright lay on one side. He endured the pain, the sameness, the unchanged routine. The nurses attended to him with great care, and for that he was grateful. He tried to be a good patient, and for that the nurses were grateful.

As much as Wright worked, he was not a wealthy man. He did not send bills to friends he treated. Many patients failed to pay money owed him, and he never went after them. Costly business investments failed, possibly because he was too busy with his work, too trusting of others to attend such matters. So here he was, a sick man with family to care for, and two daughters in college. He also worried about his patients and his research. Worse, no one could guarantee he would get well enough to resume his practice. The weakness and the helplessness took a heavy toll on his body and spirit. Louis Tompkins Wright began to lose his once stout grip on hope.

On December 19, 1939, Dr. Frank Kingdon, President of the University of Newark, delivered a moving radio address over station WOR, dedicated to the ailing Dr. Wright. "This is a story of a doctor," he began, "as true an American as you will find in this wide continent." He continued: "Tonight he is lying ill, the result of his having been gassed in the war and overworked since. I do not know whether or not he is well enough to listen to what we say, but I do know his story is good enough to be told." He went on to tell the life story of his friend whom he called a "Patriot and Physician."

Seeing his restlessness and sagging spirits, his wife arranged for a change in location and took him to upstate New York. Wright entered the Biggs Memorial Hospital in Ithaca. His mother moved to Ithaca so she could visit her son daily and help cheer him up. This allowed his wife to return home to manage family affairs. From his hospital room overlooking a lake, Dr. Wright could take in the beautiful landscape, see people moving about, birds in flight, and watch the sway of treetops whenever they acknowledged a gentle breeze.

"How Do You Like Your New Nurse?"

In the new setting, Wright seemed to rally and found reason for a more hopeful outlook for his recovery. In November of 1941, Dr. Kenneth Deegan, the superintendent of Biggs Memorial Hospital, sent a progress report to Dr. Robert Wilkerson, Wright's personal physician in New York. Deegan reported that the patient's pulse and blood pressure were good and temperature normal. He was beginning to lose some of the weight gained through inactivity. Some lesions had subsided, and his sputum showed no tubercle bacillus over the last six months. He had progressed to the point where the ultraviolet treatment was discontinued. Deegan also reported that, "The patient's general condition would appear satisfactory, and he appears to be reacting well to the little activity he has." He also thought it important to note that patient felt he was doing better.

Nevertheless Wright was still very ill. Extensive tubercle damage remained, especially to the right lung. A weak body still plagued him so despite some progress, Deegan reported that, "There would, however, appear to be no indication to significantly increase his degree of physical activity at this time."

After a while, the novelty of the new setting wore off, and Wright became restless again. He started to feel that he was no longer improving, that his progress was at a standstill. He continued to fret that because of his condition, he was unable to provide for his family. The Veteran's Administration rejected his application for benefits as a disabled war veteran. They ruled that the damage he suffered to his lungs during the war had nothing to do with his present illness. The government would not help.

Then his wife told him that their daughter Jane wanted to go to medical school. Wright did not take the news well; he became agitated at the thought. It was the reaction of a father wanting to protect his child. Would she be able to withstand the rigors of medical school in a white, male-dominated field? He need not have worried. She was of tougher fiber than he suspected. Charming and outgoing, but also bright and hard-working, Jane Wright's high grades earned her a four year scholarship to the New York Medical College. There she did so well that she was inducted into the medical honor society. She ranked third in her graduating class. Her sister, Barbara Wright, also followed the long family tradition and became a physician.

Seeing her husband become increasingly despondent at Biggs, Corinne Wright decided to bring him home. He returned in better condition than when he left, but continued to be weak and helpless. With family finances strained, Corinne Wright dismissed the nurse. The next morning she walked to the door of her husband's room and said, "How do you like your new nurse?"

Of all the bitter times, this seemed the moment of his greatest despair. He did not want his lovely wife to have to do this. He should have been a better provider. Corinne Wright saw the hurt in her husband's eyes - and the anxiety. The burden of his affliction and distress over his illness eroded his once indomitable spirit. Would he ever be able to fight off the terrible damage to his lungs and body by the phosgene gas and tuberculosis? He began to feel sorry for himself.

But Corinne Wright would have none of it. She would take care of him and that was that. And he would get well too. So Louis Tompkins Wright went through five interminable years of affliction, three in the hospital, two at home. Eventually, though, he resumed his medical practice. After the return, he tired more easily. He could do no surgery because his lungs could not withstand the fumes from the anesthetic, but there was much work ahead. His mind was undimmed and spirit reclaimed. His "new nurse," that once "fresh funny looking girl, had done her job, and she had done it well.

Eight Newly Developed Procedures

In 1947 Dr. Wright founded the Harlem Hospital Cancer Research Foundation. It's mission was to conduct clinical research in the fight against cancer using chemical agents, or what is known as chemotherapy. The challenge was monumental.

Cancer is among the most dreaded of diseases. As his eldest daughter Dr. Jane Wright once pointed out, records show that cancer has been a scourge of humankind at least since ancient times. Scientist have even found evidence of cancer in the bones of dinosaurs. Efforts to cure cancer, going back more than four thousand years, have met with limited success. When the Harlem Cancer Research Foundation was established, the best medical approach to fighting cancer had been surgery and radiation. Chemotherapy was in its infancy, and not well regarded in medical circles. In fact, the establishment looked upon chemotherapy with disdain and considered it only a cut above quackery.

One may wonder why Dr. Wright risked his sterling reputation as a physician and surgeon to enter a field with so many unknowns, with so few guidelines, with so high a probability of failure. Cancer patients referred to him were those for whom all other saving attempts had failed. But people were suffering and dying, and Dr Wright saw promise in chemotherapy as another weapon to use in the fight against cancer. He knew that in this largely uncharted field, the task would be difficult. But his decision reflected his history of accepting tough challenges.

On December 13, 1948, Dr. Wright sent a progress report to his funding agent, the United States Public Health Services in Bethesda, Maryland. In his opening statement he reported,

> The study as originally stated in our application for the grant, has been confined to chemotherapeutic treatment for inoperable cancer cases for whom no other recognized form of treatment was available. Eight newly developed procedures were employed . .

The Center studied the effect of these drugs and screened them as chemotherapeutic agents. The Wright team treated 96 cases of various malignant lymphomas and carcinomas. Leukemia, affected lymph glands, Hodgkin's Disease, cancer of the breast, skin, liver, bladder, kidney, prostate, cervix, and other malignancies were treated. Dr. Wright explained in detail the reasons for selecting each drug, the basis for dosages, and the taking of biopsies. Among the drugs administered were teropterin, bremfol, and aureomycin. Patients were not treated as objects but as humans which, in a sense, added caring for the mind to caring for the body in a positive approach. Treatment included supportive services, among them transfusions and vitamins. Visitors from companies that supplied the drugs and professors including some from the London Institute of Cancer observed treatment at the Harlem Cancer Research Foundation.

In an address delivered in 1982, Dr. Jane Wright, who joined her father at the Foundation, explained the significance of his work. "These pioneering studies," she explained, "led to 15 significant publications demonstrating important remissions in a variety of cancer in man with the use of chemotherapeutic agents." She also pointed out that the Wright team was ". . .the first to demonstrate significant remissions in patients with cancer of the breast with methotrexate, a drug prominent in the treatment of breast cancer today."

Merit Alone

Because he so strongly opposed, and openly argued against segregated health facilities, Wright was sometimes criticized as an enemy of black hospitals and of doctors graduated by black schools as well. Not so, explained his friend, Dr. W. Montague Cobb. Dr. Wright, he said, was simply intolerant of mediocrity. What he opposed, explained Cobb, was the separation of minds and attitudes and the inferior facilities that invariably went along with such separations. In his life he had seen it, experienced it, and knew its eroding effects. That is why he was an uncompromising warrior in his insistence on high standards. He never wanted black patients or any patients, to come to him and receive inferior medical treatment. When it came to people, said Cobb, Wright was "indifferent to complexion." But his stand on excellence in the interest of his patients sometimes caused him to be misunderstood.

Dr. Wright worked just as hard to build a first-class hospital library recognizing this as a necessity for a top-ranked medical facility. After a while, friends and acquaintances got together and decided to name the library, the Louis T. Wright Library of Harlem Hospital, in his honor. At the inauguration of the library, Dr. Wright proclaimed that at this hospital, "merit alone in the light of the highest standard, governs the selection of personnel."

A white doctor who later became prominent in medicine told Dr. Cobb he had interned at Harlem. He remembered having an early encounter with Dr. Wright that etched itself deeply in his memory. He said to Cobb,

> I interned at Harlem Hospital and my first service was in surgery under Dr. Wright. I had no ambitions in surgery and as Harlem was a city hospital I had not thought standards would be too high. Hence my patients histories during my first week were sketchy and rather carelessly done. To my surprise the chief of the surgeries sent for me. Dr Wright handed me my charts and said, `Young man, henceforth while you are on my service, you will write *medical school* histories. Now is that clear to you?

It was. After that, the doctor said, he was never careless or sketchy again in recording medical histories.

That experience was typical of Wright. In his intense drive toward excellence he could be very sharp with interns who fell below the standards expected of them. There were times when he was known to humiliate one of them in front of others for failure to measure up. Later Wright would call the intern into his office and talk about excellence - about being a good doctor. In these sessions, Wright always conveyed a personal interest in them, and in their professional development.

That message was often repeated. In an address to a class of graduating nurses he said:

There must have been times when you thought we were being too exacting . . .[but we try to] instill in young hearts and minds the necessity of being able to compete with all other schools in the country . . .
Be ethical to your colleagues and patients. Be sympathetic with your patients.

Make Health Facilities Color Blind

The Wright philosophy held that improvement in the health of the Negro meant improvement in the health of the nation. Poor health among any segment of the population lowered the health standing of the country. When he assessed the health of the Negro, he found their conditions was "acute," "deplorable," and "appalling." Statistic after statistic supported his claim. For instance, the "general Negro death rate was one-third higher than the general population." In the rural area it was "81% higher."

On June 25, 1952, Wright addressed the 45th Annual Convention of the National Association for the Advancement of Colored People. His subject was, "Report on the Health of the Negro." He asked the audience to imagine that there was a similar gathering of whites in a hall on the other side of town.

We and those people in the other hall probably have more similarities than differences, but most of us are Negroes and most of them are whites . . . Every Negro man in this hall is going to die at an age approximately ten years younger than the men in that other hall. Every Negro woman is going to die almost twelve years sooner than those other women.

Then came the Wright manifesto of cause, the areas of greatest consequence on the health status of black Americans.

1. *Discrimination in Housing.* Ghetto housing in this country contributes to poor health. Overcrowded conditions, substandard dwellings constitute serious health menaces.

2. *Inadequate Education.* Statistics show the health of the educated to be better than that of the untutored.

3. *Work Conditions.* Millions of Negroes are underpaid and overworked. Too often they work under hazardous conditions and when they are ill. These situations contribute to permanent disabilities and premature death. There is little time for relaxation.

4. *Discrimination in Medical Facilities.* When facilities are segregated, the quality of health care suffers. In critical situations, some Negroes have died when they were refused admission to hospitals reserved for whites.

5. *Medical Education.* Late starts in medical education experienced by Negroes contribute to poor health. Discrimination by medical schools, and medical societies has led to lack of training for aspiring health practitioners. It has hampered mutual sharing of knowledge and skills among existing practitioners.

The underprivileged must not be neglected, he declared. There must be change and reform lest the health sore fester. Five areas in particular stood in need of change:

1. *Housing Reform.* Change state laws, city ordinances, mortgage regulations, FHA policies that unfairly deny decent housing to aspiring, qualified people. Legal initiatives are imperative. There must be a change in attitude.

2. *Education,.* Improve the schools, raise educational standards. Acquire the basics, "build a necessary superstructure of highly technical specialized knowledge."

3. *Employment and Legislation.* Take an active role in the political process through united action. Organize, use the machinery of politics and don't forsake the ballot. Work to raise wages, shorten

hours and improve working conditions. Support assistance for the disabled and aged. Push for implementation of a national health insurance policy as proposed by the Truman Administration.

4. *Medical Facilities.* There should be no separation of facilities based on race. In a poignant statement Wright recalled:

I have not forgotten the death of Juliette Derricotes following an accident near Dalton, Georgia. She was allowed to die because she could not get into a local hospital. How many Julliette Derricotes have died in this country and their deaths have gone unnoticed?

5. *Medical Education.* The country should provide the best medical training "without regard to race or creed." This applies to all colleges, medical schools, and hospitals. Deficiencies, all too often found in schools at the lower level where the minority race attends, must be eliminated. Negroes are 10% of the population but only 2% of the nation's doctors. Of the 26,000 students attending medical schools, only 780 are black. Of this number, all but 195 are enrolled in the two black medical schools, Howard and Meharry.

Dr. Wright was not a pessimist. He had hope. Medical schools, medical societies, and hospitals were making small but positive changes. He firmly believed that the great health problems facing the needy could be resolved, but not within the framework of separate training and care facilities. In an impassioned plea he said, that there must be a "A sharp break from the past -- with its taboos, traditions, myths and practices, and the building of a color-blinded health structure."

"Bitterness Does Not Pay"

Dr. Wright was a public figure, an outspoken icon. As such, he was often the target of slights and criticisms, some due to his race. His wife said he did not speak openly of his hurts, instead he tried to hold his feelings within. Nevertheless, he harbored a measure of bitterness over some of the slights and attacks born of petty and selfish origin, of ignorance or narrow prejudices. He was known to stand his ground in the face of confrontations he could not avoid because of duty and principle. On two occasions he even had to draw arms in the face of danger. Once it happened while a teenager in Atlanta, Georgia to help protect his family if harm threatened during a race riot. The other time came while overseas (England) in uniform during World War I, just before moving up to the front lines in France to face America's enemies. It was the most exasperating of situations, because he was on the brink of firing, not at German soldiers, but at his own countrymen who threatened his friends for no reason other than the color of their skin.

Earlier, during his last year as a medical student at Harvard, and just before final examinations, Wright used valuable time to protest the motion picture "Birth of a Nation" because of its biased and demeaning portrayals of blacks. Several white students joined him but his stance may have earned him silent enemies. And though for many years he tried, Wright could not forget that no one at Harvard ever apologized for his unjust rejection for membership in the medical honor society, nor had the University ever acknowledged his contributions to medicine. He received no support from any medical school for his hospital, and none offered him a faculty appointment.

Corinne Wright knew her husband well; she shared his burdens. She felt that sometimes his suppressed anger would cause him to be irritable, and he would snap at others. But one day, she said, he came to the conclusion that these were harmful emotions and that his work was too important for him to dwell on such things. He said to his wife, "Bitterness does not pay. It frustrates your efforts to do things. It cuts your efficiency. Therefore it is an evil thing. It is a destructive force."

Louis Wright was a leader. Corinne Wright said that others felt her husband's strength. He inspired people and they trusted him as a fair-minded man. His prodigious memory was legendary, but a more impressive attribute was his creativity. His mind often led him to make great leaps, and he was a steady generator of ideas. Though by reputation a stern man in his insistence on medical competence, many also knew of his sense of humor and the joy in his laughter.

There was no doubting Wright's great devotion to the Harlem Hospital. He was determined that it would provide the best in medical care for its patients, regardless of race. Wright upgraded the residency program and extended the time needed to complete all requirements. He built a first class medical library and founded a journal, *The Harlem Hospital Bulletin*, which became a respected publication in medical circles. At the Harlem Hospital he never made race a measure, neither for patients or personnel.

The Steady Hand

When, as a young army lieutenant, Dr. Louis Wright, first saw the comely Miss Corinne Cooke, he was struck by the efficiency in one so lovely. In fact even as she approached her 75th birthday, Corinne Wright's beauty impressed. Louis Wright was known to acknowledge her many good qualities and he often spoke of his wife's keen mind, her unflappable nature, and admirable character. He did not earn a lot of money, as one might expect of a person of his station and active practice, because he did not focus on such matters. When he reflected on his financial status, it pained him that his wife had to sacrifice and do without, but Corinne Wright never complained. She told Dr. Bluestone of Harvard, that she believed in her husband, in his work, in his vision. She shared his hopes, dreams, and ideals.

So Mrs. Wright worked hard to make a good and comfortable home for her husband and their daughters. She was the architect who guided the girls through a good, solid education, and a well-rounded upbringing. More than her husband's confidante, she was a steadying influence for the family during tough times. Through it all, this family matriarch was active in community affairs, promoting her husband's vision of a better, healthier society. Corinne Wright was the essential element in Louis Wright's success; she completed his life, and without intent, amplified her own.

"Here Shines Integrity"

For his many battles and numerous campaigns in the interest of

medicine and racial justice, earned Dr. Louis Wright the label
"stormy petrel."   He ruffled more than a few feathers.
Nonetheless, he was not without honor and recognition. In 1938,
he was awarded an honorary Doctor of Science (D.Sc.) degree by
his alma mater, Clark University. *Life* magazine called him the
"Most eminent Negro doctor in the United States." The physician,
anatomist, and anthropologist A. Montague Cobb said he was "at
once the most productive and distinguished Negro physician yet
to appear on the American scene." In 1940, the NAACP selected
Wright for its highest honor, the Spingarn Medal, which is given
annually to an African American for exceptional achievement and
contributions.

One of the more memorable recognitions came at the 25th
Anniversary reunion of his Harvard Medical School Class. On
that occasion, his classmates cited him as having made the
greatest contribution to medicine since their graduation. In some
respect, that recognition reversed the slight of 25 years ago when
he was denied admission to the Alpha Omega Alpha honor
society in medicine. After the ceremony, the man that he believed
blackballed him from the society wrote a letter of congratulation
and said he was proud to have been his classmate. In an article
written for the *Harvard Medical Publication ,* Dr. Arlie V. Bock
praised Dr. Wright for his "charter for action." He said of
Wright:

> The alumni of the Harvard Medical School may now add to their
> records one of the most significant events in their long history .
> . . We are given to honoring men for specific achievements in
> the advance of medicine, but a demonstration of national import,
> expressing an air of spontaneous affection and respect for the
> person and achievements of a doctor is rare. . . [Wright's]
> achievements in surgery are many, his skill in hospital
> organization and service exceptional, his social service to the
> nation great . . .
>
> Here shines integrity, high purpose, and persuasive personality."

Wright did not anticipate such high praise, but he received it with pleasure and grace. Among many other recognitions: He was made a Fellow of the American Medical Association and the National Medical Association, a Fellow of the American College of Surgeons, an Honorary Fellow of the International College of Surgeons, a Diplomate of both the American Board of Surgery and the New York Surgical Society. Dr. Wright served as the first black police surgeon for New York City. After his death, the American Cancer Society awarded the Wright family its highest medal in his honor.

All Men Live And Die But Few Men Live Greatly"

As has been repeated in this discourse, Dr. Louis Wright was the consummate physician, and a caring healer. But he was an impatient man , he felt there was so much to do. His quick, creative mind was always in gear, his standards were consistently high, and he drove himself with too little regard for his own well-being. Wright's fragile health, especially his damaged lungs, was severely strained by his exhausting schedule. One day the strenuous pace, and the heavy work load overwhelmed his stout spirit but weak body. On October 8. 1952, while at home, Wright suffered a massive heart attack, and died. He was 61 years old.

Dr. Louis Wright's passing was announced on the front pages of the city's newspaper. Expressions of shock, grief and sadness came from numerous quarters and his contributions to medicine and human rights were loudly praised. The great and near great gathered for his funeral services. Dr. Ralph Bunche, first black Nobel Laureate, Williams Hastie, first black federal judge, Thurgood Marshall, later to become the first black United States Supreme Court Justice, headed the long list of mourners. Prominent representatives from the medical profession, the judiciary, city and state officials, and police honor guards were in attendance. Perhaps though, what he would have treasured most about the massive turnout, was the outpouring of grief and sympathy from, "the little people", the "common people," many who lined the streets to say their final farewell as his funeral procession went by.

Bunche delivered a moving tribute. Speaking to an overflow crowd he said

> . . .For to know Louis well, was to love him, to know him at all was to respect him. He was that kind of a man - a man of strong personality, of unyielding integrity in both intellect and principle, of unflinching courage and indomitable spirit, of warmth and dignity and understanding of his fellow-man.

> . . .In any generation there are a few such men, and they can ill be spared . . . All men live and die, but few men live greatly and leave behind them the indestructible marks of their greatness, as Louis did and has done.

Dr. Wright was buried at the Woodlawn Cemetery in New York City.

References and Materials for Further Reading

Clayman, Charles B., "Diphtheria", 1989. p. 362, from *The American Medical Association Medical Encyclopedia*, Volume I, New York: Random House.

_____, "Smallpox, 1989. p. 918, *The American Medical Association Home Medical Encyclopedia*, Volume II, New York: Random House.

_____, "Tuberculosis, 1989. p. 1013-1014, *The American Medical Association Home Medical Encyclopedia*, Volume II, New York: Random House.

Cobb, W. Montague, 1953. "Louis Tompkins Wright, *Journal, National Medical Association*, 45: 130-148.

Drotning, Phillip, T., 1970. *Black Heroes in Our Nation's History*, New York: Washington Square Press.

Green, Richard L., 1985. (ed.), *A Salute to Black Scientists and Inventors*, Chicago: Empak Publishers.

Hayden, Robert C. and Jacqueline Harris, 1976 . *Nine Black American Doctors*, Reading, MA: Wesley-Addison Publishing Co.

Logan, Raymond A., and Michael Watson (ed.), 1982. "Louis T. Wright", pp., 670-671, in *Dictionary of American Negro Biography*, Washington, D.C.: W. W. Norton.

Seymour, Schoenfeld, *1945. The Negro in the Armed Forces*, Washington, D.C.:, The Associated Press.

Thomas, Clayton L., (ed.), 1987. *Taber's Encyclopedic Medical Dictionary, 15th Edition*, Philadelphia: F. F. Davis Co..

Volk, Wesley A., and Margaret Wheeler, 1984. *Basic Microbiology*, New York: Harpers and Row Publishers.

Woodson, Carter G., *1928. Negro Makers of History*, Washington, D.C.: The Associated Publishers.

Wright, Louis T., *et al*, 1936. "A Brace for the Transportation and Handling of Patients With Injuries of the Cervical Vertebrae", *Journal of the American Medical Association*, 106: 1467.

Wright, Louis T. *et al, 1948.* "Aureomycin, A New Antibiotic With Virucidal Properties. A Preliminary Report on Successful Treatment of Twenty-Five Cases of Lymphogranuloma Venereum", *American Journal of Surgery*, 138: 408.

_____, 1949. "Treatment of Acute Peritonitis With Aureomycin", *American Journal of Surgery*, 78: 15.

_____, 1953. "Subcutaneous Injuries in the Urinary Tract", *Harlem Hospital Bulletin*, 6: 6:65.

Notes from the Louis T. Wright Papers, Courtesy of the Archives, Countway Library, Harvard Medical School Library.

Letter of Recommendation for Louis T. Wright written by Professor Lawyer Taylor, December 10, 1910.

Letter from I. Garland Penn step uncle of Louis T. Wright, to Lyman Milts, April 24, 1911.

Letter from I. Garland Penn to Louis T. Wright, May 10, 1910.

Letter of Recommendation written by Reverend C. C. Neal, May 29, 1911.

Unsigned letter to Louis T. Wright, January 5, 1912.

Letter from B. J. Davis (family friend) to Lula Penn, mother of Louis T. Wright, July 20, 1914.

Letter from Vancouver (British Columbia) Hospital, to Dr. Louis T. Wright, April 17, 1915.

Letter from I. Garland Penn to Dr. Louis T. Wright, June 21, 1915.

Letter from Dr. W. A. Warfield (Freedmen's Hospital) to Dr. Wright, July 6, 1915.

Letter from Dr. William Penn, stepfather, to Dr. Wright, July 14, 1915.

Memorandum to Miss Ovington, February 18, 1927.

Louis Tompkins Wright, M.D., *The Southwestern Christian Advocate*, July 7, 1927.

"Dr. Louis Wright Raps Separate Medical Program Conference", *Newsweek Herald,* July 30, 1928.

Newspaper Account of discrimination by Presbyterian Hospital, December 1, 1928.

Letter by Dr. Wright to Presbyterian Hospital re: Martha Hill Brown, December 18, 1928.

Letter from Dr. Dean Sage (Presbyterian Hospital) to Dr. Wright, December 29, 1928.

Minutes, Manhattan Medical Society, commenting on the Sage letter (December, 1928 or January, 1929.

Letter from Dean Sage to Louis Wright, January 9, 1929.

"Equal Opportunity, No more, no less! An Open Letter to Mr. Edwin M. Embree, President, Julius Rosenwald Fund, Chicago, Illinois, from the Manhattan Medical Society", January 28, 1931.

"Charitable Segregation: The Julius Rosenwald Fund Not Wanted by Colored New Yorkers", *The Fraternal Review*, January, 1931.

"Medical School for Jews Rejected", *New York Times*, October 16, 1935.

Wright's remarks to the New Health Center, June 24, 1936.

"Comments re: Dr. Wright in Hubert Footner's *New York, City of Cities,* 1937.

Letter from Dr. William Hinton to Dr. Wright, December 1, 1937.

Letter from Dr. Wright to Dr. Hinton, December 8, 1937.

Article about Negro Health Week, *The Afro-American*, March 26, 1938.

Letter to Dr. Wright from George Schuyler, October 10, 1938.

Dr. Wright's "Address to the Graduating Class of nurses of the Harlem Hospital, *The National News Bulletin*, February, 1939.

Statement of Principle, Address presented to the National Health Conference, circa 1939.

Letter from C. C. Stewart, M. D. to Dr. Wright, circa autumn, 1939.

Letter from H. A. Bramwell, M. D. Jamaica, to Corinne Wright, circa, autumn, 1939.

Letter from Joel Spingarn to Dr. Wright, December 20, 1939.

Letter from Harlem Hospital to Dr. Wright, December 20, 1939.

Letter from John Bourne, M.D. to Corinne Wright, circa autumn, 1939.

Telegram from A. Bok, M.D., to Dr. Wright on behalf of Class of 1915, circa autumn, 1939.

Kingdom, Frank, "Patriot and Physician", *The Crisis*, 14-15, 1940.

Letter from John Deegan, M.D., Herman Biggs Memorial Hospital, to Robert Wilkenson, M.D., November 29, 1941.

Letter from Josephine Gibson (former patient), to Louis Wright, December, 1948.

Newspaper account of the first test using the antibiotic aureomycin, *New York Times*, circa, 1948.

Report by Dr. Wright to the United States Public Health Services, December 13, 1948.

Address to the national convention, NAACP by Dr. Wright, "Report on the Health of the Negro", June 25, 1952. (Last major address).

"Louis T. Wright Library of Harlem Hospital", *Journal of the National Medical Association*, 44 (1952) 297-309.

"Honor", Tribute to Dr. Wright probably delivered on the occasion of the dedication of the Louis T. Wright Library of the Harlem Hospital.

Articles on Dr. Wright following his death, *New York Times*, October 9, 10, 11, 1952.

Eulogy to Dr. Wright delivered by Ralphe Bunche, October 11, 1952.

Cobb, W. Montague, "Louis Tompkins Wright, 1891-1952, *The Negro History Bulletin*, May, 1953.

Notes on a meeting between Mrs. Louis T. Wright and Dr. E. M. Bluestone at his office on Tuesday, August 4,1953, 1:30-3:45 P.M.

"Louis Tompkins Wright, M.D., 1891-1952; Militant Medical Pioneer", Address by W. Montague Cobb, M.D., Ph.D., at the dedication of the Louis T. Wright Surgical Wing of the Harlem Hospital, October 30, 1969.

"95th Anniversary of the Harlem Hospital", Remarks by Dr. Jane C. Wright, daughter
    of
Dr. Louis T. Wright, November 1, 1982.

Special thanks to Dr. Jane C. Wright-Jones, daughter of Dr. Louis T. Wright for providing additional information through interview and for leading the writer to the Wright Papers at the Countway Library, Harvard Medical School.

Chapter XI_____

Frederick McKinley Jones - Turning Ideas Into Inventions
(1893-1961)

When the tall man with the wavy brown hair walked around the plant, he took in every detail; his keen eyes missed nothing. He appeared to be strong and possessed of an inner quality, a presence that projected an aura of quiet confidence. By leaving his office on occasion, he could better keep on top of things and be more accessible to his men when they needed his advice or help. Though soft spoken, there was no mistaking his impatience or even exasperation with poor or careless workmanship. Still he could not bring himself to fire a man, even when the worker's performance fell short of his high standards. They had families to support, he recalled.

By choice, he worked in a plain office, not paneled or carpeted like the other executives. To him, beauty was not in such trappings but in a smoothly working switch on a machine that snapped into place with precision, a well-designed valve, or an intricate, integrated machine that got the job done. Throughout his life he had worked hard to achieve such ends. A creative man, an inventor, he did not always conform to conventional standards but he valued work and study above all else.

Frederick McKinley Jones held a management position with the United States Thermo Control Company of Minneapolis, Minnesota. He had come a long way from the circumstances of his birth in Cincinnati, Ohio, and his early years. Born May 17, 1893, Fred was the only child of poor, working class, interracial, parents. After his birth things grew worse before they got better. His story however represents a triumph of mind and spirit over an impoverished beginning and difficult times.

Fred never knew his mother. His father, a tall, red headed Irishman, told the boy that his mother was a pretty black woman but beyond that nothing is known about her. By some accounts, Fred's mother died while he was an infant, but by others, she left her husband and young child never to be seen by them again.

John Jones worked as a laborer with a railroad company. Because of his long hours on the job, he arranged for neighbors to look after Fred. Apparently he left only a few loose rules, or the rules were not enforced because the boy had freedom to do as he pleased. Sometimes Fred got into fights and other mischief, but mostly he amused himself taking things apart, and putting them together again. At other times Fred roamed the streets and chased cars. He loved automobiles, fascinated by their speed, power, and grace. John Jones marveled at his skinny little son's curiosity about how things worked.

Sometime between the ages of seven and nine, Fred lost his father. As with his mother the reports conflict, and in similar fashion. Either John Jones died when Fred was nine, and a Catholic Priest named Father Ryan took him in, or John Jones left him with the priest who lived in a rectory across the Ohio River from Cincinnati in Covington, Kentucky. By the latter account, Jones placed Fred under the care of Father Ryan so he could get an education and learn some discipline. He then returned to Cincinnati and Fred never saw or heard from his father again. So regardless of the version, Frederick McKinley Jones became an orphan at a very tender age.

The lad lived in the rectory with the priest and worked to earn his keep. He split wood, kept the fires going, scrubbed floors, shoveled snow, and sometimes even cooked. His formal schooling, spotty at best, ended at about the sixth grade level.

Living at the rectory was not an easy adjustment for Frederick because he had always been on his own, doing mostly what he wanted to do. When he lived at home, the lad never had chores nor a regular schedule to do things. Father Ryan however, believed in strict discipline and insisted on a structured lifestyle for young Fred. Nevertheless the rigid life at the rectory did not extinguish his curiosity and he yet embraced a growing passion for knowledge, especially mechanical things. He kept probing, seeing magic in how different parts made machines worked, wanting to know more about what made them tick.

Actually a ticking thing, a watch, may have been one of the first things the youngster fixed. According to an article published years later in *The Minneapolis Tribune,* while still at home in Cincinnati, he noticed that his father's watch was not ticking. "He took it apart, examined it very carefully, . . . figured out what was wrong and fixed it." Such logical thinking, and the ability to make associations suggest a mind mature beyond its years. Little Frederick McKinley Jones was only five years old when he repaired his father's watch.

Know What You Want to Be

One day the celebrated poet Robert Frost spoke to students at Miami University in nearby Oxford, Ohio. He told them that they should know what they were before deciding what they wanted to be. Frederick Jones never heard Robert Frost speak but he knew what he was - someone with a fascination for things mechanical and a talent for understanding what made them the marvelous wonders they were. Fred Jones also knew for certain what he wanted to be; a person who knew machines intimately, down to the fine detail, and the mysteries of their operation. He always wanted to fix things, and fix things he did. That was not all. Fred also wanted to make machines better, and he wanted to make new and useful things.

Not much work or activity was available for Fred outside the rectory in Covington. Nevertheless he kept busy whenever he got a break from his chores, especially when he could work on cars. Then after some seven or nine years with Father Ryan, the youngster decided it was time to leave, to strike out on his own. At the age of 14 or 16, Fred left the security of the rectory, crossed the busy Ohio River again, and returned to his hometown of Cincinnati. Arriving penniless, Fred immediately set about looking for employment. He found a car repair shop where he applied for a job. In fact he talked the owner into hiring him as a journeyman mechanic, not at the beginning or apprenticeship level. Fred had a knack for cars and he quickly proved his worth. After he had been at the shop for a while, people used to say that he only needed to put his hands on a car to make it run better.

At the young age of 19, his boss promoted him to the position of garage foreman. Before long, Fred began to indulge in his other passion - books and technical journals. He read all the mechanic books in the garage, absorbing the technical details. When he needed additional information Fred went to the library and checked out other books and journals. He learned about the internal combustion engine and the scientific principles behind them. Once he understood these principles, creativity set in. From that point he started working on racing cars because he had ideas that would make them run better and faster. Fred started building race cars before he was old enough to drive them.

Unfortunately his strong interests and talents got him into trouble. One day Fred felt such a compelling urge to see one of his cars speeding around at the races that he left work abruptly and went to the tracks. In doing so, he disobeyed his boss, a man named Crothers, who had told him not to leave work that day. Such behavior was uncharacteristic of Fred because he loved his job and it showed in the time he spent at the garage. His insubordination so angered Crothers that he gave Fred a tongue-lashing. He had specifically told him to remain at the shop and he did not do so. Just who did he think he was, running off like that? Then he suspended Fred to teach him a lesson. No doubt he intended to send a message to the other employees as well.

Years later, while being interviewed by Steven Spencer of the *Saturday Evening Post*, Jones remembered that he did not take kindly to being laid off. Miffed at Crothers, he decided he wasn't going to take such treatment, boss or no boss. He told Spencer:

Well Crothers was a swell fellow and I certainly deserved the lesson. But I was a touchy kid then and I just up and quit and decided to take a trip to Chicago to see the sights.

So off he went to the big city of Chicago. After seeing the "sights," and experiencing America's largest Midwestern metropolitan center Fred caught a train he thought would take him back to Cincinnati. He mistakenly took the wrong train however and in doing so set in motion events that permanently altered his life. When Fred realized his error, he, chagrinned at his carelessness, simply got off at the next stop, Effingham, Illinois, a town previously unknown to him. .

Hungry, Fred Jones went to the Pacific Hotel that stood next to the rail line, to get some food. There he found the owner upset and worried about his paying customers because his boiler was broken and no one could get it working again. Seeing the man's distress, Fred offered to help him with his problem. Now what did he know about steam engines and hot water boilers? Nothing. To his restless mind however, the boiler seemed like a challenge and that appealed to his curious nature. Something was broken so perhaps if he looked it over he could figure out what was wrong and repair it, like he did his father's watch. He hadn't known anything about watches either. The troubled owner accepted Frederick's offer having no other alternative to meet his dilemma.

Rolling up his sleeves, Fred got busy. He looked the boiler over, peered inside, shook things, pulled and pushed, trying to make logical connections and figure things out. But this was no car, it was no watch and Fred Jones slowly realized he had met his match. Beside, the boiler was old and long neglected, more a candidate for the dump heap than a repair job. Nothing Fred did seemed to work. After about two hours, "Mr. Fix It" was about to give up in despair and embarrassment. Fortunately a man who had been curiously watching his futile efforts, asked Fred if he could use some flue tools. If so, he would be happy to make his available. Now what the heck were flue tools? Fred knew less about them than he did boilers. Still he felt he had nothing to lose and graciously accepted the bystander's kind offer. Once he saw those flue tools however, the whole picture changed in a flash. In speaking with Steven Spencer about the incident, used a metaphor to explain:

Of course, as soon as I laid eyes on the flue tools, I knew just how those darn pipes were supposed to be fitted. If you saw a slotted screwhead and a screwdriver for the first time, it wouldn't take you long to figure out how to use the screwdriver, would it? Well, that's the way it was with the flue tools

The analogy was typical of Frederick Jones and how he perceived things. He had a way of connecting the old with the new, the known with the unknown. Armed with the proper tools, and with his own imagination, he quickly fixed the boiler. The grateful hotel owner than asked Fred to work for him. Still "smarting" over his "lesson" from Crothers, he decided to accept the offer. Anyway he had quit the job in a huff so he really saw no reason to return. Seeing the hotel job as a new set of challenges, Fred began working at the Pacific Hotel.

Hallock, Minnesota

According to the *Gopher Historian*, a man named Walter Hill, son of a prominent American railway empire builder, stopped at the hotel in Effingham on his way home. Hill needed a good mechanic to keep the machinery on his big 50,000 acre farm, operating. The locals told him about Fred Jones, the "wizard" with machines. So Hill found Jones, told him about the job, and asked the young man questions about his qualifications. He liked what he heard, about Jones' ideas, his range of experience, and his extensive knowledge of mechanical things. Satisfied with what he had heard, Walter Hill offered Fred Jones a job as a mechanic on his farm in Hallock, Minnesota.

Hallock, Minnesota is a long way from Cincinnati, Ohio and from Effingham, Illinois too. Minnesota, famed for its more than 10,000 lakes and clear blue skies, is almost in the center of the North American continent. Hallock is in the far northwest corner of Minnesota, only a few miles of North Dakota and just south of Canada. Winters can be long, the temperatures dipping far below zero on the Fahrenheit scale, producing weather more harsh than anything Fred had ever known in Cincinnati, or Effingham. Nevertheless, the opportunity to work on all those machines was a lure too powerful for him to resist. Jones took the 800 mile trip to Hallock to begin a new career.

He arrived in Hallock on Christmas Day in 1912 and found it in the grip of a howling, swirling, snowstorm. The bitter cold, the fierce weather that day, pretty much kept even the hardy Hallock residents indoors. Visibility was so low that a person could see only a few feet ahead. Still Fred Jones had no feeling of foreboding or inclination to leave.

Jones grew to like Hallock and before long it became home. A few people in the area warned their daughters to stay away from that fair skinned black man at social events, but mostly he found acceptance and a friendly environment. Jones knew what it meant to be treated otherwise, had experienced problems and meanness, and had felt the sharp sting when called a nigger. But in the Hallock community he was comfortable and perhaps most important, the job on the Hill farm brought him great satisfaction. There he could work on a variety of machines; steam engines, gasoline machines, tractors, cream separators, graders, and others. What an opportunity!

At first, Jones knew nothing about the electrical power plant on the farm so he bought books on electricity. After that, he kept the electrical plant in good working order. He also worked on the fleet of Packard cars the Hills placed in his care, keeping them running smoothly. The automobile remained his great love.

Virginia Ott and Gloria Swanson lived in Hallock some years after Fred moved away. They never met him but without inquiry on their part, heard stories about Fred Jones almost everywhere they went. Impressed by the many tales of the legendary figure who "could fix anything and make things better," they decided to write a book about his life. The two women, both professional writers, carefully and thoroughly research Jones' life and in the process interviewed many people who knew him well. The more they learned, the more impressed they became. In 1977, they published a book entitled *A Man With a Million Ideas: Fred Jones. Genius/Inventor*, about this fascinating former Hallock resident. Then in 1994, Swanson and Margaret V. Ott published a second book entitled *I've Got an Idea: The Story of Frederick McKinley Jones*.

An interesting "side" story Ott and Swanson learned about Jones revealed how he acquired the nickname "Casey". They said it started after the Hills purchased a steam tractor for their farm and sent Fred to Minneapolis to bring it back on the train. The authors wrote that upon arrival in Hallock the tractor was unloaded and Fred stood on the platform for some parting words between himself and the locomotive engineer:

> As the train pulled out, the engineer (who had invited Fred to sit in the cab with him on the trip from Minneapolis), leaned out the cab and yelled, "So long Casey Jones! Take care of your baby!" The song about Casey Jones and his Cannonball Express was being sung across the country that year. No one in Hallock knew that the man who wrote that song was Wallace Saunders, also a black man, a road house worker, and a friend of the real Casey Jones.

In the community, "Casey" took part in various social and recreational activities. He enjoyed singing with a local quartet, and played the saxophone as a member of the band. His instrument had once been an old, battered and discarded horn that he fully restored and customized for himself. Jones loved music as he did machines, making an interesting connection between the two. He reasoned that in the separate parts of each, they usually meant little or nothing. If however, the various parts of each, music or machines, are properly woven, they make the whole a magnificent work of art. Such beauty!

Jones did not always *play* music at the various social events. The tall, handsome young man, graceful on his feet, often enjoyed the company of ladies in a dance around the floor. He also took to the outdoors, sometimes fishing, other times hunting. Fishing and hunting were favorite pastimes among men in and around Hallock.

A major change occurred in Jones' life in 1916, four years after he arrived in Hallock. James Hill died, whereupon his son, Walter Hill sold the farm and moved away. Jones left the farm also and relocated to the village. There he worked in a garage owned by Oscar Younggren and helped him build race cars that Jones often drove at County fairs. "Casey" built innovations in the cars for speed and added safety features said to be 20 years ahead of his time. Before he retired Jones set speed records in and around the area that lasted for decades. His speed innovations significantly influenced the industry and his safety features, maybe more beneficial, were widely adopted.

The First Portable X-ray Machine

Among his many friends in the village, was Dr. A. W Shaleen, a local physician. Dr. Shaleen had many books and Jones often borrowed them to read and satisfy some of his curiosity about the field of medicine. Along the way he designed and built a motorized snow sled for the physician, which allowed him to reach his sick patients when deep snow made it impossible for him to travel by automobile. Typical of him, Jones came up with a new design for the snow sled and he built the vehicle cheaply out of discarded materials. For propulsion, he fitted the snow sled with an airplane propeller and for safety of the physician and others, he enclosed the propeller in a strong cage.

Jones also made several surgical instruments for different physicians and repaired medical machines when they broke down. Perhaps his most unusual and notable contribution to medicine came following one of his conversations with Dr. Shaleen. The physician expressed frustration about not being able to X-ray patients locally. By the time they made the rough and tiring trip to the city, some were worse off than they had been before leaving. If only he could X-ray the patients locally, at bedside. He could not however, because X-ray machines were too big, and too cumbersome. They had to be specially installed by highly skilled technicians in a hospital. Their cost placed them out of reach for small communities like Hallock.

Dr. Shaleen believed there could never be a portable X-ray machine capable of doing the job but Fred Jones was not so sure. What was the meaning of this word "never?" He did not know. Perhaps he could build an X-ray machine, something affordable, workable, and light enough to be portable.

First he had to learn something about X-rays. Briefly he delved into the history of X-rays learning that these strange manifestations were a form of very short wave electromagnetic radiation (0.1 to 10 nanometers) with great powers of penetration. The rays are produced when a stream of electrons, emitted from what is known as a cathode, strike a metal target, the anode, in a vacuum tube.

Wilhelm C. Roentgen, a German physicist, serendipitously discovered X-rays on November 8, 1895. With that discovery, he joined a small group of scientist who ushered in modern physics. Recognizing he had made a new and amazing discovery Roentgen carefully studied and described in great detail many properties of the invisible rays before announcing his findings to the scientific world. Still, the exact nature of these invisible rays remained a mystery so he called them X-rays as they are referred to today. Fittingly, scientists also call them Roentgen rays, after the discoverer.

The announcement about X-ray discovery was of immediate interest to scientists and non-scientists as well. Applications soon followed in medicine and also in industry. In medicine, doctors took "shadow" pictures of internal organs, both hard and soft tissue, "seeing" them without making incisions. Before long, physicians began using X-ray radiation against tumors, another weapon against cancer, and other unwanted growths in humans.

With his usual intense concentration, Jones studied the science and technology of X-ray machines in great detail. He had so much to learn. Often he and Dr. Shaleen would talk about the phenomenon after which Jones would go away and all those "ideas would go running around in his head." He put his general thoughts down, then began filling in the details, setting up the various specifications. Ott and Swanson said he went about the village collecting scrap parts he felt would help carry out his plans. He found some sheet metal here, an old spark transmitter there, a transformer that would have to be rewired. He informed Dr. Shaleen, however, that he would have to purchase the cathode tube. Step by step Casey assembled his parts. Finally it was complete and awaited a test. Would it work? Remarkably the first test showed it did.

Unfortunately some of the pictures were not consistent in their clarity. Fred spoke with Shaleen who told him not to worry. The big, high cost machines had the same problem. The physician was ecstatic. Jones was unhappy. He had new ideas he thought would make it better. Ott and Swanson told what he did:

> Fred went over to the newspaper office and got some linotype metal. He cast this metal into a big flat sheet about one quarter of an inch thick. From the side of the sheet he sawed out strips of metal. Then, after placing a film beneath the object to be photographed, he put the strips above the object and the x-ray above the metal.

The innovations worked. Much to the joy of Dr. Shaleen, and the satisfaction of Jones, the machine produced good pictures every time, not sometimes as was true of the commercial machines then in use. Swanson and Ott, as did others, declared that Fred Jones invented the first portable X-ray machine. According to Ott and Swanson, he never profited from his invention. They explained why.

> Fred's portable x-ray was used for years in the Hallock hospital. It was transported from room to room on a little rubber wheeled wagon. The idea of being paid for the hours of work put into making that machine never entered Casey's head. And it never occurred to him to apply for a patent. But within a year after Casey made his portable x-ray, a similar x-ray machine was being sold in the United States. It had been invented and patented by a German engineer named Gustav Bucky,

Making a "Talking" Movie Projector

In 1917, when the United States entered World War I, Jones enlisted. Assigned to the Minnesota 809th Pioneer Infantry Regiment, he soon rose to the rank of sergeant. Jones served his country gladly but felt humiliated by the nation's policy segregating military personnel by race. He was shipped to France with a unit of electricians that often worked near the front lines under enemy fire, until Germany surrendered in 1918. After the war, Jones returned to the United States where he was honorably discharged.

Back in Hallock, Jones noticed a surging interest in a new invention, the home radio. The home radio became possible after Lee deForest invented the audion in 1906. This unit, based on the "Edison Effect" (discovered by Thomas Edison in 1883), led to an improved vacuum tubes providing the breakthrough for the home radio. Local citizens enjoyed the entertainment and news the radio brought right into their homes from places around the country and around the world. Never had news traveled so fast to so many. Jones recognized that a new era in communication had begun. He decided to get involved with electronics, which was the basis for the radio. This was, in part, an extension of his knowledge and previous experience with electricity .

Of course Jones collected books on the subject and began his self-educational process. He studied about sound waves, and the electromagnetic spectrum. The relatively long radio wave, about which he was gathering information, was located along the spectrum opposite to the very short X-rays that he had already learned about. Just as he had improved race cars by including some of his own innovations, Jones had fresh ideas about electronics also. He developed a condenser that improved the performance of the microphone, an innovation that was adopted universally.

Among the most fascinating discoveries about Casey by Ott and Swanson was one of his "idears" he never developed. Jones thought that radios were too bulky and that there should be a way of making them lighter. What he felt radios needed was a smaller, lighter, and solid amplifier that could replace the bigger vacuum tubes. Then radios would weigh less, be more compact, and more able to withstand jarring and falling. For this Jones needed capital, local "scraps" would not do. But the idea was too revolutionary and quite possibly venture capital was limited in Hallock. Unable to raise the needed funds, Casey reluctantly abandoned the quest. In 1948, about 25 years later, John Bardeen, Walter Brittain and William Shockley, working on the same concept, invented the solid state transistors and received the coveted Nobel Prize. Casey had been on the right track.

He turned to other things. The publication, *A Salute to Black Scientists and Inventors*, edited by Richard Green, described how Jones created an interesting and entertaining sound movie system that was enjoyed ony by the people of Hallock:

> He built the first transmitter for the Hallock radio station and designed a "talking movie projector. Although a typical movie projector would cost about $3,000, Jones built one from odds and ends for less than $100. When motion pictures incorporated sound tracks, Jones built his own device using creative ideas and information he had researched.

Thomas Edison invented the silent movie and patented a device called the kinestescopic camera (1891). Later, the sound movies, or "talkies", developed after deForest discovered how to record sound directly on film. During the early years sound projectors were expensive, but worse, could not produce good sound with consistency. The theater owner in Hallock could not afford the purchase price of a sound projector so he showed only silent movies. Jones, believing he could convert the silent to a sound projector, bent to the task. Pulling together scrap supplies, he produced a workable and inexpensive sound movie projector. Many people in and around Hallock who had gone to the movies in larger cities, thought Jones' machine produced superior sound quality. That seemed plausible since Jones would not have settled for less. Once again, he had made something better and without profit to himself.

In essence Jones saved the movie business in Hallock. The owner, losing money with the silent movies was about to close his business. With the Jones projector, business picked up and he began making a healthy profit. The small village of Hallock enjoyed sound movies when most of the nation could not afford to do so. That latest invention added greatly to Jones' reputation which, unknown to him at first, was spreading beyond the boundaries of his small, northwest Minnesota home.

Joseph Numero

Joseph Numero did not know Fred Jones but had heard about him and his talking movie projector. Numero, who owned a company in Minneapolis that produced supplies for movie theaters, needed help in solving some sticky problems with his commercially produced sound movie projector. So he invited Jones to come to Minneapolis for a job interview and possibility affiliation with his company. At first Casey hesitated to accept the invitation. He liked Hallock, he was content in the small rural environment, it was home. A friend, however, urged him to go and look things over and if matters did not work out, he could always come back to Hallock.

The meeting almost never took place. When the 37-year old Jones arrived at the company, he told the secretary that he was there to talk about a job. Numero, expecting a "Mr." Jones instructed his secretary that he had no job for a "colored boy". When the secretary informed Jones he was not expected, Casey showed her the letter confirming his appointment. However flustered, Numero recovered enough to invite his visitor in for the interview. The two men began to talk.

Almost instantly Numero recognized the unusual qualities of Jones, his intelligence, and breath of knowledge. After the extensive interview, he introduced Jones to the men in the plant and upon seeing how they gravitated around him, listening intently to his every word, he knew he had found the right man. Numero hired Jones as an electrical engineer and though things did not always go well between the two strong-willed men, a bond of genuine friendship formed between them that lasted for life. At the company, Jones immediately made his presence felt to the benefit of its earnings. Cinema Supplies began selling its improved movie sound equipment to the great markets of the country. These included establishments in Chicago and Radio Corporation of America in New York. Numero saw his profits go up dramatically.

Jones created many new devices, modified and improved even more. Nevertheless he received little money beyond his salary and no official credit for his inventions. The matter of credit changed, at least partially, with his first patent for an automatic ticket dispensing machine. Designed for use in movie houses, he assigned the patent (No. 2,163.754) to Nation-Wide Manufacturing Corporation of New York City. Jones carefully crafted the machine for ease of use so the operator did not need special skills. In the vernacular of today, he made a machine that was "user friendly." His ticket dispenser, that included safeguards against jamming, a property critical to efficient operations at busy movie houses. The machine ejected each ticket in full with no partial ticket cutoffs. Built for long time use, the rugged device could operate "over long periods of time with freedom from all difficulties." It seldom called for repairs. The Jones ticket dispenser became a staple item throughout the movie theater industry.

Heat and Mosquitoes and Air Conditioning

The productive capacity of the American farmer stands among the great success stories in American history. A major problem for farmers though was in getting their products to market on a reliable and consistent basis. When transporters encountered unexpected delays on trips, or sudden increases in temperatures, or both, despite the best available insulation, ice could melt long before delivery. Under such conditions valuable commodities, meat, milk products, fruits and vegetables, spoiled, causing disappointments to those waiting for deliveries and considerable loss in revenue to all. The matter of preserving farm commodities did not concern Joe Numero and Fred Jones - at least not initially. They were successfully involved in the movie equipment business and that consumed their time and attention. Two events however, seemingly unrelated, led to a major change in direction for Numero's company.

The first incident involved Fred Jones on a hot, humid, summer night. Jones had driven out to one of several lakes near Minneapolis for relaxation after a long, hard, day. Details of what happened appeared in a story published in the May, 1949 issue of the *Saturday Evening Post*:

> He [Jones] was trying to get a breath of cool air. But every time he opened the car windows, the mosquitoes swarmed in on him, and when he closed them he continued to swelter. `Why,' he asked in exasperation, "doesn't someone make a gadget to air-condition a car, like they do in the theaters?"

After that experience, Jones went to the library. New "idears" ran around in his head but first he had to answer some questions. Had someone already made an automobile air conditioner? If so, how well did it work and what were its major flaws? Could a company profitably produce automobile air conditioners commercially? Following extensive research, Jones concluded that automobile air conditioning was an open field. That being the case, the next logical step was to learn as much as he could about the science and technology of refrigeration and air conditioning. He already knew cars and he knew them well. What he needed and what he lacked, was a solid understanding of refrigeration.

Reading books and journals, putting his ideas in new forms, combining his knowledge of the automobile with what he learned about cooling, Jones believed that an air-conditioning system for automobiles was feasible. Sketches took form. His diagram showed arrangements for switches, fuse units, wiring and connecting parts for power, location of the compressors, fans, and ducts with controls for getting cool, refreshing air inside the automobile. He then reviewed each item making sure he left nothing out and that his unit could be accommodated by the power plant of the automobile. Finally Jones went to Numero. He laid out the drawings and sketches, explaining each detail as he went along. Good try, said Numero, but he did not believe it was practical. Too heavy, he thought and the cost too high. No one would buy it. The company would lose money. Reluctantly Jones set his idea aside, similar to the time he stop working on the solid transistor project.

There are times when dreams and thoughts, even those that appear unfeasible, lay dormant, perhaps somewhere in the subconscious mind. Then something triggers that thought and it emerges, though not always in recognizable form. Numero thought he had dismissed Jones' "idear" about cooling automobiles when the second connecting event took place. During a golf outing he bet a playing partner that his [Numero's] company could place a workable refrigeration system in a transport truck to protect perishable goods against spoilage. To Numero, it was a joke, he was not in the refrigeration business. Nonetheless, to his unsettling surprise, his golfing companion took him up on he bet. He delivered a truck to Numero's firm asking him to fit it with a workable refrigeration system, as he had said he could do. The move caught Numero off guard.

Others had tried to refrigerate the transport truck but they had failed. Numero tried to wiggle out of the commitment. In the meantime, Fred Jones learned about the situation and saw he truck out on the lot. Quickly he altered his plans for air conditioning the car, gathered his men and, almost catlike, "pounced" on the job. Air conditioning and refrigeration - both in essence the same and operate on the same principle. Jones lost little time in seizing the opportunity.

Jones had known that earlier truck refrigeration systems failed largely because the units could not stand the jarring, vibration and pounding as the trucks sped down all kinds of tough roads.

Most systems were too heavy, too bulky to be practical. Jones drew on his days when he built race cars that had to withstand such shaking and pounding. He made his vehicles safer but also lighter and won races because they survived the grueling contests. Back then, he had come up with plans that helped "shockproof" his cars. On more than one occasion Jones had resolved tough problems of fitting some device in a space so small that no one else thought it could be done.

When he finished with the truck, Jones had devised and installed a rugged refrigeration system, yet more compact and efficient than the others. It could deliver, and it could take the pounding. For the first time a truck refrigeration system worked successfully. With its success, fresh food product entered a new era, and the eating habits of American permanently changed.

Even so, Fred was not yet satisfied. He believed he could make his system work better. Soon after installing the first model, Jones worked on improvements. The original model, placed under the truck and out of the way, cooled quite well but Jones noticed it sometimes got clogged with mud from the road. The system could easily be cleaned off but the requirement posed an inconvenience. With a slight redesign, he located he system over the cab. The arrangement also placed the system out of the way and did not use storage space. Jones went on to improve the environmental air control in the commodity storage area to maintain optimum freshness. *The Minneapolis Tribune*, reported that Fred Jones "revolutionized refrigerated transportation." After the truck refrigerator proved successful, and seeing a market in the field, Numero formed the United States Thermo Control Company of Minneapolis.

Serving His Country - Again

As noted earlier, Fred Jones joined the armed forces during World War I where he helped make electricity available to the Allies near the front line. During World War II, Jones contributed even more to the war effort as a civilian. The *Gopher Historian* reported on some of the several ways Jones helped America during the war through his inventions:

> When the United States entered World War II, . . . Jones adapted his portable cooler to many military uses. He designed automatic units that were flown to field hospitals that were in the South Pacific. Some contained blood serum and others medical supplies which had to be kept at exact temperatures. He built cooling units that were taken to islands in the Pacific and were taken to jungle outpost by helicopters. He made others to be used on airplanes for the benefit of wounded soldiers, Some of his units could produce heat or cold according to need.

No doubt Jones air conditioner saved lives. In the hot, stifling heat of the Pacific War Zone, wounded Americans often lay in hospital planes long periods of time before being cleared to take off in dangerous areas. It was healthful and comforting to have Jones' cooling system operating during the delay. Spencer said that Jones' system could also cool "the engine nacelles[separate enclosures for aircraft engines] of B-29s in the Pacific. This allowed a speedup of the reconditioning of motors. Without this help, the mechanics had to stop work every few minutes."

Refrigerated Rail Cars

After his successful innovations of the truck refrigeration system, Jones turned his attention to the refrigeration of railway boxcars for the shipping of farm produce. He called one of his first railway inventions, "Methods and Means for Air Conditioning." His patent application, No. 2, 696,086, was noticeable in its clarity, thoroughness, and attention to details. He made 37 detailed drawings covering every facet of the system. His accompanying narrative indicated that Jones had included in his research the best conditions needed for food preservation, accounting not only for the best temperature ranges but also for optimum conditions of humidity to maintain produce in the freshest condition possible. Jones considered specific needs of different products shipped and accommodated them as well. The versatility of his systems will be further described later on. Jones always worked to provide maximum freshness, and prevention of early spoilage when food is removed from refrigerated conditioning. At one time he observed:

> Foods which have been preserved by severe freezing can be kept in practically perfect condition for a year of so if they are maintained at temperatures ranging between -10°F and 0°F. However, some of these foods, such as fish, poultry, orange concentrate, strawberry and the like, will either spoil or change in flavor in a matter of hours if their temperature is permitted to rise as much as +20°F.

Jones' refrigeration inventions maintained a temperature of 0°F or lower for a "substantial period of time." He design delivered cooling or heating depending on need. Jones also invented and installed on his units, control panels that allowed operators to monitor the internal conditions of the cars and to control temperature and humidity as needed.

Another useful feature of the unit was the flexibility of railcar use. Unlike the old ice and brine cars, operators could remove the Jones refrigeration units when desired and use the cars for purposes other than refrigeration. The fuel supply necessary for operating the [refrigeration]"could be removed in a few minutes, and if wanted, could be replaced by another unit." As to cost, Jones' system was distinguished by its economy of operation.

Jones and Numero went on to build air conditioning units for ships, airplanes, and of course, cars. Thus the dream of an inventor, born on a hot humid night in the midst of swarming mosquitoes, became a reality. The benefits of this technology in terms of health, comfort, and nutrition have been enormous, no doubt far outstripping anything that even Fred Jones envisioned. Thermo King was soon doing business into the billions of dollars annually.

Flying Leaps to the Top of the Mountain

In all, Jones patented 60 of his inventions. As indicated, he created scores of worthy items that he never patented and therefore did not receive credit for them. After going to work for Numero, most of his patents pertained to refrigeration, but not all. He also invented a two-cycle engine, a unit that could heat or cool, a self-starting engine, and an automatic ice cream machine.

Over the years, many people sought Jones' advice on technical matters, college-trained engineers among them, some with graduate degrees and others with years of experience. Jones respected these people of letters with their formal training and learned from them. He sometimes fretted about own his limited formal education, considering this lack a handicap. Nonetheless, Jones' professional judgment of people was based more on what they could do and how they thought, not what degree they held or did not hold. Sometimes though, he criticized what he saw as shortcomings in the educated, especially young and inexperienced engineers. He told Steven Spencer that some of them "never realize when they have the wrong answer - don't know how many zeroes they have to have before the decimal point." He felt that they worked too much with figures and not enough with the real thing. Jones believed that figures should be secondary - a sort of measuring cup to prove an estimate.

Casey Jones believed that mathematics was a valuable tool to help convert the abstract to concrete reality but always it was the mind that conceived the possibility and mathematics was the servant of that possibility. He would agree with the 18th century mathematician Carl Gauss who proclaimed that "Mathematics is the Queen of the sciences," but also saw it as the Enabling.Prince of technology.

In his approach to inventing, Jones would start with something that existed, then dream, of something that did not. He would begin with something concrete, move to the abstract and return with a new product, concrete and complex yet simple, out of an abstraction. An acquaintance, in describing his genius and unusual qualities of mind, said that Jones could take flights of imagination without having to grope along the usual step-by-step process to reach his goal. Jones, he averred, "was not fettered by conventional thinking," but could simply take a "flying leap to the top of the mountain." Ever mindful of his fellow workers, Jones would back down from the mountain "cutting steps" for others to follow and himself to trace.

"I Would Rather Work and Study"

As mentioned earlier, Fred Jones and Joseph Numero became great friends. Nevertheless it was not unusual for the two men to fight over one company matter or another. Sometimes they fought so hard that onlookers would think they had fractured their relation forever. But always, the men would talk, mend fences, and renew their bonds.

As for money, Jones had a history of owning little. Before going to work for Numero, he would fix or make things for people at little or no charge. At times he gave credit and some never paid him. What money he had, Jones often gave away to friends. Despite his position at Thermo King, and contributions, "Casey" Jones owned no part of the company. When asked why he replied simply, "Didn't want to. You get too much money and you lose touch. " Jones never wanted to lose touch with his work. As he told Jay Edgerton of the *Minneapolis Tribune*, "I would rather work and study than do anything else I know,"

On the other hand, Numero made sure his friend remained in good financial health. He never forgot that Jones was a primary factor in the company's billion dollar success.

"First, Don't Be Afraid"

A few other words about the Jones character. Spencer pointed out that a lot of what Jones learned over the years was "hammered out on the hard anvil of experience." He learned much from reading, of course, having a great capacity for comprehension and retention and he absorbed knowledge by listening to others. Though he never returned to Hallock to live, he retained a fondness for its people. In turn, Hallock residents were proud of him. When they visited Minneapolis, many would look him up. Sometimes, when friends would come by, usually unannounced, Fred would drop everything, much to the dismay of his workers, and take the "home folks" out on the town. Several Hallock residents landed on the Thermo King payroll, because of Fred Jones.

Despite his social nature, one could not call Jones a talkative person. Robert Smith recounted how Jones once gave a rare "little speech" to the Phyllis Wheatley society when they honored him for his inventions and contributions to society. As noted elsewhere in this book, Phyllis Wheatley was born in Africa about 1761. Brought to Boston as a slave, and later set free, she was one of the first women in America to publish a book of poetry. It was read and praised in this country and abroad.

Speaking briefly to the Wheatley Auxiliary, Jones' short address threw light on his philosophy of life, which philosophy grew out of his years of work, struggles, and success. Said the sage,

> There are three ways you get to be successful. First, don't be afraid to get your hands dirty. Second, you have to read. You don't have to buy books. Use the libraries. And third, you have to believe in yourself. Don't listen [when] others tell you you're wrong. Remember, nothing is impossible.

"My Head is Like a Machine"

While a young man in Hallock, Jones married an attractive Swedish woman but sadly, the union did not last. Fred Jones was too undisciplined with his odd working hours and he spent too much time away from home. He would give his money away to friends in need so, because of his generosity, Casey often came home broke. After the breakup of his marriage, Fred Jones thought he would never wed again. "What woman would want to put up with a person like me?" he asked, wistfully. Even his workers found him difficult with his lightning swift mind, near perfect memory, and nonconformist ways.

Still this man who never really had a family occasionally felt a void that work and his restless mind could not fill. That changed when he met, and a year later married, Louise Lucille Powell. Of German background and Jewish faith, Lucille's first husband died while she was pregnant with their only child, a son. Somehow she understood Fred better than most. Her patience and disposition, which served to cope with his eccentricity, also gave direction to his days. In turn, Jones loved his new wife and appreciated her qualities. He often said to her that it was his great misfortune that he had not met her 20 years sooner. How different his life would have been, and how much better. Lucille made his house a home and he was comfortable in it. When he came in from work, she would play records of his favorite music as it helped him unwind. He best liked Irish songs, perhaps a legacy of his father, and interestingly enough, compositions by Chopin. Once while listening to a beloved tune, he said to Lucille, "Listen mama, see how it all fits together?" To him, good music and a well-designed machine were alike, their parts all fitted together.

With his Lucille, Fred finally had someone to share his inner feelings. She told Ott and Swanson about the time he reached into his soul and revealed why he did not sleep very well. He told her he had all those ideas running around in his head. "My head," he said, "is like a machine. It won't let me rest. If only I could turn it off." It was a revealing insight into the mind of a genius.

It pleased Lucille to see how Fred and her son quickly bonded. Fred felt good about his new situation and looked forward to being a husband and father, who would send his son to college someday. At last he had something missing all his life-- a family. The Joneses live in an apartment that had been built for Fred above the factory.

Unfortunately, tragedy soon struck when their young son unexpectedly died of leukemia. Together, the couple grieved their loss, grateful for the solace they found in each other. Later when Lucille's mother became infirm she asked Fred if it would be all right to take her in. "Its your mother", he said. Of course it was all right. He couldn't understand why she felt the need to ask.

Succeeded Where Others Failed

Though not acclaimed nationally, Jones was not without recognition. In 1944 the American Society of Refrigeration Engineers made him a member. Several times he went to Washington at the request of the federal government to serve as a consultant to the United Department of Defense, the United States Bureau of Standards, and the Army Quartermaster Corp.

Jones' enthusiasm for his work never waned but the ravishes of age, and personal neglect began to erode his once great stamina. As his health declined, he spent more and more time in the hospital. On one occasion, he underwent brain surgery but his mind continued to be sharp, his prodigious memory remained intact, and ideas continued "running around in his head." Even as his condition worsened, Jones maintained a positive outlook, an optimistic view of his life. He told a nephew of his wife that he had few regrets. He had enjoyed a good life and lived pretty much as he wanted to live.

On a winter day, February 21, 1961, Fred Jones could no longer continue his valiant fight for life. He died of lung cancer. Only death stilled his active mind and put to rest the ceaseless parade of ideas in his head. In the end, the words of Pindar, written around 5 B.C. seemed applicable to him. Wrote Pindar:

> I will work out the divinity that is busy within my mind and tend the means that are mine.

After his death, a great tribute of love from his wife. She told Ott and Swanson:

> Life with Fred was never dull . . . We had only 15 years together, but I wouldn't have missed them for anything.

Funeral services for Frederick McKinley Jones were held at Hodroff and Sons Mortuary in Minneapolis. His body was interred at the Fort Snelling National Cemetery.

On July 10, 1977, 16 years following his death, a significant honor was bestowed on Jones when he was inducted posthumously into the Minnesota Inventors Hall of Fame. At the request of his widow, Lucille Jones, J. A. Numero, the honorary chairman of Thermo King, accepted the member plaque for his old friend. The plaque included an inscription that read in part, that Frederick McKinley Jones "succeeded where others failed."

References and Materials for Further Reading

Burt, Jr., McKinley, 1969, *Black Inventors of America*, Portland OR: National Book Co.

Edgerton, Jay, "Crack Engineer Shuns Praise: Work and Study are Fun to 'Genius'", *Minneapolis Tribune*, May 4, 1949.

"F. M. Jones in Minnesota Hall of Fame," *Midwest Motor Transport News*, 6:9, December, 1977.

"F. M. Jones, Thermo King Official, Dies," *Minneapolis Tribune*, February 22, 1961.

"Frederick McKinley Jones: Black Genius," *Gopher Historian*, 1-4, Fall, 1969.
Green, Richard L., (ed), 1985. *A Salute to Black Scientists and Inventors,* Chicago: Empak Enterprises, Inc.

Hayden, Robert C., "Frederick McKinley Jones, 1895-1961," in Logan, Rayford and M. Winston (eds) 1892. *Dictionary of American Negro Biography*, New York: W. W. Norton and Co.

Havighurst, Walter, 1969. *The Miami Years, 1809-1969*, New York: W. W. Norton and Co.

Hertz, Will, "Way Found to Keep Produce Fresh," *Minneapolis Tribune*, February 5, 1951.

Ott, Virginia and Gloria Swanson, 1977, *Man With a Million Ideas*, Minneapolis, MN: Lerner Publishing, Co.

Ploski, Henry and James Williams, 1989, "Frederick McKinley Jones," *The Negro Almanac*, New York: Gale Press.

Scientific American, 1981, *Scientific Creativity and Genius*, New York: W. H. Freeman and Co.

Smith, Robert T., "Tribute to Fred Jones" *Minneapolis Tribune*, February 16, 1977.

Spencer, Steven M., "Born Handy," *Saturday Evening Post,* 31, 153-155, May, 1949.

Toppins, Edgar, 1971. *A Biographical History of Blacks in American Since 1528,* New York: David McKay, Inc.

Chapter XII_____

Percy Julian-Born To Be A Chemist

Casting furtive glances around him to see if anyone were looking, the young lad raced quietly to a fence surrounding the school. He pulled himself up, and peered across the yard into the open windows of the building and tried to make out just what those youngsters, fortunate enough to be enrolled in a chemistry class, were doing. As he watched one student heat some substance unknown to him, the wistful youth wondered if someday, somewhere he might be able to study chemistry.

For a while, he imagined himself in that school, learning, and having fun with science. Lost in fascination, he did not hear footsteps approaching from behind. Suddenly, a harsh, authoritative voice jolted him back to reality. "Hey boy, get away from here!" The startled youngster looked around and saw a policeman pulling him down from the fence. Quickly he released his hold, dropped down, and raced away - from the fence, the school, and the chemistry class. As he ran away, the youth heard the policeman telling him not to come back. It was not a friendly voice.

The young boy, Percy Julian, was black. The high school in his segregated hometown of Montgomery, Alabama, was for whites. Alabama had no public high school for blacks, except in faraway Birmingham. That school, overcrowded, poorly financed and without a science laboratory course, could hardly serve Percy in his thirst for chemistry.

Never Settle for Mediocrity

Percy Lavon Julian was born April 11, 1899 in Montgomery, Alabama, the oldest of six children. Among his siblings were two brothers, James and Emerson, and three sisters, Mattie, Erma, and Elizabeth. Their parents, James and Elizabeth Adams Julian, had as a goal that their children would have the best education possible. Though firm in discipline, they provided an environment that was warm and caring. In this family of modest means, pride, self worth, and hard, honest applications of mind and body were promoted as virtues. Persistence in quest of chosen goals, they felt, offered the best promise of achievement and other worthy rewards.

So it was that best efforts toward excellence was the centerpiece of the Julian family tradition. These values came to James and Elizabeth Julian from their hard working parents who knew slavery before they tasted the freedom that came after the Civil War. Elizabeth had the major responsibility for rearing the family and she provided a steady hand. Her husband's job as a railroad mail clerk kept him from home on long train runs.

When James Julian was traveling it was his wont to strike up conversations with passengers, and when he met a "well-educated person" he often asked them to recommend books that would help educate the mind. As soon he could afford to do so, Julian would purchase the books, which included Homer, Shakespeare, and other classics.

Julian had became attached to philosophy, elocution, and mathematics. He read the books he purchased, encouraged his children to read them too, and to understand their content.

If these sessions did not make clear the James Julian's emphasis on excellence, a single incident, which became a part of the family lore left no doubt. Percy Julian recalled the time when he proudly showed off a paper where he had received a grade of "80" in school. His father however, was unimpressed. He explained to his son that an "80" was mediocrity for which he should never settle. His goal, he explained, should always be a "100". The sharp retort left young Percy a bit stunned but he never forgot that simple lesson, and as the astute James Julian no doubt intended, nor did his siblings.

Percy had great admiration for his father. He once described the family patriarch as a man of formidable intellect. With pride he told of his father's self education, and disciplined habits of mind. "He was a mathematical genius," Julian said, and "he had that gift of imagination and correlation that could have made him a most brilliant scientist."

Why a Chemist?

Despite the unpleasant incident outside the high school, and the dim prospects to study chemistry, young Percy told his parents that he wanted to be a chemist. The announcement greatly perplexed his father. Why, he wondered, would the boy want to be a chemist? Whoever heard of a black chemist? A lawyer perhaps, a physician, yes. But not a chemist because that would mean becoming a teacher. If he became a teacher, why he would starve to death. He strongly urged his son to study medicine and become a physician instead.

Many years later, Dr. Anna Julian, the wife of Percy Julian, told the writer a story she believed to have influenced the young lad's feelings about becoming a physician. Young Percy took a paper route in his neighborhood to earn pocket change. During that time, physicians routinely made house calls. One day as he delivered papers, Percy happened upon a scene that gave him pause. He overheard a doctor telling a patient that he would not write a prescription she needed because she owed him money. Disturbed, Percy decided if physicians must behave that way, he did not want to be one.

DePauw University

While James Julian contemplated where Percy might go to college, he met a woman passenger on a train where he worked She caught his attention with her deportment and literary breath. The woman attended and graduated from DePauw University

Greencastle, Indiana. Impressed, James Julian decided that if DePauw could produce such a person, then it should be a good school for his Percy. There his bright young son could have his mind challenged and get a solid education. Why at DePauw, maybe Percy would forget this ridiculous notion of becoming a chemist, and study medicine instead. Right there he decided that Percy would go to school at DePauw University.

So it followed that Percy applied to DePauw and the school accepted him for admission. The day of his departure for Greencastle, Indiana was one of memorable drama. The family gathered at the train station and bade good farewell to the first of their family ever to attend college. After the kisses and embraces, Percy boarded the train and sat near a window. Looking out, he saw his diminutive grandmother. Now well into her 90's, her once quick, nimble fingers had picked a record 350 pounds of cotton in one day. He saw his grandfather who waved a hand with two fingers missing. An angry slave owner had them cut off when he discovered the black man could read and write. His mother stood there, sad to see her eldest leave, but sending him off with her love. Next to her stood his father. To Percy, his goodbye salute seemed to urge him to go out there and "make it 100."

Many miles separate Montgomery, Alabama, from Greencastle, Indiana. Montgomery, with a population of over 30,000, was a deep south city in culture and tradition. Greencastle, a small college town located in the Midwest differed in customs, habits, dialect, topography, buildings and climate. Montgomery had a large black population, rigidly segregated along racial lines. When Percy arrived at DePauw, he was the lone black student enrolled. Such changes called for a considerable adjustment by the 17-year-old.

Percy had not the luxury of a gradual acclimation to the rolling hill country of Greencastle, Indiana, its institutions, and its people. He settled down quickly, and went about his business. First Percy found a place to stay, then a job to supplement his small scholarship.

Unfortunately neither Percy nor his father anticipated the heavy class load he would have to carry. When officials at DePauw examined his record, they judged his academic background too impoverished to classify him as a regular freshman. Especially he lacked the Latin and English background required of DePauw students. So they sent Percy to Ashbury Academy to earn "proper" high school credentials. Percy attended Ashbury for two years while carrying a full load at the University.

Meanwhile, he found work as a shoeshine boy at a barber shop in the Village of Greencastle. Later, Percy worked for a campus fraternity where he waited tables and started the furnaces each morning. His pay consisted of meals and free lodging in the attic. He earned extra money by playing the piano and saxophone with a small band. Although versatile in the music he could play, Julian was most fond of jazz, spirituals, and the classics. He enjoyed a lifelong love of music.

The extraordinary demands imposed by work, academic overload and his extra-curricular activities might have been daunting to a person without his uncommon ability and staunch determination. Percy understood his situation, but he remembered some things taught at home, about how serious application of mind and effort could serve one well in difficult times. It also must have been of considerable help that Julian met with a friendly reception at DePauw and Greencastle. Mostly, he remembered his years there with favor.

Despite the heavy work and study loads, Percy Julian established a brilliant record at DePauw. When James Julian saw how well his son had done, he quickly decided that his other five children should go to DePauw and get a good education. They must first get a sound high school background and avoid the difficulties that Percy encountered. His decision was quite bold, seemingly based more on a dream than reality, because his income could hardly meet the cost of so ambitious a plan. James Julian however, was as resourceful as determined and he came up with a plan. He decided to move his entire family to Greencastle. Then he went to his superiors and persuaded them to change his train route so that Greencastle, not Montgomery, would be his home base. Once in Greencastle, the Julian children must have made their parents proud because all six of them received a bachelor's degree from DePauw. All continued their education and went on to earn professional or graduate degrees. Both of Percy's brothers became physicians.

Feeling Betrayed

As much as he respected his father's views, young Percy Julian knew that he still wanted to be a chemist. At DePauw, he met Dr. William Marshall Blanchard, a chemistry professor who influenced his career and a became a lifelong friend.

The professor, Dr. Blanchard grew up in North Carolina. He joined the chemistry department at DePauw in 1901. Over the next 40 years, Blanchard placed his imprint on the chemistry department and the university as well. In his publication, *History of the Chemistry Department at DePauw University: 1837-1987*, Professor Donald J. Cook referred to Blanchard as a person unusually dedicated to the academic guild. He described him as a man of foresight but also of compassionate nature. Dr. Cook said that under Blanchard, the chemistry department grew in statue and earned respect in the academic community.

During Julian's student years at DePauw, Blanchard was professor and chair of the chemistry department. The white professor from North Carolina and the black student from Alabama came to know and like each other very well.

Articulate and well versed, Julian became quite involved in campus affairs and was a popular figure. Drawing on his religious background, he often spoke at the campus chapel. His reputation and impressive oratorical skills brought him to the attention of a white congregation in a nearby community who, one summer, made him a substitute minister. He also dug ditches and worked on various construction jobs.

By his senior year, Julian had earned the highest cumulative average in chemistry. He was also a Phi Beta Kappa scholar and valedictorian of his graduating class. Approaching the end of his undergraduate studies, Julian contemplated graduate school and eventually the doctorate in chemistry. Of course he did not have the money but the chemistry department had a long-standing tradition of finding fellowships so its majors who so wished, especially the outstanding ones, could continue their education. As the days went by, Julian's classmates would tell each other where they were going . . . to Illinois . . . to Michigan . . . to Ohio State and other graduate schools. When Julian could not respond in kind, they simply said that apparently they, were saving the best for last. Percy, they said, would surely get one of the "plums," like Harvard, Yale, University of Chicago, or the like.

An anxious Julian waited . . . and waited. Then he began to wonder, where was the plum. Finally with the suspense becoming too much to bear, Julian went into Blanchard's office and asked, "Professor, did you get me a fellowship?" Blanchard told Julian he had been expecting him. He thought he would come. Holding up a handful of letters, he told Julian he had written to many universities and received many replies. They accepted the other students he nominated but all rejected Julian. It would be a waste to educate a black man to the doctorate in chemistry, they said. They argued that industry would not hire him. If they did "the white boys would sabotage his work" and exasperate the project director. White universities would not accept him on their faculty. One letter suggested that Blanchard persuade his "bright colored lad" to go south and teach in a black college. The writer said, he wouldn't need a Ph.D. to teach there.

Julian listened to Blanchard, stunned. His plans, so confidently conceived, suddenly smashed and lay in ruins. No fellowship after all and the painful realization that scientists he held in awe, respected scholars, champions of scientific objectivity, rejected him, not on merit, but race. Hurt, humiliated, and feeling betrayed by these men of science, Julian fought hard to check tears of disappointment.

Blanchard, sympathetic and discomfited by Julian's obvious

pain, tried to reach out. He told his star pupil that he had arranged an interview for him about a teaching position. The president of Fisk University, a black institution, would be on campus the next day. Then he offered words like. "Don't be discouraged," and "I'm sure you are going to make a good teacher."

The past flashed across Percy's mind. Four years of hard work and sacrifices, his father the "wise man," asking, "Do you wish to starve to death?" No doubt he thought of Elmo Brady, also of Alabama. In 1916 Brady became the first black in American history to earned a Ph.D. in chemistry. Would he, like Brady, be forever shut out of the nation's great universities, reputable laboratories and most of its libraries? Was his father right? Was he destined for the fate of Elmo Brady? Crestfallen, Julian started to leave. Remembering his upbringing, he stopped at the door, turned to the professor, and thanked him "properly" for trying to help. Then he left.

Still the Pursuit

Though bitterly disappointed, Julian kept the appointment with Fisk University President Fayette Avery McKenzie. The interview went well. Julian accepted an offer to teach chemistry at Fisk in Nashville, Tennessee. The small, private, historically black institution, was founded in 1866, only one year after the Civil War. In class Julian found bright students, curious, and eager to learn. He worked hard to stay ahead of them, but more important, he felt they deserved the best he could give. Now more than ever he wanted to attend graduate school to become better prepared. Not pleased with some of his lectures in organic chemistry Julian sent one set to Professor Blanchard for his comments. Replied his old mentor, "Your lectures are so clear I am going to tear up some of my own and use yours instead."

Meanwhile, Julian had an opportunity to attend medical school but turned it down. He still wanted to earn the doctorate in chemistry and continued to look for a way to do so. After two years at Fisk, he received an Austin Fellowship for graduate study. With this support, Julian enrolled at Harvard University in 1922. He worked with the respected chemist E. P. Kohler and conducted investigations involving chemistry of unsaturated systems. Julian earned a straight "A" average. In 1923, one year after entering Harvard, he earned his master's degree in organic chemistry.

Julian then applied for a teaching assistantship to continue his studies toward the doctorate. That was usually not a problem for students with a stellar record as he had earned. Harvard refused him, giving as reason that its white students, especially from the south, would object to having a black man as their teacher. Once again, the merit of his performance could not overcome the hindrance of his race.

Natural Product Chemistry - A Beginning

Julian stayed around Harvard for more than another year. He worked odd jobs, lived on a bare-boned budget, took courses in physics and biology, hoping to eventually obtain grant support for further studies. Nothing came. Again he remembered his father asking if he wanted to starve to death.

West Virginia State College for Negroes offered Julian a teaching position. Though the salary was small, it rescued him from further poverty. Julian went to West Virginia State as the chair and sole faculty member in the chemistry department.

Several times Julian spoke about his hero Dr. Elmo Brady. He believed that Brady's isolation from the community of scientists blunted his growth and affected what contributions he might have made to science. In a sense, he now lived in academic isolation not unlike that of Brady because there were no colleagues in chemistry. Julian was the chemistry professor, laboratory instructor, lab assistant, janitor, equipment, materials and supply manager. His facilities contrasted sharply with those at the institution he had just left.

Under such conditions it would have been easy for Julian to

become dispirited. Yet this proved to be a critically important period in his life.

Some observers of historically black colleges have pointed out that many of the early presidents were dynamic leaders and spellbinding orators. Perhaps such skills helped them and their constituencies overcome the complex social, political and economic restrictions under which they worked. At West Virginia, Julian met such a leader in the president, Dr. John W. Davis. The president no doubt recognized the potential in his young faculty member. The two men talked at length. Davis encouraged Julian to conduct research on his own, even if his laboratory was almost bare.

Julian accepted the suggestion and began working on some experiments. While at Harvard he had become interested in the relatively new field of "natural products" chemistry. His experiences with E. P. Kohler opened his eyes to the great possibilities in this science. He mastered many of the complex and delicate skills needed for research and the basic theoretical tenets upon which natural product chemistry was based. His understanding of organic compounds, their unique bonding capacities and the chemical behaviors of carbon compounds, proved useful in this endeavor. Julian became fascinated by the possibility of duplicating or synthesizing in the laboratory, products found only in nature. Such knowledge had incredible possibilities in medicine, food, clothing, buildings, transportation, communication, and many aspect of life. To get started, Julian repeated some experiments pioneered by Ernest Spaath, renown chemist of the University of Vienna. Spaath had successfully synthesized such chemicals as nicotine, found in the leaves of tobacco, and ephedrine, useful in treating asthma and hayfever.

Howard University and Miss Anna Johnson

Julian remained at West Virginia only one year before accepting a teaching position at Howard University in Washington, D.C. A more comprehensive institution, Howard also had better facilities and a budget. When he arrived, officials asked Julian to design the new chemistry building that had just been funded, a request he eagerly accepted. The resulting facility grandly served generations of students and faculty thereafter standing as an unspoken tribute to one Percy Lavon Julian.

While at Howard, Julian met a petite and attractive young sociologist named Anna Johnson. Ms. Johnson, a native of Baltimore, Maryland was in Washington on a research project assignment. She had recently earned the masters degree in sociology from the University of Pennsylvania, where, such was her record that some faculty there urged her to return and study for the doctorate. A few years later, Anna Johnson did just that and earned a Ph.D. in sociology at Pennsylvania. She was the first of her race and gender to do so. A half-century later another black female, who somehow knew of Dr. Anna Julian, called her with the news that she was the second black female to earn the same degree from Pennsylvania. Dr. Julian was elated by the news but sad that it took so long to happen.

Like Julian, Anna Johnson, an excellent student, was inducted into the prestigious academic honor society, Phi Beta Kappa. Professor Helen Edmonds, distinguished historian and humanities scholar of North Carolina Central University, said that Johnson had been a child prodigy, with a gifted mind that equaled that of her brilliant future husband, Percy Julian. Friends described her as low key, quiet and gentle, but of strong character. She never complained about her limited financial base, or difficulties encountered due to race and gender. Her application of a good mind and effort, and such support as was available, led to her success.

Shortly after her arrival to the nation's capital, Anna Johnson heard about Percy Julian from friends and acquaintances. They described him as an interesting man, charming and witty, conversant with many topics, not just science.. They said he could also be boring because eventually he would start talking about chemistry until their eyes glazed over. Julian would launch into long discussions about complex chemical reactions, drawing structural formulas in the air with his fingers pointing out radicals and functional groups. He would take his imaginary compounds and rearrange them to form new substances like moving furniture in a room, to create new arrangements with new functions , little of which they understood.

After they met, Johnson found the professor to be charming and witty as reputed, but not at all boring. The two soon became friends. Perhaps her early interest in chemistry was a factor as Johnson initially planned to major in the science. She switched to her other interests, sociology and English, only when it became apparent that her mandatory off-campus living arrangements made it impossible for her to meet the time demands required by chemistry laboratory assignments. Johnson liked sociology because of its focus on people, her special interest being in structures and dynamics of families in different cultures.

Vienna and Ernest Spaath

The difficulties at Harvard in getting support for further studies did nothing to blunt Julian's efforts and determination to pursue the doctorate in chemistry. A few years after his appointment to the faculty at Howard University, Julian was awarded a study grant by the General Education Board, which was funded by the Rockefeller Foundation. Because of his interest in natural product chemistry, Julian sought to study under Ernest Spaath at the University of Vienna. Toward that end, he submitted an application for admission in competition with a long list, including indigenous and foreign seekers, for the few openings available. A jubilant Percy Julian received a letter from Vienna informing him of his acceptance. The short preparation time before school opened forced him into feverish planning and making ready for travel and several years of stay abroad. Clearly among the most challenging of his tasks was educating himself in German, the language of use in Vienna. Julian pushed himself through a crash course in German and spent as much time as possible during the ocean voyage in intense study. Upon his arrival in Europe, he felt comfortable with the language and after a few months in Vienna learned to understand and speak the Viennese dialect as well.

Julian met with cordial reception, both at the university and in the broader Viennese society. He encountered no reservations or qualifications due to his race or nationality. In this environment, he fully applied his great powers of concentration and made admirable progress in his studies. According to Bernhard Witkop, fellow students and faculty admired Julian for "his passion for hard work and study, his profound knowledge of chemistry, and his astounding memory." One of Julian's friends at Vienna, Josef Pitkin later wrote to Bernard Witkop that among other things, Julian was "particularly noticed for his neatness, the cleanliness of his work bench." Witkop also said Spaath was a "critical, pitiless examiner" and not given to high praise. But of Julian he said, "An extraordinary student, his like I have not seen before in my career as a teacher!"

Julian himself never fully explained his reasons for going to Vienna to study. No one doubts that his interest in natural product chemistry ranked high in his decisions. His friends though, often gave another reason. They knew of his love for opera and there was no better place to indulge in such passion than Vienna. There he never had to concern himself with being denied admission due to race. In Vienna, he took full advantage of his opportunities to attend opera productions.

As much as he immersed himself in his studies and research, the urbane and affable American also enjoyed an active social life. Beside attending the opera he played tennis, swam in the Danube, went skiing - once, and took excursions about the country. Julian was also a frequent guest at social functions, and sometimes he entertained others. Somehow he found time to refine his piano skills and improve his technique by taking lessons. At other times he entertained his friends by playing classical musicals. He introduced them to original music from America, mainly Negro spirituals and jazz. In letters home, Julian shared many of his experiences with family, friends, and with Anna Johnson.

None of this distracted Julian from his studies. He applied himself industriously. His research also went well. Julian passed the long and grueling doctoral examination, that one writer said was appropriately called the *Rigorosum*. He wrote a thesis   on the alkaloids of a herbaceous plant called *Corydalis cava*. This area of investigation was of particular interest to him as many organic alkaline substances are useful in producing synthetic medical products like atrophine and quinine. In 1931, two years after his arrival in Vienna, Percy Julian became only the third African American to earn the doctorate in chemistry.

Dr. Percy Julian left Vienna with cherished memories, including a full measure of intellectual and social freedom, rich camaraderie, and acceptance of him as an equal. These conditions helped in his communication with others in his field, to their mutual benefit. As he left Vienna however, a major international crisis was in the making. Nazism was on the rise, soon to sweep the European continent.

The Return

Dr. Julian returned to Howard University with renewed vigor. He could not wait to get down to work. His two major goals were to build a leading department of chemistry at Howard and to synthesize the drug Physostigmine (Eserine). The synthesis of Physostigmine was said to be so difficult that some respected scientists said it could not be done.

Physostigmine is an alkaloid compound and at the time, was only available by extraction from the Calabar bean. The alkaloids, as a class of compounds, are nitrogenous groups and most commonly found in plants. Physostigmine is an ingredient in eye drops used to treat glaucoma. An estimated 15% of all blindness among adults in the United States is caused by this disease.

Scientists had determined the chemical composition and molecular structure of physostigmine. The formidable scientific puzzle was how to duplicate in the laboratory this compound that was only found in nature. Such a discovery was even more difficult during Julian's time when the chemical synthesis of natural products was more in its infancy.

Julian investigated the physical and chemical properties of the natural product. He conducted an extensive search of the literature for other chemicals known to have properties similar to the compound in question. Then he tackled the tough problem of trying to find out the precursors, involving the precise order of development required to duplicate the substance found in nature. When at last he felt the desired substance had been synthesized, confirmatory tests had to be run with great care and exactness. Only then could he announce a new synthesis. Julian had persuaded one of his friends from Vienna, a most able chemist named Dr. Josef Pikl, to come to America and work with him on the project. Undaunted by the challenge, and with a sense of optimism and excitement, the men began their search.

Again however, Julian encountered a major disappointment, this one related not to race but campus politics. According to his longtime friend and respected physician/scientist Dr. W. Montague Cobb, short-sighted people of less than honorable intent covertly opposed Julian's presence at Howard. Cobb, a professor at Howard, called them "forces of evil," who betrayed a good man, and undermined his work. Deeply disappointed, Julian resigned his position at Howard. With no facilities, and out of a job, his research efforts stalled.

Come to DePauw. Your Work Must Continue.

At DePauw University, William Marshall Blanchard now Dean of the College of Liberal Arts learned about Julian's plight. Blanchard told Julian that his work was too important to stop now. He found support grant money for the project from private sources and invited Julian to return to DePauw and continue his work. Blanchard provided needed facilities and asked Julian to direct research projects of seniors and graduate students in chemistry.

Professor Emeritus Donald Cook described Julian's work at DePauw as impressive. He wrote that:

During the next three years the quantity and quality of research papers turned out by Dr. Julian and his students were phenomenal for an institution of the size of DePauw.

Witkop, said of Julian's work at DePauw: "Thirty beautiful senior theses. . . 11 . . . publications in 4 years. . . [and most] read more like doctoral dissertations . . . "

Soon after the move to DePauw, Julian and Pikl resumed their research with a minimum of delay. In a series of publications, they reported progress toward synthesizing essential intermediate products. In their fourth paper, they announced the first synthesis of a compound called d, 1-Eserethole, which all but completed their project. However, another scientist also reported progress toward synthesizing physostigmine. In the last of a series of ten papers, Sir Robert Robinson of Oxford claimed to be the first to synthesize d, 1-Eserethole. Julian studied Sir Robinson's procedures and noting that they were different from his own, became skeptical of the Englishman's product. A debate followed in Europe and America about which product, Robinson's or Julian's was d, 1-Eserethole.

Some of Julian's friends and supporters, including persons at Harvard and DePauw, advised him not to challenge Robinson's claim. Robinson was a respected scientist, older, and more experienced. To challenge him was risky and Julian's reputation could be permanently ruined before his career got started. Even Pikl, Julian's assistant was apprehensive.

Julian respected the British scientist and openly held him in high esteem. Nevertheless he was confident he had obtained the product as claimed and would not relent. Instead, the American moved with dispatch. He quickly provided evidence showing the two compounds, his and Sir Robinson's were different and that laboratory tests confirmed that his compound, not that of Robinson was identical to the natural product. Cook called Julian's fifth and last publication in the series, "The Complete Synthesis of Physostigmine, undoubtedly the most significant publication to come from this institution [DePauw]."

Letters and telegrams from several American and foreign scientists congratulated Julian on being the first ever to synthesize physostigmine.

Leaving DePauw Again

As noted earlier, Julian went to DePauw on a temporary line supported by funds Dean Blanchard had raised. After four years and the successful synthesis of physostigmine the grant expired. Blanchard however, wanted to keep Julian at DePauw as a regular faculty member. Toward that end, he nominated Julian for a tenure-track faculty position in the department of chemistry. The Depauw University Board of Trustees took up the issue, but voted to deny the appointment. Like many during this time, they did not feel a black person should hold a regular faculty position at their institution.

An unnamed source then moved to nominate Julian for a faculty position at the University of Minnesota. When it became clear that the Board of Regents would not accept a black candidate, he withdrew Julian's name before the board met.

The cumulative effect of so many setbacks and rejections in his long struggle to use his scientific talents, caused Julian to despair and feel that he would find never find a place academia. The words of his father must have echoed again. He then considered industry where many of his former DePauw students found employment.

Success did not come immediately, but on the strength of his publications and well-trained former students the Institute of Paper Chemistry in Appleton, Wisconsin offered Julian a position with its research staff. Unfortunately, before he could report for work, the company learned that an old city law banned Negroes from being "bedded or boarded in Appleton overnight." In deference to the law, they rescinded the offer but vowed to campaign for a change in the law. Sadly though, for Julian, it was another setback.

Fortunately, the story did not end there. One member serving on the board of Institute of Paper Chemistry, W. J. O'Brien, took a great interest in Julian. As a Vice President of the Glidden Paint Company, O'Brien decided that if Julian was half as good as his reputation, he wanted him for his company. To him, the man's race was not an obstacle. So, during a break in the meeting, O'Brien contacted Julian by phone and offered the chemist a position with Glidden. President of the American Chemical Society Max Tisler said that when O'Brien hired Julian he decided, "I won't say anything [to other company officials] about who he is; I'll just hire him."

Of particular interest to O'Brien, was Julian's success in isolating the sterol called stigmasterol, from the Calabar bean. Two scientists, Fernholz and Butenandt, had isolated stigmasterol from the soybean. O'Brien's company wanted to find use for their tons of soybean oil by products, and they believed Julian's experience with the Calabar bean could be beneficial for Glidden in its mission. Julian accepted O'Brien's offer to work at Gliddens as Assistant Director of Research. When he arrived at the Chicago plant in January 1936, the company had changed its mind. A surprised Julian learned that he was not the assistant director but the Director of the Soya Product Division! The affiliation with Glidden marked a turning point in Julian's life. He made productive use of his knowledge, experience and considerable powers of imagination. Glidden benefited even beyond the dreams of O'Brien. Over the next four decades the Soya Products Division moved from a losing proposition to the company's most profitable division.

Julian's affiliation with Glidden was also important on a personal basis. He had always felt that if he ever got married, he had to be able to offer something to a wife. It was not that he objected to his wife working, or to her having a career. He just felt he should be able to care for his family, whether or not his wife worked outside the home. Now that he had this position with Glidden, he believed he could assume the responsibility. For the first time, James Julian did not need to worry that his chemist son might starve to death. On December 24, 1935, Percy Lavon Julian and Anna Johnson, married.

The Synthesis of Substance S

As was his wont, Julian assumed his new post with enthusiasm and a sense of purpose. An industrial setting is vastly different from academia, but he appeared to make the transition with considerable ease. Julian immersed himself in his new job and worked long hours.

The story of Julian's association with Glidden as Director of the Soya Research Division was one of great activity. According to Witkop, it was Julian's mission to head a team that would "exploit every ingredient of soybean oil."

In 1948, Hench and Kendall of the Mayo Clinic announced a discovery that cortisone was an effective anti-inflammatory agent for treating symptoms of arthritis. Cortisone also could be used to treat several other health related conditions including Addison's Disease, certain allergies and acute leukemia. The Mayo Clinic announced extraordinary results, and many hailed cortisone as a miracle drug.

Originally, researchers and pharmaceuticals extracted cortisone from the cortex or outer capsule of the adrenal glands located on the kidneys of cattle. The amount of cortisone in each gland is minute and not easily extracted. That made cortisone so expensive that only a few could afford the treatment. Even so, the demand far exceeded the small supply.

Like many other chemists, Julian attempted to synthesize the complex hormone. He set as his mission to find a way to synthesize the compound and produce the drug inexpensively on a large scale. Max Tishler described what happened:

Scarcely had the announcement of the Mayo Clinic come, when Julian published a new synthesis for Reichstein's S, which is also present in the cortex of the adrenaline gland and which differs from cortisone in lacking only an oxygen atom in position-11. In contrast to the previous synthesis, Julian's procedure was practical, and made Substance S available in commercial quantities. . . Julian's process is probably the most widely used. . . [and is] marked by simplicity and high yield. . .

In an address "On Being Scientist, Humanist and Negro," Julian explained his approach. He reasoned that:

> Nature has a mechanism for introducing into cortexolone the missing oxygen atom, thus producing Cortisone. Nature's procedure in this regard, was not yet known to chemistry. . . "

With that realization, he set about solving the complex puzzle of synthesizing cortexolone from soya products. Carefully and meticulously he put into effect the images created in his mind and succeeded in synthesizing cortexolone, or Compound S. - After this synthesis cortisone could easily be produced with the simple addition of an oxygen atom, and produced on a mass scale. Thereafter the price of cortisone dropped from more than four hundred dollars per treatment to a few cents. The drug then became available to hundreds of thousands of people who suffered from the crippling effects of arthritis. Julian's procedures became the model for producing hydrocortisone compounds.

Many More Products from the Soya Division

Other major scientific and industrial breakthroughs came out of Julian's division. He and his associates synthesized the male hormone testosterone, and the female hormone progesterone. Testosterone is essential for normal growth and development of the male accessory sex organs. It affects many metabolic activities and has other medical applications. Progesterone plays an essential role in reproduction, mammary gland development and controls normal menstrual cycle functions. These drugs, previously in limited supply, then became available in large quantities, and at affordable prices.

Julian later discovered a way to stabilize Lecithin against rancidity. His division could then produce Lecithin Granules, a food supplement. From lecithin, scientists can obtain other important organic products such as stearic acid, glycerol and choline.

Perhaps not as dramatic, but very important, Julian and his

associates made soybean meal an active ingredient in nearly all animal feed including feed for poultry. Glidden protein plant became a world leader in isolating and producing pure vegetable protein on a mass scale. Witkop explained that this success resulted from Julian's ingenious procedure to "adjust the size of the protein molecule to fit particular applications." He also said that Julian "put into production, on a daily, multi-ton output, a process for the isolation, with controlled properties, of the major protein species of the soybean." He obtained another inexpensive material used for "coating and sizing of book and magazine paper, the coating of labels that permitted improved printing, and the waterproofing of cartons."

Julian foresaw that the soybean protein could be produced inexpensively and "millions of protein-starved people" in underdeveloped countries could be fed. He also conducted studies into the metabolic pathways of Vitamin D. Julian and his associates coaxed Vitamin D_3 from the soybean, leading to the manufacture of Vitamin D. The United States Navy used his Aero Foam, another soybean product synthesized by Julian' division, to extinguish gasoline and oil fires during World War II. Aero Foam helped to save the lives of thousands of United States fighting men.

Other Areas of Investigations

It is interesting to note that many of Dr. Julian's scientific breakthroughs were medically beneficial. Perhaps he remembered that his father wanted him to be a medical doctor, and that both his brothers became physicians. He gave his brothers something to work with. Interestingly enough, just as Julian's father wanted him to go into medicine, so did he want his son Percy Jr., to become a chemist. But Percy Jr., became a lawyer instead. Chemistry is not out of the family, however, as his granddaughter is a chemist.

Julian also conducted studies that threw light on tryptophan. Tryptophan is an amino acid necessary for normal growth and

development. It is a precursor of serotin, a chemical important in
nerve transmission. According to W. Montague Cobb, Julian
worked out the intricate kyneurine pathway, an intermediate of
trytophan, and did work on the yohimbine ring structure. His
work on the yohimbine plant provided useful instructions on the
study and structure of many other alkaloid groups. Among scores
of other studies, Julian investigated the chemistry of indoles, a
product of bacterial decomposition of trytophan. He conducted
research on various steroids, soya phosphatides, soya proteins and
 extensive other investigation into the sterols.

It is apparent then that despite Julian's rich contributions to
applied chemistry, he made contributions to basic knowledge
also. In analyzing Julian's various scientific ventures, Max Tishler
said that "In the course of his intensive steroid study, much new
and valuable chemistry has evolved including new compounds
and new reactions." Tishler went on to credit Julian with a
number of "firsts" in his studies of the steroids. He mentioned
many of his new syntheses that he described as "facile"
procedures. "Indeed," said Tishler, Julian's monograph on the
Chemistry of Indoles, . . . is a classic reference work for
students and investigators in this field." Oberlin's Professor Luke
Steiner explained the breath of Julian's work.

> "[He] . . . demonstrated his chemical competence and creative
> imagination in applied chemistry by securing a number of patents
> for the making of desired substances from plant products, but he
> kept on publishing in pure chemistry an impressive series of papers
> on indoles, sterols and steroids, and conjugated systems.

Others said of Julian that he had a mind that could decipher
and retain an exceptional amount of information. Anna Julian
said that her husband read widely and knew what others were
doing in the field and that his great strength was his imagination.
His co-workers spoke with admiration about his diligence, and
also his sterling powers of creative thoughts. Ideas poured out
faster than anyone could keep up with them. This gift of
imagination served him well in seeing connections among

fragments. He had a passion for chemistry.

The Entrepreneur

In 1953, Julian left Glidden to form his own company. This may be considered a bold and courageous move since banks refused all his loan applications. To start his company, he invested his personal resources. First he founded the Julian Laboratories. Eventually, he expanded to foreign countries opening branches in Mexico and Guatemala. Later he founded the Julian Research Institute followed by the Julian Associates, Inc. To get his business enterprise going, he wisely enlisted the able assistance of his wife. Her organizational skills, good business sense, and unflappability were valuable assets in the hectic environment of getting started, and meeting all kinds of deadlines. She performed several duties and in her own words, did "lots of bookkeeping." His staff, including the science work-force, looked like a miniature version of the United Nations.

Julian established the Mexico branch of Julian Laboratories because wild yams grew there. He had discovered that wild yams were a better source for the syntheses of Substance S than soybeans. Later, when he learned that even more of the plants grew in Guatemala, he opened another branch in that country. His company became a world leader in producing Substance S from yams.

After more than a decade of being a corporate executive, supervisor and bench scientist, Julian sold the Laboratories to Smith, Kline and French Laboratories. He became a consultant to them as well as to Upjohn Co. and Ciba, Ltd., of Basle, Switzerland. He remained as president of Julian Research Institute and continued his studies until his death.

Percy Julian and the Humanities

Friends spoke of Julian in terms of his "urbane" manners, good humor, and wit. He had an excellent command of language and a gift for words. Many simply called him an accomplished scholar with a compelling gift of oratory. Consequently, he received many invitations to speak. In constant demand as a speaker, he addressed both scientific and non- scientific gatherings. Julian could quote poetry and various other passages from literature, including the Bible, and do so with ease. Music was a favorite hobby and he was familiar with all the great jazz artists and classical spirituals.

Julian read with interest the philosopher C. P. Snow's discourse on the gap between science and the humanities with interest. He agreed with Snow on two points: that a chasm existed between the disciplines and that the consequences were lamentable. He argued, though, that Snow should have included the black scientist in his analysis, finding it "ironic that in this controversy the Negro Scientist has been overlooked." According to Julian, if Snow had included this group, he would have found new information, and might have realized that the circumstance of living in a segregated society placed unique demands on the black scientist. The black scientist, said Julian, "had to concern himself with the problems of his fellow man as humanist, while at the same time, pursuing his career as best as he could as a scientist." In the very act of his living and working, in him (or her), the two disciplines were joined.

Science, Philosophy and Society

Julian believed that scientists had an obligation to seriously engage moral and ethical issues affecting society. At the Northwestern University's 1973 Klopsted Lecturer, he said. " Through the ages, value judgment has played a directive role in man's endeavor - from Socrates . . . to Longfellow. "Socrates" he said, argued that the wise man will " pattern himself after . . . that City [of God] . . . and in doing so will set his own house in order!"

He quoted a Longfellow poem to help make his point that the scholar should hear and feel. Therefore the "scholar's abstract findings," should be used to "broaden knowledge of the physical world" and make a better life. Julian believed that despite some seemingly intractable problems in society, he believed in hope. He said to his audience:

> Hope stands firm through the darkness of failure until the dawn of understanding breaks-knowing it will break; knowing that there must be and there will be a light that conquers shadows.

Is science moral or amoral? In the Klopsted Lecture, he said that "Science is a man-made discipline, and I fail to see how we may separate a man-made discipline from man himself."

How should science be judged? Julian felt that the worth of science should not rest solely on its contribution of material things but also on its value to "an ordered natural world in which we live."

In the laboratory, Julian deferred to the best known theories and laws that predicted and explained the behavior of nature at the molecular level. For this, he used his creative imagination and powers of rational thought to cause changes in the molecular world, never before attained outside nature. But he held that science was a human endeavor, not to be divorced from the human soul.

Julian also believed that scientific ability was universal. Therefore, one can find gifted persons in science in any race, or culture. He believed that opportunity, tolerance, and encouragement were essential if the innate scientific talent was likely to emerge. In an interesting metaphor, Julian likened the American ghetto unto a desert as far as nourishing and developing talent. It required, he said, "almost dreamers and fools to think of education" toward a science career. Even as in the harshness of a desert there are flowers that bloom, so were there ghetto fools who dared to dream, to "follow their urges toward pure science." Optimistically, Julian envisioned a society, however reluctantly, gradually opening the doors of opportunity. Perhaps out of his own experience, bolstered by his faith in the goodness of people, Julian predicted a "new breed of humanness in the scientists who overcame the ghetto handicaps. This new breed would better understand the need for ethics and morality to guide the use of scientific triumphs and technology. He predicted that " instead of the stultified heart, his own trying experiences will generate deep human compassion."

The Ordeal

Julian's rise to recognition and prominence in the scientific community did not exempt him from slights due to his race. Once he was invited by a college in Illinois to speak and to participate on a panel. He remained after the conference to converse with some people in attendance before going to the hotel where other guests had already checked in. He never got past the door. Stopped at the entrance, he was informed that the lodge did not accommodate "coloreds" and was given a train ticket back to Chicago. So while the other panelists spent the night in comfort he rode home in a train passenger seat. On another occasion Julian was invited to a meeting of scientists at a club in Chicago, but one hour before the conference was to convene he received a phone call telling him not to come because no Negro could attend a function there.

One can only wonder if these and similar slights ever impeded upon the creativity of this proud man or any person. Periods of anger and recrimination, however brief, would have been understandable. Nonetheless, those who knew him well declared that there were no lingering effects and no bitterness. His friend Helen Edmonds said of him, "He was a man too busy to hate."

Perhaps the greatest test of his forbearance came after Julian purchased a house in a Chicago suburb. Before he could move his family, arsonists attempted to burn the house down. Even after they occupied the residence, some tried to make their lives unpleasant, using subtle and not so subtle tactics. One woman in the neighborhood, considered emotionally unstable, paraded up and down the street in front of the Julian's home. She would stop passing motorists, point to their home and yell out, "n-----s live there, n-----s live there!"

A few months later, while Julian and his wife were in Baltimore for the funeral of his father, someone bombed his house. The device exploded near the rooms of his sleeping children, Percy Jr., then 11, and Faith, who was seven. Faith Julian remembered being jolted out of her sleep by the earsplitting blast. Oddly enough, her first reaction was not fear, but a sudden awareness of a "strange and horrible smell." Looking out into the darkened night and seeing a part of her house demolished, she knew something was terribly wrong. Suddenly she saw a man running away from the house. The intruder jumped into a car that sped off into darkness.

Anna Julian was a person of uncommon grace and warmth. Nonetheless, in the face of these travails she recalled how the family resolve strengthened. When asked if they ever considered giving up, she answered very quietly but firmly, "Never. As long as you run, you will be forced to continue to run. There comes a time when even at the risk of your life, you say, enough is enough."

During those early and trying days Julian vowed that his family would not be prisoners in their own home. They would not be afraid to step out the door. So. for their protection, this normally mild-mannered man patrolled his spacious lawn, with a rifle at the ready. He rejected help less others might suffer for coming to their aid. Later he began pruning his shrubberies, and planting his beloved tulips, his rifle still close by. Once while digging in the dirt, he heard the woman mentioned earlier, screaming to passing motorists. Standing up, he parted the shrubberies to get a better look. Just then his antagonist spotted his rifle on the ground. Frightened, she ran away, never to return.

Despite these incidents the Julians did not have to stand alone. Anna Julian spoke about "people of goodwill who gave support and reassurance for the stand we took." Unknown to them, a Jewish couple learned of a plan to cut off the Julian's water supply. They explained to the village official that cutting off the flow to the Julians would deprive other households of water as well. Another citizen threatened action in the court. The official never took the threatened action.

Following the bombing, many people expressed outrage against the violence. The *Chicago Sun* condemned the "cowards whose mad prejudice drove them to commit a felony" against a man who had relieved much suffering, and saved many lives. In an open letter published in the *Sun*, a group of Oak Park citizens declared, "We welcome them [The Julians], to Oak Park and are honored that they should want to live among us. We assure them that we wish to do everything in our power to make them our real neighbors." Thus courage and goodwill were joined, and the Julians stayed without further discord.

The Calming Influence, The Rudder

Faith Julian believes that had her father not been a scientist, he would have been a farmer. He loved to putter around in his lawn and did so whenever he could. Each spring, thousands of the colorful tulips he planted still trill at the first sign of spring. He also bought a farm not far from Greencastle. An old, rustic log cabin built by the former owner, an Irish immigrant, still remained on the farm. Julian renovated it and the family spent many pleasurable hours there. It was a place to relax and greet friends. James Julian, then retired from his job as a railroad clerk, loved to go out to the farm "to do what he could do." And Dean William Blanchard was among the welcomed guests. There was lots of work to do on the farm where Julian grew corn and other vegetables and it felt good. Out in the field he could roll up his sleeves and sweat doing physical labor. He enjoyed the farm immensely.

Julian often mentioned the important role his wife Anna played in his life. Faith said that in all that he accomplished, her mother was his lifeline. She gave meaning to his life. She said:

My mother provided the calming effect for my father whenever he grew impatient or agitated. She saw how dedicated he was and the long, hard hours he worked, so she was always there for him and made sure there was balance in his life. She arranged for social outlets that he thoroughly enjoyed. Despite his considerable social skills, without her intervention, his work would have consumed all his time. Also during difficult times, when things seemed not to go right, she was his gyroscope, his rudder.

Service, Honors and Recognitions

As busy as he was, Percy Julian gave much valuable time to public service. So did his wife. He held membership on governing boards of at least eight colleges and universities, including DePauw, University of Chicago and Southern Union College, Alabama. He was active in many civic organizations, among them, the Commonwealth Edison Environmental Advisory Council, NAACP Legal Defense and Education Fund, National Institute of Arthritis and Metabolic Diseases. Julian served on the boards of the National Negro and Professional Committee of the Legal Defense and Educational Fund, National Conference of Christians and Jews, and Chicago Urban League. He was also an officer in his church. Julian was an invited member or fellow of many learned societies including: The American Institute of Chemists, Phi Beta Kappa Associates, National Academy of Sciences, American Association for the Advancement of Science, and New York Academy of Science.

His service was not limited to organizations. Perhaps unfortunate for the scientific world, and society at large, he was often interrupted while absorbed in some scientific research problem, and asked to help some social cause or address a social crisis.

Julian received many honors and recognitions. Some 19 honorary doctorates from a range of colleges and universities, such as Northwestern University in Evanston, DePauw, Howard University, Oberlin College, Michigan State University, Fisk University. Sigma Xi honored him with its Proctor Prix Award. Other recognitions included the Chemical Pioneer Award from the American Institute of Chemists, and the Merit Award from the Chicago Technical Societies. Julian was among the first African-American inducted into the American Inventors Hall of Fame. The NAACP gave him its Spingarn Medal; Phi Beta

Kappa its Distinguished Service Award, DePauw its coveted "Old Gold Goblet", the Decalogue Society of Lawyers honored him with the Distinguished Merit Award, Choplin State (1968), Murray State (1972), and Illinois State at Normal (1975) named buildings in his honor.

When he retired as professor and chairman of the chemistry department at DePauw University, Donald Cook suggested a name for the new science building erected on the campus. Cook said the building should take an "honored name of one whose life and achievements would kindle a new heritage". He thought no one met those qualifications better than Percy L. Julian. In response to his convincing proposal, and support of the president, the DePauw Board of Trustees approved Cook's nomination and in 1980, on "Old Gold Day," DePauw University rededicated and renamed its new building the *Percy L. Julian Science and Mathematics Center.*

Percy L. Julian died April 19, 1975. Each year DePauw celebrates his legacy with a Percy L. Julian Memorial Lecture. Because he was widely viewed as both a scientist and humanist, scholars from the scientific world alternate with a humanist scholar in presenting the lecture.

Schools in such places as Chicago, Louisiana near New Orleans, Phoenix, Arizona and Oak Park, Illinois bear his name. At the Percy L. Julian Junior High School in Oak Park, a student named Carrie Lawson published a poem in her school's brochure called "Percy Julian":

Percy Julian . . .
A man of strong beliefs
Civil Rights
Brotherhood
A humanist Percy Julian . . . A common man,
A loving husband,
Devoted father
A teacher and counselor

Percy Julian . . .
A man of great achievement
Chicago man of the year - 1950

National Academy of Science member
Proctor Prix Winner
Soybean discoveries that changed medicine
forever and saved lives

Percy Julian . . .
A scientist . . . but more.

References and Materials for Further Study

Bims, Hamilton, 1975. "Percy L. Julian Fights for His Life," *Ebony*, 94-104.

Cobb, W. Montague, 1971. "Percy L. Julian, Ph.D., 1899-," *Journal of National Medical Association,* 63: 143-150.

_____, "Onward and Upward," Lecture: Presented at the Annual Percy L. Julian Memorial Lecture, DePauw University, April 28, 1977.

Cook, Donald, *Chemistry at DePauw, 1837-1987*, Greencastle, Indiana: DePauw Association of Chemists, 1987.

DeKruif, Paul, 1946. "The Man Who Wouldn't Give Up," *Reader Digest*, 113-118.

Edmonds, Helen, Come Down to Kew Gardens - In Lilac Time - It Isn't Far From London," Lecture: Presented at the Thirteenth Annual Percy L. Julian Memorial Lecture, Julian Science and Mathematics Center, DePauw University, April 11, 1989.

Green, Richard L. (Ed). *A Salute to Black Scientists and Inventors,* Chicago: Empak Publishers, 1985.

Haber, Louis, *Black Pioneers of Science and Invention,* New York: Harcourt, Brace and World, 1970.

Julian, Percy L., 1974. "The Engineering Scientists as Scholar and Humanitarian," *ChemTech*, 4:131-134.

_____, "On Being Scientist, Humanist, and Negro" in Wormley, Stanley L. and Lewis H. Fenderson, ed. *Many Shades of Black,* New York: Morrow and Company, 1969.

McDermott, William, F. 1963, "Chemist With A Cause," *The Rotarian,* 102: 24-26.

Press, C. Jaques C., *American Men and Women of Science*, New York: Cottell Press, 1972.

Tishler, Max, "Percy L. Julian, the Scientist." Paper "(Presented when Dr. Julian received the Honor Scroll of the Chicago AIC Chapter, Nov. 13, 1964 at Chicago, Illinois)"

"The House That Joyce Built," *Fortune*, 95-171 (May, 1849)

Volwiler, Ernest, "Percy Julian, Citizen and Co-Worker, Paper-condensed version-presented (" . . . when Dr. Julian received the Honor Scroll of the Chicago Chapter, Nov. 13, 1964, at Chicago, Illinois.)

Winslow, Eugene, (Ed.) *Black Americans in Science and Engineering: Contributors of Past and Present*, Afro-American Publishing Company for General Electric Company, 1988.

Witkop, Bernard, "Percy L. Julian - April 11, 1899-April 19, 1975, in *Biographical Memoirs*, National Academy of Sciences, 52:223-268 (1980).

Special appreciation to the late Dr. Anna Julian, widow of Dr. Percy Julian and Ms. Faith Julian, daughter of Dr. Percy Julian, for granting the writer an interview.

Chapter XIII_____

Charles Drew-Pioneer Blood Plasma
Scientist
(1904-1950)

by S. Maxwell Hines

Charles Richard Drew was born to Richard and Nora Burrell Drew on June 3, 1904 in Washington, D.C. He was their first child. Of Charles' four siblings, one died in infancy, but Joseph, Nora and Eva lived to maturity. At first the family lived in the large, sixteen-room house of Charles' maternal grandparents. Their home was at E. Street, NW in a middle class, racially-mixed neighborhood known as Foggy Bottom. Up to eighteen members of the extended family lived together at one time and there was strong bonding among them. Eventually though, Richard moved his growing family out of his father's house and settled in Arlington, Virginia.

Charles' father, was a carpet-layer by trade. Financial circumstances forced him to drop out of high school before he could graduate. Nonetheless, on the strength of his intelligence and industrious nature, Richard Drew rose above his humble beginning, and became financial secretary of his union. That would not have been of particular distinction except that he was the only African-American member of Local 85 (Carpet, Linoleum and Soft Tile-Layers Union). Charles' mother, Nora, was a teacher before her marriage to Richard. At her husband's insistence, she left teaching to devote herself more fully to her family. This she did with singleness of purpose and dedicated application of mind and energy.

The entire family was active in the Nineteenth Street Baptist Church. It appears that this was a favorite of most African-American bourgeois of Washington, D.C.

Early Life

Beside his church activities, young Charles worked as a paper carrier. His paper business grew to where he had to hire six boys to meet the demand. He also spent much time developing his all-round athletic skills. Charles participated in swimming, football, basketball and track. In each sport he excelled. While he was in elementary school, the boy seemed more inclined to devote himself to athletics than academics. Although opportunities were extremely limited for black athletes, Charles' early career ambition centered on sports.

He attended Dunbar High, a segregated school in Washington, D.C. Dunbar was considered by many to be among the better public schools in the country. Over the years, many of its principals were graduates of Harvard, Oberlin, Dartmouth and Amherst. Dunbar placed strong emphasis on academics, but supported athletics as well.

Charles earned four varsity letters and twice was awarded the James E. Walker Medal for an all around athletic performance. His schoolmates voted him `best athlete,' `most popular student' and `student who has done most for the school'. He graduated in 1922.

The Scholar Athlete

In the fall of 1922, Charlie entered Amherst College in Massachusetts on an athletic grant. Again, he was a star athlete. He was the only first year student to be awarded a varsity letter for track. As a sophomore, he became a star halfback on the football team. Charles was awarded the Thomas W. Ashley Memorial Trophy as the member of his class who contributed most to athletics. Though never in any serious academic difficulties Charles clearly did not live up to his academic potential because of his emphasis on athletics. While a member of the Omega Psi Phi Fraternity, the second oldest African American social fraternity in the United States, he co-authored its hymn. Charles earned his bachelor's degree at Amherst in 1926.

Upon graduation, Charles decided he wanted to study medicine. He planned to enter Howard University but was short of funds. To earn enough money for medical school, he accepted an appointment at Morgan College (now Morgan State University), in Baltimore, Maryland, serving as Athletic Director and teacher of biology and chemistry. After working and saving money for two years, Drew applied to Howard Medical School but was rejected because he needed two more credits in English.

Though it was a bitter pill for him to swallow, the rejection only served to make him more determined. He applied to McGill University in Montreal, Canada and was accepted. Drew considered this as fortunate, not only because of the admission, but because McGill allowed him to compete in intercollegiate athletics as a graduate student.

Drew entered McGill University in 1928. He competed in athletics where he excelled. In the high and low hurdles, the high jump and broad jump, Drew won Canadian championships.

Unfortunately he had to face up to the painful truth that none of this paid any bills. So to meet expenses, Drew worked as a waiter. Still short of cash, he swallowed his pride and borrowed money from his former coach and former classmates at Amherst. That was not an easy thing for him to do. Now the stakes were higher, and feeling he now could not fail the young American therefore applied himself more seriously to his studies.

His more intense study efforts paid off. By the end of his third year at Amherst, Drew had done so well that his good grades earned him a $1000 Rosenwald scholarship grant. Due to his strong academic performance he was inducted into Alpha Omega Alpha, the academic fraternity at McGill for medical students. Charles Drew also ranked among the top five of his class on a competitive examination and was awarded the Williams Prize for academic excellence during his fifth year at McGill.

Drew graduated from McGill in 1933 with a Doctor of Medicine and Master of Chirurgie (Surgery) degree (M.D.C.M.). He did his internship at Montreal General Hospital. Dr. Drew remained at Montreal General for his residency.

Dr. Drew liked Montreal very much, finding the city fascinating. There he also enjoyed the most color-blinded experience of his entire life. But in 1935 his father died and the sense of deep loss led him to return home. In Washington, D.C., Drew applied for a position at the Howard University Medical School. He was offered an appointment as instructor of Pathology. Although the pay was small, he welcomed an opportunity to help his people. His appointment to the faculty of the very institution that rejected his application as a student gave him more than a small measure of satisfaction.

Progress in Medicine And Medical Research

Dr. Charles Drew arrived at Howard in 1935. After the first year, besides teaching pathology, he was appointed Assistant in Surgery at the Medical School and Surgical Resident at Freedmen's Hospital. Freedman's was the teaching hospital affiliated with Howard University. The next year, Drew was named Instructor in Surgery and Assistant Surgeon at the hospital. He so distinguished himself that during his third year he was recommended by the head of surgery, Dr. Howe, to a two-year fellowship for advanced training. The fellowship was funded by the Rockefeller Foundation. It was the first such fellowship ever offered through Howard.

In 1938, Drew went to Columbia University in New York, and its affiliate Presbyterian Hospital. He received advanced training in surgery. Drew worked with Dr. John Scudder, Assistant Professor of Clinical Surgery, on his research in fluid balance, blood chemistry and blood transfusion. Little did Drew know that this work and his association with Scudder would lead to his most recognized achievement in medicine.

During his stay at Columbia, Drew also became a prolific writer. His scientific reports, while complex, were always clear and cogent. His writings flowed elegantly without distracting from the content. Between 1939-40, Drew was author, co-author (with Scudder and others), or contributed to the writings of ten articles and one book. Although most of these articles involved hematology (the study of blood), also included was an article on surgery, his first love. Drew's work and expertise in hematology overshadowed other achievements but he also concentrated on honing his surgical skills while at Columbia.

Lenore

The year 1939 was an extremely busy one for Dr. Drew. Beyond his surgical residency, and intense study of the properties of blood, a new person came into his life. While traveling by automobile to a medical conference in Tuskegee, Alabama, he and his companions stopped in Atlanta to visit some friends. There he met an attractive young lady named Minnie Lenore Robbins. She taught home economics at her alma mater, Spelman College. When Drew left Atlanta and continued his journey to Tuskegee, he thought a great deal about her. He knew he had to see Lenore Robbins again. After attending the two-day conference, Drew boarded a train for New York. Upon reaching Atlanta, he got off the train, and in the middle of the night, headed for the Spelman dormitory where Miss Robbins lived. Despite the lateness of the hour, he insisted that the matron wake her up so he could talk to her. Just three days after he met Lenore Robbins, the smitten Dr. Drew asked her to marry him-immediately. Though flattered by this impulsive show of love and affection, Miss Robbins was a bit more pragmatic than the young doctor from Howard Medical School. She felt it would not be prudent or proper to rush into so important a commitment as marriage. It was spring, and she agreed to marry him in the fall, if all went well and they still felt the same.

So with this promise, Drew took his leave. He boarded the train and when he was settled in his seat, began writing a letter - to Lenore. He told her about his work at Columbia, and shared with her his goal of becoming an exemplary surgeon. He wrote about his hopes to train an elite African-American surgical force that would have its own research-based school of thought in medicine. When Lenore wrote back that his letters were not very romantic, he effortlessly adjusted his tone and wrote what could have been considered sonnets to his love. Drew quoted poetry of others and added poetic verses of his own. Lenore found beauty in his writings and the effect was altogether pleasing. For the rest of his life, Drew wrote Lenore regularly whenever they were apart.

Back in New York, Drew threw himself into his work. He began to direct his attention to the field of blood transfusion. The matter of blood transfusion and preservation had long been the research focus of Russian scientists. Unfortunately, the research was spotty, scattered, and followed many divergent lines of inquiry. Drew launched into an intensive study of the known research and coalesced the findings into a more usable form. This along with his and Scudder's findings, led to Drew becoming a leading expert on whole blood preservation. The research culminated in a doctoral dissertation entitled 'Banked Blood'. The work was comprehensive and the original draft was said to be the size of the New York telephone book.

In May 1939, Drew sought permission to study for the Doctor of Science Degree in Medicine. Columbia University agreed. But the Rockefeller Foundation opposed the move feeling that the time was not ripe for an American of African descent to undertake such an advanced study. Drew however, persisted (Time was over ripe). Finally, the foundation yielded to continued efforts by Drew, his advisors and sponsors, and agreed to support him.

Meanwhile, in June of 1939, Lenore Robbins traveled to Washington, D.C. to meet the Drew family where she received a favorable reception. That having been done, the couple began making wedding plans. Lenore had promised Drew that if all went well and they felt the same, she would marry him in the fall. Apparently all did go well and on September 23, 1939, with the arrival of fall, Charles Roberts Drew, and Minnie Lenore Robbins became husband and wife.

In New York, the newlyweds found a small West 15th Street flat that they shared with another couple. Drew continued his work and study at Columbia and Lenore joined him as one of his laboratory assistants. The Doctor of Medicine was conferred upon Drew by Columbia University in June of 1940. He was the first member of his race to earn such a degree. After earning his second doctorate, Charles Drew returned to Washington, D.C. this time with his bride, and resumed his duties at Howard University.

Blood Banks

Early in World War II, England suffered terrible casualties at the hands of the German Air Force. The country was desperately in need of blood. It came as no surprise when the Royal Air Force of England asked for and received 5,000 liters of blood from the Presbyterian Hospital in America. With the escalating need for blood transfusion to save the lives of servicemen and civilians, there was an obvious need for further research on blood preservation, especially for the front lines of battle. Drew was asked to help so he returned New York. There he joined Scudder in a race to seek better and more reliable means of banking and preserving whole blood. It was difficult to maintain blood banks near the battlefront and whole blood spoiled within a short span of weeks. Moreover, blood did not travel well. Drew and other investigators realized that the red blood cells were responsible for the rapid deterioration of whole blood. At this point several questions formulated in his mind. What if blood plasma were used (Plasma is the fluid portion of blood absent of red blood cells)? Could it save lives as effectively as whole blood? Would it survive travel better? Would it be easier to preserve?

Drew decided to pursue this line of investigation - a bold decision on his part. Based on his and Scudder's research, and the cumulative investigation of other American doctors, Drew began clinical trials on the use of blood plasma. He carried out the actual trials himself at Presbyterian Hospital. Results confirmed his hypothesis that blood plasma could be stored for long periods without deterioration. It was also confirmed that blood typing was not required before being administered. There were no serious adverse reactions even when used in large quantities.

In June of 1940, the results of the clinical trials were made public. Almost immediately the Board of Trustees and the Board of Medical Control went into action. Drew's findings were quickly incorporated in the planning as `Blood for Britain' program was established. The Red Cross provided the financial support needed to put the project in action. A massive `Blood for Britain' program was mounted to send blood plasma to the beleaguered country and its allies for use in treating the thousands of casualties sustained in the war effort.

With his research completed, and the blood program in place, Drew returned to Howard again. Scudder and Dr. C. P. Rhodes of Memorial handled the technical details of the program. The success of the program was not the only joy in Drew's life. During this period their first child, Roberta was born. They called her "Bebe," for Blood Bank'.

Drew did not remain at Howard very long. His former instructor and friend, John Beattie had become director of the Army Blood Transfusion Service in England. He suggested to his English colleagues that the program would be well served with Drew directing the project. After they were shown his credentials the group quickly agreed. Losing no time, Beattie cabled the following request to Drew: "Could you secure five thousand ampoules of dried plasma for transfusion work immediately and follow this by equal quantity in three to four weeks?" To this request Drew replied: "There are not five thousand ampoules of dried plasma in the whole world but assistance will be forthcoming."

Drew's task as medical supervisor of the Blood for Britain program was to coordinate the collection of plasma from nine hospitals for shipment abroad. He developed a set of procedures for blood collection and processing that protected against the shipment of contaminated plasma. Drew continued to supervise the program until Britain developed a viable blood program of its own. Later the Blood Transfusion Association commented: "Since Drew who is a recognized authority on the subject of blood preservation and blood substitutes and, at the same time an excellent organizer, has been in charge, our major troubles have vanished." Drew had helped Britain buy valuable time in its fight against Germany. In January 1941, his work completed, he returned again to his post at Howard.

Unfortunately, Drew did not leave the blood program with complete satisfaction. While completing the paperwork for the Blood for Britain, program he began studies on mass production of blood plasma, in collaboration with the United States Army, National research Council, Red Cross, and Blood Transfusion Betterment Association. Two immediate problems confronted him. One was the shortage of donors. The other problem was the policy restriction that the blood donors had to be white. The same restriction was enforced in the Blood for Britain program, even in the face of their dire need, because of the racial segregation policy of the US armed forces. In 1941, the War Department of the United States sent out a directive that:

> For reasons not biologically convincing but which are commonly recognized as psychologically important in America, it is not deemed advisable to collect and mix Caucasian and Negro blood indiscriminately for later administration to members of the military forces.

This policy countered the long held view by reputable scientists the world over that the blood of all *homo sapiens* was alike regardless of race. For that reason the policy troubled Drew. Type A blood of one race was type A in all. Why sacrifice life-saving procedures in so critical a time on the altar of racial prejudice? Some speculated that Drew ended his association with the program over the intolerance shown by the armed forces concerning the issue. Others say that Drew held a press conference and denounced the policy publicly but no record of such can be found.

Promotions, Honors and Recognitions

In April 1941, Drew took an examination given by Johns Hopkins that certified him a surgeon by the American Board of Surgery. He did so well that in October 1941, he was named the first African American examiner for the American Board of Surgery. Shortly after, Drew was promoted to Professor of Surgery at Howard and appointed Chief Surgeon at Freedman's Hospital.

More honors followed. Tuskegee Institutes's John A. Andrew annual clinic awarded him the E. S. Jones Award for Research and Medical Science. Less than two years later, in June 1943, the American Soviet Committee on Science appointed him to membership on the strength of an article he published on the advances made by Soviet hematologists.

In January 1944, Howard promoted Drew to the position of Chief of Staff at Freedman Hospital. In June the same year, he received the NAACP's Spingarn Medal for his work in hematology. The Spingarn Medal is the highest award offered by the NAACP. Just over a year later, the National Medical Association named Drew chairperson of its surgical section. The National Medical Association consisted of African American physicians. The organization was founded when the exclusionist policy of many of its chapters, barred Americans of African descent from membership in the American Medical Association. Howard promoted Drew again, this time to the position of Director of the Freedman's Hospital. He held that post from 1946-1948. Also, in 1946, the American-Soviet Medical Society elected him vice-president, and the US Chapter of the International College of Surgeons made him a fellow. He became a surgical consultant to the United States Surgeon General in 1949. Drew also received honorary doctorates from Virginia State and Amherst College.

In the summer of 1949, Charles Drew finally took a vacation - of sorts. Actually it was a working vacation. He traveled to Europe as one of four consultants to the Surgeon General. His mission being to inspect American military medical facilities in Europe, he assessed the facilities and recommended changes as necessary for improvement.

When he was not working, Drew enjoyed the cultural offerings of Munich, Nuremberg, Paris and London. Of course he shared all of his experiences in Europe with Lenore through his letters. As usual, the letters were poetic and romantic, while also chronicling his adventures in Europe. His European exploits read like a travel log that invited readers to share experiences with him. He returned to Howard at the close of the summer. It was the only vacation he ever had.

A Genial Man, A Demanding Teacher

For all his accomplishments, the American Medical Association never accepted Drew into its membership. He repeatedly submitted applications accompanied by endorsement of prominent members of AMA. All efforts failed. The local chapter would not accept him and the national office responded to his letters of protest by reiterating that membership in the organization was decided solely by doctors of local chapters.

When Drew returned to Howard, his focus changed from researcher to the fulfillment of a dream he had shared with Lenore in his first letter to her. He began to devote most of his time to training African-American surgeons. Charles Drew was a genial man, but as a teacher, a most demanding taskmaster. His mission was to prepare African-American surgeons who could meet the highest standards of excellence anywhere. Perhaps his own experiences made him acutely aware of the demands the world was going to make on them. He was as free with his advice and admonition as with his personal resources when it came to his students. He wanted them to get the best education possible so they would be ready to define the `Negro School of Thought' in medicine, a most intriguing concept, that he always envisioned. He kept in personal touch with most of his graduates and followed their careers closely, with great pride and interest in their successes.

Despite national and international fame, Drew never lost the personal touch. In constant demand as a speaker for both lay and professional groups, the physician-surgeon-teacher-medical researcher, found no task too large and none too menial. Drew gave free counsel and service to numerous local communities and small hospitals. He made many trips to cities to help open doors to black surgeons. Indeed, he fought tirelessly for equality and fair play in the field of medicine. His unrelenting campaign led to many barriers being lowered.

Tragedy

On April 1, 1950, Drew and four other physicians were motoring to a conference at Tuskegee Institute in Alabama. It was a long journey. Although tired after a full day at work, he and his companions decided to drive all night since there were few overnight public accommodations for black Americans. At 7:30 the next morning they were traveling along State Highway 49 in North Carolina. Drew was at the wheel. He dosed off and the car careened off the road. It flipped several times before finally coming to a stop. The other passengers were thrown free but Drew's foot was caught in the brake pedal and the car rolled over him. Passers-by called an ambulance from the nearby town of Burlington and Drew was rushed to the Alamance General Hospital. He suffered severe and extensive injuries. After examining Drew, doctors decided not to move him to a hospital with better facilities for fear he might die en route. His left leg was nearly severed, his neck was broken and his vena cava, (the large vessel that returns blood to the heart) was ruptured. Blood transfusions were administered but were of no use because his ruptured vena cava prevented blood circulation. Several very capable and experienced physicians attended Drew but their efforts were futile. Charles Drew died mid-morning at the age of forty-five. His family later wrote a letter to the physicians expressing satisfaction with the care Drew received.

Drew's body lay in state in the Andrew Rankin Chapel of Howard. There a memorial was observed April 5, 1950 at 1:00 P. M. His funeral services were held in the family church, the Nineteenth Street Baptist Church, and officiated by Reverend Jerry Moore. Drew was survived by his wife, Lenore Drew, his daughters Roberta "Bebe," age nine, Charlene Rosella, age eight, Rhea Sylvia, age six and his son Charles Jr., age four. A memorial fund was established in his name. Also, an Amherst Drew Memorial Scholarship Fund was established to aid premedical students at Drew's alma mater.

Posthumous Honors

After his passing several public schools, medical schools and parks across the country were named in honor of Dr. Charles Drew. On October 13, 1976, his portrait was unveiled and hung during a ceremony at the National Institute of Health in Bethesda, Maryland. His was the first portrait of an African-American to be placed among those of Nobel Laureates and center directors. On June 15, 1977, the Charles R. Drew Blood Center of Washington, D.C. Red Cross Building was dedicated. The United States issued a commemorative stamp in honor of Drew in 1981. On April 5, 1986, a six -foot granite marker holding a bronze commemorative plaque, was built and dedicated at the site of Drew's fatal accident.

Charles Richard Drew is best remembered for his work in hematology, but his 45-year life benefited much more. He left behind insightful research that remains relevant today. His personal writings continue to be treasured by those who read them. He also left behind sports records that attest to his athletic prowess. The legacy that he would treasure most however, is the number of his African-American surgeons who have made contributions to the art of healing and who continue to train the next generation of surgeons, just as he had intended.

References for Further Reading

Adams, R. L., 1964. *Great Negroes Past and Present,* Chicago: Afro-Am Publishing.

"Charles Richard Drew: 1904-1950," 1950. *Negro History Bulletin,* 13.

Cole, C. W., 1950. "Citation for the Award of the Degree of D.Sc. to Dr. Drew by Amherst College," *Negro History Bulletin,* 13 (9).

Curtis, J. L., 1971. *Blacks, Medical School and Society,* Ann Arbor, Michigan: University of Michigan Press.

Downing, L. K., 1939. "Contributions of Negro Scientists", *The Crisis,* 46 (4).

Drew, C. R., 1950. "Negro Scholars in Scientific Research," *Journal of Negro History,* 35, 135-40.

Haber, L., 1970. *Black Pioneers of Science and Invention,* New York: Harcourt, Brace and World.

Haskin, J. 1992. *One More River to Cross: The Stories of Twelve Black Americans,* New York: Scholastic, Inc.

Love, S., 1992. *One Blood: The Charles R. Drew Legend and the Trauma of Race in America,* Ann Arbor, Michigan: University Microfilms International.

Love, S. 1992. *Dedication and Unveiling of the Dr. Charles R. Drew Memorial Marker: Alamance County, NC, April 5, 1986,* Graham, NC: Alamance County Historical Properties Commission.

Mahone-Lonesome, R. 1990. *Charles Drew,* New York: Chelsea House.

Wynes, C. E., 1988. *Charles Richard Drew: The Man and the Myth,* Urbana: University of Illinois Press.

*Chapter XIV*_____

Jane Cooke Wright -
Mother of Chemotherapy
(1919-)

Dr. Jane Cooke Wright stands among the few early workers who showed chemotherapy to be a valuable tool in the fight against human cancer. During a career span of over forty years, she and her colleagues made important discoveries through arduous, disciplined research, supported by their belief that cancer in humans is ultimately controllable. This is her story.

Family Background

Jane Cooke Wright was born November 30, 1919 in New York City, and raised there. Her father, Dr. Louis Tompkins Wright, a native of Atlanta, Georgia, was a prominent New York physician, surgeon, medical scientist, and civic leader. Her mother, Corinne Cooke Wright, a native of New York City, taught in elementary school until the birth of her first daughter, Jane. The Wrights' only other child, Barbara, was born shortly afterward.

The Wright sisters are members of family with a long history of medical practitioners. Their father received his M. D. degree from Harvard University Medical School. He graduated with honors and ranked fourth in his class. As a physician, medical scientist, and medical educator, Dr. Louis Wright broke new ground in several areas (See *Louis Tompkins Wright, Chapter*

X). In addition to his medical practice, Wright served for 24 years as chairman of the national NAACP Board of Directors. His long and vigorous fight for human rights led one observer to call him a "stormy petrel for justice."

Returning to family history, in 1881, Dr. Ceah Wright, former slave and paternal grandfather of Jane and Barbara, earned the M. D. degree at the new Meharry Medical College of Nashville, Tennessee. Meharry's mission was to prepare physicians to meet the critical medical needs of blacks as they emerged from over 300 years of slavery. In 1896, their step grandfather, Dr. William Penn, earned his M. D. degree from the Yale Medical School, the first of his race to do so. In 1952, an uncle, Dr. Harold West, who held a Ph.D. in biochemistry was installed as the first black president of Meharry Medical College. Earlier he worked on the team that synthesized threonine, an amino acid essential for the normal functioning of the human body.

That these men, and the families who supported and encouraged them, could aim so high in the shadows of slavery, and achieve such lofty goals, speaks with praise of their abilities and character. The next two generations, following Louis Wright, all women, became physicians of mark and continued a remarkable family tradition of more than 100 years in medicine.

Education

Corinne Wright carefully guided the children's early education. She enrolled them in private schools noted for their high academic standards and well-rounded programs. They attended the Ethical Culture Schools for their elementary education, and for high school were enrolled in the Fielston School. From the very beginning Jane displayed a fondness for learning and each day when it was time for school, it was as if the sunlight broke into her eyes. She took part in almost all activities but as she knew her mother expected, and she preferred as well, lessons always came first. They were a challenge, a joyous adventure. The sciences and mathematics were her favorite subjects but her ease of grasp also suggested a high aptitude for these disciplines.

She likened solving mathematical problems to having an interesting hobby. It was fun. Once she went beyond an assignment in her biology class when she persuaded her mother to buy an embalmed cat. She meticulously dissected the animal, showing unusual skills, and carefully examined the various systems: circulatory, digestive, nervous, genito-urinary and skeletal. Jane came away from that experience with a thorough knowledge of the animal's anatomy and what was to her an exciting adventure.

The eager young student with the piercing eyes, so like her father's, adored art, most especially paintings in oil and water color. Later she put her talents to practical use when chosen art editor of the class yearbook. In athletics she proved to be an strong and accomplished swimmer. Chosen captain of her school's swim team, Jane set records in the 100 yard breaststroke and backstroke that stood for many years. She also studied modern dance with Tamiris and Hanya Holm, respected names in the field. On December date, 1937, she danced with the acclaimed Holm group in the grand performance of "TREND" at the Center Theater in New York City. It was a memorable occasion. In her young life she approached everything she did, academics, sports and the arts, with equal determination, always with intensity.

Jane graduated from Fielston in 1938. The following fall she enrolled at Smith College in Northampton, Massachusetts. Her rigorous secondary school education served her so well that she easily made the adjustment to college, finding it no more demanding than Fielston. She arrived at Smith already well versed in French so in college she expanded her academic interest to include German and added physics to her other sciences of strong interest. Fascinated with the "new" language, she moved into the German House to further improve her skills. That moved paid dividends because German soon became her best foreign language. She continued her interest in outdoor activities by adding skiing, to her continuing interest in swimming and dancing. As in high school, Jane Cooke Wright kept an amazingly busy schedule.

Wright took all the required and distribution courses at Smith and as in high school, consistently earned excellent grades. Before graduation she took the colleges' demanding comprehension examinations. The examinations included items from English, a foreign language (French or German), history, government or philosophy, and science or mathematics. She prepared diligently for these tests, leaving nothing to chance. As a result, she and passed each test without difficulty. Students at Smith also had to pass a swimming test but with her championship skills in that sport, this requirement posed no challenge at all.

With an interest in almost everything, and similarly her success, Jane Wright really had no idea what she would do after college. For that reason, she did not at first lock into any particular course of study. She seriously contemplated art, but only briefly. Her father suggested she should consider something more practical in case of future hardship. By the end of her sophomore year, Wright's favorite subject was physics but she did not believe that discipline offered a professional future for a woman. After considerable deliberation, and some agonizing over the matter, she settled on the standard premedical major. Next she informed her father about her decision. The news caught him by surprise and though inwardly pleased he worried about her chances in a tough field dominated by white males. She in turn was equally surprised when her sister Barbara followed her into medicine.

In all this, Wright regarded with appreciation, her good fortune. Her parents supported her in all her endeavors and this backing strongly counteracted the prevailing attitudes of gender and racial discrimination. She remembered her college years at Smith College with fondness, feeling they were good years. She surmised that her experiences, in and out of the classroom, represented a valuable stepping stone to her personal growth and were critical to her future career.

Medical School

During her senior year at Smith College, Wright applied for admission to medical school. She could not be considered for Harvard, her father's school, because that medical school did not accept women at the time. Her excellent academic record at Smith College proved very beneficial when she earned a four-year scholarship to the New York Medical College. She was one of the two women graduated by Smith College in 1942 who went to medical school.

Along with a sense of pride and achievement, the scholarship was also of personal significance. Her father had fallen seriously ill, disabled by tuberculosis. Severe damage to his lungs by an enemy gas attack during World War I, exhausting hours devoted to medical practice, and tough civic battles weakened him and he became susceptible to the debilitating disease. Those were difficult times but the staunch fortitude of her mother set examples for the whole family. So with Corinne Wright's encouragement and strong emotional support, young Jane Wright regrouped. With the support of her scholarship she continued her education and did so without additional drain on the already burdened family financial resources.

Wright enrolled in medical school shortly after the United States entered World War II. The nation's institutions were mobilizing to assist in the war effort. The New York Medical College, like many across the country, eliminated vacations and accelerated its programs. The tough curriculum had to be completed in three years instead of four, making the demands on students heavier and more intense. Nonetheless, this was the kind of challenge that appealed to Jane Cooke Wright. Contrary to her father's apprehension, Wright enjoyed a favorable reception at the New York Medical College. She often commented that never did she experience any obvious problems or negative event associated with her race or sex. Soon she was well on her way to becoming a doctor.

Despite the taxing schedule, Wright scored well in medical

school. On the strength of her excellent medical school record she was inducted into the Contin Society, the medical honor association at the school. (Later, Contin became affiliated with the national medical honor organization, Alpha Omega Alpha Medical Society). During her "senior year" Wright was elected president of the Contin Society, vice president of her class and literary editor of the yearbook. In 1945, the New York University School of Medicine bestowed the M. D. degree, with honors, upon Jane Cooke Wright. She ranked third best in her class.

Dr. Wright interned in the field of internal medicine at the Bellevue Hospital in New York City, then spent two years of residency (the second as chief residence) at the Harlem Hospital. The Director of Surgery was Dr. Louis Wright, her father.

In 1945, while in residency, Dr. Jane Wright married a bright young attorney, David Jones, a graduate of the Harvard Law School. In her professional life, she continued to be Dr. Wright but in private she was Mrs. Jones. She once remarked that as Mrs. Jones she could attend social functions with minimal possibilities of listening to other peoples medical woes but as Dr. Wright such respite, welcomed after a long hard day, was not assured.

The couple had two daughters, Jane and Allison. Eventually their daughter Jane earned her M.D. degree then specialized in psychiatry. The other daughter, Allison, earned her Ph.D. degree in clinical psychology. These successes made a mother proud, paid a noble tribute to their late father, and continued a family tradition in medicine for yet another generation, the fourth.

The Call

Dr. Wright completed her residency, passed the New York State Medical Examination with high marks, then "hung out her shingles". The young physician, eager to begin-and well prepared, set up private practice in busy New York City, where she grew up. Interestingly enough, despite her outstanding medical school and residency record, and her shaping environment, that is, a family with a long and distinguished history in medicine, no clinic or institution chose to offer her an appointment. Yet if there was a slight in this, she appeared to take little if any notice and there is no evidence that she pursued any such appointments. Instead the new Dr. Wright focused on building her medical practice and attending to the needs of her patients. Later she agreed to an appointment as physician for a public school in New York City. Immersed in her work, the increasingly busy healer had no idea that this would be a short career. Just as she began to settle into her practice, her father asked her to join him in his ongoing cancer research at the Harlem Hospital. The request caught her by surprise but she quickly recovered and told her father yes. By that decision, Jane Cooke Wright, M.D., set the course that defined her career, and the remainder of her professional life.

Dr. Wright's father was recognized as arguably the most skilled surgeon in New York City. As a physician, and as a clinical researcher, he engineered several noteworthy medical advancements recorded in his 96 published papers. For example, in contradiction to the then prevailing wisdom of the medical profession, he showed that the Schick Test could successfully test for diphtheria in dark-skinned African Americans. His invention of a neck brace for persons suffering injuries to the neck and cervical vertebrae was widely used in the medical profession. The elder Wright conducted the first clinical tests using the antibiotics aureomycin and terramycin.

In 1947, her father founded the Harlem Cancer Research Foundation. It was perhaps the most challenging venture of his active life. Two years later, in 1949, he invited his physician daughter Jane, to join the staff as a member of his research team. The basic purpose of the foundation was to find chemotherapeutic agents that would control or better yet, cure cancer. In this ambitious quest, the Harlem Cancer Research Foundation investigated the effects of many anticancer drugs on human cancer on two fronts, the laboratory and in clinical settings.

Jane Wright often spoke and wrote of cancer from a historical and a personal perspective. She described cancer as an ancient mystery that predated recorded history. The dreaded disease starts in just a single cell among the billions of cells in the human body and for some reason begins to grow uncontrollably. Often, it spreads throughout the body. If such abnormal growth is not controlled, or the involved cells not removed, the spread of cancer usually continues until the host dies. What makes the fight more difficult is that there are more than 100 different kinds of cancer that can start in any part of the body. Each kind of cancer in each part of the body pose unique and difficult medical puzzles. The nature of a particular cancer depends on the site of cell origin. There are cancers of the lungs, breasts, prostate, colon, skin, and other parts of the body. Tumors or neoplasms (new growths), which start in the surface epithelial cells, are called carcinomas or "solid tumors." (Epithelial cells are found in the outer covering of the skin, lining of the body cavities, ducts and tubes). When the abnormal cells originate in the lymph nodes, it is called Hodgkins's disease or lymphosarcoma. When abnormal cells begin in a mole, the cancer is called malignant melanoma. Leukemia is cancer of the white blood cells.

Of course not all tumors are malignant or cancerous. When not malignant the growth is benign, meaning not spreading, and it poses no health threat. But how is one to know? To find out whether the growth is benign or malignant, doctors conduct a biopsy. They remove a small amount of tissue. Then medical specialists called pathologists, examine the cells under a microscope to detect the type of tumor and the site of origin. This information is important since different types of cancer behave differently and require different treatment.

The Harlem Research Cancer Foundation

The Harlem Cancer Research Foundation accepted patients when surgery and radiation failed. As mentioned earlier, , the Center specialized in the use of cancer chemotherapy, the treatment of cancer by chemical agents (or drugs).

Dr. Jane Wright threw herself into the cancer research projects without reservation. Her resolve served her well in making the transition from caring family medical doctor to researcher and caring physician. In her new role, she would need to draw on all her background in science, recent medical school acquisition, versatility and more. If she did not already know, she soon learned about the serious complexity and grave difficulties of the fight against cancer as a chemotherapist. Chemotherapy as a weapon against cancer was in its infancy so though she worked with hope, there was no illusion about a quick cure. Nonetheless, in this Herculean task to help suffering humanity in one of humankind's greatest scourge, she would be working with her father, who she greatly admired, and that in itself was a great incentive.

The young physician learned a lot working with him. He was the consumate physician, a penetrating analyst with immense experience, skillful hands and was a veritable font of creative ideas. She saw close up the compassionate healer who cared deeply about people in need. These exemplary qualities, including his uncompromising drive toward excellence also made him a demanding taskmaster. This, however, proved not a problem for one who shared his values so the boss' daughter experienced no problem in being a part of the team.

It was not long before father and daughter began publishing papers together on their research findings. One of their early reports announced achieving remission in patients with neoplastic diseases using an alkalating agent called triethylene melamine. An alkalating agent introduces an alkyl radical (CH_3) that may interrupt the function of essential cell components.

As a stop of last resort, so to speak, the Wright investigators found the triethylene melamine treatment encouraging. It was one of the agents that helped eased somewhat, disappointments in the midst of suffering and the inevitable loss of some patients. Each step forward provided a modicum of relief and shed new light on the often confounding, emotionally challenging effects of the tough cases they treated. Under the strong leadership of Dr. Louis Wright the team maintained a steady course and pursued, with determination, their mission to help find cures for cancer. They understood the Importance of their work in this new, unexplored, territory they took some solace that every new victory, even small ones, added to other small victories, in the battle against cancer.

The Baton is Passed -- Suddenly

Then tragedy struck. About three years after she joined the Cancer Research Foundation, Dr. Wright's father suffered a fatal heart attack. The sudden and shocking loss brought pain. Sadness, tears, and overwhelming grief descended on her. Nonetheless, even as she and her family grieved Dr. Jane Wright vowed to remember her father. She decided that the greatest tribute she could pay to this fallen warrior, this giant of a figure, would be to continue the work he started. She pledged herself to that task. Then, in a show of faith and confidence in the young medical scientist, the board appointed her Director of the Harlem Cancer Research Foundation. She enlisted the help and support of her associates and the work continued apace.

The new Director inherited a staff consisting of a biologist, a chemist, a pathologist, a hematologist, a tissue culturist and several clinicians (surgeons, internists, and radiation therapists). She often referred to her associates with pride and cited them for their ability, dedication, and contributions. Such was the competence of her staff that several of them went on to make good in other locations. One associate, Dr. Jewell Plummer Cobb later became president of the University of California at Irvine. Another, Dr. Dorothy Walker, went to Howard University as a professor and research biologist.

Making Gains, Innovations, and Developing Guidelines

In any meaningful research, it is important to keep up with developments in the field. What were other investigators trying, when, how, with what results, and under what conditions? Dr. Wright read widely, reviewing all the literature she could find on other developments in chemotherapy research and developments.

At conferences, local, state, national and international, she listened intently as other researchers presented papers about their findings and she read papers of her own. At these gatherings she also conferred with numerous research scholars, domestic and foreign, and exchanged valuable information about a common foe. These activities, along with papers she published in widely read medical journals, often brought comments and questions, not infrequently sparking debates among practitioners. This is common when one's works are deemed significant, it is a time-honored and valuable tradition, helpful in advancing any field of endeavor.

In 1955, Dr. Wright left the Harlem Research Cancer Foundation to accept an appointment at the New York University Bellevue Medical Center where she continued her research. She remained at Bellevue for twelve years before moving over to her alma mater, the New York Medical College.

As intimated earlier, when Jane Wright joined her father, very few medical centers used chemotherapy treatment to combat cancer. In this new and yet to be proven field only a few visionaries dared called it the "Cinderella of Cancer Research." "Most physicians", Dr. Wright observed, "simply ignored chemotherapy as a possible tool in the fight against cancer." Noted cancer researcher Dr. Ezra Greenspan of Mt. Sinai Hospital said bluntly that "Cancer chemotherapists . . . were generally deemed by their confreres to be dreamers, misguided fools or charlatans." He went on to aver that "Cancer chemotherapy is perhaps the most chemically challenging, stressful, and manipulative area of modern therapists." Chemotherapy had to survive several decades of blunt criticism before it finally attained respectability in medical circles.

Still the Wright team persevered in the use of several anticancer drugs. In 1951 for instance, they announced successes in treating solid tumors. They were the first to report regression in breast cancer using the folic acid antagonist, methotrexate. Most investigators were using this agent only to treat Hodgkin's disease lymphosarcoma, and the leukemias, but not with solid tumors. Wright's results were confirmed by Schoenbach and co-workers at the Mt. Sinai Hospital in 1952.

Ezra Greenspan took note of their work. He cited the Wright team for achieving" . . . a 32% regression rate with methotrexate alone, in a mix of patients with skin, subcutaneous, and chest wall metastasis . . ." Later, other investigators began using up to a five-drug combinations, several of which included the drug methotreate.

Wright and associates also investigated the effectiveness of using different drugs sequentially. This was another innovative procedure. Some of their patients, afflicted with "metatastic breast cancer improved significantly and survived seven to ten years." Wright's experiences led her to announce that "There is increasing evidence that prompt poly-chemotherapy after `curative' surgery in the early clinical stages of the disease could save thousands of lives annually."

In 1960, Wright and associates recorded another "first." They achieved drug-induced remissions in the skin cancer known as "mycosis fungoides" with the systematic use of the folic acid antagonist methotrexate. Mycosis fungoides is a troubling fungus-related malignancy. Previously, radiation was the only effective treatment of this cancer.

A pet project of Dr. Wright was to work out a method to predict the effect of a given drug upon a patient's cancer. She believed that this could be achieved by growing a tissue culture of the patient's malignant cells in a test tube, which is *in vitro*, then treating it with a specified drug. To test this hypothesis, she and her associates treated cancer tissue *in vitro*, and administered the same drug to some patients, or *in vivo*. The results were encouraging. When they ran similar tests on a series of patients, and treated them by the regional perfusion technique, they achieved a 70.7% correlation. By the perfusion technique, a high concentration of drug is administered to the regional area containing the tumor, such as the leg for example. In some cases, they obtained an even higher correlation, 81.25%.

Sometime later, Anne Hamburger recognized their technique as an important step forward. In the 1981 as guest editorial for the *Journal of Cancer Institute*, she wrote: " The work of Wright *et al*, in the 1950s, provided the guidelines to other investigators using this approach."

This was a significant contribution because then there were few guidelines for any chemotherapy procedures. Seizing upon the possibilities of their new approaches, the Wright investigators went on carefully as they developed and used different procedures for administering the drugs, always attending very closely to the patients. Sometimes the drugs were given orally, sometimes intravenously and at other times, intramuscular.

They also incorporated procedures developed by others in their research, often making specific changes to improve their effectiveness. For instance, Dr. Oscar Creech of New Orleans introduced what he called an isolation perfusion technique for a more safe method of delivering a larger concentration of chemotherapeutic agents to tumors. Robert Hayden, in his book "Nine Black American Doctors," explained how the Wright investigators proceeded:

> The perfusion technique involved locating the major artery and vein serving the cancerous area. Using a special needle, the artery and vein were connected. Tourniquets were used to prevent chemicals from leaking out of the circulation detour into the rest of the body. Then the chemical was pumped into the needle connecting the two blood vessels.

With this technique, and the application of several drugs, 32 out of 52 patients showed some tumor regression. Dr. Frederich Coulomb performed all of the perfusions for the group. They used the perfusion technique and the antitumor antibiotic Dihydro-E73 to treat several patients with squamous cell tumors of the head and neck area and the vulva. Dr. Wright reported "striking and significant carcinolytic effects . . . which lasted for months. This drug, however, is no longer available."

Later Wright discovered that the best results using the regional perfusion technique were with the antibiotic Actinomycin D in patients with advanced malignant melanoma. Five of the ten patients with melanoma exhibited tumor regression following treatment. Of these, three patients with tumors in the legs had complete disappearance of all tumors. At the time of her report, in 1967, the three patients were alive and well, and had been free of all diseases for over four and one-half years. In twenty-three patients who were treated only intravenously with Actinomycin D, and not with the perfusion technique, no regression of the melanoma was seen.

Making the Tough Decisions

How does the chemotherapist go about the vital but complex mission of trying to save lives of cancer patients using chemotherapy, while guarding against doing harm? As indicated earlier, the team carefully developed and followed specific procedures and guidelines for their investigations. First they considered only those drugs that had shown antitumor activity in carefully controlled animal tests. That of course, was only the first step because though a drug may have shown promise in animal tests, that was no guarantee they would be of value in humans. In an article published in the *New York Journal of Medicine* in 1961, Dr. Wright made an interesting observation:

[The] lack of correlation between the results of drugs against tumors in the mouse and in man is probably due to the fact that the mighty mouse will tolerate many drugs in dosages twenty times higher than the human can tolerate. It is interesting that the sensitivity of tumors to drugs from man and the mouse is similar in tissue culture.

Such findings however, were significant in helping to shape guidelines for their investigations. Wright followed the premise that "since drug dosage cannot be extrapolated directly from animal studies, it was necessary to carefully explore drug dose levels and schedules." Typically, when her team selected a drug for use, they conducted tests against a broad range of human tumors to learn which types were sensitive to a given group.

In an article published in 1962, she explained more fully what they did and the procedures they followed. The essay on "Cancer Chemotherapy Reports," disclosed their experiences with 25 different anticancer drugs in over 1000 patients. Wright wrote:

> For a drug to be of clinical importance in the control of neoplastic disease, it must produce tumor regression and other signs of clinical improvement at a dosage level which does not produce intolerable side effects or death of the patient.

The Wright team took great care to establish safe human dosage schedules for each drug. Then they treated the patient using single drug therapy and adjustments were made to fit individual tolerance. They realized that tolerance of one individual to a drug therapy might change over time. Also, the tolerance of a given individual might be different from the tolerance of another. So always, Wright was extremely cautious in the administration of cancer chemotherapeutic agents. If even mild drug toxicity occurred, she would temporarily stop therapy until all such signs disappeared. Then she would resume therapy at a lower dose. With the achievement of complete remission, that is, complete tumor disappearance, they ended therapy for as long as the patient remained free of the disease. Sometimes the researchers achieved complete remission without toxicity. Under certain controlled and well-monitored conditions, they ended therapy in patients who showed partial tumor regression.

In her exacting work with patients who suffered from advanced cancer, what rewarded Dr. Wright and associate most, and sustained their determination, was seeing patients improve. One patient, a nine-year-old girl, had advanced Hodgkin's disease. She received a single drug treatment of triethylene melamine (TEM). The young patient quickly responded to the treatment and showed signs of improvement. Dr. Wright continued the treatment and eventually all signs and symptoms disappeared and then released the patient. Unfortunately, a few years later, the cancer recurred so the team started TEM therapy again. For the second time all evidence of the disease completely disappeared. Dr. Wright reported that the patient "was living well when last seen 28 years since institution of therapy, with three healthy children."

To keep going, such research efforts must have support from grants. Yet, despite the major contributions they made to the field of cancer chemotherapy, fund raising was difficult - always uncertain. The federal government through the National Institute of Health, National Cancer Center and the United States Public Health Center provided most of the support received by the Wright team. Inexplicably, the Wright team never received a research grant from the American Cancer Society despite their applications and contributions to the field.

More Dr. Wright on History

Jane Cooke Wright published her cancer research findings in 135 scientific papers and contributed chapters in nine books. She read scores of papers before local, state, national and international groups. She was driven, and more than anything else, wanted to find a cure for cancer. At the same time, she wanted to help educate the public about cancer, to inform them, to remove myths, and misconceptions that could prove detrimental to their health. Dr. Wright understood the importance of enlisting an educated public as a major ally in the fight against cancer. Despite many difficulties, she continued to be hopeful and in an article "Cancer Update 1987" she wrote:

> Progress in the control of cancer has been significant and steady. With the development of new active anticancer drugs, better analogues, new refinements and strategies, further improvement in the efficacy of cancer chemotherapy will occur . . . Among newer exciting developments in cancer treatment are those occurring in tumor immunology with such biological response modifiers as the interferons, immuno-regulatory peptides, monoclonal antibodies, interleukine 2 . . . Most important is research into the causes,

prevention, and early diagnosis of cancer and other modalities of cancer research.   Each new discovery brings us closer to the ultimate conquest of cancer in man.

In May of 1992, Dr. Wright gave a talk on "Discoveries" at her Smith College Class 50th Reunion.   She noted that except for war and accidents, the major concerns in the United States lay in the conquest of heart disease, cancer and strokes.   These diseases, she said, accounted for 71% of all deaths in the United States, with cancer ranked second as the leading cause.   Of course, cancer is global, like many other diseases.   It occurs in "every country . . . in both sexes and at every age."

Placing cancer in historical perspective, as she did more than once, Dr. Wright pointed out that cancer "has been found in the bones of dinosaurs of 70-220 million years ago, in . . . mammals from 10 million years ago, and in man from 2500 B.C." She told of attempts to eradicate cancer by the Egyptians as far back as 3000-2500 BC by cauterizing "with a hot iron."   Crude surgical procedures were performed by the Egyptians and Greeks in desperate attempts to find a cure.   Beyond this, perhaps this most significant advancement in surgery as a treatment, took place in the 1880s following the developing of "safe anesthesia and antisepsis procedures."   In 1895, Roentgen discovered x-rays and a year later the Curies discovered and isolated radium. Following these discoveries, radiation therapy as a treatment for cancer began.

She pointed out that the modern era in cancer chemotherapy began with a chance discovery, or serendipity.   In 1942, there was an accident in the harbor of Bari, Italy. A U. S. Naval vessel ladened with mustard gas sank, releasing a large volume of its contents.   Sailors were poisoned and they developed a condition known as pancytopenia or destruction of the red and white blood cells.   Taking note of this development, the U.S. Chemical Welfare Service started a large scale screening program of hundreds of sulfa and nitrogen mustard compounds that were found to inhibit growth of animal lymphoid tissues.   A few other researchers took interest.   In 1946, Gilman and Philips at Yale, tried using tris-nitrogen mustard. They reported improvement in a patient with lymphosarcoma, a malignant tumor of the lymph nodes. Shortly afterward, Dr. Y. Subarow and his co-workers at Lederle Laboratories developed the folic acid antagonists. In 1948 Dr. Sidney Farber of Boston, reported his epoch-making discovery that the folic acid antagonists produced remission and an increase in the life span of children with acute leukemia. Farber, widely known as the "father of chemotherapy", was one of the first outside advisors to the Harlem Cancer Research Foundation.

So Jane Wright saw significant changes over the years in the struggle against cancer, many of them she helped to advance. She remained firm in her conviction that, based on the evidence, there were good reasons to continue research in the use of chemotherapy as a weapon to do battle with cancer. Her confidence being bolstered by the emergence of new and more weapons she spoke encouragingly, and pointed out that,

> In the last 50 years new anti-cancer chemicals were steadily developed . . . Approximately 6,000 compounds out of 60,000 tested in the animal screening program of the United States Government and private industry have been found to have antitumor properties. [Today}, development in the use of chemical agents in man are encouraging . . . the relative increase in survival rates in the past two decades is due in large part to chemotherapy . . . The role of chemotherapy in management is continuously changing and involving to that the best is yet to be determined.

Wright identified areas where headway was made against cancer, among them were Hodgkin's disease, lymphosarcoma, leukemia, rhabomysarcoma, Wilms' tumor (kidney tumor in children), choriocarcinoma of the lung and breast cancer. Progress was indeed being made on all fronts against a difficult foe.

China, The Soviet Union, Mount Kilimanjaro

Dr. Wright's prominence as a chemotherapist brought attention to her work and many requests to serve on projects and various task forces. For one such project, an international expedition, she agreed to lead a delegation of cancer researchers in the Citizen Ambassador Program of People to People International, to China, Eastern Europe and the Soviet Union. On these journeys she learned first hand a lot about what cancer researchers and practitioners were doing in other lands. Her hosts in turn, proved eager to learn from the American as they had read many of her published papers.

Wright later served on the Board of Directors of the African Research and Medical Foundation. From 1973-1984 she held the post of Vice President of that organization. To help improve medical care in far-flung places, the foundation instituted the practice of mobile medicine and flying doctors in East Africa.

During the summer of 1957, Dr. Wright undertook a medical mission to Ghana at the request of the U. S. State Department. In 1961, she visited Kenya, representing the African Research and Medical Foundation. There she worked on a medical safari from the Ngong Hills to Loitokitok on Africa's storied Mount Kilimanjaro. She later remarked that "the care and treatment they [the safari] brought to the people, the benefits that followed, and the interaction with the people brought their own rewards."

Some Thoughts About Her Tasks

What sustained her in face of the difficult fight against so formidable a foe as cancer? When the question was put to her, Dr. Wright paused briefly, her brow knitted ever so slightly. For one thing, she approached the task with a "can do" attitude. She knew progress would be slow at times, often uneven, but the hope for a breakthrough never vanished. Every little step meant progress, every new territory explored, every innovation tried, and failures also, taught lessons. She thought that those entering the world of cancer research needed a "bent for science." How much of that trait was "nature" and how much "nurture" she left for the learning psychologists to decide. Progress also depended on other factors. These include, sound policy, good organizations, effective leadership, funding for personnel, equipment, and materials. In a few well chosen words Dr. Wright added:

> In conclusion, it is our purpose to extract from . . .experiences, whenever possible, the fundamental natural laws so that the inevitable new, improved drugs can be used immediately at maximum efficiency.

An Active and Varied Life

From her childhood, Dr. Wright always lived an active life, a veritable bee hive of activity. Her intense, energetic investment in cancer chemotherapy research would have exhausted most people. Somehow, she did much more. She was a wife, mother, and daughter and her care extended beyond her nuclear family. When her mother's health started to decline, she brought her home and cared for her until she expired. She also lost her husband who died following an illness brought on by a rare disease contracted during a trip abroad. Dr. Wright raised her daughters during what she called "a difficult time for young people."

Dr. Wright also served on the Board of Directors of Medico, a service of Care, and with Blue Cross-Blue Shield. In higher education, she was appointed to a tenure position as professor in the New York School of Medicine. At Smith College, she served for ten time-consuming years on the Board of Directors. Appointed Associate Dean of the New York School of Medicine in 1967, she was the first woman in America to hold that position. When she became an administrator, Dr. Wright remembered her father. She recalled that he was a strict hospital director. He expected his staff to be "properly dressed" and altogether professional in demeanor and appearance. She wondered what he would have done in an era when men wore long hair, jeans and earrings.

Among several professional organizations that accepted her into membership was the prestigious American Association for Cancer Research (AACR). It is the largest organization in the world devoted entirely to cancer research. She also served four years on its Board of directors. The AACR recognized her among those women internationally who made significant contributions to cancer research.

Wright was among the seven founding members of the American Society of Clinical Oncology (ASCO). She served as secretary-treasurer of the organization for three years. Formally established in 1968 with a roster of 60, the membership rose number dramatically to 8,800 by 1980. Today Dr. Wright holds an emeritus membership in the society. Among others of her professional affiliations include the American Cancer Society, New York City Division, the Medical Advisory Board of the Skin Cancer Foundation, and the New York Cancer Society. From 1971-72 Wright was elected president, the first woman to hold that office. Today she remains active in consultant roles and serves on visiting teams to various hospitals in and outside the city. She has also been a consultant to the state supported Roswell Park Cancer Institute in Buffalo, New York, the first exclusively cancer research center in the United States.

In 1964, the president of the United States, Lyndon Baines Johnson, invited Dr. Wright to join a distinguished group of medical personnel to serve on the President's Commission of Heart Disease, Cancer and Stroke. The chair of the commission was the famous heart surgeon, Dr. Michael E. DeBakey. When Johnson convened the commission at the White House he emphasized the urgency of their task and the goal of their mission:

> Unless we do better, two thirds of all Americans now living will suffer or die from cancer, heart disease or stroke. I expect you to do something about it.

The cancer subcommittee, on which Wright served, recommended that regional cancer centers be established around the United States. It was adopted and included in the report to the president.

For 21 years, from 1966 to 1987, Wright worked on various committees with the Department of Health, Education, and Welfare (now Health and Human Services). From 1966 to 1970 she spent four intense, grueling, and draining years on the prominent National Cancer Advisory Committee.

For Exceptional Service

Many honors and awards recognized Wright's contributions to the advancement of medical science. Here are a few: She was cited for "important contributions to research in clinical chemotherapy", by the American Association for Cancer Research, this a prestigious recognition by her peers. Smith College presented her its distinguished Smith Medal. Women's Medical College of Pennsylvania conferred upon her an honorary doctorate, the Doctor of Medical Sciences (DMS), and Denison University the Doctor of Science (DSc). Thelma Perkins included her in the CIBA-GIGY list of *Exceptional Black Scientists* and the Smithsonian Institute featured her in its exhibit of "Black Women: Achievement Against Odds." From the Women's Division of the Albert Einstein School of Medicine, she received the "Spirit of Achievement Award". Among other treasured awards were the Susan Smith McKinney Medical Society Award, and the Otelia Cromwell Award from Smith College.

The Greatest Reward: "To serve with heart and mind"

Dr. Jane C. Wright retired in 1985 after a long and productive career in cancer research. Nonetheless the "Mother of Chemotherapy" remains active, constantly urging researchers to persevere in the field she helped develop from its early childhood. She has faith in its future, based on results already obtained.

Wright credits certain particulars for her opportunity. In a speech delivered during 1992, she was moved to say,

> My contributions were possible because of fortuitous circumstances. I was in the right place at the right time and became engaged in research on chemotherapy when only a few were working on drugs.

When her father opened the doors to cancer research, Dr. Wright applied a good mind and strong work ethics to the risky task. She tends not to dwell on some tough personal and professional encounters but is far more likely to acknowledge the absence of racial or gender prejudices than to complain about their impeding presence. Public recriminations when her work was undermined, complaints when warranted support was withheld or breakthroughs not recognized, take back seat to praise for those who cooperated and gave needed assistance No doubt her father would have been proud of her and her accomplishments. Her motto seemed to be that it is better to appreciate that which she has or had than to deprecate that not forthcoming. When asked about her many honors she said that all were important and she treasured them in her heart. Nevertheless she observed that "The thrill of clinical investigation and the joy of healing are the rewards of medicine." Her work was best summed up on February 3, 1982 when she gave a speech at a high school in Stamford Connecticut. She said:

> I am one of those who has had the fun of a creative medical family, and a special kind of joy working for sick people. There is a deep satisfaction in knowing you are a part of a continuing process and program, that you have picked up where others have left off and others will pick up where you left off. One is drawn to these things, not because of financial reward but ultimately because of the desire to serve with the heart and mind.

References for Further Reading

"CIBA-GEIGY To Present Dr. Wrights's Portrait to Du Sable Museum", *1985. CIBA GEIGY News Release.*

"Dr. Jane C. Wright Returns to NYMC as Associate Dean," 1967. *Intercomm 1*:18, New York Medical College.

"Dr. Jane Cooke Wright Aids Attack on Cancer," 1968. *Scope Weekly, 12*-13, February.

Dr. Jane C. Wright, Physician and Therapist," excerpted from *Women Pioneers of Science*, by Louis Haber, 1980. *Daisy,* 6:22-23.

"Dr. Jane Wright Honored by Local Corporation," 1985. *Newswire, 22-23,* February.

"Dr. Jane C. Wright Portrait Presentation," 1985. *CIBA-GEIGY.* November 10.

Echman, Marga, 1967. "Two Names Are Better Than One," *New York Post Weekend Magazine, 29,* April 27.

Greenspan, Ezra., 1982. *Clinical Interpretation and Practice of Cancer Chemotherapy,* New York: Raven Press.

Hamburger, Anne W., 1981. "Use of In Vitro Tests in Predictive Cancer Chemotherapy," *Journal of National Cancer Institute,* 66: 981-988.

Hayden, Robert, 1976. *Nine Black American Doctors,* Reading, MA: Addison-Wesley Publishing Co. Inc.

Jenkins, Edward S., 1989. "The Remarkable Dr. Jane Cooke Wright," *Afro-Americans in New York Life and History,* 13, 57-63.

Okon, May, 1967. "Why We Can't Solve the Cancer Problem," *New York News,* 4, 34-35, November 19.

"Postscript to a Career," 1988. *Images,* New York Medical Colleges, 18-19, Fall.

"Salute to Eight Senior Women Scientists; Jance C. Wright of New York City," [International], 1945. *Cancer Report,* 117, 1045.

With L. T. Wright, A. Prigot, S. Weintraub, 1950. "Remissions Caused by Tri-Ethylene Melamine in Certain Neoplastic Diseases: A Preliminary Report," *Journal of the National Medical Association,* 43, 211-240.

_____, 1952. "The Effect of Folic Acid Antagonist, A-Methopterin, on the Level of the Circulating Eosinophilus in Humans, " *The Journal of Hematology,* 7:743-748.

Wright, Jane C., et al, 1957. "Investigation of the Relationship between Clinical and Tissue Culture Response to Chemotherapeutic Agents on Human Cancer, *New England Journal of Medicine,* 257:1207-1211.

With J. P. Cobb, 1959. "Studies on a Craniopharyngioma in Tissue Culture. I. Growth Characteristics and Alterations Produced Following Exposure to Two Radiomimetic Agents," *Journal of Neuropathology and Experimental Neurology,* 18, 563-568.

Wright, Jane C. 1961. "A Survey of Medical Conditions in Ghana in 1957," *Journal of the National Medical Association,* 53, 313-320.

Wright, Jane C., "A Visit to Kenya and Tanganyika in 1961," *Journal of the National Medical Association,* 53, 327-334.

With D. C. Walker M. M. Lyons, 1967. "Sensitivity Testing in Primary Cultures of Human Tumors

Wright, Jane C., 1962. "Clinical Drug Dosages and Duration of Therapy of the Cancer Chemotherapeutic Agents," *Cancer Chemotherapy Reports No. 16.*

With D. C. Walker, "A Predictive Test for the Selection of Cancer Chemotherapeutic Agents for the Treatment of Human Cancer," Journal of Surgical Oncology, 7, 381-393.

Wright, Jane C., 1984. "The Thrill of Clinical Investigation and the Joy of Healing Are the Rewards of Medicine," in *Black Women Against the Odds,* Washington, D.C.: Smithsonian Traveling Exhibition Service

Wright, Jane C. 1984. "Cancer Chemotherapy: Past, Present, and Future-Part I," *Journal of the National Medical Association, 76*: 773-784. .

Wright, Jane C., 1984. "Cancer Chemotherapy: Past, Present, and Future-Part II," *Journal of the National Medical Association, 76*: 865-875. .

The author is grateful to Dr. Jane C. Wright who provided additional information and insights for this chapter through interview.

Leon Roddy - The Spider Man
(1921-1975)

Leon Roddy paused at his work for a short breather. He took the big handkerchief from his back pocket, wiped the perspiration from his brow, and from the back of his neck. Then he went to his brow again. Leon looked at the clock. He had three more long hours of labor in the stifling heat before the end of the workday. The youngster stuffed the handkerchief back into his pocket, took a deep breath, then returned to work.

Leon tried to focus on other things to combat the heat with his mind. His thoughts went to the early morning hours when it was a bit cooler. Just after dawn he and his father, Floyd Roddy arrived on the grounds of the Amarillo Flour Mill in Amarillo, Texas, and reported for work. He vividly remembered approaching the plant and seeing the tall stacks silhouetted against the dawning west Texas sky. When they arrived, his father gave an order he dreaded to hear. "Well Leon, today you go down into the bin."

Leon was one of the three children born to Floyd and Mattie Roddy in Whitewith, Texas. His father had worked for many years in the flour mill located in the Texas panhandle. Now he was a foreman and he thought his son might want to follow him and work his way up too. But Leon never wanted to work at the mill; he had other ideas. His father did not realize that he planned to finish high school and go to Texas College, a Methodist school over in Tyler, Texas. He had his heart set on college and that is what he finally told his father. Floyd Roddy was a good man but he could also be stubborn. He explained to his son why he took a dim view of his plans to attend college:

> I'm sorry Leon, but I sent money to your brother for a whole year for his education at Wiley College down in Marshall, Texas, only to find out the boy never even enrolled. No, I am not wasting any more money on schooling for you or your sister beyond high school. Maybe you'd better come to work at the mill with me. On the other hand, if you are bound and determined to go to that college, come to work anyway so you can earn your fee.

That was how young Leon came to work at the mill. On most days things were not too bad. His father had him doing a variety of jobs, scooping wheat from the bin to the conveyor belt, or unloading boxcars of grain that came from Forth Worth. Sometimes Floyd Roddy had Leon selling company finished products out of the warehouse to the "locals." That was easy. But at certain intervals, the big flour mills had to be cleaned out. That meant someone had to go down into the bin and labor in the stifling heat to get the job done. Sometimes the temperature down there went as high as 140 °F.

Momentarily, a flush of anger went with Leon down in the bin. On the other hand, he knew he could earn more money for college at that job - $2.50 a day instead of the $1.50 he was getting for the other jobs. For a black teenager in northwest Texas during the late 1930s, that was about as good as it got. He was young and healthy, and the thought of earning more money for college was the motivation he needed to continue the hard work.

Leon attended high school in nearby Sherman, Texas. He really liked school. English, mathematics, and foreign languages were among his favorite subjects but nothing outranked biology. John Tonnette, a dynamic teacher taught biology and he made the subject come alive. It did not take Tonnette long to recognize Leon's special aptitude for science. When he saw the youngster's unsatiable curiosity and love for biology, Tonnette encouraged his star pupil to go to college and major in biology. Many years later, speaking to a state conference of Louisiana secondary school science teachers, Roddy paid tribute to his high school mentor saying, "Mr. Tonnette was good teacher, an inspiring man. He influenced me a lot, and when I finished high school, he helped get me a scholarship to partially pay for a college education."

In high school Leon managed to stay at or near the top of his class in every subject. Interestingly enough, his fiercest competitor was his girlfriend Martha. Before every exam, he would go over to her house and they would study together. (Somehow they always managed to enroll in the same classes). After studying Leon would walk a short distance from the house, stop and call back, "Martha, I'm going to beat you tomorrow." But it did not always turn out that way.

It so happened that his biology teacher was also his football coach so the two had more than one common interest. Football was Leon's best sport. He also played basketball, describing himself as a "scrub" on the team. In addition he joined the debate team where he reveled in the intellectual challenge.

Outside school, Leon took on odd jobs to earn pocket money. Along the way, he learned to clean and press clothes, a skill that came in handy during his college days.

With a small scholarship from Texas College, and his earnings from the flour mill, Leon finally said goodbye to his family and friends. He left the Texas panhandle and enrolled in college, determined to major in biology. At Texas College he found a one-man biology department, a Professor Hilliard who opened his eyes even more to the wonders of life science. Hilliard made Leon his laboratory assistant where he fulfilled the terms of his scholarship. This gave him a chance to spend more time in the laboratory, which was greatly to his liking. There he learned lots more about biology and the requirements for conducting good, precise, laboratory experiments.

On weekends, Leon worked at a cleaning and pressing shop in Tyler. He collected clothes, cleaned and pressed them, then made deliveries. Soon he knew almost everyone on campus and all knew him.

But Leon never neglected his studies - they came first. His grades were as good in college as they had been in high school. Floyd Roddy took note of his son's good scholarship despite working two jobs to meet his expenses. Eventually, convinced that Leon was of serious intent, the elder Roddy reconsidered and began sending money to help his son remain in college.

Being so involved, and focused on matters of priority, the years at Texas College went by swiftly. As he entered his senior year, relatives back home began to look forward to the idea that their young Leon would be the first member of his family to earn a college degree. That gave him a good feeling but he also pondered his life beyond college. Perhaps he could go to graduate school, maybe even study for the doctorate. Before he reached that mark however, circumstances beyond his control intervened. On Sunday December 7, 1941, Japan shocked the United States with a devastating surprised air attack on its big base in Pearl Harbor, Hawaii.

The attack destroyed most of the United States fleet in the Pacific, practically demolished the airforce stationed there, and inflicted heavy casualties on U. S. military personnel. President Franklin Roosevelt reacted swiftly. On Monday, December 8, 1941, referring to the Japanese attack as "a day that shall live in infamy," he appeared before the United States Congress and asked that a State of War be declared against Japan. Congress quickly agreed. Then Germany and Italy on one side, and the USA on the other, declared war against each other. Thus the USA joined the Allies, Great Britain, Russia, French Exile and the Commonwealth nations, against the Axis Powers, greatly expanding the scope of World War II. A global conflict of unprecedented scale in human history, raged.

The United States mobilized the most massive military machine in its history. Able-bodied young men volunteered, or were drafted into the armed forces and many women enlisted in special units. Leon Roddy joined millions of others in being called to service. One week before his graduation, the military inducted him into the U. S. Army.

The Great War in Europe

Texas College conferred the bachelor's degree on Roddy, with high honors, *in absentia*. Meanwhile, he went to Camp Walters in Mineral Wells, Texas for basic training, and from there to Camp Beale, California. There he joined an artillery battalion for brief but intense training before sailing to England where they learned to use the howitzers.

By that time battles in Europe had escalated in intensity as the Allied launched a massive military campaign against a powerful German military machine. The Allies invaded Western Europe and in fierce battles liberated France, Belgium, Luxembourg, Poland and others from Germany. Shortly after the invasion Roddy's unit was moved to France where they took up position near the famous French Maginot Line. Almost immediately they engaged a retreating but stubborn and still dangerous German Army. Roddy's artillery unit was assigned to the 9th Army under the command of the storied General Omar Bradley. For a short time they also fought under the command of the offensive minded General George S. Patton, sometime called "Ole Blood and Guts." When they completed their mission with Patton, Roddy's unit returned to Bradley's command where they continued to fight German forces in several vicious, intense, battles. They could not know however that the worse lay ahead.

Around Christmas, the coldest and most miserable winter in a century descended on Belgium and northern Luxembourg. In a desperate attempt to turn the tide of battle in their favor, Germany's Fuehrer Adolph Hitler ordered more than 500,000 troops to mount a furious counter assault against a thin, stretched out American line in Belgium. Before light broke the dawn, crack German Panzer units, the elite SS troops, and an assortment of old and young troops made a lightning attack across the frozen battlefield, catching the Allied forces by surprise. Nonetheless, the Allies fought back. Called the "Battle of the Bulge," this campaign was said to be the bloodiest conflict in military history. The loss of lives was staggering. In that single conflict the numbers killed and wounded on both sides rivaled casualties suffered during the United States Civil War

Roddy's unit swung into action. Fighting fiercely among the roar of cannons, screeching shells, tanks, and rifle fire, they began to punish the enemy. Refusing to be intimidated, they held their position and, as Roddy recalled years later, "We did not lose a foot of ground and not a man [prisoner] to the enemy." The "Battle of the Bulge" marked a major turning point in the war. A few miles away, 100,000 other black non-combat soldiers volunteered for infantry duty to bolster the fighting manpower in Europe. One unit, the 66th Armored Infantry Battalion, spearheading for Patton's armored division, joined the fight in the Battle of the Bulge, held the lines then forced the Germans into retreat. History takes little note of the role played by these all black units, and movies about the European campaigns ignore them. Nonetheless they fought and died in France, Belgium, Luxembourg, and across Germany to the Austrian border. Like other Americans and their allies, they helped turn the tide of battle - and the war.

The enemy fell back, continuing to fight, but never mounted another major offense. American and British warplanes controlled the skies. The Soviet Union took the offensive on the Eastern Front, drove Hitler's forces Leningrad, and invaded Germany itself. On May 7, 1945, Germany surrendered and, the terrible war in Europe ended.

On every continent, and around the globe, those who fought with the Allies or supported them celebrated the victory in Europe. Still the war, especially for the United States and her Pacific Allies, continued. After a series of stunning victories in the Pacific at the beginning of the war, the Japanese were now suffering reversals as American led Allies put them on the defensive. Despite losing, the enemy fought fiercely, remained a dangerous fighting force, still able to inflict heavy loss of life and machines on American forces. Then the United States unleashed a new and terrifying weapon of war, the atomic bomb, on the Japanese cities of Hiroshima and Nagasaki.

Never had the world witnessed, or except a few, even dreamed of such massive human made destruction and loss of life and lingering pain, as inflicted by a single mighty explosion in each city and may it never happen again. On September 2, 1945, fearing another atomic bomb attack, possibly on Tokyo itself, Japan surrendered, ending World War II. Peace came just one day before Roddy's unit was to be shipped from Europe to the Pacific war zone.

Graduate School at Last

Roddy received an honorable discharge from the United States army and immediately began making plans for graduate school. The admonition of his former Professor Hilliard to attend graduate school, never left him. Like thousands of war veterans, he received support for his education under the GI Bill of Rights. Roddy enrolled at the University of Michigan, eager to begin.

To the dismay of this ex-soldier, things did not go well at Michigan. Never before had he been unhappy at school. Though he scored well on tests, and kept his average high, nearly always he received Cs as his final grades in zoology courses. Only by taking courses in botany, where he consistently received As, did he manage to maintain a B average. His classmates, and for that matter, his professors were "standoffish" and generally uncommunicative. Only one of his white classmates, a young man from Mississippi, spoke with him. The two men would talk about biology, exchange information, swap ideas, and speculate on the meaning of developments and exciting breakthroughs in the field. In times of rare leisure, they talked about society in the north and south, their reception at Michigan, and about life. A strong bond formed between the black and white southerners, and they became friends for life.

The Dragonfly

One bright spot in zoological studies at Michigan changed Roddy's professional life. He needed an elective to complete his requirement for the master's degree so he enrolled in a seminar at the University Museum. The instructor, a Professor Rogers, was conducting research on a large winged insect call the dragonfly (*order Odonata*). During this seminar Roddy became fascinated with entomology, the study of insects.

At the end of the term, Rogers had a talk with Roddy.

"You've done well in this course," he said, "I think you should do further study in entomology, As you know, we don't offer a degree in entomology here, but why don't you go to Ohio State. They have a good program and I can recommend you to a friend over there."

Roddy thanked his professor, and graciously accepted his offer of recommendation. He felt excited about the possibility of studying for the doctorate in entomology and submitted his application for admission to Ohio State University with dispatch. The following summer he enrolled at Ohio and began his doctoral program in entomology. Continued enrollment through the academic year strongly beckoned but now married, and with a wife and child to support, he needed to work. As soon as possible though, a determined Leon Roddy planned to resume his studies in entomology.

Returning to his native Texas, Roddy accepted an appointment as a biology professor at Tillotson College. He taught there two years, then resumed his formal program in entomology at Ohio State. Arriving in Columbus, Ohio in January, the wintry cold stood in sharp contrast to the milder Texas climate but not as cold as it was in Michigan, nor the bitter winter he spent fighting the Germans in Europe during World War II. Fortunately, the isolation he experienced at Michigan proved far less a problem at Ohio State and in this more liberating environment he found it easier to concentrate on his work. If anything, whatever isolation he experienced was self-imposed. He told the writer about an unexpected experience:

I was put into an office with other graduate students studying entomology. After a few months they went to my major professor and complained that I didn't associate with them. I was segregating myself. But I had learned at Michigan that as a black man, I was to keep to myself. At Ohio State they invited me to things, but I didn't attend-fearful that I would run into problems that I did not want to encounter at this time. But my professor called me in and said, `Roddy, the other students say you won't have anything to do with them-that when they ask you a question, you answer and just clam up'.
I could see that he was sincere so I tried to explain that I had encountered many problems while studying for the masters and that

I had come to believe that among students of science, all were prejudiced. `Forget the past, he said. This is a better place.'

So it turned out to be. Except for one inexplicable final grade, it was a better place for Roddy. He buried himself, first in his studies, then the research for his dissertation. In 1953, after just seventeen more months at Ohio, Roddy met all requirements for the Doctor of Philosophy degree in entomology. More than that, the experience largely restored his faith in the integrity of the scientific community. Roddy came to believe that some scientists were as open-minded and objective in their personal lives as they were in the laboratory. Years later, in recognition of his research and publication, Leon Roddy was honored as one of the top alumni of the Department of Entomology.

One Thousand Insects.

Dr. Leon Roddy went looking for work again. He turned down several opportunities to teach at northern universities, saying, "Somehow I felt needed back home." Three historically black institutions made offers: one in Florida, one in his native Texas, and one in Louisiana. After visiting each of these institutions, he accepted a position at Southern University in Baton Rouge, Louisiana. Interestingly enough, Southern offered the lowest salary but had the largest, and what he believed was the most progressive biology department among the three. Most important, Southern also offered courses in entomology. The chairman of the biology department, J. Warren Lee impressed him very much. He later learned that Lee also earned his Ph.D. at Ohio State. "I never met a finer man than that guy," Roddy recalled. "He went out of his way to help me. But he also worked the stew out of me."

And work he did. Roddy arrived at the Baton Rouge, Louisiana campus in the middle of the hot, humid, summer. The university was experimenting with a 12-week summer session so that its more able and hardworking students could earn a baccalaureate degree in three years. The teaching hours were long, and the classrooms and laboratories were crowded.

After living in Ohio for nearly two years, Roddy that found the summers in Baton Rouge took some getting use to-especially with his exhausting load. He knew heat in Amarillo but it was different-drier, far less humid. The weather and workload seemed almost too much to bear and as he contemplated his situation, a brief wave of frustration swept over him. How long could he last under these energy-draining conditions? How could he get into his research? Where was the time? Where was the support?

After one long day of lecturing and conducting class laboratory experiments, Roddy went to his desk and collapsed in an old swivel chair. He was tired. The biology department was housed in a building near a bluff that overlooked the Mississippi so today he swung his well-worn oak desk around and gazed at the large Spanish moss draped oak trees that bordered the lovely campus and separated it from the river below. Observing the lush foliage on the river's banks, he might have thought about Mark Twain who wrote about "The steep verdant slope . . . at whose base the [Mississippi] river flowed endlessly to south to the Gulf of Mexico. He could have reflected on the words of Langston Hughes, a visitor to the campus at Southern who wrote:

I bathe in the Euphrates when dawns were young,
I built my hut near the Congo and it lulled me to sleep.
I looked upon the Nile and raised the pyramids above it.
I heard the singing of the Mississippi when Abe Lincoln
went down to New Orleans, and I've seen its muddy
bosom turn all golden in the sunset.

Sometimes when atmospheric conditions were "right", a multi-hued sun would sink in the west, and splash the skies with a churned red-orange-yellow color mix that reflected off the Mississippi below, at the bend. The sky was "right" today and Roddy took in the impressive scene. It was a kind of reward from nature after a hard day-providing generously a free, relaxing experience before calling it quits.

Small wonder that he did not hear Professor Rome, the quiet, serious botanist, approaching him. He had these insects, collected in Louisiana but unclassified. Could Professor Roddy-no, (of course he *could*) *would* he care to identify them? Surprised but drawn to the sample, a hesitant but firm yes-yes he would. The weariness forgotten, the young scientist eagerly went to work on the collection that contained over a thousand different insects.

Insects have existed at least since the Devonian period more than 400 million years ago. For sheer numbers and adaptability, insects surpass any organisms in the macro-world. In size they range from a few millimeters to around 30 centimeters (practically a foot). In comparison, of the 1.7 million known species of plants and animals, an amazing 750,000 or about 44.5% are insects. One scientist estimated that there are about 30 million species of insects. They can be found on and beneath the ground, on and beneath water surfaces, as high as 3,000 meters (About 10,000 feet), in glacial north, in deserts and rain forests, in cold mountain streams and hot springs, almost everywhere except the polar ice cap.

The katydid sings, cricket shrills, mosquitoes buzz, lightning bugs blink and glowworms eerily glow. Ladybugs devour aphids, termites chew up old trees, praying mantises and dragonflies eat insects. Even the despised cockroaches eat lice and bedbugs.

The milkweed butterfly, monarch butterfly, tiger swallowtail are pictures of grace and beauty. Other insects pollinate flowers, making crops possible. Bees make honey and beeswax, silkworms make silk and from fruit flies many secrets of genetics were revealed.

On the other hand insects literally challenge mankind for supremacy of the world. The corn borer, potato beetle, boll weevil, and locusts inflict huge crop damage. Termites undermine structures of wooden buildings, mosquitoes and flies transmit diseases including malaria, cholera, sleeping sickness, West Nile virus and typhoid fever. Not to be overlooked are insects that bite and sting like wasps and mosquitoes and, fleas and lice bite and cling, humankind and domestic plants animals, causing illness, discomfort and sometimes death.

Roddy first confirmed that each animal in the collection was an insect (class insecta) as not all small crawling creatures fall into that category. Insects have three body parts: a head, thorax and abdomen with three pairs of legs attached to the thorax. They have one or two sets of wings (apterogota), or no wings pterogota). Scientists place all insects into the kingdom Animalia, phylum Arthropod, class Insecta and some 30 different orders. Examples are Diptera (flies, mosquitoes, gnats); Hymenoptera (bees, wasps, ants), Odonata (dragonflies, damsel flies), and Phasmida (walking sticks).

Carefully and meticulously Roddy studied the minute parts of the insects before him, working into the night. He took notes, all carefully organized, his scientific habits of mind placing a high priority on accurate, detailed descriptions. Sometimes he made dissections and careful, neat, drawings, all the while marveling at the unique structures of these well-adapted creatures.

Occasionally the professor paused, wiping the sweat from his brow and the back of his neck like he had done years ago while working at the flourmill. He catalogued each animal using the technical language of the entomologists, names like *tomaxys, calcitrans, pyrausta nubilis, blissus leucopterus, pieris rapae.*

Finally it was done. More than one thousand different insects, all found in Louisiana, many classified for the first time. It was 5:00 A. M. the next day. Leon Roddy had worked through the night and in a few hours he had to meet his first class.

The Spider Man

A few weeks later Lee walked down the hall to Roddy's office with a collection of spiders. The chairman wondered if Professor Roddy would identify them for use in a class of invertebrate zoology. During their discussion about the project, Lee suggested that Roddy might want to do some research on spiders, a relative of the insect, since so little was being done in their study, especially in Louisiana.

Spiders are often mistaken for insects. Though both are arthropods, they differ. Spiders are placed in the class Arachnida, and order Araneae. The name *Arachnida* comes from a mythical Greek character, Arachne. Over 50,000 species and 2500 genera inhabit the earth from sea level to high mountains, and almost every conceivable place on earth. They have existed at least since the Devonian period.

Adult spiders have eight legs, they are all wingless, and have two major body sections, cephalothorax and abdomen. There is great variation in size.

Though trained as an entomologist, Roddy had also studied the spider. He knew that few animals were as misunderstood as the spider. Myths and legends abound. Science fictions often portray them as gigantic, sinister, almost indestructible monsters, bent on devouring people and wrecking havoc on property. "Not so," said the bayou scientist. None every reach such gigantic size. They range in length from only 0.5 mm to 9 cm. Moreover, he explained, "Only two spiders native to North America are poisonous: the brown recluse and black widow."

The truth, as Roddy so often declared, most spiders are harmless and many are of great benefit to humankind. They are important in helping maintain a balance in nature. Spiders help to keep insects in check. Their silk webs, the lightest, finest, and strongest known, have long been the best objects for use in optical instruments. Scientists use some spiders to test the effect of certain drugs. Nevertheless, Roddy was well aware that most people believed any spider could deliver a potent bite.

Weaving spiders, come not here,
Hence, you long-legged spinners, hence!
Beetles black, approach not near;
Worm nor snail, do no offense.
-From "A Midsummer Night Dream"

The spider collection led to a second turning point in Roddy"s life. Soon he could be found out in the field, studying spiders in their native habitat in the bayous, swamps, flatlands and hills, as well as homes and other buildings of Louisiana. Nothing deterred him. Not the underbrush, not the weather, not even when an occasional venomous water moccasin snake defiantly claimed territorial rights. Nonetheless, when a bobcat objected to his presence, Leon Roddy vacated the area with new-found speed. When you are facing what is pound for pound one of the meanest, most vicious animals known, you look elsewhere for spiders.

Roddy began to publish his findings and read papers at professional conventions. This brought such attention to his work that soon others began to recognize him as a foremost authority on spiders in the state and nation. Letters came from as far away as several foreign countries requesting copies of papers he had published in scientific journals. He discovered new species of spiders including the first one he named *drassodes louisianus.* As one of the few systemists in the world he classified thousands of spiders for other international authorities on arachnids. He also collaborated with W. J. Gerst the curator of arachnids at the American Museum of Natural history in Washington, D.C. All told, Leon Roddy identified more than six thousand spiders.

Included among his publications were detailed descriptions of several new species of the clubionid spider. Roddy announced that the clubionid could be found in various parts of the United States and Canada, and that two European species were "apparently becoming well-known in the Pacific Northwest."

It is little wonder that to his students, colleagues and other friends around campus Roddy became known as "The Spider Man."After a feature story in the magazine section of a Sunday issue of the New Orleans *Times Picayune,* Louisiana's largest newspaper, the name became more widespread.

Roddy was a champion of the spider and its benefits to humankind, The toxin of most spiders has no effect on humans, he often said to anyone who would listen:

> We don't really appreciate the spider. The animal is insectivorous, so spiders consume an enormous quantity of insects that would otherwise plague man, his crops and domestic animals. They do far more good than harm. Their web is used for making sights in microscopes and other optical instruments. As far poisonous spiders, there is only one native to this state-the black widow. The feared tarantula and brown recluse are not native inhabitants of Louisiana.

Even the black widow spider shies from man. Despite the publicity, there is only one case where we know the bite was fatal.

Even the bite of a feared tarantula, he repeated often, though painful was not dangerous to humans and in fact, many people kept them as pets.

Roddy became an expert on spiders because of his scientific curiosity and keen mind. But his years of research were not easy. He conducted most of his field and laboratory investigations at his own expense, without benefit of support dollars from his institution, the government, or private firms. Despite these handicaps, he shared his findings with the scientific community through publication and reading papers at conferences. He also spoke to elementary and secondary teachers, students and civic groups. Beyond expanding knowledge about our natural world, a worthy objective, his work had practical applications as well.

One case involved the United States Army. They wanted to know if its troops stationed in the Bay St. Louis, Mississippi area might be exposed to poisonous spiders and requested the services of Professor Roddy. After a three month investigation, he informed the base commander that the only poisonous spider was in the area was the black widow spider and she only rarely.

"The Spider Man" never denied a request made of him. On another occasion a woman in the north central area of the state suffered a painful spider bite as she lay in bed. Worried that it might have been a brown recluse, the victim crushed the animal flat and saved it. Having read an article about a scientist working on spiders at Southern University, she immediately called him for help. Would he tell her if she had been a victim of the brown recluse? If so, might this specie have infested the area?

Roddy traveled to the woman's home and identified the spider as the brown recluse. Bites of the brown recluse are rarely fatal but the sore can be long lasting, and other complications can develop. Treatment by a doctor is important so Roddy quickly gave needed information to the woman's physician. Immediately thereafter the "Spider Man" launched some scientific detective work. After careful but extensive field investigations, he found no evidence of the brown recluse in the area. He hypothesized that the spider had somehow been brought in from elsewhere. . Roddy continued his search for spiders in the marshes, vegetation, flatland, and in the rolling pine tree covered hills in the northern territories of the state. He studied their anatomy, did some work on their physiology, studied their habitat, unique behavior, marvelous workmanship, lifestyles and relations to their environment. Though bitten more than once, he remained undaunted in his study of a valuable but misunderstood creatures and member of the ecosystem. Years later the Harvard biologists explained the importance of Roddy's kind of work. Wilson wrote that, "Every ecologist can tell of studies delayed by the lack of taxonomic expertise." Roddy provided that kind of expertise in the world of spiders, an area of great need. He went on to say that when the organisms of the earth are classified, we will have a better, clearer understanding of living things and of life.

The lean, bronze-skinned Leon Roddy was an affable man with an engaging personality. Always approachable, his baritone voice and west Texas accent still in evidence, he enjoyed a good laugh. People tended to like him and he enjoyed the companionship of others. In his rare spare time he would play a round of golf with his friends, or watch the Southern University Jaguars play football on autumn Saturday afternoon. He also enjoyed fishing for bass in the bayou country.

A proud man, Roddy was devoted to his family. He had three daughters, Stephanie, Michelle and Robbins, and a son, Leon from a previous marriage. His wife, Marian Daniel Roddy grew up in North Carolina, where she was born. The Roddys met at Southern.

Leon Roddy's dedication to his research matched his dedication to humanity. He firmly believed that a better understanding of the spider could contribute to an elevated quality of life for humans though that was not the popular view extant. Even so there were some acknowledged his works. Though all were cherished, the citation by the Ohio State University Department of Entomology, the Texas College Distinguished Scholar and Teacher in the Field of Biology Award, stood out.

Roddy pursued his research with the spider indefatigably though he lamented the absence of research support for the work he was doing. In moments of despair brought on by the lack, he would entertain the notion of going back to entomology where he could find research dollars. Nonetheless, he continued to reveal new and exciting things about the arachnid until his strong constitution became weakened by an affliction. On June 22, 1975, at the age of 54 years, Leon Roddy lost his gallant fight with cancer. But none who knew him and his work could doubt that he was truly "The Spider Man."

References and Materials for Further Reading

"Leon Roddy-Man Who understands Spiders," 1962, *Ebony*, 17: 64-71.

Roddy, Leon, R., 1966. "New Species, Records of Clubionid Spiders", *Trans. Amer. Micros. Soc.*, 85: 399-407.

Sammons, Vivian O., 1989. *Blacks in Science and Education*, Washington, D.C. Hemisphere Publication.

Vietmyer, Noel, 1989. "Who Needs Spiders, Believe it or Not, -We Do"!, *Reader's Digest,*, 135:137-40.

Wilson, Edward O., 1985. "The Biological Diversity Crisis", *Issues in Science and Technology*, 2:20-29.

Most of the material for this chapter was drawn from personal interviews with the late Dr. Leon Roddy and based on recorded interviews. The title of his dissertation was "A Morphological Study of the Respiratory Horns Associated with the Puparea of some Diptera,, Especially Ophyra Anescens.

Chapter XVI_____

Reatha Clark King - Chemistry of the
Halogen Compounds
(1938-)

After the benediction, the congregation moved out of the sanctuary. Amid handshakes, nods, and small talk, the members of the Mt. Zion Baptist Church of Moultree, Georgia, gathered in pockets and groups on the grounds outside. Young Reatha Clark felt good. She always did at her church services. Yet on this day, she experienced a certain sadness as well. In a few days she would leave Moultree for a small Methodist College in Atlanta, called Clark College. She looked forward to enrolling in college, but she knew she would miss her family, friends and church.

Outside their home, church was the center of life for Reatha, her two sisters Mamie and Dorothy, and her mother, Ola Clark. Church members seemed to take an interest in its young people and they encouraged those who showed promise. They admired the Clark children because of their strong work ethics and uncommon success in school. "You youngsters have such good heads," they would say. "You are so apt and all. You just must make something of yourselves." Often they simply said, "Just keep on keeping on." Reatha and her sisters felt the warmth and strength of the people's sincerity, and were encouraged. Mrs. Clark, in her quiet and calm demeanor, graciously acknowledged the recognition accorded her daughters.

Reatha Belle Clark was born in rural Pavo, Georgia, April 11,

1938. The second of three daughters, her parents were Willie and Ola Watts Campbell Clark. Mrs. Clark formal education, all in an impoverished school system, was limited. She had only a third grade education, but she was astute, industrious, and of strong character. With an uncanny ability to manage for her family, she got the most out of her meager resources. Willie Clark, a farm worker, could neither read nor write. Nonetheless folks respected his ability to "figure things out." Despite his lack of literacy, those who knew him, called Willie Clark a "smart man." So when anyone spoke of the Clark sisters, they used such terms as "diligent," "industrious," and "dependable," like their mother. And they were "smart too," like both their parents. Unfortunately, while the children were still young, the marriage failed, and Willie and Ola Clark separated.

Willie Clark signed on with a farm labor camp in Florida as a migrant farm laborer. It pained the children when he left and they felt robbed of part of their legacy. Many years passed before Reatha Clark saw her father again.

After the marriage broke up, Ola Clark took her children and relocated to Moultree, Georgia. There she found a low paying job as a domestic, the only employment available to her. She often worked more than one job, putting in long hours for small pay. The children's father occasionally sent money, but never much, never often, and never in dependable fashion.

Many years later, a determined Reatha located her father on a farm in Florida. She wanted him to meet her husband and the grandsons he had never seen. Willie Clark showed her about the farm and spoke with pride about how he could operate all the machines. He told his daughter that he was sorry he had not done better by his children. He said that he really wanted to send more money when they were growing up but he had to depend on other people to mail things for him. Since he could neither read nor write, he did not trust others to do the right thing; he feared they would cheat him. His daughter listened, accepted her father's explanation, and forgave him. Upon hearing his story, one of her sisters could not and would not accept his excuse.

Mrs. Clark did lots of sewing because she wanted to make sure her daughter always "looked presentable." Reatha and her sisters pitched in to help whenever they could. They earned money by helping farmers gather tobacco from the fields and stringing the leaves together. During cotton-picking time, they took to the fields. There was no other way for young black girls to earn a few dollars.

None of the farm work was easy but picking cotton really tested their mettle. In the oppressive, humid heat of August, the relentless sun offered workers no relief except an occasional drifting cloud that gave a fleeting moment of welcome shade. When picking cotton, the hard pointed ends of the open bolls could pierce the fingertips, drawing blood of a harvester not skillful or careful enough in the plucking. The arduous, sweaty labor strained the workers back, shoulders, and sometimes knees; the sacks of cotton collected had to be pulled or toted to the scales for weighing before returning to the fields. Cotton pickers usually earned no more than $2.50 for 100 pounds and picking more than 100 pounds a day was not easy.

The Clark sisters always worked with gritty determination, taking no time for play and little rest breaks. They had good work ethics learned from examples set by their parents. In the fields, though in their minds this kind of work was temporary – a mean toward a better end, they labored under self-imposed high standards of excellence. After all, like the church people encouraged, they would make something of themselves.

Of course there were lighter moments in Moultree. Each year the church, of progressive mind toward its youth in this rural setting, sponsored a summer camp and Ola Clark always made sure her children had the opportunity to attend. Reatha remembered with pleasure the outdoor activities including games, the singing, the Bible lessons and other attractions. An outgoing person, she enjoyed all camp activities, but best of all the company of many good friends.

A Place to Learn

School however took preference as Ola Clark placed high priority on a good, solid, education for her daughters. But studying and attention to homework was   never a problem in a family that took

Great pleasure. in learning. Always the sisters encouraged and supported one another.

As the Clark children progressed through school, they sometimes reflected on church members' admonishment to make something of themselves. From time to time they pondered, "What were they to make of themselves?" They had no counselors to point the way to careers and other than their teachers, they had no professional role models. Their less than extensive travel offered not enough exposure to guide them. Years later Reatha Clark summed up their dilemma:

> . . . during those early years, there was no encouragement to us Black girls to try to become scientists. Becoming either a hairdresser, teacher, or nurse represented the reality of a better job for young Black women. Women in these jobs became our main source of role models both in person, and in our books.

Neither Mamie, Reatha or Dorothy selected hairdressing as their first choice. When Mamie was graduated, she decided to study nursing at Dillard University in New Orleans. Reatha considered following her older sister but only briefly. "One nurse in the family is enough," she said. So again the great and as yet unanswered question: "What? What should she make of herself? Well - what about a teacher? Now if a teacher, what kind of teacher?"

She decided that home economics teachers impressed her the most. They seemed to work with an air of confidence; their professionalism seemed evident in the way they carried themselves. In a speech delivered at Spelman College in 1989, she revealed her plans to make something of herself:

> When I graduated from high school in 1954, I set as my goals to be a home economics teacher and later to return to Moultree to teach in the local high school. I left Moultree, Georgia in 1954 to attend Clark College in Atlanta with this as my career goal.

Reatha Clark finished high school as valedictorian of her class. In recognition of her strong academic standing, Clark College offered her a scholarship. The scholarship was an absolute necessity since almost no money could come from home. Somehow it seemed fitting that Reatha Clark would attend Clark College.

Clark College

To her good fortune, the year she arrived on campus, a Dr. Alfred Spriggs headed the department of chemistry. Spriggs, who earned his Ph.D. in chemistry from Washington University in St. Louis, Missouri, came well   prepared. Students found his enthusiasm for chemistry infectious. Like many her classmates, Reatha had never seen a black person with a Ph.D. in chemistry.

Reatha enrolled in her first chemistry course because it was required of all home economics majors. There she met Professor Spriggs who immediately challenged his students. Spriggs, a dynamic personality and outstanding teacher,   was also a demanding taskmaster who set high standards in his classes. He took his students on exciting and fascinating journeys through chemistry. The   professor had a knack for making clear to students concepts they tended to find most baffling. He taught them *how* to study chemistry so they could master fundamental concepts and principles. Spriggs showed connections as he explained how chemistry was important to other sciences. Then he spoke about career possibilities in chemistry and chemistry-related fields. Reatha had never heard such things before. How wonderful is this science called chemistry!

Professor Spriggs did more than teach chemistry content. He helped students understand the organization, structure, and nature of the science. Through him, students explored various subbranches of chemistry and he often gave riveting accounts of new research initiatives and amazing new breakthroughs. Then he told them there were black chemists out there. From time to time he talked about some exciting research they were doing.

Dr. Spriggs encouraged students to prepare themselves academically and emotionally, to go beyond Clark College. They should think about graduate school, not just Washington University where he had attended, but any good, reputable, graduate school. He outlined what he felt were basic requirements for success in graduate school including coping skills to meet the mental, physical and social demands. Then he told them they could meet these demands, that they had the ability and would have the knowledge. Reatha Clark remembered Spriggs as a man who "preached from the pulpit of possibility." The energetic professor instilled a 'can-do' attitude in his students.

Another chemistry professor, Dr. Henry McBay also impressed her. He taught his students that *blacks can do science.* The historical proof, the record of black achievement in science left no room for doubt. At various times he would explain that the real significance of George Washington Carver for instance was his role as the first and greatest chemurgist of his time. Chemurgy is the application of chemistry to agricultural products.

Reatha Belle Clark began to experience a new awakening. The dream of becoming a home economics teacher faded as she became increasingly drawn to chemistry. After the first semester, she realized how much she loved the subject. For the rest of her college career, she approached each term eagerly looking forward to the next chemistry course. If the course had a reputation for being "one of the tough ones," so much the better. With her competitive nature for such challenges, intensity, and so powerful an interest, it is not surprising that she switched her major from home economics to chemistry.

The Hard Realities of Life

Either the change in major from home economics to chemistry was an act of faith and courage, or the proverbial *brash impetuousness of youth.* A bachelor degree in home economics carried with it a good promise of a job as a teacher- if not in Moultree, then somewhere else. A bachelor degree in liberal arts with a major in chemistry meant almost no possibility of employment for a black person, especially a young black female. Reatha realized that a major in chemistry meant graduate school but that required money she did not have. Just meeting her financial obligations to Clark College was a constant struggle. So how could she ever go to graduate school? She did not know.

Reatha worked in the registrar's office for thirty-five cents an hour. None of the money came to her as the earnings were part of her scholarship package. That package covered only part of her expense. Her mother helped as best as she could, but on her small domestic pay, and with two daughters in college, there was not much to go around. Sometimes Mrs. Clark would send carefully selected "second choice" items she thought would look good on her lovely daughter. Reatha, in turn, received them with gratitude, and wore them well.

Still the money problems remained. At the end of every semester she was in debt to the college. By policy Clark College did not allow students to take final exams if they owed money to the institution. Without final exams, there would be no grades, and without grades for the previous semester, students could not register for the new semester. Reatha could not pay her bills, but she did not want to give up either. "Keep on keeping on" the folks back home would say. Now she had to find how.

Fortunately Reatha came across a slim reason to hope. Through the campus grapevine she learned that a student could petition to have some bills deferred. The appeal process involved making a request directly to Dr. Brawley, president of the college.

The thought of having to face the president with such a request was daunting. Nevertheless, the idea of going home, just as she was really getting into college chemistry gave her the courage she needed. When she met President Brawley, Reatha learned to her surprise that he knew about her, and knew that she was an honor student. The president and the college were committed to retaining its students if at all possible, especially its promising students. Reatha Clark was all of the above and President Brawley allowed her to take the final exam. After that, at the end of each semester, a financially-strapped Reatha Belle Clark showed up at the president's office and asked his secretary for an appointment to see him. Hearing her voice the president would call out to his secretary, "Is that Reatha Clark out there?" When the secretary answered in the affirmative, he would say, "All right, go ahead. Let her know she has my permission to take her exams."

"Study With Pencil in Hand"

Thanks to this unwritten policy Reatha remained at college where she could "Keep on keeping on." She continued to maintain a high average, and her chemistry grades were especially good. Then she enrolled in organic chemistry and for the first time ran into some sticky problems. In the other chemistry courses, she could quickly grasp the principles, see patterns and relationship, and apply her strong mathematical ability with success. Principles, theories, and laws yielded to her sound study habits and thinking skills. Like her father, she could "figure things out." It seemed though that organic chemistry placed a heavy premium on rote memory. Concepts and patterns were more elusive. While her grades were good in organic chemistry she was not up to her usual standards and she struggled to maintain her usual high level. Reatha was not happy with the extent of her conceptual grasp of the subject.

One day she and a classmate ran into Dr. Spriggs in the hallway of a classroom building. As usual he asked about their well-being. The two young students immediately began complaining about organic chemistry and their problems with the course. Spriggs listened, then gave them a two-sentence bit of advice. "The trouble," he told them, "is that you don't know how to study the subject. Study organic chemistry with pencil in hand." That simple bit of wisdom turned out to be a gem. After that, organic chemistry began to fall in place.

Pulling Effects and Pushing Effects

Somehow, despite her heavy work and study schedule, Reatha Clark found time for participation in various campus activities. Every year, during what was originally *Negro History Week*, now

African American History Month, several related activities took place at Clark College. Reatha participated in these activities every year, sometimes directly involved, other times as part of an audience. She said of her experiences,

> Black heroes became a part of my consciousness. The men and women we learned about, and those who came to speak to us during that week became my heroes. They had a *pulling effect* on my life while the likes of Dr. Spriggs had a *pushing effect.*

In addition to the above Reatha Clark was inducted into Beta Kappa Chi, an honorary scientific society. She was active in the campus student government, and on the social front was initiated into the Delta Sigma Theta Sorority. During her senior year, students selected her as "Miss Clark College," the campus queen. The honor recognized her standing among her peers in the college community, her leadership, scholarship, and to quote the inventor/poet Lewis Latimer, her *matchless form of charm and grace.*

Believe - Inside!

At the beginning of her senior year, Reatha Clark faced new problems requiring tough decisions about her future. She passionately wanted to attend graduate school but had not the slightest notion about where the money was coming from. If by some stroke of good fortune she obtained the money - what graduate school should she attend? Professor Spriggs had urged them to go to some *good* graduate school. As she had done four years earlier, the bright young woman from Moultree took stock of some people she held in high esteem. Where did Professor McBay, Dr. Benjamin Mays, President of Morehouse College, and Professor Spriggs attend graduate school? She noticed that the University of Chicago appeared most often so partly on that basis, and the reputation of the chemistry program there, she decided to apply for admission to that University. Still the major question remained – where would she find the wherewithal?

Another concern was atypical of Reatha Clark but it was

understandable. For the first time she questioned her readiness. Clark College had been a good place for her; its excellent and dedicated faculty held their students to high standards while urging them to do their best-always. And she had grown, measurably. But Clark was a small, somewhat under funded, black college in the South. Was she, coming from such a school, prepared for a large, prestigious, and world-famous institution like the University of Chicago? Some of her classmates shared her apprehension.

Enter Dr. Spriggs again. Somehow he sensed their concerns and between classes, spoke with them informally. Of course they were good enough. Of course they could make it. They had the ability and the background to succeed. Out of his own experiences, and the path he took toward the doctorate, he saw enough in them to give him faith. "I believe in you, he said. "Now you must believe in yourselves - inside." As for the money, he urged them to keep working, learn well, have hope, and never despair.

The students thanked their professor and, renewed by his encouragement, went their way. For Reatha, it was a time for further reflection. Spriggs had said, *believe!* The folks back home had said, *Just keep on keeping on.* The messages seemed the same.

Then came the wonderful news that Reatha had been awarded a Woodrow Wilson Fellowship to attend graduate school. She applied for admission to the University of Chicago and was accepted. Shortly after the good news though, she faced two new problems - one of them very troubling.

Family Pulls Together - Again

Family members, including her extended family, had always anticipated that Reatha would attend college, then return to Moultree and teach. When she told them she would not be coming home, but instead would soon travel north to enroll at the prestigious University of Chicago for graduate work in chemistry, they were a bit puzzled. It seemed to them that being a college graduate was indeed quite an accomplishment, especially since she also finished with such high honors. What need did she have run off to some far away graduate school? And why would their lovely young Reatha want to spend her time in some smelly old laboratory anyway? Even more important, a worried aunt warned her: "If you get too much education, you would scare the men away and wind up being an old maid."

Nevertheless the family wanted what was best for their own. If she really wanted graduate school, she had their blessing. Go ahead, *make something of yourself.*

That settled, a much weightier problem remained. Her mother desperately needed surgery. Doctors diagnosed her condition sometime ago, but with two children in college, she delayed the operation and continued to work. The doctors wanted to operate immediately, saying she should wait no longer. Ola Clark also knew she lacked the money to pay for the treatment and after surgery she faced an extended recuperation period. She had hoped that with her two oldest daughters out of school, the family could combine their resources to meet medical expenses.

Reatha Clark now faced a dilemma. The fellowship offered her the cherished opportunity to attend graduate school. She could study chemistry at an outstanding university and work toward an advanced degree. Moreover, for the first time in her life, even including high school, she could study free of money worries. Yet she could not abandon her mother at a time like this.

The family convened and weighed their options. It did not take long for the children to decide. Their mother must have the surgery. Then Mamie Clark announced a solution. She would enlist in the army as a nurse. Out of her salary in the military, she would pay for the operation and other expenses. That would allow her sister to enroll in graduate school.

That settled, Ola Clark agreed to have the operation. Surgeons removed some twelve tumors from her body. Aided by her remarkable resiliency, she astounded everyone by making a complete recovery. Before long, Ola Clark resumed an active life.

A Chicago Winter

From Atlanta, then a growing Southern city, Clark moved to the much larger Midwestern city of Chicago, second only to New York in population. That, and changing from a small, all black undergraduate institution, where she knew or recognized everyone, to a large, research international institution with few black students, and where she knew no one, called for major adjustments.

The University of Chicago began as a denominational institution, just like Clark College, but was now private. Where all her chemistry classmates at Clark had been black, at Chicago, Reatha Clark found none of her race in the chemistry department. Gaining admission to the university was fiercely competitive and its student body highly selective. Nevertheless, Reatha Clark made the transition among the elite with remarkable ease.

Clark's counselor at the University was pleasant but minced no words during their first meeting. He explained what she later described as "the realities of my new life" at Chicago. The counselor told her:

> At Clark College you were a big fish in a little pond. Here is another level of size and comprehensiveness. Here also is a different mix of students and what may be your greatest intellectual challenge.

Clark listened very carefully and took seriously his words. She learned from him but felt not the least intimidated, She never thought it would be easy but here was her chance, her opportunity to continue along the path of becoming a good chemist, a legitimate scientist. The challenge issued by her counselor only served to stimulate her and strengthen her steel resolve. Reatha Belle Clark stood ready to begin.

Nevertheless there was one factor to which she paid deference. As the season changed, she found the bitter, cold winter of Chicago, with its snow and powerful arctic winds unlike anything she has ever experienced in her native South. Her mother received a letter. It read in part, "Please, send the long johns!"

Thermochemistry

Clark decided to major in physical chemistry and her counselor suggested she repeat her undergraduate course in that one subject. He pointed out that the University of Chicago used a different text and he wanted her to become acquainted with its content and the areas of particular emphases there. The counselor did not want her to begin at a disadvantage. Clark took his advice. She used the opportunity to map the intellectual and paradigmatic terrain at UC, to acquaint herself with the department, its philosophy, orientations, dynamics, and expectations.

When Clark arrived, physical chemistry at UC was largely a domain of white males. There were few women, and as mentioned earlier, no other blacks. On the strength of her intellectual ability, background, and strong study habits, she scored high in her classes - just as she had in undergraduate school. Her warm and friendly nature, and ability to mingle, served her well in the scientific community. Those about her, responded in kind. "The people," she recalled, "were great."

Physical chemistry is one of the five major sub-branches of chemistry. It is a necessarily rigorous subject since other divisions look to it for the theoretical bases to explain and predict their own chemical observations. The field demands a solid background in abstract mathematics. Theories and laws of physics, especially in thermodynamics, must be mastered to make sense of the complex chemical reactions and energy transformations that take place. At the University of Chicago, Clark also found considerable activity and great excitement among scientists about solid state physics and chemistry. The expectation that they were on the verge of a major breakthrough fueled enthusiasm all around and Clark could clearly feel the energy extant. Always inquisitive, she took note of what the scientists were doing, and what they anticipated. Nevertheless, after careful consideration, she realized that her strongest interest was in the more classical fields of thermodynamics and thermochemistry. Moreover, the work of the thermochemist was basic to most other scientific disciplines. In thermochemistry many intriguing problems remained unsolved.

The thermochemist, as do all physical chemists, applies laws of physics in elucidating chemical properties and their characteristics. Especially do they rely on the laws of thermodynamics (that deal with principles of heat, entropy and absolute zero) in making precise determination of heat of reactions and behaviors of systems in equilibrium. These are elusive tasks. In minute detail, physical chemists discover and describe the conditions under which chemical reactions take place, especially the reactants, and at various stages, products, temperatures, pressure, and energy absorbed and released. Many such reactions are exceedingly complex, and reaction times vary from being agonizingly slow to almost instantaneous. Whatever the speed of reactions, physical chemists must identify all intermediate products and measure them with accuracy and precision. Such information is fundamental to scientific progress in many fields.

Clark earned her master's degree at the university and continued work toward the doctorate in physical chemistry. Based on her strong academic record, she qualified for additional fellowship support after the Woodrow Wilson Fellowship expired. Her research project involved the study of heats of formation of intermetallic compounds. Her assignments demanded long hours of exacting measurements, and complex mathematical applications. She had to create and design new and special materials and equipment to carry out the reactions. Then she would run her experiments, collect and organize her data for analysis, synthesis, and interpretation. It is in the area of designing the research to break new ground, and in interpreting abstract mathematical data that perhaps impose the greatest demand.

Sometimes, despite all effort answers seem elusive or even unobtainable. Such difficulties sorely test the ingenuity, patience, stamina, and determination of the scientist to "keep on keeping on". When Clark faced such challenges, she called upon her tenacity and habits of intense atttention, traits acquired as a child, and refused to despair. Highly imaginative, she would draw upon her uncommon powers of concentration, locate the problem and then devise new, creative approaches. Nature makes tough demands on those seeking her secrets, but may reveal a few of them to the inquiring mind that

Keeps on pressing on.

The Networks

In her department Clark was able to work in an atmosphere of mutual respect, which is important among scientists. In such a setting, scientists can agree upon positions or air differences in a quest for truth. Aided by her wit, intelligence, and intense involvement, Clark made great strides at Chicago.

She also made friends and forged close relationships outside the department. A mind that is capable of conceptualization tends to do so in various settings. Perhaps it should not be surprising that one day it suddenly dawned upon her conceptualizing mind, that without a conscious effort on her part, she had formed several "networks of friends," and that occasionally they overlapped. She had a "chemistry network" and an "other science network". The latter included people in other branches of chemistry such as organic chemistry, biochemistry, etc., mathematics, earth science, physics, and computer science. A circle of friends where she lived became the "Beecher Hall network." That network consisted of various ethnic groups: blacks, whites, and foreign students. At the International House where she ate on Sundays, she had a "cafeteria network." Each of these "networks seemed to form naturally, and they enriched her life immeasurably. She said of them: "Such interactions broadened my horizons, and greatly contributed to my intellectual growth."

It was through one of these networks that Clark made an important and enduring connection. During a rare time off, she and a few network friends (quite likely the Beecher Hall network), went to a basketball game in the city. The opponents were two historically black schools from the South: Fisk University of Nashville, Tennessee, and Morehouse College of Atlanta. While at the game, she met N. Judge King Jr., a native of Birmingham, Alabama. Judge King attended Morehouse College and majored in chemistry during Reatha Clark's enrollment at nearby Clark College. It is quite possible that they may have fleetingly seen one another.

After his graduation, King moved to the City of Chicago where he was now teaching chemistry at the Englewood High School. He planned to enroll in graduate school and earn an advanced degree in chemistry in the near future. The two young people had much in common and for some reason the basketball game became less important, even to the Morehouse alumnus.

Judge King made it a point to arrange a second meeting with Clark and one meeting led to another. Such are the ways of life that not all bonds are the kind that physical chemists study in the laboratory.

The aunt of Reatha Clark who fretted that her niece's education might cause her to become an old maid, need not have worried. In December of 1961, Reatha Belle Clark and N. Judge King were married. She was 23 years old.

The Partially Opened Door

One year later, in December of 1962, Mrs. Reatha Clark King completed all requirements for the doctorate. At the Spring Commencement of April 1963, the University of Chicago conferred upon her the Ph.D. degree in chemistry. Dr. King had just celebrated her 25th birthday. With both her education and marriage achieved, her concerned aunt could now relax.

Earlier in the year, and in anticipation of her graduation, Dr. King sent out applications for employment as a chemist. The Civil Rights Movement had opened some doors for qualified women and minority scientists though not all doors were opened, and others not very wide. Despite her degree from a prestigious university, outstanding academic record, and sunny disposition, she encountered various and subtle forms of racial and gender discrimination. Corporate and education recruiters interviewed Dr. King but none offered her a position. Invariably interviewers asked if she was married and did she plan to have children. Men seldom if ever had to answer such questions.

The National Bureau of Standards

Her keen mind and life experiences, first in the South, later in the North, facilitated observation and judgment in recognizing both overt and subtle biases. Nevertheless, despite these experiences she refused to blame every negative experience on race and/or gender prejudices. She knew people of genuine fairness in every racial or ethnic group, and except in rare instances when she briefly harbored thoughts not quite noble, she possessed the maturity, toughness, and strength of character to rise above such experiences. The job search continued until her persistence paid off. In January 1963, Dr. King accepted a position as a research chemist at the National Bureau of Standards, whereupon the family moved to Washington, D.C. One reason she accepted the position in the nation's capitol was so her husband could enroll in the graduate program in chemistry at Howard University and the couple could remain together.

Shortly after her arrival, the Bureau assigned Dr. King to an exacting project investigating the heats of formation of gaseous fluoride compounds. The problem under investigation had been worked on by two previous research teams, but the difficulty of finding or developing a material that could contain the highly corrosive oxygen difluoride, and its furious reactions, impeded any progress.

Her team had to discover a different and workable approach to the tedious and hazardous problem. So King and her co-investigators first conducted a thorough review of the literature. They needed detailed information about successes, problems and failures of previous attempts. Then they went "back to the bench," designed and tested many materials for carrying out and studying the reactions. Their project was crucial to aspects of the National Aeronautical and Space Administration (NASA) including the success of its space program. Like all their research initiatives, the Bureau placed a high premium on accuracy and precision.

For three years, the team worked with various materials as they designed and developed special equipment to carry out their research. Finally they achieved their goal and completed the research project with such exacting measurements as to draw high praise from bureau superiors.

Reatha King published several significant papers, some as author, others as co-author, on the heat of reactions for fluorides and intermetallic compounds. One paper that reported on the highly unstable compound chlorine trifluoride, proved to be consequential in its application to rocketry. One gets a clear sense of the kind of compound she worked with, and its special nature, and the need for accuracy in the opening statement of her article. She reported:

> Chlorine trifluoride is a vigorous flourinating agent which combines spontaneously with many other compounds and elements. This fluorine-containing oxidizer is easily liquified, and for this reason has applications different from those of other However as with the fluorine-containing oxidizers, the special applications of chlorine trifluoride, such as its use in rocket propulsion, require accurate thermochemical data.

She further noted the paucity of studies on the heat of formation of chlorine trifluoride. She successfully made the difficult determination of the heat of formation at 298.15 °K (or 25.15 °C). The heat of formation in this study was determined using flame calorimetry since this method was judged most proficent in eliminating formation of mixed halide. Procedures and results were described in detail, including all sequences of reactions. She found the heat of formation of chlorine trifluoride (ClF_3) to be 164.65 $\pm$ 5.14 kJ mole^{-1}.

King's publication on "A Thermochemical Study of Some Lava Phases," was reproduced in two other languages: French and German. Another publication where King reported her findings on "Fluoride Flame Calorimetry," appeared in Sweden.

Some assignments came with short notice and little or nothing to go on because almost nothing had been done in that area. In such cases, it was necessary to start "from scratch." One such assignment came at the end of a work day that had been particularly draining. Weary from the long, tough day, King had looked forward to going home, and resting. Then came the problem along with a sense of urgency, and of course demanding of the high standards of accuracy and precision that the bureau always required. Having looked into the problem however, the challenge and the intrigued brought renewed energy. Soon she lost all track of time or consciousness of fatigue. Far into the night she labored, devising, testing, redeveloping as the hours stretched toward dawn. In the end her efforts paid dividends and she solved the problem. Nonetheless that did not terminate her work. She tested and re-tested the sample until no doubts about the accuracy and precision of her results remained. When she reported her findings, it was 3:30 A.M., the next day.

King's work formed the basis for resolving an important interagency government dispute. R. L. Jack, chairman of the Trial and Guarantee Survey Board wrote a memorandum to King informing her that, " . . . your efforts enabled us to advise representatives of a large, west coast steamship company, and a Gulf coast shipbuilding corporation, that a rerun of the new $15,000,000 cargo vessel would not be required."

In recognition of her work the Bureau cited King with an outstanding performance rating. Shortly thereafter the Bureau awarded her with a promotion for her work on flame calorimetry of fluoride compounds. Her supervisor, Dr. George T. Armstrong said that her study was " . . . remarkable for its completeness, and for the thoroughness with which all aspects of the problem was investigated." She also won the Meritorious Publication Award for her paper, "Fluoride Flame Calorimetry II: The Heat of Formation of Oxygen Difluoride."

In addition to their heavy load of work and study, the Kings added to their family. Reatha King gave birth to a son, N. Judge III about two years after joining the Bureau. The second of their children, son Scott was born three years later. N. Judge Jr. continued his studies and completed all requirements for the doctorate in chemistry at Howard University. Nassau Community College in New York offered him a faculty position as a professor of chemistry.

Reatha King worked as a research scientist with the Bureau for over five intensive, often dramatic, and highly productive years. She always felt, and often proclaimed, that the Bureau, and the good teams she worked with, provided an environment that significantly augmented her professional growth. She felt good about her progress, and took pride in the contributions she made to science. It was therefore with mixed feelings that she resigned from the Bureau to begin a new career.

Academia

It had been just over a decade since she left rural Georgia, but changes in King's life had been many and profound. What remained as a constant however was the importance of family. From her upbringing, Reatha King learned that family was central and whenever asked for her role model among figures she held in high esteem, she would quickly point to her mother. So, as much as she enjoyed working at the Bureau, when her husband had a position elsewhere, Reatha King felt her family needed to remain together. The Kings relocated to New York City where Reatha King joined the faculty of York College to teach chemistry. York, a new campus in the City University of New York (CUNY) system, was in the process of building. She adapted quickly and the entire resilient King family made the transition to this different environment with relative ease. Both Dr. Kings soon settled into their respective new and busy world of academia, at their individual institutions.

Professor Reatha Clark King soon discovered that she thoroughly enjoyed teaching chemistry. She drew upon her rich experiences as a research chemist to help her students explore the "real world" of science. The enthusiasm, sincerity, and masterful teaching of her former professors like Spriggs and MacBay, influenced her pedagogical style. There were wonderful years at York as Professor King became enmeshed in the life of the new campus. She helped to design the science curriculum for the new institution, which despite it being a long and tiring task, was gratifying in its good results. Later she took on the additional task of teaching physical science, much to her delight.

Before long King assumed administrative duties as Assistant Dean of Natural Sciences and Mathematics. In that position, and at 32 years of age, she supervised over 80 people. Not long afterward she was promoted to Associate Dean. To better prepare for the complexities of administration, and feeling she could better serve with formal training in business and exposure to current trends and thinking in the field, King took a sabbatical leave and enrolled in Columbia University where she earned an MBA degree.

Metropolitan State University

King remained at York College for nine years. In 1977 she left the CUNY system, to become president of Metropolitan State University in St. Paul, Minnesota. Previously she had resigned her job with the Bureau of Standards and Measurement and gone to New York because her husband had a job there and the family had to stay together. This time he resigned and moved to Minneapolis, for the same reason. The parents returned to the Midwest although in another region and the boys moved from the east for the first time in their young lives.

It is no small jump from a Deanship to become president of a college. Assuming the role of a college president, also a great challenge, King drew on her previous experiences at the Bureau and York College and assumed the new position with typical intensity, imagination, and enthusiasm. She assumed the presidency of Metropolitan with a vision of educational initiatives along with a "work together" philosophy. Under her leadership, a mission to serve the people of the region through education took new meaning.

The eyes see there materials for building,
See the difficulties too, and the obstacles
. . . the dream becomes not one [person's] dream alone,
But a community dream
-from *Freedom's Plow* by Langston Hughes

With this combination the enrollment at Metropolitan College increased nearly fourfold. The number of graduates outstanding increased five fold, perhaps an even greater achievement since it indicated that more of its students were graduating. Metropolitan expanded its curriculum, adding nursing, computer science, a graduate program in management, and a special outreach program for the disadvantaged. Also, during her presidency, Metropolitan received several citations for outstanding achievements in serving its constituency.

President King earned widespread acclaim in recognition of her vision and leadership. Such national figures as Harvard president Derek Bok and Theodore Hesburgh, then president of Notre Dame, praised her progressive administration, curriculum expansion and services important to the constituents of Metropolitan. Said Hesburgh of King, "She has made Metro State both respected and accepted by all the powers that be, in the community."

King served as president of Metropolitan State College for eleven years until 1988 when she resigned to take another appointment. Moving to the corporate world, she accepted a position as President and Executive Director of the General Mills Foundation, also in the city of Minneapolis. Upon leaving Metropolitan College, she received several messages of appreciation and good will. One of them read in part:

President Reatha Clark King,

When you became Metropolitan State University president in 1977, you compared Metro State to a seed that had been planted, but had not reached its full potential. Eleven years of your cultivation has seen that seed blossom, developing strong, deep roots.

Your own background and roots helped you to focus on Metro State's needs. You knew what issues were important. Through your vision and leadership Metro State has moved to the forefront of innovative higher education, now becoming positively anchored in the metropolitan community. Your positive influence will be felt at Metro State for many years to come. . . ."

The administrators, faculty, staff and students of Metropolitan State University, Oct. 26, 1988.

Science and Scientists

In 1989, Dr. King delivered an address that reflected on the importance of her scientific experience. Under the title, *"B*ecoming a Scientist. My Most Important Career Decision", she told her audience:

... I would emphasize again how much my scientific knowledge and discipline of behavior came from education as a scientist have provided such a marvelous beginning for my work as a university president and a foundation executive ... Young people especially often fail to realize that scientific education is flexible and that it can prepare one to function in various careers.

In a conversation with the writer, she expressed some of her views, and shared philosophical thoughts, on science and scientists:

To Be a Good Scientist: To be a good scientist one must have ability, curiosity, energy and patience. The scientist should be concerned about how his or her science is put to use - whether in beneficial or harmful ways. Scientists should consider the consequences of their discoveries. In this regard, scientists should be a part of the public forum.

Science and minorities: It must be understood that blacks have the ability to do science. We still suffer from the stereotype that there is no scientific ability among blacks. But blacks should be encouraged to go into science beginning at the elementary level.

To ensure that blacks are brought into science, make certain that they are informed about the various fields and careers in science. Minorities need to be shown how science can empower.

I cannot say at this time that the scientific community is totally fair to minorities and women, but the situation is improving even in the face of lingering stereotypes in some places, that minorities and women are 'not as good as.'

Science and Support: To carry on science, and advance the frontiers of knowledge, scientists need equipment. To promote the advancement of science requires imagination. Funds are needed to carry on scientific research. Development of new theories and the testing of old must be a constant concern. Science will advance because men and women are naturally curious. Government policy profoundly affects the direction science will take.

Science, Technology, and Religion: I experience no conflict between science, technology, and my religious faith.

Family and Moultree's Values Remain

She grew up in an economically impoverished situation but considers herself wealthy in having lived in strong and caring home and community environments. They sowed the value seeds that shaped her character and outlook on life. Family traditions of striving and seeking excellence, church members and neighbors, friends and teachers urged her along. They encouraged her to apply her intellect, often with such words as, "use your good head," and "make something of yourself." That was easier said than done because in her path were the proverbial hills and molehills, and mountains to climb. There were valleys too, and wide rivers to cross; nothing came to her without her trying. By virtue of her tenacity, her unyielding faith, "intensity," and determination, she placed herself in the path of possibility, prepared herself well and seized every opportunity. In the process, Reatha Clark King earned a Ph.D. in the rigorous field of physical chemistry, and became a research scientist for the United States Government. Later she became a college professor, associate dean, dean, and at the age of 39, a college president. Today she is president and executive director of the General Mills Foundation.

It is evident in her demeanor that the reward she has always cherished has been the satisfaction of a job well done. Yet, she is also appreciative when others judge her efforts to be praiseworthy. Many have. Several institutions awarded her honorary doctorates, among them: Carleton College, Alverno College, Rhode Island College, Seattle University, Empire State College, Marymount Manhattan College, Smith College, Nazareth College of Rochester, and William Mitchell College of Law.

In 1988, King was cited as Twin Citian of the Year for Minneapolis-St. Paul, Minnesota. In 1992, and in subsequent years, *Ebony* magazine listed her among the top 50 black executives in corporate America. CIBA-GEIGY included her among Thelma Perkins' *Exceptional Black Scientists* poster series.

King serves on many educational, corporate and community boards. Among them: The University of Chicago, Carleton College, the American Association for Higher Education, Minnesota Mutual Life Insurance Company, H. B. Fuller Company, and Norwest. She has presented numerous lectures, appearing throughout this country and abroad. Overseas, she has spoken to audiences in Japan, Israel, the Philippines, Tanzania, and Bangladesh.

How she effectively manages so many engagements defy easy explanation. Nevertheless, something of the way she views the complexities of her times came out in a speech she delivered at the University at Buffalo in 1990. Addressing a racially mixed audience of university and community people at the annual Martin Luther King Jr. Commemoration she said, "Some will say these are the best of times; others will say these are the worst of times; I simply say these are real times."

Dr. King, though soft-spoken, calm, of unflappable demeanor, is also strong, tough, and can make hard decisions. Perhaps the string of successes she has enjoyed in her admirable careers is due largely to her approach. In every case King was always "intensely involved" and from each received "great satisfaction." Knowledge gained from one position proved useful for the next round. With her unusual insight, and ability to connect experiences, she sees relations among her diverse careers. She said of her various positions: "Each new position has been a process, not of leaving but of combining or adding to."

It is a long journey from a laborer in the cotton and tobacco fields of Georgia to an executive suite in corporate America. But the basic values she learned while growing up in Moultree, Georgia remains with her. Along with her warm, gracious, and professional style, she has a special talent for sizing up the dynamics of her environment and putting things in perspective. She takes pride in her family and they remain central in her life. Husband N. Judge King Jr. is a businessman in the aviation industry. Their oldest son N. Judge III, is a graduate of the Minnesota Medical School. Their second son Scott earned a degree in mathematics from Morehouse College. The words "Just keep on keeping on," still ring.

References and Publications for Further Reading

"An Educator: Her Roots and Her Vision. Reatha Clark King, President, Metropolitan State University," *Reflections*, October 26, 1988.

Decker, Ruth, 1985. "The Chemistry is Right," *ESC News.*

"50 Top Black Executives in Corporate America," *Ebony*, 47:108-116, 1992.

Letter to Dr. R. C. King from R. P. Hudson, Chief of Heat Division, IBS, enclosing her "Meritorious Publication Award." The award was in recognition of her paper, "Fluorine Flame Calorimetry II. The Heat of Formation of Oxygen Difluoride." April 10, 1969.

Letter to Dr. G. T. Armstrong from R. L. Jack, Chairman, Trials and Guarantee, Survey Boards, U. S. Department of Commerce, praising the work of Dr. King's report on the "analysis of fuel oil from USNE SEA LIFT sea urials, May 2,"Perkins, Thelma, 1982. "Exceptional Black Scientists," *CIBA-GEIGY Poster Series.*

Swanson, William, 1989. "1988 Twin Citian of the Year," *Twin Cities*, 12: 44-47.

An incomplete list of publications by R. C. King

"Social Problems and the Ethics of Preventive Maintenance," in Hausman (ed.), 1992, *Insights on Global Ethics,* Camden, Maine: Institute for Global Ethics.

From a video tape of an address delivered at the University at Buffalo, Buffalo, New York, 1990 at the annual Martin Luther King Jr. Commemoration.

"Becoming a Scientist. My Most Important Career Decision". Paper read at Spelman College, Atlanta, Georgia, 1989.

"The Changing Student: A Resource for Improvement of Educational Services," *National Forum*, p. 22, 1985.

With G. T. Armstrong, "Fluorine Flame Calorimetry" in Sunner, Stig and Margaret Mansson (ed.), 1978. *IUPAC, Experimental Chemical Thermodynamics (Vol. I), Combustion Calorimetry, New York: Pergamon Press.*

With G. T. Armstrong, 1970. "Fluorine Calorimetry III. The Heat of Formation of Chlorine Trifluoride at 298.15 °K," *Journal of Research, of the National Bureau of Standards*, 74A: 661-668.

With G. T. Armstrong, 1968, "Constant Pressure Calorimetry with Fluorine II. The Heat of Formation of Oxygen Difluoride," *Journal of Research of the National Bureau of Research*, 72A: 113.

"The Heat of Formation of Aluminum Carbide," *Technical News Bulletin, National Bureau of Standards*, 1965.

With G. T. Armstrong, 1964. "Heat of Combustion and Heat of Formation of Aluminum Carbide," *Journal of Research of the National Bureau of Standards*, 68A: 661-668.

With O. J. Kleppa, 1964. "Heat of Formation of Some Selected Laves Phases," *Aceta Metallurgica*, 12: 87-97.

With O. J. Kleppa, 1962. "Heats of Formation of the Solid Solutions of Zinc, Gallium, and Germanium in Copper," *Aceta Metallurgica*, 10: 1183.

With O. J. Kleppa and L. S. Hersh, 1961. "Heats of Mixing Silver Nitrate Mixtures," *Journal of Chemical Physics*, 35: 1975.

The author obtained much of the material in this chapter through an interview with Dr. Reatha King.

*Chapter XVII*_____

Shirley Ann Jackson- Theoretical
Physicist
(1946-)

For a long time Thelma Perkins poured over volumes of materials: books, journal articles, letters, patent applications, newspaper articles and various other documents about African American scientists. She also traveled, consulted with historians, scientists, families, and acquaintances of her subjects. Her mission: to compile a short list of twelve African Americans who had made significant contributions to science and technology. The CIBA-GIGY Corporation where she worked, approved her proposal and supported the project. From a list of well over a hundred possibilities, she checked and rechecked before her list became final. Then, where possible, she made contacts with those on her list or families of the deceased. One of her calls went to Dr. Shirley Ann Jackson, a theoretical physicist then working with the Bell Telephone Company in Murray, New Jersey. Perkins explained her project and invited Dr. Jackson to a ceremony where she would be honored as one of the select twelve *Exceptional Black Scientists.*

Jackson hesitated. She appreciated the honor but preferred to stay away from the limelight. She did not want anyone to make too much of her achievements, render premature judgment, or give unwarranted praise for what she had done. The late, extraordinary chemist Percy Julian often expressed the same sentiments. Beside, science was something she loved, she had so much yet to do and there were still many unanswered scientific questions. Perkins however, found her record impressive and from peers of Dr. Jackson she heard words of respect and admiration for her work and the breakthroughs she had made in theoretical physics. Nonetheless Jackson might still have begged off the recognition except she also felt that this project could help send the word to young women and minorities that they too had a place in science. The tribute provided a larger forum for her message that minorities and women can and should be equal partners in the scientific and technological enterprises. She felt the *Exceptional Black Scientists Series* had the potential to reach doubters on both sides of the fence and it was consistent with her own mission to help dispel deeply entrenched doubts. Jackson once spoke to Joan Whitlow about mental blocks and misconceptions:

> There is a psychological factor that keeps Blacks disinterested in science and math . . . Many people do not see these as concepts accessible to them.

Then in deference to Perkins' CIBA-GEIGY recognition she said,

> If I can motivate some Black child to study a little harder, or help some Black student come through some discouragement, or make that discouragement temporary instead of permanent, then that's great, that's fine. That's the . . . reason I did it.

In accepting the honor, Jackson joined an elite list of scientists that included Percy Julian, Ernest Just, Jane Wright, Charles Drew, Reatha Clark King, Jewell Plummer, David Blackwell, W. Montague Cobb, Lloyd Ferguson, Augusta White, Samuel Kountz, and Jennie Patrick. CIBA-GEIGY commissioned the accomplished artist Ernest Crichlow of Brooklyn to do the portraits of honorees. Large, attractive posters of the scientists were reproduced in color, and made available to interested persons and institutions nationwide. The response was overwhelming and even after several printings the demand far exceeded the supply. In 1992, at a grand ceremony, Thelma Perkins presented the original paintings to the Schomberg Library of New York where they now remain for others to see and study.

Stinging Insects and Fungi

Shirley Ann Jackson was born in Washington, D.C. August 5, 1946, the second daughter of Beatrice and George Jackson. Her mother was a social worker and her father a postal supervisor. The Jacksons strove to instill a sense of pride and positive self worth in their children and they made special efforts to foster those values in an environment of caring and support. They also taught them that one needed to know how to handle success *and* failure, good times *and* tough times equally as well.

The Jacksons took the matter of education seriously. So when Shirley decided to participate in a science fair, it was not a surprise when her father enthusiastically urged her on. Both parents were always there to help their children but they also expected them to help themselves.

Shirley attended Roosevelt High, a racially segregated school in the nation's capitol. She excelled in all her classes, but enjoyed science and mathematics the most. Early in her life Shirley showed a gift for those subjects but bolstered her talent with arduous efforts and hours of study. She believed then, and does so today, that a gift is not to be taken for granted but should be "nurtured, honed, and refined." A talent not used could become ineffective, atrophy, or even be lost. Therefore, despite her "natural gifts", she worked diligently to improve herself.

For some reason, during her growing up years Shirley had a fascination for insects, the most abundant macroscopic animals on planet earth. Some considered her a bit odd because she collected critters that most people tended to avoid, like the bumblebee and yellow jacket. She showed no fear of them or their sting. After their capture she would design her own experiments to answer some question she had about their behavior. She also studied molds and other fungi in her environment, along with bacteria, the microscopic plant-like organisms. Such curiosity and habits of mind came in handy when she decided to enter the science fair.

For the fair, Shirley wanted to investigate the effect of certain environmental conditions on the growth of bacteria. Realizing that she did not have the materials and supplies needed for her research Shirley looked around her home and began collecting various discarded objects that would serve as substitute. For a while though, the spunky youngster worried that her makeshift project might not compete favorably against others where students had more sophisticated scientific ware. Her fears proved to be unfounded as the Jackson project won first place.

Shirley enrolled in the rigorous, accelerated mathematics and science program in her school. Years later she praised the teachers at Roosevelt High for their caring, and for setting standards of excellence as their goals. The teachers, she recalled, respected the students with the result that the students respected themselves. The faculty message to them was *You are somebody. You can and should make meaningful contributions to society. Prepare yourself to do so.* Though her teachers provided a warm environment, there was no coddling, rather they offered them a dose of "tough love" in an academic setting. Good work habits, high standards, and responsible citizenship were the expectations.

In 1957 the Soviet Union made scientific and technological history when they placed the first artificial satellite, called *Sputnik,* in earth orbit. That astounding achievement gave the Soviets an apparent lead in space exploration and a possible military advantage over the United States. Stunned, the U. S. government swiftly expanded the space program and provided federal grants to upgrade teacher preparation, sponsor new curricula in science and mathematics, and to identify, encourage and educate bright young minds interested in the sciences, mathematics and engineering.

Students at the all-black Roosevelt High School heard the call but they also perceived a serious dilemma and daunting contradiction. They did not doubt that the nation needed top scientists, mathematicians and engineers, nor their own ability to help meet the need. On the other hand they believed that black Americans would encounter barriers to their ambitions, that they would not be accepted in the scientific community because, simply *that is the way things are in this country,* So typically, Roosevelt students, including the brightest, inclined toward a "What's the use" attitude.

The faculty at Roosevelt High School would have none of it. They urged the students to prepare themselves and knock on doors. They agreed that things were not perfect, and that blacks yet faced many obstacles in science and technology. Nonetheless some opportunities were opening up. They saw change, slow, but change nonetheless. They did not want their students to give up. About her teachers Shirley Jackson once said:

> Since [leaving Roosevelt], I have met students who are not as lucky as I was. Their abilities have been neglected by some educators simply because they are members of some minority group about which those educators harbor damaging misconceptions.

Over and over Jackson cited others who encouraged her during those critical growing up years. Not only her teachers but family and church members too. She told Joan Whitlow:

> Everyone called me the "brain", but my family, neighbors, teachers, and fellow church members respected me and encouraged me to do well.

MIT

Shirley finished school at Roosevelt High 1964. An honor student, and valedictorian of her class, she received a Martin Marietta Aircraft Company Scholarship (1964-68), and a Prince Hall Mason Scholarship to help with her education. In the fall of 1964, she enrolled at the Massachusetts Institute of Technology. Jackson applied to MIT because of its world renown programs, especially in the sciences, mathematics, and engineering. Of its 9,000 academically elite students, less than 0.2% were black. Shirley decided to major in the area of her greatest interest, physics. She loved physics and decided this would be her focus. More than in any of the fundamental sciences, that is among biology, chemistry and physics, she could combine her love of science and mathematics. Nationally, about 95% of those seeking a bachelor's degree in physics were men, and less than 5%

women. Fewer than 2% were African-Americans. At MIT, less than
0.2 % of its students, all academically elite, were black. Shirley
Jackson was one of the few women, and lone African-American in
her physics class Despite this picture, she enthusiastically looked
forward to getting a good education at this world class institution.
Here she would become a scientist.

Then came the down side. Her classmates distanced themselves
from her so she had to work and study alone. The forced isolation
differed sharply from the friendly camaraderie of her high school days
and she felt the sting. Years later, in reference to that period she said,
simply, "I was not always welcomed by my fellow students."

Her ostracism did not stop with the men. In an interview with Ann
Gibbons she said, `The irony is that the white girls weren't working
with me either.' Gibbons went on to report that "The white women
refused to sit at the same table with Shirley in the cafeteria and made
it plain they did not want her in their study groups."

So in 1964, at arguably the top engineering school in the world,
attended by some of the most intellectually gifted young minds,
Americans and foreigners, Shirley Jackson had no choice but "to
work alone." Whether driven by ignorance, apprehension, prejudice,
or some or other factors, students avoided her. Their attitudes tested
her mettle and all the values of self-worth and determination of spirit
that she learned at home, high school and church. Jackson did not
pretend to be unaffected by the experience. Instead, she
acknowledged that during those days, she felt lonely and somewhat
despairing at first. But then she put things in perspective and in
further discussion with Gibbons said,

I went through a down period, but at some level you have to decide you
will persist in what you're doing and that you won't let people beat you
down.

She chose to persist. Her gift of mind and strong work habits served
to counter her quarantine and initial low spirit. At home, in her
church, and at school they had told Shirley and her peers, that they
were worthy and worthwhile Americans. She heard their message and
believed them in heart and mind. And why, she reflected, was she at

MIT? To get a good education of course, like other Americans from all over the country - and students from abroad. She had no obligation to apologize for her presence.

Shirley worked in the materials lab where she learned much, and delighted in the science experiences there. Despite her other difficulties, what she learned about material science affirmed her her conviction that she chose properly in selecting MIT to study. She remembered thinking that MIT was "one of the greatest scientific schools in the world, and we [blacks] need to be in all kinds of schools." She never doubted that she would remain in place until the day of graduation.

Jackson earned good grades in her class and gradually some of her fellow students began to accept her and she them. Thus in time she adapted to MIT, and the institution to her. Then she began to branch out, and do other things as well.

On campus Shirley helped organize some of her minority schoolmates and they prodded the university into working for a more diverse student body. University officials were not insensitive to her ideas and they showed a willingness to listen and work for change. On the strength and sincerity of their cooperative efforts, MIT made progress toward diversity and the institutions's president gave Shirley Jackson much of the credit.

The Study of Forces and Energy

When she selected physics, Shirley Jackson enrolled in one of the oldest of the scientific disciplines. Physics can be traced back beyond the glory days of the Greeks to ancient civilizations in other lands and continents. Oddly enough, though the science is old, the name is relatively new. It was not until about 1840, that an English philosopher, William Whewell coined the name physics. Prior to that, physicists were called usually called Natural Philosophers.

From a historical perspective, physics is divided into two categories, classical and modern physics. As stated by the author Richard Brennan, "Classical or Newtonian physics refers to the scientific studies made prior to the introduction of the quantum theory." Many scientists contributed to the munificent achievements of classical physics but the most celebrated of them all is Sir Isaac Newton. Newton's powerful and monumental works, compiled in the book *Principia,* dominated physics for well over two hundred years. Like many intellectual giants, his encompassing theories rested on the discoveries of many predecessors, among them Copernicus, Kepler, Galileo, Descartes, and others. Science is cumulative.

Modern physics is concerned with matter on the atomic and sub atomic scales. Its foundation rests primarily on Max Planck's quantum theories, Niels Bohr's theories on behavior of ultimate particle, Ernest Rutherford's law pertaining to radioactive disintegration, and Albert Einstein's dominate theories of relativity. These scientists, and such figures as Henri Becquerel. Wilhelm Roentgen and Marie and Pierre Curie, were most responsible for ushering in modern physics at the beginning of the twentieth century. Of course, as with all of science, there were other important contributors as well.

Central to the theories of modern physics is that both matter and energy are made up of discrete units, or quanta". It is a highly abstract science. Shirley Jackson, the spunky young lady they used to call "the brain" looked forward to learning physics by studying with the prestious faculty at MIT.

In physics Shirley studied Newtonian physics including mechanics, thermodynamics, electricity, sound, light and optics. As she progressed through undergraduate school and beyond, she also studied subjects in modern physics. Whether classical or modern physics, Shirley found each exciting, and interrelated, each preparing her for more sophisticated knowledge of the science. Eventually, her interested turned more firmly to modern physics.

Physics helped Shirley to understand much more about the vast, macroscopic world of time and space, *the cosmos,* where distances are so great as to be measured in light years. Physics also led her into the minute micro world where events may be so fleeting as to be measured in nanoseconds, and particle size in nanometers, picometers, femtometers and attometers. The strange and bewildering subatomic particles, some apparently without mass, are among the mysterious yet fundamental units of the universe. Jackson's studies took her from the complex, concrete, physical world, to an even more challenging universe of abstract physics. Here she had to use intricate, abstract mathematics as essential tools. At this point, highly abstract mathematics is the only mean of interpreting results, solving problems, making discoveries and developing new theories. The physicist's important tools include differential calculus, integration, limits and series. These are progressively more abstract and rigorous. Beyond that, the physicist must rely on the purely abstract mathematics called linear algebra (matrix). Some physicists also draw on topology, which involves the fundamental properties of shapes. With these tools, the scientist is more prepared to move into matrix mechanics, wave mechanics, and quantum mechanics. Of course the most essential in all this is for the theoretical physicist to have great powers of concentration, imagination, and exceptional intuitive powers.

Shirley Jackson successfully completed her undergraduate studies at MIT and in 1968 received her bachelor of science (SB) degree. Because of her record, scholarship offers came from other institutions for graduate studies. She decided to remain at MIT and set her course for the doctorate. Shirley majored in theoretical physics with a concentration in elementary particle physics. Her major professor and graduate advisor was Dr. James Young, "the first full-time tenured black professor in the physics department" at MIT and a rarity among major universities of the nation.

Scientists have long accepted the theory that matter is particulate in nature. The field of elementary particle physics, involves a continuing search for, and understanding of the "fundamental" units or particles of the atom. Their overall goal is to better understand the nature of our world and the universe. Such understanding, properly used, can be beneficial to the quality of life for humankind.

At the turn of the century, scientists knew little more than that the atom was composed of electrons, protons and neutrons. They devised clever procedures and constructed ever more sophisticated instruments to gather additional knowledge about these unseen particles. Gradually scientists compiled impressive and exciting new knowledge about subatomic particles. They measured their electric charge, mass, movements, spin, energy, and various behavioral traits. Then to their surprised they began to discover undreamed of "new" particles coming out of the nucleus of the atom. Going into the 1930s and continuing today, scientists have discovered and described many such emanations. Out of the protons and electrons, they discovered smaller, strange particles called quarks. So far they have detected six different kinds of quarks. They found things like the baryons, leptons, the neutrino, muon, pion, and a dazzling array of highly elusive others. In this field, in additional to the skills and knowledge mentioned, great intuitive and imaginative powers are essential. This is the world Shirley Jackson selected for her life's work.

Social Responsibility; Historical "Firsts"

Because of her excellent academic record at MIT, Jackson received grants from the National Science Foundation, the Ford Foundation, and the Martin Marietta Aircraft Company. The money enabled her to meet the high cost of graduate education. As she progressed in the tough program, Jackson learned that no female American of African descent had ever earned a doctorate in physics from MIT. Nonetheless, she saw no reason to back off from what appeared to her as a natural course of action.

Despite her heavy academic load, Jackson also found time for community service. She crossed the Charles River and tutored young children in the section of Boston known as Roxbury. She also volunteered her services in the children's surgical ward at Boston City Hospital and worked hard on campus to promote change.

While she was in graduate school, an assassin's bullet ended the life of the Nobel Laureate and human rights leader, Dr. Martin Luther King Jr. Saddened but influenced by King's philosophy of promoting social change through nonviolent activism, Jackson decided to honor his memory in a positive way. She came to believe that to help build a just society, institutions as well as individuals must change. Toward that end, she co-founded the Black Student Union at MIT. The organization took a positive thrust and sought to improve student life on campus. The members also helped recruit more black American students. MIT President Dr. Paul E. Gray appointed her to the Task Force on Educational Opportunity. Gray remembered the complexities of the problem, and the role Shirley Jackson played. He said:

> Before 1968 we had only a handful of black American students as freshmen each year. The lack of easy and visible handles on the problems from our viewpoint, the anger and despair felt by the few black students on campus, and their frustration at the lack of progress, which was shared by all, made for a heated and tense atmosphere in our group . . . honest differences in perspectives were often more evident than shared objectives.
> Shirley Jackson stands out in my mind as being one of the best bridge builders during that difficult time. . . . Her manner was always calm, unassuming and reassuring.

Jackson's approach was consistent with her philosophy. She believed that to affect changes in the institution it was necessary to be a part of it. The change agent, she felt, should first know the institution, its history, goals, beliefs, structure, operational procedures, dynamics, and loci of influence. Jackson also felt that the change agent must be credible because credibility empowers reasoned and reasonable demands for change. That approach won support on the campus and enrollment of minority students at MIT increased significantly.

Jackson never set out to make history but she did so nonetheless. Among her record of firsts are: the first female African American to earn a bachelor's degree in physics at MIT, the first of her race and gender to study energy particle physics theory, and she was the first and only American student of African descent in her department. In 1973, at the age of 26, she became the first African American female to earn a Ph.D. in physics from the Massachusetts Institute of Technology. In addition, she was first of her race to earn a Ph.D. in any discipline from MIT, and the first black American female to earn a Ph.D. in physics in the United States. In a few short years Shirley Ann Jackson established an impressive record and blazed a lot of trails. But of her intent, she told Angela Cowan:

> My only goal was to pursue opportunities and to contribute to physics and technology. Physics is fascinating, and being in an exciting place working on exciting and important problems is very rewarding.

Her achievements, which subsequently served to inspire other minority women, did not appear to Jackson as anything remarkable. In a revealing comment, she told Celeste Knox, " . . . what I did reflected the poor state of the advancement of women and minorities in certain disciplines."

Post Doctoral Studies and Bell Laboratory

During 1973-74, and 1974-76, Dr. Jackson worked as a research associate in theoretical physics at the Fermi National Accelerator Laboratory in Batavia, Illinois. Also during 1974-75, she spent time at the European Center for Nuclear research in Geneva, Switzerland as a visiting professor. Later, Dr. Jackson conducted research at the International School of Subnuclear Physics in Sicily, the Stanford Linear Accelerator Center, and the Aspen Center for Physics. At these places she conducted experiments on theories of strongly interacting elementary particles. Ann Gibbons explained the kind of pressure under which the young scientists worked. Jackson told her, `if you give a physics paper, it had better be good - because people will remember.' Then Gibbons added, "When Jackson gave a paper, it usually was good."

In 1976 Jackson accepted a job at A&T Bell Laboratory at Murray Hill, New Jersey. She worked in the area of condensed theoretical physicist, where she studied gases, films, and semiconductors. There she completed the transition from the academia to industry. At Bell, she changed her focus from theoretical particle physics to theoretical condensed matter physics. This area of physics included work with gases, solids, and semiconductors.

High energy physics and condensed matter physics each call for special preparation. There are some areas of overlap but also significant differences. How then, could a person trained for years in one area of specialization make a successful transition to another area of specialization? Part of the answer lay in Jackson's broad preparation in physics, mathematics, statistics, computer science, and work in the materials laboratory at MIT. She also brought to condensed matter physics, a thorough knowledge of subatomic particles, including of course the electron. A grasp of the nature and behavior of the electron is critical to the science of solid state physics. Studies pertaining to semiconductors, superconductors, elastic bodies, thermal energy, magnetic fields, and optical properties of matter use models developed by elementary particle scientists.

In addition to her training, Jackson possessed certain essential personal qualities developed and honed since her youth. These included versatility, insightfulness, and the courage to occasionally make unorthodox decisions. Her ability to simplify and unify vast and apparently disparate information served her well. Even as far back as her childhood days, Jackson showed a capacity to make the imaginative leap, another useful ability. In her present work, she had to be able make sense of phenomena measured in nanoseconds, and realize something weighty is there, or was there, or that nothing of import is there at all. From a bewildering array of data, she had to separate insignificant from the significant, to use abstract mathematics and abstract thinking to predict, to test, to confirm, and ultimately to relate all this to the "real" world. These factors help to explain in part, her ability to successfully make the transition.

At the AT&T Bell Laboratory, Jackson also had to recast her style of work. When she first went to MIT, out of necessity she learned to work alone. What was a virtue in one setting however, proved to be a problem at Bell. Jackson explained To Gibbons, her situation:

> [Upon joining Bell Laboratories], I was still pretty much a loner. I tended to pretty much do my own thing, and that is not always the best way to do things in science. That's why when women are isolated-or blacks or any minority-it can be very destructive.

Recognizing the operational culture of the workplace in her new position, she tried hard to change her style. But that was not her only problem. When Knox asked how she was initially received at the Bell lab she said:

> Backlash, because of the press I received when I graduated from MIT. I think it was more difficult for me to build personal and professional relationships with some of my peers . . . Some people probably expected more from me than they would have from a person they just met. Others felt I was being overplayed. In general, minorities and women are expected to prove themselves more.

Speaking this way, it was not her intent to point fingers. Her purpose was to simply describe the social forces sometimes at play in the scientific workplace, in this case as it pertained to her. Despite its celebrated regard for objectivity, science is after all a human institution with human strengths and weaknesses. The experience that Jackson described may in part help explain her sensitivity to overpraise. That, and her own values.

Choosing the Right Problem

Jacob Bronowski once wrote that "The creative mind looks for hidden likeness." He said that this search for unrecognized likeness "engages the whole personality" and tremendous concentration." That would mean for the theorist, availability of blocks or stretches of time. Without such time, great investment of resources by a research laboratory may be wasted, or an idea or insight could be lost- never to be reclaimed. Moreover, mental toughness is required so that when disappointing setbacks are encountered, as is almost sure to happen at one time or another, the will, and the creative potential must not be blunted. By her own admission, Jackson has always been focused and as she said, "I don't like to lose."

None of this is of much import if the research scientist does not select the right problem, ask the right question. At Bell, Jackson had, as she explained, a lot of latitude to select what project she wanted to explore. She had no direct supervisor nor specific projects imposed upon her. She would, as she explained to Celeste Knox, "inform my department head of the research . . . [and] make appropriate requests for . . . resources, equipment and support." The most important step, explained Jackson, which is critical to all else, is to select the right problem and to ask the right question.

After working on her project, Jackson would publish a memorandum of her findings for internal circulation. Then she would (1)state the research pursued, (2) explain why what she did was important, (3),describe the results, (4) explain why the results obtained were important, (5) discuss "what impact the results [could] have on building up the scientific and technological base important to A&T . . ." and to her discipline.

The memorandum, which would give precise details of her research procedures and findings, would be carefully reviewed for possible benefits to the company. Then, "if no proprietary restraints are found", the research could be published in an appropriate scientific journal. Judgment of its reception by the scientific community would be made, at least in part, by who and how many technical groups extended invitations for talks on the publication. Based on these criteria, Jackson and her research resulted in several breakthroughs. Some of her important work included the Landau theories of charge density waves in one and two dimensions; transport properties of random systems; correlation effects in electron hole plasmas, channeling in metals and semiconductors, two dimensional yang-mill gauge theories; and neutrino reactions. Cowan reported that other areas of investigation by Jackson included:

> . . . the electronic and optical properties of wide-bandgap semimagnetic semiconductor superlattices that have potential for use in blue/green lasers and other optical devices.

Ronald Mickens reported that already Jackson has published well over 100 scientific papers and abstracts. He found them in such journals a *"Annuals of Physics, Nuovo Cimento, Physical Review, Solid State Communications, Applied Physics Letters,* and *Journal of Applied Physics."*

An Active Life

Despite her heavy schedule, Jackson made time for other things. Married to a physicist, Dr. Morris Washington, the couple has one son. About her family, Jane Whitlow wrote:

> Jackson discusses very little about her private life. She cherishes her privacy and shies away from publicity. She is a wife and mother, and she takes neither lightly. She has published over 100 scientific papers and abstracts, and more are sure to come. Scores of papers, have been presented to national scientific conventions, large universities and small colleges, and different civic groups.

Jackson holds membership in leading scientific societies. These include the American Physics Society, the National Science Academy, Sigma Xi, National Society of Black Physicists (Past President), the National Institute of Science, the American Association for the Advancement of Science, and the New York Academy of Science among others.

Jackson sits on the Board of Trustees of the Massachusetts

Institute of Technology and Lincoln University. The Committee for the Education and Employment of Women Scientists and Engineers is one of many state and national groups that benefit from her service. She is a member of the Delta Sigma Theta Sorority, past Vice President of the MIT Alumni Association, and the Director of the New Jersey Research Corporation. The list is long.

"Carpe diem"

The work of Dr. Shirley A. Jackson has contributed to a better understanding of the nature of the universe through her research on fundamental particles. Her study of minute particles is essential to a comprehension of nature as a whole. The theoretical biologist Ernest Just, who spent his life investigating the living cell and its subunits said, "Although we may deal in particulars, we return finally to the whole pattern woven out of these."

As mentioned earlier, Jackson does not want to be the object of over-praise or measured for an elitist crown. So she has had to work hard not to feel uncomfortable when others give her recognitions or honors for the scientist she has become and for her public service. Nonetheless, the honors and recognitions have come on the merit of her achievements. A few of them include her election as fellow in the American Physical Society, "Woman of the Year" by the Lenape (New Jersey) Professional and Business Women, member of the Board of Trustees of Lincoln University and recently elected a life member of the Board of Trustees at MIT, the Candace Award from the National Coalition of 100 Black Women, Outstanding Young American Award, in 1976 and 1981, and of course the GIBA-GEIGY Exceptional Black Scientist Poster Series recognition.

Out of her own experiences Jackson has some interesting advice for a good education.

1. Good mathematics and verbal skills are essential, not only for scientists and engineers, but for everyday life.

2. We must triumph over the psychologically impeding barrier that makes us think blacks cannot be successful in science and mathematics.

3. Schools must teach problem-solving skills, and provide instructions that help young people see relationships and recognize patterns. Students should then be taught to unify concepts and to see the whole picture.

4. Employment discrimination against blacks, other minorities and women who hold advanced degrees in science serves the guild poorly. (Because of this, she has given time and energy to help promote fairness in employment and continues to do so).

Shirley Jackson has accepted being a role model out of a sincere sense of responsibility. At the Ciba-Geigy's ceremony where she was honored, Jackson explained how, through her science, she can best serve that end. She remarked:

> I have accepted the responsibility for being a role model because of my still somewhat unique academic credentials in the Black community and my efforts to increase the Black representation in the scientific community. But I must continually remind others, particularly media people, that I am a scientist. My first responsibility as a scientist is to be a productive researcher, which is, in fact the best role model I can be."

Shirley Jackson recalled that when she was graduated from high school, a teacher wrote in her autograph book, *carpe diem*. She learned that the words meant "seize the day and get the most out of each day." In 1992, she moved to Rutgers University where she continued her research and worked with graduate students. More recently she accepted the challenging role of Chairperson of the United States Nuclear Regulatory Commission. Established in 1975, the agency must protect "public health and the environment by ensuring the safety and security of civilian uses of nuclear technology and materials used in the United States. In 1999, she became president of Renssalaer Polytechnic Institute." For Shirley A. Jackson, Ph.D., *Carpe diem* still obtains.

References and Further Reading

Asimov, Isaac. *1988.Understanding Physics,* USA: Dorset Press.

Brelin. Christa (ed). *1992. Who's Who Among Black Americans,* Detroit: Gale Research, Inc..

Brennan, Richard. 1992. *Dictionary of Scientific Literacy,* New York: John Wiley and Sons, Inc., .

Bronowski, J. 1982. "The Creative Process," in *Scientific Genius and Creativity,* New York: The W. H. Freeman Company..

Brown, Frank and Mandeline Stent. 1977. *Minorities in U. S. Institutions of Higher Learning,* New York: Praeger Publishers.

Cattel, Jaques, (ed.) 1989. *American Men and Women of Science,* R. R. Bowker, New York. .

"CIBA-GEIGY Presents Jackson Portrait to MIT", *Columbus, Georgia Times,* January 26, 1983.

Cowan, Angela Y., "Shirley Jackson Honored by Rutgers," *Bell Lab News* 31 (6): 4, (March 19, 1991).

"Doing It . . ." Jackson's Excerpta," *The International Newsletter,* 3:1 August, 1982.

Gibbons, Ann, 1993. "Gaining Standing-by Standing Out: Pathbreakers", *Science,* 260, 393.

Just, Ernest E, 1939. *The Biology of the Cell Surface, Philadelphia:* P. Blakiston's Sons and Co.

"Jackson portrait given to MIT", *MIT Tech Tally,* December 8, 1982.

Martin, Brian, and Cornelis Spronk. 1991. *Physical,* New York:

Knox, Celeste, "Choosing the Right Problem to Solve: An Interview With Shirley Jackson", *National Women History Month Newsletter,* 4, 1988.

"Portrait Presentation", *The Westchester County Press,* January 6, 1983.

Smith, Jessie Carney, *Notable Black American Women,* Detroit: Gale Research, 1992.

Statistical Abstract of the United States, 1968. United States Department of Commerce.

The Power of Discovery, The Challenge of History, African Americans in Science, 1996, Hartford, CT: Aetna Calendar Corporate Communication

Whitlow, Joan, 1982. "Physicist Directs Blacks to Science, *The National Leader.*

INDEX

Williams, cont'd
heart, -86
Freedman's Hospital, 81-85,
Gresham, Walter, 81, 85
Guersey, Orrin, 70
Hall, George, 78, 88, 89, 92
home surgery, 75
Idlewild, 89, 90, 91
Janesville, Wisconsin, 70
Janesville Academy, 70-71
marriage 85, 89
Mr. Mason, 68-69
Mrs. Jones, 73-74
Morais, Herbert, 79
mortality, Freedman's, 79
National Medical
Association, 86--87
politics in medicine, 85-86
Palmer, Henry, 71-73, 85
Patterson, Lillie, 67, 85
Price: Ann Wilks
(grandmother), 67-68, Henry,
67-68,
Provident Hospital, 75-78, 81,
86,-89, 92
return to Chicago, 86
Rockford, Illinois, 69
St. Luke Hospital, 88, 89
Southside Dispensary, 75
standards of excellence, 76,
77-78
stroke (Dr. Dan), 90-91
tributes, 91
Walker, Alice, 85
Williams: Alice Johnson, 85,
89, 90, Daniel Jr., 66-67, 68
Sarah, 66, 67, 68, 69, 70,
Anne, 66, Florence, 66,
Henry Price, 66, 71, 85, Ida,

66, Sally, 66, 70
Woods, Granville, 94-115
at sea, 94
"Black Laws," 96-
birth, 95
Edison, Thomas, 103-105,
117
education, 96, 97-98, 111-
112
electricity, engineering, 97
engineer, train locomotive,
97, 98
fate of some inventions, 111
Gilligan, John, 113
honors, recognition, 113
Inventions: airbrakes for
trains, 106-108, amusement
apparatus, 110-111, electric
conduit, 109, electric
railway system, inductive
telegraphy system, 105,
electro-magnetic brake
system, 107, electromotive
railways, (overhead
conducting system), 109,
galvanic battery, 106-107
induction telegraph system,
102, relay instrument, 105,
telephone and electricity
transmission, 100-101,
telephone and railway
telegraphy, 101, steam
boiler furnace, 98-100
Latimer, Lewis, 104-105
patent applications, 98-99
Phelp(s), 103-104
Simmons, William, 98, 101,
102
train accidents, 101- 102